SILENT SERIAL SENSATIONS

SILENT SERIAL SENSATIONS

The Wharton Brothers and the Magic of Early Cinema

BARBARA TEPA LUPACK

CORNELL UNIVERSITY PRESS
Ithaca and London

First published 2020 by Cornell University Press

Printed in the United States of America

Library of Congress Cataloging-in-Publication Data

Names: Lupack, Barbara Tepa, author.
Title: Silent serial sensations : the Wharton brothers and the magic of early cinema / Barbara Tepa Lupack.
Description: Ithaca : Cornell University Press, 2020. | Includes bibliographical references and index.
Identifiers: LCCN 2019031429 (print) | LCCN 2019031430 (ebook) | ISBN 9781501748189 (paperback) | ISBN 9781501748202 (adobe pdf) | ISBN 9781501748196 (epub)
Subjects: LCSH: Wharton, Theodore. | Wharton, Leopold, 1870–1927. | Wharton Studio (Ithaca, N.Y.) | Motion pictures—New York (State)—Ithaca—History. | Silent films—New York (State)—Ithaca—History. | Film serials—New York (State)—Ithaca—History.
Classification: LCC PN1993.5.U772 L87 2020 (print) | LCC PN1993.5.U772 (ebook) | DDC 791.43/75—dc23
LC record available at https://lccn.loc.gov/2019031429
LC ebook record available at https://lccn.loc.gov/2019031430

Front cover image: The Whartons, Leopold (left) and Theodore (right), filming in 1918 with Marguerite Snow (center). Courtesy of the History Center in Tompkins County, Ithaca, New York, Wharton Studios Collection.

Back cover image: A photograph of the Whartons, actors, and crew enjoying a break between filming, circa 1916–1917. Courtesy of the Division of Rare and Manuscript Collections, Cornell University Library.

In memory of three remarkable women in my life:
Jane Tepa, Olga Kuchciak, and Maria Tepa

★ ★ ★ ★ ★

And,
as always,
for Al

For where thou art, there is the world itself,
With every several pleasure in the world.
Henry VI, Part 2

CONTENTS

Illustrations

PREFACE

An adventurous and headstrong heroine is drugged, shanghaied, and even declared dead before being electrically resuscitated, but nonetheless she persists in tracking her father's killer. A gang of devil worshippers resorts to mind control, astral projection, levitation, and thought photography to tyrannize an adolescent girl in an attempt to steal her fortune. A clever forensic detective who relies as much on science as on intuition uses a laser-sighted pistol, a portable seismograph, and other gadgets and inventions to outwit his opponents. A mysterious faceless villain terrorizes his victims with psychological tortures even more horrific than the actual physical torments he inflicts.

As contemporary as such cinematic devices might seem, they actually date back more than a century to two pioneering filmmakers, Ted and Leo Wharton. Among the best and most prolific serial motion picture producers of the silent era, the Wharton brothers were the creative force behind such landmark serials as *The Exploits of Elaine* and *The Mysteries of Myra*, whose topical story lines, sophisticated cinematic techniques, and special scenic and lighting effects helped to establish the language and define the conventions of the genre.

I discovered the Whartons while researching the Norman Studio in Jacksonville, Florida, for my books *Richard E. Norman and Early Race Filmmaking* and *Early Race Filmmaking in America*. Curious about the existence of other surviving silent film studios, I was surprised to learn that, in the early 1910s, the Wharton brothers established a successful independent production studio in Ithaca, New York, where they created some of the most acclaimed and highest-grossing films of the decade. Those popular serials, which aroused the enthusiasm of audiences worldwide, played a vital role in the evolution of cinema as a mass medium and as a form of entertainment for people of all ages and backgrounds; and they became forerunners of today's ubiquitous crime and mystery procedurals and sensation-filled commercial blockbusters.

I was especially fascinated by the Whartons' close and often complicated association with some of the most influential figures in the early movie industry, from actors and actresses such as Francis X. Bushman, Pearl White, and Irene Castle, who starred in their productions, to publishing magnate William Randolph Hearst, who provided some of their financing. I realized that their own story was as interesting as the plot of one of their serials.

Researching the Whartons, though, was a challenge. As with most silent films, the majority of their pictures are not extant, while those that do survive are often in fragmentary or corrupted form, making it impossible to assess the entire body of their work firsthand. Fortunately, I was able to make use of the Wharton business records and film materials archived in the Division of Rare and Manuscript Collections at Cornell University, the History Center in Tompkins County, Ithaca city newspapers, and film and trade journals from the 1910s and early 1920s. Those materials gave me an opportunity to examine contemporary accounts of the brothers' filmmaking ventures. Information about the Wharton-Rubenstein family graciously shared by family historian Karen Longley was invaluable in outlining family connections and relationships. Memoirs by and anecdotes from Wharton Studio cast members, film crews, and film extras allowed me to re-create much of the "lost" history of those early years. The Wharton Studio Museum (especially executive director Diana Riesman), the "Ithaca-Made Movies" website established by Terry Harbin, the "Serial Squadron" DVDs produced by Eric Stedman, the *Ithaca Silent Movies* programs written by Aaron Pichel, and the library and film holdings at the George Eastman Museum, the Moving Image Section of the Motion Picture, Broadcasting and Recorded Sound Division of the Library of Congress, and other archives afforded me links to stills, photos, and other materials that proved immensely helpful, while the discovery of a handful of rare film scripts, three of which are reproduced in the appendixes to this volume, provided insights into the Whartons' actual filmmaking.

Unmatched in their day and still widely imitated in ours, the Whartons were undeniably sensational filmmakers who not only made an invaluable contribution to cinema history but also captured the special magic of early filmmaking.

ACKNOWLEDGMENTS

My thanks to the Rockwell Center for American Visual Studies at the Norman Rockwell Museum, Stockbridge, Massachusetts—and especially to Stephanie Plunkett, deputy director and chief curator, and Jana Purdy, project manager—for a fellowship that allowed me the opportunity to conduct some of the research for this study and for ongoing encouragement of my work. Thanks as well to Humanities New York, especially Sara Ogger, executive director, Michael Washburn, director of programs, and Scarlett Rebman and Joe Murphy, grants officers, for a grant to support my work on early and silent film in central New York.

Thank you to Cornell University Press, especially Michael McGandy, senior editor and editorial director, Three Hills, for his graceful shepherding of this project and his support and encouragement throughout. I am grateful as well to Mahinder Kingra, editor in chief; Susan Specter, senior production editor; Glenn Novak, copy editor; the readers, who offered excellent suggestions for revision; and to everyone at the press who assisted in the production.

Many people lent generous assistance and offered important contributions:

In Ithaca, where the Whartons established their independent studio and achieved their greatest fame, I am grateful to Diana Riesman, cofounder and executive director of the Wharton Studio Museum, whose encouragement of this project from its inception has been unwavering and whose assistance has been invaluable; former executive director Rod Howe and director of archives and research services Donna Eschenbrenner at the History Center in Tompkins County, who extended a warm welcome, provided access to their archives, allowed me to use stills from their Wharton Studios Collection, and answered questions that arose; the Division of Rare and Manuscript Collections, Cornell University, which afforded me access to their collections, especially the Wharton Releasing Corporation Records and other related film materials; Julie Simmons-Lynch, Cornell University, whose Wharton timeline was an excellent starting point for my research; and the Arch Chadwick Collection of Wharton Studio Photographs, Ithaca College.

In Rochester, where the Whartons collaborated on a wartime project with George Eastman: I thank the George Eastman Museum, particularly Deborah Mohr, former assistant librarian, Richard and Ronay Menschel Library, and Virginia Dodier, former associate librarian, for their generous assistance and support, and Ken Fox, head of library and archives, and Stephanie Hofner, research facilitator, for sharing their expertise and creating such a genial working environment. Sophia Lorent, curatorial assistant, Moving Image Department, kindly screened several episodes of *The Exploits of Elaine* for my viewing; senior curator Paolo Cherchi Usai shared his tremendous expertise in silent film by answering a number of my questions on exhibition practices; and Jared Case, curator of film exhibitions, has been enormously helpful in promoting the Whartons through the Finger Lakes Film Trail. At the Robbins Library, University of Rochester, Rose Paprocki graciously assisted with research questions.

In Texas, where the Whartons spent part of their childhood, my sincerest thanks to Karen Longley, family historian, whose ongoing investigation of the Wharton-Rubenstein family has been immensely useful in documenting the brothers' early years and preserving their history.

In Saint Louis, where both Whartons gained early acting experience, I am grateful to Jason D. Stratman, assistant reference librarian, Missouri History Museum Library and Research Center; Ray Steinnerd, Missouri History Museum Library volunteer; Adele Heagney, reference librarian, Saint Louis Public Library; and William "Zelli" Fischetti, assistant director, State Historical Society of Missouri.

In Santa Cruz, where Ted Wharton struggled to open a new film studio after leaving Ithaca, my thanks to Deborah Lipoma, local history librarian, Santa Cruz Public Libraries.

In Washington, DC, Rosemary Hanes, reference librarian at the Moving Image Section, Library of Congress, provided me with the script from the first episode of *The Mysteries of Myra* that appears in the appendix to this volume and also other information about Wharton films, and Mike Mashon, head of the Moving Image Section, Library of Congress, shared materials and expertise.

In Colorado, thanks to Steve Friesen, director, Buffalo Bill Museum and Grave, Golden, for providing me with stills from *The Indian Wars*.

I am grateful as well to Kevin J. Harty, La Salle University, for his ongoing support and his careful reading of the manuscript; Mary Huelsbeck, assistant director, Wisconsin Center for Film and Theater Research, for her interest in the project and her encouragement; Christy Acevedo, for her help in securing Wharton ancestry documents; and Maryanne Felter, Cayuga

Community College, for assistance with questions about the Film Company of Ireland. My thanks as well to the many libraries and archives that provided me with materials, among them the University of Rochester, the University of Virginia, SUNY/Buffalo, Harvard University, Yale University, New York University, Temple University, Duke University, the University of Michigan, the University of Nebraska–Lincoln, the Museum of Modern Art, the UCLA Film and Television Archive, the Wisconsin Center for Film and Theater Research, the New York Public Library, the Boston Public Library, the Dallas Public Library, and the Santa Cruz Public Library.

I have benefited immensely from the work of many remarkable film historians, especially those who have studied the serial. Among them are Richard Koszarski, Terry Ramsaye, William Raymond Stedman, Buck Rainey, Kalton C. Lahue, Ed Hulse, Alan G. Barbour, Kevin Brownlow, David Bordwell, Shelley Stamp, Christine Gledhill, and Ben Singer. Their studies have been of immense value and have helped me to shape and clarify some of my own ideas.

I thank my friends and colleagues who offered support, especially Donna Bliss, Mary Young, and MaryKay Mahoney.

And last, but never least, I am grateful to my husband Al, for his careful reading, his judicious editing, his unconditional support—and for so much else.

NOTE ON SPELLING

In early film reviews, newspaper articles, and similar documents, the names of actors and the roles they played sometimes vary in their spelling. For example, former editor, film producer, and International Film Service manager Edward A. MacManus occasionally appears as Edward McManus or Macmanus; actor/director Maclyn Arbuckle as Macklyn, Maklyn, or Maklin Arbuckle; and Wharton property man Al Tracy as Al Tracey. Leo Wharton's wife used both her married and maiden names and appears at times as Bessie Wharton, Bessie Emerick, Bessie Emerich, and Bessie (or Besse) Emrick. I have tried to standardize and regularize the spellings, citing the correct (or preferred) form. The exception is direct quotations or correspondence. In those instances, when a variant form of a name or a variant spelling occurs (even if incorrect), I have preserved it.

Similarly, in quotations in the text and in the scripts that appear in the appendixes, the misspellings, inconsistencies, and infelicities have also been preserved.

In contemporary trade journals and publications, the titles of the episodes of the Wharton serials and the names of the characters in those episodes are sometimes inconsistent in their wording or spelling. The variants are usually noted in the endnotes.

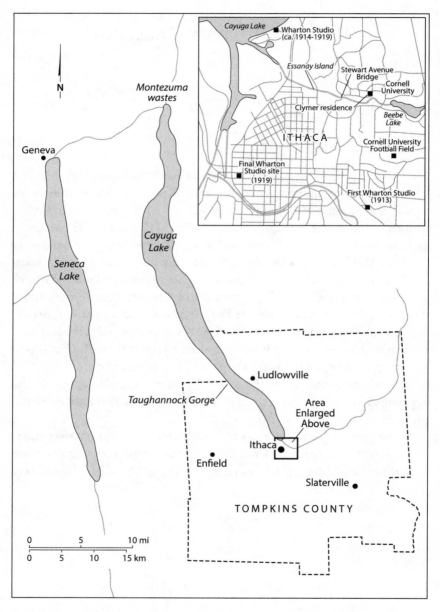

FIGURE 0.1   Map showing Wharton shooting locations in and around Ithaca, New York.

SILENT SERIAL SENSATIONS

Introduction
The Sensation of the Serial

Going to the movies. For most Americans in the mid-1910s, it was both a special event and a weekly ritual. Movie houses, many of them grand downtown "palaces" with names like the Rialto or the Majestic, had begun springing up across the country to accommodate the growing demand for moving pictures. Some theaters, called "atmospherics," were decorated to resemble exotic locales—a Spanish courtyard, for example, or a South Asian temple; others boasted crystal chandeliers, gilded plasterwork, and other opulent trappings. Outside, their triangular marquees lined with tiny blinking lights and their extravagant sidewalk displays tantalized moviegoers with the promise of new visual excitements.

Since moviegoing in those days was an occasion, patrons dressed accordingly: women donned their most fashionable hats; men wore their good suits. Inside the theater, they would be escorted to their seats by uniformed ushers or usherettes (who were "attractive, but not so pretty" as to compete with the on-screen entertainment).[1] By the time the lights went down and the plush velvet curtain came up, moviegoers were already on the edge of their seats in anticipation of the spectacle and sensations that awaited them: A hair-raising car chase? A massive train wreck? A runaway hot air balloon? A daring rescue from a steep cliff or a burning building? Perhaps a wild animal attack?

Glass slides immediately preceding the picture advised women to remove their hats ("Madam, How Would You Like to Sit Behind the Hat You are

Wearing?"), cautioned men not to smoke, and warned that "Loud Talking or Whistling Is Not Allowed." At the larger theaters, an ensemble of musicians or sometimes an entire orchestra would start to play, a signal that the show was about to begin. Even at the smaller neighborhood houses, a solo piano player or organist provided a musical accompaniment, either improvised or from cue sheets, to establish the appropriate atmosphere.[2]

If the audience was lucky, the theater might be conducting some kind of giveaway that day—a doll, or maybe a paper mask, a calendar, a souvenir booklet, or a puzzle. Though not as elaborate as the "dish nights" or "bank nights" that became so popular in the post-Depression years, those giveaways created an additional incentive for attendance. As the projectionist changed reels (which usually ran twelve to fifteen minutes each), patrons took advantage of the intermission to visit the concession stand—something that theater managers encouraged, because it augmented their business (and, on rare occasions, generated almost as much income as the box office did).[3] In the more elaborate theaters, "cry rooms" in the back allowed mothers to calm their babies and still watch the show. Neighborhood theaters lacked such amenities but nonetheless offered the same exciting entertainments and opportunities for socializing, which contemporary journalist Mary Heaton Vorse described as a "series of touching little adventures with the people who sit near you."[4] For families who saved up their nickels and dimes, a visit to the movies became a regular Saturday outing—and ultimately, for many, a cherished memory.

Throughout much of the 1910s, one particular kind of production kept moviegoers coming back to the theaters week after week: the serial motion picture. Typically two-reel action-packed films that ran for ten, fifteen, or more installments, those serials often ended with a cliffhanger and a promise "to be continued next week." Episodically structured and suspensefully plotted, they not only served as the precursors of the popular installment dramas and crime procedurals that have become staples of modern network and cable television programming; they also anticipated the extended incremental storytelling methods and "thrilling episodes of inescapable fatality and hair-breath escapes" that later filmmakers would exploit in commercial blockbusters such as the *Star Wars* series and the Indiana Jones and Marvel movie franchises.[5] Like those later megahits, serial pictures—effectively the blockbusters of their day—teased their narratives in clever ways in order to sustain filmgoers' curiosity until the release of the next installment.

Late nineteenth- and early twentieth-century entertainments had largely been geared to social class: the upper classes frequented the "legitimate" theater, while the lower classes flocked to vaudeville shows and nickelodeons.

But, as Ben Singer observed, the serial originated at a fortuitous time, when the newer theaters were being built and mainstream elements in the film industry were trying to broaden the market by making "innocuous middle-brow films suitable for heterogeneous audiences," including the predominantly working- and lower-middle-class and immigrant population that had supported the incredible nickelodeon boom.[6]

The transformation that American cinema was experiencing in those years, like the remarkable technological and social advances that shaped it, was certainly profound. As motion pictures evolved from an inexpensive, fleeting amusement into the nation's first truly mass medium and a respectable form of entertainment for people of all backgrounds, their visual grammar, narrative paradigms, industrial structure, and audience all solidified.[7] And serials played a considerable role in that transition, which was arguably the most critical and consequential in cinema's history. With their fast-paced, expansive, action-filled extended story lines, they were, as Richard Koszarski wrote, "among the first attempts to develop very long and complex screen narratives, and they served as a useful bridge between the short film and the feature during the crucial 1913–1915 period."[8]

The Significance of the Serial

Not merely a significant development in themselves, serials also helped to forge a strong link between the print and the film industries. As the visual equivalent of the nineteenth-century serialized fiction craze—that is, the installment publication of stories by popular authors such as Charles Dickens, Anthony Trollope, Mark Twain, and Harriet Beecher Stowe in journals and newspapers—early serials drew on many of the same devices, from the elaborate and often improbable plot twists and cliffhangers to the blatantly melodramatic appeals to the emotions. Film producers quickly realized that, just as the readers of serial magazines a decade or two earlier had devoured each new installment by their favorite authors, avid moviegoers would rush to the theaters every week to follow the adventures of their favorite stars. By incorporating the new technologies of automobiles, trains, steamships, airplanes, and submarines that fascinated contemporary viewers—and by capitalizing on events that were timely and topical—producers knew they could rouse the interest of their audiences and ensure their regular attendance.

At the same time that film serials harked back to their nineteenth-century literary roots, they looked ahead, creating exciting synergies across multiple media. Whereas the cross-promotions, cash-prize contests, and numerous tie-ins to popular magazines and newspapers expanded the movie base, print serializations of the serial film stories increased that base even more. Since moviegoers who had read the story readily paid to see it brought to life on the screen, such collaborations resulted in sizable profits for both media and initiated a fan culture that exploded with the proliferation of movie magazines, newspaper film columns, and other joint promotions. As Shelley Stamp observed, because movie fans "were encouraged to connect together various versions of the story available in print tie-ins and on screen, asked to sustain their engagement over multiple installments, and invited to enhance their enjoyment by cultivating an interest in the star's private life," the fans themselves became a central catalyst in the narrative.[9]

Moreover, like the early race pictures that influenced the migration of southern blacks and their acculturation to their new northern homes, serials had a vital cultural and social impact. Shown in big-city movie houses and small-town theaters nationwide, they helped to Americanize immigrants and foster a sense of community, while simultaneously creating an awareness of global culture. And by making weekly theater attendance a habit for tens of millions, they facilitated the rapid growth of one of the nation's most profitable industries.[10] With the looming threat of war, their furious action and unambiguous characters provided a much-needed diversion for adults and children alike, for whom movies proved to be the most affordable, available, and influential form of entertainment in the early decades of the twentieth century.[11]

In particular, serials served to increase patronage by women, who only recently had come to regard film-going as a respectable activity. As seedy nickelodeons gave way to elegant new movie palaces, women began attending the pictures in record numbers; and although the figures vary, it is estimated that by 1920, they comprised 60–75 percent of the audience. Since their attendance not only boosted the box office but also elevated cinema's cultural cachet, movie theaters tried to woo female patrons in various ways, from physical design modification (improved lighting and ventilation, mirrored common areas, perfumed deodorizers) to merchandizing tie-ins with local store owners.[12]

As the primary consumers in their families, women were in a position to influence their families' choice of entertainment,[13] and often they came to the movie houses with their husbands and children in tow. Yet they also started attending on their own, so that, "as independent customers, they could experience [different] forms of collectivity" through shared reception and public interaction.[14] For young urban working girls and rural wives and mothers alike, the serial heroines offered new models of independence, ambition, and athleticism, and illustrated the freedoms and opportunities to which they aspired. And their perils brought vicarious thrills.

As early film historian Lewis Jacobs observed in his pioneering critical history *The Rise of the American Film*, those heroines were especially influential because their physical prowess and daring had a real-life analogue. In many ways, it paralleled "the real rise of women to a new status in society—a rise that became especially marked on America's entrance into the war, when women were offered participation in nearly every phase of industrial life."[15] At the same time, serials revealed what Ben Singer called "the oscillation between contradictory impulses of female empowerment and the anxieties that such social transformations and aspirations created in a society experiencing the sociological and ideological upheavals of modernity."[16] To understand the significance of the serial is therefore to recognize its essential role in both American social and cinema history.

The Serial's Evolution

The serial form can be traced back to an early twelve-part Edison production, *What Happened to Mary*, whose first installment was released on July 26, 1912. Though more accurately considered a series rather than a true serial, *Mary* employed a similar format: its narrative line was composed of a distinct beginning, middle, and end, and its dozen one-reel episodes were filled with considerable physical action and suspense.[17] But unlike the chapters of a serial, those episodes were autonomous and lacked the sequential continuity that defined the genre.

Edison's production had its genesis in a "remarkable story of a remarkable girl" published in early 1912 in McClure's *Ladies' World* magazine, one of the most widely read periodicals of its day, in which an abandoned baby named Mary is rescued by shopkeeper Billy Peart. Paid five hundred dollars to raise her, Peart is promised another thousand if he finds her a suitable husband when she comes of age. Years pass. But after Peart locates a likely candidate, the now-eighteen-year-old Mary rejects the choice. Having learned the curious circumstances of her "adoption," she takes a hundred dollars that she believes is rightfully hers and leaves town in search of the truth about her origins. In a prelude to the many contests, premium offers, and novelty tie-ins eventually associated with the serial drama, readers were given clues and encouraged to submit three-hundred-word entries to the *Ladies' World* guessing Mary's whereabouts, with a cash prize for the winner.[18]

The gimmick added enormously to the story's popularity. Not surprisingly, more "Mary" stories—and more gimmicks—soon followed, the most successful one devised by *Ladies' World* editor Charles Dwyer and Horace G. Plimpton, general manager of Thomas Edison's Kinetoscope Company. In the summer of 1912, the two men came up with the idea of printing a new "Mary" story in each issue of the magazine, with prizes for readers who correctly guessed what was in store for the heroine in the next installment. The same week that the magazine was published, Edison would release, nationwide, a film version of that month's narrative. Their hope was that the two ventures would be mutually supportive. By targeting the female audience that constituted the primary readership of popular periodicals (particularly of the romance-adventure stories that began appearing in newspapers and magazines in the early 1890s and in "girls' book" series),[19] they believed they could simultaneously increase the circulation of the magazine and the attendance at the theater. The idea worked beautifully. Sales of the magazine rocketed to more than a million copies a month. According to Buck Rainey, "*The Ladies' World* jumped ahead in the circulation war with its competitors and Edison realized a nice profit on the films."[20]

In the series, the eponymous heroine Mary Dangerfield (played by Mary Fuller, a principal player in the Edison acting company), after learning the circumstances of her adoption and rejecting Peart's proposed suitor (William Wadsworth), embarks on adventures that take her from New York to London and ultimately uncovers the secret of her identity. Each installment was self-contained and could be understood and enjoyed independent of the rest. Yet while the question of how and when Mary would obtain her $10,000 inheritance created a modicum of suspense for the audience, the one-reel films lacked the cliffhanger ending and the other "thriller" devices common to later serials,[21] and ultimately the connecting narrative proved too diffuse and the intervals between major plot incidents too long.[22] But like the six-part sequel series *Who Will Marry Mary?* that was released a year later, *What Happened to Mary* featured the same heroine in each of the episodes, allowing viewers a familiarity with the character without demanding sequential regularity in the story line.

Similar series followed. Among the most popular was Kalem's *The Hazards of Helen* (1914–1917), which—at 119 installments of twelve minutes each—was the longest series ever produced. Its quick-thinking heroine Helen was an exceedingly capable and clever telegraph operator. No matter how dangerous or dramatic the situation in which she found herself—whether confronting bandits or stopping runaway trains—she resolved it by her own wits, rarely relying on a man for assistance or protection. Another Kalem series, *The Ventures of Marguerite* (1915), starred Marguerite Courtot as a young heiress who attempts to escape the many schemers, foreign agents, and kidnappers who want to steal her fortune—one of the most common plot lines in early series and serial pictures.

Most film historians now agree that the first true motion picture serial was *The Adventures of Kathlyn* (1913–1914), produced by the Selig Polyscope Company of Chicago. Following the example of Dwyer and Plimpton's highly effective cross-promotion for the *Mary* series, producer William Selig approached the *Chicago Tribune* about the prospect of allying his production of *Kathlyn* with the newspaper, a tie-in promotion that editor James Keeley believed worth a try. And so, for the opportunity to establish what *Moving Picture News* called the first such extensive "co-operation [to be] enjoyed in the motion picture business," the *Tribune* paid Selig $12,000.[23]

Based on a story by Harold MacGrath with a screenplay by Gilson Willets, *The Adventures of Kathlyn* was produced in thirteen two-reel episodes, the first of which was released on December 29, 1913, with new installments following at two-week intervals. At the same time the episodes were playing in the theaters, people could read a serialization of the stories in the *Chicago Tribune*, with a later novelization of the complete series published in 1914. The promotion was an unqualified success: the *Tribune's* circulation jumped 10 percent, a fact that was duly observed by other papers such as the *Los Angeles Times*, the *New York Sun*, the *Boston Globe*, and the *Philadelphia Record*, all of which soon established similar serial connections of their own.[24] Selig also initiated other effective publicity gimmicks, such as the free distribution to all *Photoplay* magazine subscribers of a special edition of the MacGrath novelization of the series, illustrated with stills from the film.

Unlike earlier series pictures, *The Adventures of Kathlyn* was an actual serial in which the stories were not self-contained but rather carried over to the next installment. One of its defining elements (and a common element in subsequent serial productions) was the cliffhanger ending, which created what Pathé serial writer Frank Leon Smith termed a "holdover suspense."[25] That meant that the heroine was left dangling—sometimes literally—until the next episode, and so was the audience, who could only guess what the outcome might be. Starring as the daring Kathlyn was "the Selig Girl" Kathlyn Williams, an attractive young actress and comedian who had studied at the American Academy of Dramatic Arts in New York City. Selig had already featured her in a number of one- and two-reelers that incorporated the wild animals he amassed in his animal park in just outside Los Angeles and leased to other filmmakers.

In announcing *Kathlyn's* release, the Selig Company explicitly noted the serial aspect of the film, describing it as "a series of 13 two-reel subjects . . . [that] will end in such a manner that the person who has seen one of the

FIGURE I.1   Now considered the first true serial motion picture, *The Adventures of Kathlyn* (1913) was a huge hit with movie audiences.

series will instantly realize that there is more to come, and be on the lookout for the next picture."[26] The serial followed Kathlyn as she goes to India in search of her father Colonel Hare (Lafayette "Lafe" McKee), who the late king of Allaha decreed should succeed him. Upon her arrival, she is informed by the devious Prince Umballa (Charles Clary), who covets the kingship, that the colonel is dead, leaving her as the heir. Umballa, it seems, plans to force her into marriage and then to rule as her consort. But American hunter John Bruce (Tom Santschi) comes to her aid. Over the next few episodes, usually with Bruce at her side, Kathlyn faces mortal danger—in the jungle, in a ruined temple where she is menaced by a hungry lion, at the foot of a volcano as it begins to erupt—before Umballa is exposed and punished for his deception and she is reunited with her father (who is not dead after all) and affianced to Bruce.

With its fearless heroine who attracted women moviegoers and its "blood-and-thunder dynamism of action" and strong male-hero figure who appealed to men, the serial was an instant hit. Its popularity, in fact, extended well beyond the episodes themselves and into the culture.[27] Newspapers and magazines splashed Williams's face on their covers, making it virtually impossible for people to pass a newsstand or shop front without seeing her image. Couples danced to a hesitation waltz named in Kathlyn's honor and sipped Kathlyn cocktails; women wore Kathlyn-style coiffures; and men carried souvenir postcards with her image. A song "Kathlyn, Dear Kathlyn" was published and performed, and Kathlyn's name was used to promote products as diverse as slippers, face powders, and cigars. Kathlyn became one of the most popular names for babies, too—including a baby elephant. The serial even spawned a 1916 feature-length film that used the same cast and crew.

Many of the serial productions that followed from other studios employed a similar formula: a beautiful young heroine in distress, threatened by a villain who covets her fortune or some other object of great value. Universal's first serial, *Lucille Love, the Girl of Mystery* (1914), for example, had been converted virtually overnight from a two-reeler into a fifteen-part spy drama starring Grace Cunard as the eponymous heroine who is pursued around the world by a spy intent on stealing the top-secret military documents in her possession.[28] Each "tense, nerve-gripping, awe-insuring" installment, as Universal promised, kept moviegoers on the edge of their seats.[29]

Initially considered little more than a novelty, the serial quickly became an all-out craze. Terry Ramsaye, in his landmark study *A Million and One Nights*, likened its spread to a "break out [of] smallpox in an Indian village in midwinter."[30] In furious competition with each other, studios rushed to get their own versions into production. In January 1914, Edison released the first chapter of the twelve-part *The Active Life of Dolly of the Dailies*, which was based on stories by *New York Sun* drama critic Acton Davies and serialized and syndicated to sundry newspapers. As the title suggests, Dolly Desmond, played by popular actress and serial veteran Mary Fuller, was an intrepid female reporter for the New York *Daily Comet*, whose beat took her all over the city and whose "active life" found her facing many dangers, from a kidnapping to a Black Hand bomb.[31]

Around the time that Edison was producing *Dolly*, Thanhouser Film Corporation was busy shooting *The Million Dollar Mystery*, another serial project produced in conjunction with the *Chicago Tribune* with the intention of boosting that newspaper's circulation. In the picture, when Florence Hargreave's father (Sidney Bracey) terminates his connection to a secret Russian organization that he had joined in his youth, Countess Olga Petroff (Marguerite Snow) and the other members of that group vow revenge and determine to secure his million-dollar fortune for themselves. After the elder Hargreave outwits the group and escapes in a balloon (a surprisingly common plot device in both stage and early film productions, which played to the fascination with new transportation technologies), the gangsters come after Florence (Florence "Fearless Flo" La Badie) to compel her to reveal the money's secret hiding place. Despite numerous close encounters—on an airship, in the path of an oncoming train, in a seaplane, in quicksand—she eventually frustrates their evil and greedy plan.[32]

The twenty-three-part serial (1914) had its own special promotional gimmick: the final chapter was left unwritten, and readers and viewers were encouraged to submit the best idea for the serial's conclusion. Advertisements for the contest promised the winner would receive "$10,000 for 100 words." Interest in the serial was maintained by having William J. Burns, head of the renowned International Detective Agency, provide clues to the public through a national movie magazine. And the "thriller," which incorporated numerous advanced production techniques, "returned $1.5 million on an investment of $125,000, making it one of the most financially successful cliffhangers ever produced."[33]

Unfortunately for Thanhouser, the sequel *Zudora* (1914), which consisted of twenty two-reel episodes, did not meet with the same success. Renamed *Zudora in the Twenty Million Dollar Mystery*, it was renamed yet again, this time as *The Twenty Million Dollar Mystery*, in order to capitalize on the original production. Because its story, though suspenseful, was confusing, Harold MacGrath was brought in to make a midcourse correction. But the serial, like the later reedited version released in ten parts as *The Demon Shadow* (1919), disappointed both its audience and its backers.[34]

Peril-Prone *Pauline*

The Pathé serial *The Perils of Pauline* (released beginning March 23, 1914), on the other hand, produced by newspaper tycoon William Randolph Hearst, not only heightened interest in the genre; it also immortalized its star, Pearl White, and became the most famous of all the early chapter plays. Derided by film historian Anthony Slide as "badly written and badly directed" and attacked by other historians as "appalling beyond belief . . . crude and inept," *Perils* nonetheless became an enormous hit with filmgoers. "The magic that burned this film into the national consciousness," Richard Koszarski explained, "was clearly not just coming from the screen" but was part of a larger cultural phenomenon created by the massive Hearst press campaign.[35]

Hearst had been quick to recognize the potential of motion pictures and to appreciate the rewards they could reap for him and his empire. In late 1913, in a joint venture with Selig, he began producing newsreels that were released under the title *Hearst-Selig News Pictorial* and distributed by the General Film Company. Those newsreel negotiations confirmed his belief that motion pictures were the "modern development of the publishing business" and convinced him of the viability of a serial idea. As Louis Pizzitola writes in *Hearst over Hollywood*, to make up for time he felt he had lost, Hearst contacted both Edward A. MacManus, the former editor and film producer who was behind the profitable *What Happened to Mary* series, and Charles Pathé, one of cinema's four pioneering Pathé brothers, for their help in planning the launch of his ambitious serial project. Hearst then engaged writers Morrill Goddard, the editor of Hearst's *The American Weekly*, and Morrill's brother Charles W. Goddard (who would later collaborate with brothers Ted and Leo Wharton on the writing of *The Exploits of Elaine*). In close cooperation, the three worked on story ideas and came up with the serial's plot and characters. Within a matter of weeks, the twenty-chapter script was complete.

Hired to direct were Louis J. Gasnier, whose affiliation with Pathé dated back to 1899, and Donald MacKenzie, who also assumed the role of "Blinky Bill" in the serial. Paul Panzer, whose association with Ted Wharton had helped him secure the role, played the heavy, Raymond Owen (later renamed "Koerner," to make him sound more German and even more sinister in the wartime era). Crane Wilbur appeared as the love interest and hero, Harry Marvin. But it was Pearl White who was the undisputed star. As Pauline Marvin, the ward of wealthy mogul Sanford Marvin, she was the personification of the era's free-thinking, independent "New Woman." Although she loves Harry, Pauline resists Sanford's urging to wed because she first wants "to see the world" and to embark on her own career as a writer. After Sanford's death, Pauline is bequeathed a large inheritance, with the provision that should she die before marrying Harry, the inheritance will pass to Sanford's secretary Koerner, who immediately begins plotting ways to eliminate her and acquire the fortune for himself. The episodes find her in constant mortal danger, facing a host of threats from Chinese ruffians, fanatical Japanese patriots, Sioux Indians, even river pirates. But with Harry and her devoted dog usually at her side, she survives every near-fatal mishap that Koerner orchestrates, from a faulty parachute to a rattlesnake hidden in a bunch of flowers.

As the irresistible but peril-prone Pauline in Hearst's landmark serial, White became an instant celebrity. With the juggernaut of Hearst's publicity machine solidly behind her, she was propelled to full-fledged stardom and became one of the most popular film actresses of the silent era.[36] On Sunday, a day when the entire family was likely to read the newspaper, each of Hearst's syndicated publications featured an eagerly awaited illustrated episode of *Perils*. At the same time, Hearst drama critic Alan Dale (the pseudonym of Alfred J. Cohen) published self-serving reviews of the serial, which in turn would be widely quoted or reprinted in other magazines and trade journals. Photographs of White appeared almost daily in the Hearst press, and Hearst's publicists promoted her as the ideal of young womanhood: beautiful yet modest, daring but sensible.[37] Pearl, in short, was everywhere.

Like his advertising, Hearst's marketing of *Perils* was unsurpassed. In addition to the 147 film prints sent out weekly to the exchanges for distribution (rather than 30, which was the norm) and the weekly print serializations of the episodes, Hearst offered $1,000 in prize money to the person who could guess the plot of Pauline's next adventure. He even rolled out a popular song, "Poor Pauline," to celebrate the heroine and to perpetuate her appeal. Not surprisingly, interest in Pauline quickly spread to all parts of the world. *Perils* "became nearly as popular in China and Russia as it was in the United States, creating [White as] one of the first international film stars."[38]

The Whartons' Role in Serial History

While *The Perils of Pauline* was neither the best nor the most innovative of the early serial motion pictures, it remains the most emblematic of the American serial craze. But it was the pioneering serials produced by filmmakers Ted and Leo Wharton that would have the most profound and sustained impact on the genre. The intriguing character types, topical themes, and advanced special effects that the Whartons introduced not only expanded the possibilities of the serial form and established many of its conventions but also provided a model for incremental storytelling and holdover suspense still employed by filmmakers and television producers more than a century later.

From their box-office-busting thirty-six-part *The Exploits of Elaine* (1914–1915), which was recently recognized by the U.S. National Film

Registry for its cultural and historical importance, to the landmark supernatural thriller *The Mysteries of Myra* (1916), which depicted actual occult magical practices; from the newsroom mystery *Beatrice Fairfax* (1916), which celebrated the modern working woman and inspired a series of "girl-reporter" pictures, to the military preparedness picture *Patria* (1917) and the patriotic serial *The Eagle's Eye* (1918), which captured the country's wartime mood and anxiety, the Whartons spoke directly to the concerns of their age and to the interests of their audiences.

Drawing on their own experience in both the performance and production aspects of the business, the Whartons were able to attract first-rate talent. Their pictures starred some of the most popular performers of the day—big names such as Francis X. Bushman, Beverly Bayne, Irene Castle, Milton Sills, and Pearl White—and introduced or featured actors such as Lionel Barrymore, Warner Oland, and Oliver Hardy who would go on to distinguish themselves and find fame in Hollywood's sound films. They also fostered the careers of the skilled technicians behind the camera such as cinematographer Ray June and director Wesley Ruggles, who won great acclaim in the industry.

In their technique and their content, the Whartons embraced technological and scientific innovation. Interweaving contemporary events into their scenarios, they incorporated harrowing escapes, thrilling stunts, and even a few "cliffhanger" scenes shot on actual cliffs and gorges around Ithaca, New York. And it was there in Ithaca that the brothers established their independent Wharton Studio, where the pictures they created brought excitement to their audiences and energy to the town, which for a time became an impressive center of filmmaking.

Yet the story of the Whartons is much more than an account of two pioneering filmmakers who became the most sensational serial filmmakers of their day. It is also a singular portrait of the burgeoning movie industry at a critical and transformative point in American social, political, and cultural history.

CHAPTER 1

Seeking "Old Opportunity"

Ted Wharton knew that show business would be a tough profession to crack. The early years that he spent on and behind the stage, though, gave him an invaluable introduction to virtually all aspects of the entertainment industry, especially to the performance and production of melodrama (the predominant form of theater in the late nineteenth and early twentieth century). They also taught him the technical and improvisational skills that would serve him well as he graduated from vaudeville performance and legitimate stage acting to direction of film shorts and production of serials, particularly since he—like his brother Leo and other pioneering filmmakers in those transitional years of the early 1910s—was often experimenting as he developed the conventions and devices that would become staples of later cinema and television.

Getting into the Business

Theodore ("Ted") William Rubenstein (later changed to Wharton, his mother's maiden name) was born on April 12, 1875, in Milwaukee, Wisconsin.[1] His parents William and Frances ("Fanny") Rubenstein, sister Eugenia Alice ("Genie," born 1864), and brother Leopold Diogenes ("Leo," born 1870) had emigrated from England in 1873.[2] William, who was originally from Bohemia, worked as a merchant in Milwaukee; Fanny kept the house. By 1880, the Rubensteins had relocated to Hempstead, Texas, where Ted was raised. (He later joked in a newspaper interview, "When I was four years of age, my parents moved to Texas, and, feeling duty-bound, I went with them.")[3]

After William's death in 1882, the family moved to Dallas, where young Ted held short-term jobs as a messenger for Bankers and Merchants National Bank and as a clerk in the auditor's office of the Texas and Pacific Railway.[4] But even at an early age, he felt the draw of the theater and determined to make his career in the entertainment industry. Over the next decades, he sought out various positions both in the business end of the profession and on the stage as an actor,[5] gaining the confidence and the expertise needed to break into the burgeoning film business.

While still in his teens, Ted secured a job as assistant treasurer and then treasurer of the Dallas Opera House. Although that experience deepened his passion for the performing arts, he realized that "life would be more interesting on the stage than 'counting the house.'" So, in 1895, he moved to Saint Louis, where he spent two seasons acting with the Hopkins Grand Opera Stock Company.[6] The company, which advertised itself as being "composed of popular favorites who [had] won their way to public recognition through artistic and meritorious effort,"[7] was organized and operated by the honorifically titled "Colonel" John D. Hopkins, a former associate of P. T. Barnum and a prominent and colorful figure in vaudeville management in the Mississippi Valley for over three decades. A small-time actor turned big-time impresario, Hopkins introduced the popular daylong "10–20–30," a low-admission continuous show that comprised drama and between-the-acts vaudeville and drew large and enthusiastic audiences into his circuit of theaters.

The Grand Opera House building that Colonel Hopkins took over in the mid-1890s was a familiar and cherished local landmark. And while the programs he offered there varied, one thing about them remained constant: they were always sensational. One week's bill, for example, included the nineteenth-century melodrama *The Two Orphans* starring the popular Kate Claxton, who had created the lead role, along with European acrobats and hand balancers, singers, comedians, dancers, a hanging wire performer, and a hat manipulator. In fact, it was not unusual on any given day for acts as disparate as Fulgora, an impersonator of world famous generals, and Professor de Berssell, a "funny French modeler in clay," to appear on stage beside bamboo bell ringers and thoroughbred racehorses.[8]

Surviving programs confirm that Ted appeared in numerous "continuous performance" productions at the Hopkins Grand Opera, where he occasionally worked with his brother Leo, who was also a member of the company. In January 1896, for example, the brothers had small roles in William Haworth's

FIGURE 1.1   Both Ted and Leo Wharton performed at the Hopkins Grand Opera in Saint Louis. Occasionally, as in *The Ensign* (January 1896), they appeared together.

The Ensign. Originally performed in Washington, DC, in early 1892, the five-act naval war drama was based on the *Trent* Affair of 1861, an international diplomatic incident that occurred during the Civil War and threatened war between the United States and Great Britain. An American warship, the USS *San Jacinto,* had intercepted the British mail packet RMS *Trent* and removed two Confederate diplomats who were bound for Britain to enlist military and financial support for the South. Unwilling to risk war, President Lincoln resolved the crisis by disavowing, but not apologizing for, the actions of the *San Jacinto*'s captain and releasing the envoys.[9]

Widely performed, *The Ensign* was a hit with both theatergoers and actors. (Film pioneer D. W. Griffith, who played the role of Lincoln in a production at the Alhambra Theatre in Chicago in the early 1900s, would later lift some of the Lincoln scenes for his film *The Birth of a Nation*.)[10] It was likely quite familiar as well to the audiences who viewed the Hopkins staging in Saint Louis, in which Ted, billed as "T. W. Wharton," appeared as Sergeant Black, an officer from the *San Jacinto,* while Leo, billed as "L. D. Wharton," was cast as Lieutenant Henry Fairfax, the judge advocate. Featured on the same bill with *The Ensign* that week were several vaudevillians, comedians, musicians, and another "specialty of merit": a demonstration of the "American Bio-graph," leased from the American Mutoscope Company at the outrageous cost of $500 a week. Said to be "the most marvelous invention of the age,[11] that early motion picture device may have whetted Ted's curiosity and pos-sibly given him his introduction to the emerging cinema industry.

Colonel Hopkins's influence in the entertainment industry was broad and far-reaching,[12] and his Saint Louis company provided an excellent train-ing ground. Yet even in the waning years of the nineteenth century, New York was the place where most American actors aspired to be, and Ted was no exception. So when the opportunity arose to join the company of the Lyceum Theatre to act in conventionally staged dramas that carried more cultural prestige and legitimacy than the vaudeville in which he had gotten his start, he happily relocated to New York.[13]

Considered to be quite modern at the time of its construction on Fourth Avenue in 1885, the Lyceum—with an interior designed in part by Louis Comfort Tiffany, an electrical installation said to have been supervised by Thomas Edison himself, and amenities such as an elevator car—was home to a stock company that included many of the most talented actors of the day, some of whom went on to find success on the silent screen. Established by playwright Steele MacKaye and producer Gustave Frohman (one of three Frohman brothers who were active in show business), the company evolved from the original Lyceum School of Acting to the New York School of Act-ing and finally to the American Academy of Dramatic Arts. After debt forced MacKaye and Frohman to sell their interests, Gustave's older brother Daniel became manager and producer, a position that he held for more than two decades, even after the old Lyceum Theatre was razed in 1902 and the new Lyceum opened on Forty-Fifth Street in the heart of the Broadway Theater District.

The company performed numerous plays each year—more than eighty during Daniel Frohman's tenure—and also employed troupes of actors and musicians who toured the plays, most of which were sensational melodra-mas or historical dramas. During his time at the Lyceum, Ted worked with highly regarded actor (and later silent screen star) E. H. Sothern; and he acted alongside other members of the company in productions such as *The Sporting Life* (1898), a popular four-act, sixteen-tableaux melodrama written by Cecil Raleigh and Seymour Hicks about a young British lord who incurs heavy debts and must decide whether to allow his horse to throw a race in order to redeem his losses.[14]

After his appearance in *The Sporting Life*, Ted transferred to Charles Frohman's Empire Theatre Company, which, like the Lyceum, was famous for the stars that it developed—among them William Gillette, John Drew Jr., and Ethel Barrymore (whose brother Lionel would later be cast in the Whartons' *The Romance of Elaine* serial). Brother to Gustave and Daniel, Charles was a noted theatrical personality who is credited with creating the star system on Broadway. A great promoter of playwrights, he was the force behind multiple hits before his untimely death in May 1915 during the torpedoing of the *Lusitania*,[15] a tragic event that would prove central to several of the Whartons' later serials.

As part of Empire's stock company, Ted appeared in *The White Heather*, a successful British melodrama written by Henry Hamilton and Cecil Raleigh, in which a scheming nobleman is willing to go to any extreme to maintain his position of privilege.[16] The play—which ended with a spectacular underwater diving operation to recover a lost ship's log that confirmed the legitimacy of the marriage of the nobleman to the woman he "ruined" and the paternity of their child—was scenically outstanding, full of the plot and character exaggerations that defined the genre. An unqualified hit, it premiered on November 22, 1897, and played for 184 performances, during which time "the Academy of Music, large as it is, hardly suffice[d] to accommodate the audiences the play attracts to its doors."[17] Ted also appeared in a supporting role in another Frohman production, *A Marriage of Convenience*, a four-act comedy of manners that opened on November 8, 1897, at the Empire Theatre and starred prominent actor John Drew.[18] A period piece set in the time of Louis XV and based on *Un mariage sous Louis XV* by Alexandre Dumas, the play, originally adapted for the British stage by Sydney Grundy, was an excellent study of a newlywed husband, the Comte de Candale, who is "all worldliness and ease," and his charming "girl-bride," who is "all innocence, truth and timidity." According to the *Tammany Times*, it "pack[ed] them in like sardines."[19]

Since aspiring actors often moved between theaters and up to better companies, it was hardly surprising that, at the urging of his cousin Lena Rubenstein, Ted soon left the Empire Theatre to join the New York company of Augustin Daly, another influential theater manager, critic, and playwright. Lena, the wife of actor Creston Clarke (nephew of Edwin and John Wilkes Booth and son of Junius Brutus Booth, all of them distinguished stage actors) and herself a frequent performer on the New York and London stages under the name Adelaide Prince, had earlier spent almost five years with Daly, whom she introduced to Ted.[20]

Widely considered "the autocrat of the stage," Daly exercised tight, almost tyrannical control over all his productions. At the same time, he advanced the careers of the actors in his company—Ada Rehan, Maurice

Barrymore, Maud Jeffries, Tyrone Power Sr., and Isadora Duncan, among them. Ted became part of the stock company, and upon Daly's death in 1899 he assumed the position of stage manager for the road tour of *The Great Ruby*, a "perennially interesting pageant melodrama" that appealed to young and old alike and that would be revived several times over the next decade (with Leo Wharton appearing in one of those later productions).[21] The play was the kind of big, splashy, turn-of-the-century production that audiences had come to enjoy. Revolving around the theft of a large ruby from a Bond Street jeweler's wife by a gang of thieves, it offered numerous excitements and plot contrivances typical of the melodrama of the period, including frequent changes of scene that ran the gamut of fashionable English life. In the exciting climax, the jewel thief tries, unsuccessfully, to effect his escape by jumping into a balloon, a scene that, the *Argonaut* reviewer observed, "in theatrical parlance, [was] 'simply great'" and eclipsed anything seen in other productions.[22]

The staging of such a fast-paced melodrama was certainly a challenge, but evidently one that Ted welcomed, since he subsequently assumed similarly demanding positions with other New York production companies. His last two seasons of theatrical life were spent as manager of the famous Hanlon Brothers' *Superba* company and as acting treasurer of Hammerstein's Victoria Theatre in New York.

Superba, as its name suggests, was nothing short of superb. A "unique mechanical and pantomime spectacle" that drew heavily on the popular traveling circus tradition long linked to theater,[23] it was created, arranged, and performed by the Hanlons, whose vaudeville act originally consisted of six British-born brothers.[24] All were talented gymnasts and acrobats who eventually became successful theatrical producers and are now considered by some to be the fathers of musical comedy.[25] In 1890, the three surviving brothers created their final production, *Superba*, a pantomime that grafted their signature acrobatic slapstick onto fairy-tale plots with remarkable tricks and transformations, and each year for the next two decades they reworked it to feature all-new machinery and technical gags. *Superba* afforded them an ideal opportunity to combine their physical stunts with spectacular stage settings and magic that drew on the new technologies that were revolutionizing the entertainment industry. The pantomime's three acts, Mark Cosdon writes, were filled with a bevy of chorus girls, a series of scenic spectacles, and gruesome displays that included guillotines, a haunted studio with furniture that moved on its own, chariots pulled by lobsters, fire-spewing dragons, circus freaks, revolving stages, and even a trip through the Saint Louis World's Fair.[26] The *Boston Globe* marveled at the "fairies, fiends, sea nymphs and sea

FIGURE 1.2 Before going into the film business, Ted Wharton served as manager for *Superba*, a "pantomime spectacle" that inspired some of the special effects the Whartons later incorporated in their films.

monsters, domestic animals and wild beasts, whales, mermaids, sea serpents and vistas glowing with jewelled iridescence" that were summoned onstage during one of the performances.[27] Such visual spectacle no doubt stirred Ted's imagination and inspired some of the ghostly apparitions and stunning special effects he later incorporated into *The Mysteries of Myra* and other of his serials, as well as the circus sequences in *Beatrice Fairfax* and in the "Shoestring Charlie" circus pictures that, at one point, the Whartons planned to produce.

On the other hand, Ted's position at Hammerstein's Victoria Theatre and his close association with its founder, mogul Oscar Hammerstein, taught him equally valuable practical lessons about the entertainment business. After the failure of his Olympia Theatre, Hammerstein had been hard pressed to secure the necessary funds to build the Victoria in 1899. So, during the construction, he insisted on keeping the budget as lean as possible, instructing his crews to use debris from the demolition of the original building on the site to fill the walls of the new theater, and even purchased and installed secondhand theater seats to keep costs down. Money continued to be a concern for Hammerstein as he transformed the Victoria from a prominent vaudeville house into a legitimate theater in 1904. And while, over the succeeding years, the risk proved profitable, the memory of the fiscal hardships was not lost on Hammerstein—or on Ted Wharton, who, as the theater's acting treasurer, oversaw its finances.

A Tough Game

Despite the proficiency he had acquired in stage production and management, Ted knew that theater was "a tough game to buck" and that finding "old Opportunity was even harder." So he began pursuing new possibilities in the entertainment business. "I was wandering through 59th Street, near Columbus Circle, bemoaning my sad fate," he later recalled, "when I happened to glance upward and notice a sign [for 'Moving Pictures, Admission 10 cents']. I have often wondered how the man who painted that sign knew that I had just that amount in my pocket." As he came out of the theater—one of the first in New York City to be exclusively devoted to motion picture exhibition—he was dazzled by the sudden glare. "I mistook [it] for sunlight, but I soon discovered that it was old Opportunity, brighter than ever. He took me gently by the arm and whispered in my ear: 'Here's your chance, my boy—write Moving Picture Stories.'"[28]

Ted's interest in the motion picture industry was further aroused by his visits to the old Edison Studios in Manhattan, after which, on his own, he began writing screenplays that revealed his aptitude for the craft. Twenty-eight of the thirty freelance scenarios that he submitted to the Edison Company, *Motography* reported, were immediately accepted.[29] And once the Edison Company recognized Ted's unusual theatrical background as both actor and manager, they offered him the position of technical scenario writer (later scenario editor) and studio supervisor of the Edison Studios in 1907, which he readily accepted.

The original Edison production facility, the first movie studio in the United States, was called the Black Maria. Established in late 1892 for the purpose of making film strips for the Kinetoscope (a forerunner of the motion picture projector),[30] it was built on the grounds of Edison's laboratory in West Orange, New Jersey, and closed when Edison moved to a more sophisticated glass-roofed studio in Manhattan in 1901. Another facility, located at Decatur Avenue and Oliver Place in the Bronx, opened in 1907, just around the time that Ted joined the operation. It is unlikely that Ted ever worked directly with Thomas Edison or even with Edison's former assistant W. K. L. Dickson, who had been responsible for overseeing the development of the motion picture system during the studio's early years before he left to join Biograph. But he had the chance to collaborate with directors like Alex T. Moore, who focused on shifting the studio's productions away from "actualities" (news footage) and toward the creation and distribution of "story films," which were becoming increasingly popular with moviegoers. And he crossed paths with Edison directors Harold M. Shaw, Oscar Apfel, Charles Brabin, Alan Crosland, J. Searle Dawley, and Edward H. Griffith, all of whom went on to enjoy successful Hollywood careers.

There is no record of the pictures at Edison in which Ted might have been involved, which is unsurprising, since most of their early productions went largely or wholly uncredited. But there is no doubt that the Edison Company provided him with excellent insights into both the possibilities and the pitfalls of the early film industry, lessons that proved vital as he continued to make his way in the profession.

The following year, Ted was hired by Kalem, another major motion picture company, to establish its first indoor studio. Kalem had been founded in 1907 in New York City by Chicago businessman George Kleine and Biograph veterans Samuel Long and Frank J. Marion, who amalgamated their initials to create the company's name.[31] Under the direction of Sidney Olcott, who had been lured away from Biograph, Kalem produced a number of successful pictures, some of which were filmed at a branch office in Jacksonville, Florida, and others on location in Ireland. Anxious to expand its national base of operations beyond New York, Kalem sent representatives to investigate and to open new facilities in California, first in Glendale and Santa

Monica and then in Hollywood, where the company eventually took over the Essanay Studio in East Hollywood. By 1914, three years before it was sold to Vitagraph, Kalem had earned a reputation for its serials, which included the 119-episode *The Hazards of Helen*. And the sixteen-episode *The Ventures of Marguerite*, released in October of the following year, 1915, solidified the company's reputation as a maker of "series of supreme quality."[32]

Making Films for Pathé

Ted Wharton, though, was not involved in any of Kalem's serial productions. By 1910, he had already left the company to join Pathé Frères, to assist in the opening of its American studio and then to serve as its director.[33] Founded in 1896 in France as the Société Pathé Frères (Pathé Brothers Company) by Charles, Émile, Théophile, and Jacques Pathé, the company—under Charles's supervision—soon became the world's largest film equipment and production company. After acquiring patents from the Lumière brothers and partnering briefly with Georges Méliès, Pathé designed an improved studio camera, began making its own film stock, expanded to include a chain of movie theaters, and created newsreels that were shown in theaters worldwide. At the new American studio in Fort Lee and Jersey City, New Jersey, Pathé produced *The Perils of Pauline* (1914), a serial in which Ted Wharton—by then making films at his own studio in Ithaca, New York—had a peripheral involvement.

As early as 1910, while in Pathé's employ, Ted began directing one-reelers based on his own notes and scenarios.[34] The pictures usually took just a few days each to film; and the actors, often uncredited and drawn from the same pool of company performers, played a variety of different roles. Popular actor Billy Quirk, for instance, who appeared in numerous Wharton shorts (and whom Ted at least briefly considered for a starring role in his later serial, *Beatrice Fairfax*),[35] was cast in parts as diverse as boyfriend and burglar, conductor and country lout, Mexican and eccentric Frenchman. Similarly, actress Octavia Handworth, who often appeared alongside Quirk and whom Ted also regularly employed, portrayed a settler's wife, a countess, a Roma, and an African American. And like virtually all the actors in the company, both Quirk and Handworth performed their own stunts.

Since Pathé made very few directorial attributions for its 1910 films, it is difficult to assign a definitive credit to all but a handful of the pictures on which Ted worked. Many of them, though, were short westerns, which played to the curiosity of urban and suburban audiences about the disappearing and mythified frontier and which, that year alone, accounted for about 20 percent of the films released in the United States.[36] Ted's westerns typically had a simple and often melodramatic plot formula, featuring a hero who saves the day and a villain who receives a comeuppance for his crimes. In his *The Gambler's End*, for example, "ne'er-do-well" Herbert Ralston swaps identities with a dead man in order to make a fresh start but is struck down in a hail of bullets fired by friends of the cowboy he had killed. (Paul Panzer later recalled his fortuitous casting in that role. "Mr. Wharton had selected a natural type for the art—a man who looked like a gambler—but the poor fellow could neither act nor ride horseback. I happened to drop into the studio that day. Mr. Wharton welcomed me with open arms. I took the other fellow's clothes and the scenes that had been exposed were retaken. [Afterward] Mr. Gasnier offered me a salaried position in stock. Then came five happy years, finishing with the wonderful serial 'The Perils of Pauline.'")[37]

While all of Pathé's westerns proved to be popular, the "Indian pictures" were a particularly big draw for moviegoers, who seemed endlessly fascinated by the exotic nature and cultural practices of Native Americans. Ted's sympathetic story lines and excellent photography in pictures such as *The Maid of Niagara* evoked Indian life and scenery in a way that was rarely seen.[38] In that romance of forbidden love, after his beloved Red Doe is selected to go over the Niagara Falls as the annual sacrifice "to propitiate the Spirit of the Cataract," young Iroquois brave Esoomgit wades into the torrent to his own death, believing that they will be reunited in the Happy Hunting Grounds. Although the plot of the film was unapologetically sentimental, the special effects were reported to be exceptionally beautiful, with the view of the falls imparting the "impression of grandeur."[39]

Another of Ted's shorts about forbidden love, *The Appeal of the Prairie*, told the story of Sioux warrior Lonefox, who rescues a half-dead prospector, John Henderson. Years later, Lonefox gets a job at Henderson's bank but is set up for the theft of some notes by fellow worker Charles Holstein. Although Henderson acquits his old friend, he refuses him consent to wed his daughter, whom Holstein is courting. An angry Lonefox considers committing a violent act of revenge, but his better nature wins out. Instead, he destroys the diploma that symbolizes his assimilation and accommodation to the "white" world and decides to return to the West, where his father welcomes him back to the tribe.[40] Among his own people, he can revert to the manners and customs of his race. As Mary B. Davis suggests in *Native America in the Twentieth Century*, that resolution was inevitable in early films, since the prospect of love between Native Americans and whites was almost always doomed or had tragic consequences.[41]

Ted's pictures for Pathé, however, were not limited to westerns and Indian stories. He also produced numerous successful comic shorts, which usually relied on familiar twists and devices such as mistaken identity. In *A Simple Mistake*, for example, after the ponderous Mrs. Hallate watches her husband depart for a trip, the slightly built Augustus Slip (Billy Quirk) wanders by and is immediately smitten. What follows is a comedy of errors, as Mr. Hallate, having missed his train, returns home and is mistaken by a police officer for the man whom his wife has reported as an unwelcome intruder. Before the matter is resolved, Hallate suffers various indignities: he is ousted from his house, thrown out of the second-floor window by the officer, and locked into the back of a police wagon. Meanwhile, Augustus tries to escape discovery in some humorous ways, hiding himself behind a curtain and taking refuge under the couch. Augustus was featured in another of Wharton's comedy shorts, *The Hoodoo*—one of many "hoodoo"-themed pictures produced around that time—in which Augustus receives a legacy from his late uncle. Expecting a large fortune, he inherits instead what appears to be an ancient statue of a little Indian god, which brings him nothing but misery until he smashes it and finds the plan of a secret diamond mine inside.[42]

Unfortunately, some of Wharton's Pathé comedy shorts drew on stereotypes of African Americans that had evolved from the popular minstrel acts and "Tom shows" of the mid- to late-nineteenth century and that reflected

FIGURE 1.3 *How Rastus Gets His Turkey*, a blackface comedy that Ted Wharton produced, drew on familiar stereotypes from nineteenth-century minstrel shows.

the retrogressive racial views of his day. *How Rastus Gets His Turkey* (alternatively titled *How Rastus Got His Turkey*), for example, played on a familiar stereotype, depicting Rastus—a name that was often applied generically to the character type—as allergic to work and addicted to stealing.[43] The short opens on the day before Thanksgiving, as the shiftless Rastus, described as "black as ink," determines to find a holiday turkey for his wife Eliza and their family. With no money to purchase a bird, he decides to steal one from the butcher and, when that fails, from the yard of George Green, one of the butcher's customers. After a series of comic misadventures and chases, all ends well for Rastus: by the next morning, there is a fine turkey on the family's table.[44]

Still other shorts that Ted produced for Pathé were highly sentimentalized melodramas that recalled the "10–20–30" shows and the stage "mellers" (melodramas) in which he had earlier performed. *Dad's Boy*, based on a scenario written by Ted, starred Henry B. Walthall, who would go on to find fame in D. W. Griffith's *The Birth of a Nation*.[45] John Chester, a country store-keeper, mortgages his store to raise money for his son's college tuition in the hope that, after graduation, the son will return home to become his business partner; but the boy decides to practice law in the city instead. Unable to pay the mortgage, Chester watches sadly as the sheriff forecloses on his property. Unknown to him, however, the son, apprised of his father's plight, buys the store and returns it, debt-free, to his loving parents.[46]

Ted also starred Walthall in another melodrama, *Waiting*, whose scenario he wrote and whose story line he would later rework in one of his Ithaca pictures. A young man who proposes to his sweetheart is told by her father that she is not old enough to marry. Urged to go west and "wait" for a few years, the suitor does so and makes good. When he receives the happy news that his sweetheart will be joining him, he leaves for the station, nosegay in hand, only to discover that her train has gone over a bridge, killing everyone on board. Desolate, the young man scatters the flower petals on the train platform and returns home. But every Thursday for the next few years, he gathers a little bouquet and drives to the station, where he believes he will meet his bride. Then, one day, after returning from the station, he sinks into a chair, grasps a picture of his sweetheart, and has a vision of her coming to him; in that moment, he closes his eyes and dies.

Part of Ted's skill in producing shorts for Pathé was his cleverness in incorporating modern technologies such as airplanes and automobiles that he knew excited audiences and drew them into the movie houses. In one such comic short, *The Motor Fiend*, a speedster dreams that all speed limits have been abolished and that his automobile has been equipped with a "joy meter," which allows him to track every object he runs over, from dogs and hens to policemen and, ultimately, to his own mother-in-law, which brings him the most "joy" of all. And in *The Champion of the Race*, Ted used an endurance race as a device for getting Helen's father George Brown to consent to her marriage to James Gordon, the man whom she loves, rather than Harry Castleroy, the man whom her father wants her to wed. After placing a $20,000 bet that he will win the race, George Brown finds himself stranded on a boat with Castleroy just as the contest is about to begin. But, with Gordon's assistance, the daring Helen (who anticipated the independent and free-spirited "New Woman" heroines of the Whartons' later serials) enters the race in her father's place and wins both the bet and the big trophy, prompting Brown to accede to her choice of spouse.[47]

At Essanay

Despite strong ties to Pathé, in late 1911 or early 1912 Ted decided to leave the company for a better opportunity at another studio: Essanay. Founded in Chicago in 1907 by George K. Spoor and Gilbert M. Anderson as the Peerless Film Manufacturing Company, the business was renamed Essanay to reflect the founders' initials. Anderson's success as popular cowboy star "Broncho Billy" helped to establish Essanay's reputation, while the company's association with Charlie Chaplin, whom Essanay lured away from Mack Sennett and his Keystone Studios, and with screenwriter and eventual gossip columnist Louella Parsons solidified it. Essanay soon expanded its operations, first to Colorado and then to California, where the company later relocated its permanent offices in Los Angeles—although Ted, who was based in the Chicago studio, where he was producer and director (roles that, in those days, were essentially interchangeable), was not directly involved in the expansion.

Parsons remembered her first meeting with Ted, "a young man with a shock of dark hair and an ambition to give the screen some real thrillers. . . . He had invented the serial for Pathé and had come to Essanay at what was considered a huge salary for those days." Despite his somewhat stern exterior, he proved to be a kind and encouraging friend who helped many people, actors and directors alike; and he quickly established himself as "a daredevil among directors" who had little interest in passionate love scenes but instead sought out different and exciting types of stories—even though, as Parsons recalled, "no one had more of a knack for bringing pathos to the screen than this brilliant young man."[48]

Using both the experience that he had gained at Pathé and his new authority at Essanay, Ted began writing and directing short films. Over the next two years, he completed numerous one-reelers, releasing as many as one per week through Essanay's ambitious "Five-a-Week" programming (that is, five new short pictures every week). As he had done at Pathé, Ted drew his acting talent from the studio's company of actors, which at the time included Beverly Bayne, Bryant Washburn, Dorothy Cassinelli, Martha Russell, Helen Dunbar, Harry Mainhall, Frank Dayton, Harry Cashman, and E. H. Calvert, several of whom would later join Ted's Ithaca company. The biggest celebrity of all, though, was Francis X. Bushman, the handsome actor dubbed "the King of Movies," who, like many early film stars, had broken into movies by way of the stage. Bushman, though, had a distinct advantage: as a former body-builder, he possessed an athletic appearance and an enviable physique, which—along with his classic profile—made him easily recognizable and helped turn him into a matinee idol admired by men and beloved by women. (Although he was already married with five children at the time that he began his film career, the studio kept his marriage a secret so that it would not jeopardize his enormous popularity with his many female fans.) Almost immediately, Bushman became the headliner in many of Ted's Essanay pictures.

Filmed over a period of two to three days, those pictures—whether romances, comedies, or adventures—usually had a simple and often hokey story line. In *Napatia, the Greek Singer*, for instance, the young fireman Billy Arnold (Bushman) is attracted to a beautiful singer. After being locked away in her room by her mean foster father, Napatia sets some papers on fire, knowing that neighbors will report it and Billy will come to her rescue.[49] In *The End of the Feud*, young mountaineer Jim Parker (Bushman) and his sweetheart Rose Simpson marry, despite their dueling families' opposition to their relationship. One day, after their child Millie wanders into the clearing where the two clans are fighting, she works magic with her sweet smile and ends the hostilities forever.[50] An infant brings about a similar transformation in *Swag of Destiny*, turning Flinty McNeal from a crook into a good family man.[51] And in the fantasy romance *Neptune's Daughter*, Charles Fleming (Bushman), a young artist, woos Neptune's daughter Undine, who assumes human form in order to wed him. After a quarrel, during which Fleming tells her that he longs for his old sweetheart, Undine begs her father to allow her to return to the sea. Fleming, though, soon regrets his desertion and follows her to ask forgiveness but finds only her lifeless body. At that moment, he awakens and realizes it has all been a dream (a common plot resolution in early films).[52]

Ted also starred Bushman in pictures such as the poignant *The Magic Wand*, a modern fairy tale in which a young girl played by "Baby" Harriet Parsons (daughter of Louella Parsons, who wrote the scenario) steals a "magic" wand from a school play in the hope of improving the lot of her destitute mother,[53] and in the sentimental drama *The Turning Point*, in which Widow Baker is swindled by Dan Walton, who takes her money and issues her a worthless stock certificate in a gold mine. But seeing a photograph of his mother, who reminds him of the widow, Walton is filled with remorse. Following Baker to her country cottage, he returns her money and "proves himself a man."[54]

Although Ted wrote most of his own scenarios, like other early film producers he often drew material from classic sources, a practice that helped allay censors' concerns. *The Virtue of Rags*, for example, was a drama based on Dickens's *A Christmas Carol* that told the story of a callous landlord named Grouch (played by Bushman) who discharges a kindly debt collector after he fails to collect the rent from an impoverished widow.[55] Only after a dream in which he has the experience of being destitute and outcast himself does the landlord see the error of his ways and learn charity. "Regenerated" through the virtue of rags, he restores the widow to her rooms, installs new furniture for her, and leaves with the satisfaction of knowing he has made reparation for her long years of misery.[56] Still other shorts like the Secret Service–themed *The Eye That Never Sleeps* introduced story lines that Ted would take up again in later serials such as *Beatrice Fairfax* and *The Eagle's Eye*.[57]

A few of Ted's Essanay pictures were especially heavy-handed in their moralizing. In *The Voice of Conscience*, whose scenario he cowrote with Harry Mainhall, he explored the consequences of an unfortunate but haunting act. When wealthy Frank Craig is killed in a hunting accident by his friend Jack Tenny (Mainhall), William Sherman (Bushman), the sweetheart of Craig's daughter, is tried for the crime. Just as Sherman is about to be convicted, Tenny bursts into the courtroom, confesses, and dies—"a victim of conscience"—in the arms of the sheriff.[58] *Sunshine*, also based on an original story by Ted, told a similarly sentimental tale. Although convicted murderer Joe Roberts (Mainhall) initially refuses to talk, eventually he confesses to Father O'Brien, a friend from his childhood, that he committed his crime to protect his sister, Sunshine. After she ran away to be married, her would-be lover betrayed her and left her ready to jump from a bridge into the black waters below. Finding her so desolate, Joe kills her betrayer and exults over the fact that "the dead scoundrel will never steal another girl's smile." The picture ends with O'Brien making an entry in his record: "Joe Roberts died August 13th, 1912. Sunshine Roberts, entered convent August 13th, 1912."[59] Despite the picture's maudlin subject, critics praised its innovative techniques, especially the creative use of superimpositions during the confession scenes, a device that Ted would use again in several of his later films.[60]

Another story of loss and redemption, *From the Submerged* (1912), Ted's most thematically and technically sophisticated short for Essanay, is now considered one of the masterpieces of silent film. Charlie (E. H. Calvert), a young homeless man, is saved from suicide by a mysterious stranger (Ruth Stonehouse), who urges him to look to heaven for hope. Two years later, after Charlie has reconciled with his dying father and come into the family fortune, he gets engaged to a wealthy socialite. Along with a group of friends, they attend a "slumming party," where they visit a bread line that is distributing food to the poor—the very same bread line where Charlie received help when he was in dire need only two years before. After the fiancée finds humor in the plight of the suffering men, Charlie breaks off their relationship and returns to the park to search for the young woman who had earlier saved him and whom he has never forgotten. When he encounters her again, she is in despair: "the poor girl, more wretched and ragged than ever, [has come] to cast herself into the bleak waters" from the bridge near the spot where they first met. But Charlie consoles her, marries her, and brings her back to his home to share the wealth she never suspected that he possessed.[61]

FIGURE 1.4 Wealthy friends with little compassion for the poor attend a "slumming party" in Ted Wharton's *From the Submerged* (1912).

The film (one of the rare early Ted Wharton pictures to survive) is especially notable, as Michael Glover Smith observed, for the "social criticism, the ironic juxtaposition of wealthy and poor characters, the bread line scenes, the musical editing rhythms and the use of an internally rhyming structure (e.g., bookending the film with scenes in the same park)," all of which "show the obvious influence of D. W. Griffith's groundbreaking *A Corner in Wheat* from 1909" and which in turn may have influenced other directors, such as the Estonian-born French director Dimitri Kirsanoff.[62] The most indelible scenes, though, are those that depict the humanity of the suffering and hungry men in the bread line, who are quick to give away their own food to those who need it even more than they do, in a stark contrast to the self-centered and self-absorbed wealthy partygoers who exhibit little humanity of their own.

From the Submerged confirmed that Ted Wharton was already one of the most accomplished young directors of his day, and it suggested that more good things lay ahead for him.

CHAPTER 2

Taking a Parallel Path

Leo Wharton believed that he was born to perform, and his early years proved him right. Born Leopold Diogenes Rubenstein (later changed to Wharton) on September 1, 1870, in Manchester, England, Leo moved with his parents and sister Eugenia to Wisconsin and then to Hempstead, Texas, where he spent part of his childhood.[1] During that time, according to his later industry biographies, he was called "Six Shooter," a nickname likely derived from the town of Hempstead, which was known as "Six-Shooter Junction."[2] After his adventurous disposition caused him to run away from home at the age of eleven, he became a fancy roller skater on the vaudeville stage, an act that earned him a surprisingly good salary. He also made the acquaintance of Minnie Maddern Fiske, one of the leading American actresses of her time, who is credited with introducing audiences in the United States to the works of Norwegian playwright Henrik Ibsen and later with leading the fight against the Theatrical Syndicate, which controlled the U.S. theater industry for almost two decades in a monopoly similar to the one that Thomas Edison established in 1908 for the burgeoning movie industry. Mrs. Fiske reportedly "wanted to adopt [Leo] and make a great actor of him." But "her kindness to him made him think of home and mother[,] so back he went to his own people."[3]

After returning to Dallas, where his widowed mother Fanny was living, Leo worked a number of short-term jobs, among them as a clerk for the

Sanger Brothers Department Store (1889–1890) and as society editor for the *Dallas Morning News* (1891–1892).[4] The call of the stage, however, was still strong, so he ventured again into the theatrical world, joining the acting company of Jennie Calif, one of the best and most popular companies on the road, at a salary of "$8 per week and cakes."[5] Over the next few years, he assumed small roles in a number of productions with other companies, eventually moving into better (although still mostly supporting) parts.

Dallas, though, was still home, so Leo kept returning, for both short visits and longer stays. A Dallas city directory published in 1894, in fact, listed him, under his original surname, as the business partner of Harry A. Hurt. Their firm of "Rubenstein & Hurt, Stereopticon Advertisers" prepared advertising slides to be shown in theaters on the "magic lantern" projectors that were a popular form of entertainment and education before the advent of moving pictures. That enterprise likely gave Leo his first exposure to the early film industry and piqued his curiosity about the new medium that was revolutionizing entertainment. While in Dallas, he married a young woman, Jennie Leach, with whom he had a daughter, Marie (born 1893); but the marriage was short-lived, and he was soon back out on the road performing with various traveling troupes and small acting companies.[6]

Hitting the Stage

Leo's earliest documented stage appearance was in 1893, in the play *The Fairies' Well*, a picturesque and romantic Irish legendary drama starring young Irish actor George H. Timmons that received positive reviews wherever it played. According to the *Worcester (MA) Daily Spy*, Timmons was supported by a good company that included Leo, billed as L. D. Wharton.[7] (By then, for professional purposes, he—like Ted—had dropped his Jewish surname "Rubenstein" and adopted the less ethnic-sounding "Wharton," likely as a way of ensuring a broader range of roles for himself as an actor.) And the *Philadelphia Inquirer* wrote of a local performance of *The Fairies' Well* that the audience was large and enthusiastic, and that "the play is pure in tone, refined in sentiment and is enlivened by sweet singing and clever dancing" and realistic scenery.[8]

After a few years of such itinerant acting, Leo was able to secure steadier employment at the Hopkins Grand Opera in Saint Louis, where his brother Ted was already performing. As part of Colonel Hopkins's theatrical company, Leo assumed various stage roles in the popular daylong "continuous performance" programs that Hopkins pioneered, which combined live drama and between-the-acts vaudeville. One such role was that of Adolphus, a "dedicated lover," in the four-act "screaming comedy" *Rooms for Rent*, set in present-day Saint Louis and staged in late December 1896. The play was part of a larger bill that included pyramidists, operatic sketch artists, and acrobatic comedians, all of whom elicited cheers from the audience.[9] The following month, Leo appeared in Hopkins's staging of the naval war drama *The Ensign*. In the role of Judge Advocate Lieutenant Henry Fairfax, Leo performed opposite his brother Ted, who played an officer from the American warship *San Jacinto*—and for once, Leo received the higher billing.

As one of the company regulars, Leo appeared in other plays that the Hopkins company staged, including "the great Southern drama" *The Octoroon* in March 1897, in which he was cast as Colonel Poindexter, the auctioneer and slave salesman who presides over the sale of the tragic heroine Zoe Peyton. The explosive and long-running five-act play by Dion Boucicault (based on the 1856 novel *The Quadroon* by Thomas Mayne Reid), an antebellum melodrama second only to *Uncle Tom's Cabin*, drew large crowds to the Saint Louis theater and provoked much discussion about interraciality, slavery, and abolition.[10] Billed as "L. D. Whorton" [*sic*], Leo also had a small role in the Hopkins production *The Romany Rye*, about a "learned hero" (the "Romany Rye" or "Gypsy Gentleman" of the title) who chooses to live among and learn from the Roma during the Victorian age.[11]

Although Leo knew all too well how peripatetic an actor's life could be, he nonetheless left the Hopkins Grand Opera and went back on the road in the hope of making an even bigger name for himself on stage. To that end, over the next few years he moved frequently and performed in a variety of productions throughout the South and the Midwest. Though much of his work was in supporting roles, in November 1898, at the Crescent Theatre in New Orleans, he was fortunate to enact a rare principal role as British Lord Green Goods in Charles Blaney's *The Hired Girl* (later novelized as *The Hired Girl's Millions*). Set in the dormitories of Vassar College, the comedy had a slight plot, "created only to hold the special parts together, and to give them a stage setting": Green Goods arrives at Vassar intent on finding and winning the coed with the most money, but he is outwitted at every turn by the hired girl.[12] Little more than "a general collection of features and tricks in the musical line," the fast-paced farce—one of many contemporary "collegiate capers"—proved so entertaining that it filled all the seats in the theater.[13]

At the Lyceum in Cleveland in October 1899, Leo's performance as "the Clean Man" in a revival of Charles Hoyt's farce *A Day and a Night in New York* brought him to the playwright's attention and led to a much larger part in another of Hoyt's productions, *The Liberty Belles*.[14] Staged at the New York City theater that Hoyt managed for a few years (known as Hoyt's Madison

Square Theatre, later simply Madison Square Theatre),[15] the elaborate musical revue was typical of the popular stage shows, yearly parodies, and topical extravaganzas such as Ziegfeld's "Follies" and the Shuberts' "The Passing Show" that never failed to please audiences. *The Liberty Belles* incorporated many familiar comic devices of the era—hijinks at a girls' school, secret elopements, intruding and moralizing uncles—but while the music and songs were neither "exceptionally bright [nor] catchy," the presence of twenty-one attractive women known as "Klaw & Erlanger's Troubadours" made the stage "alive with light and life and color."[16]

Also in New York City, Leo performed the role of Duval, a member of the Diamond Gang, in a revival of *The Great Ruby* mounted by Louisiana-born showman Henry Greenwall, who had earlier worked with Leo at the Crescent in New Orleans. Originally staged by Augustin Daly (for whose traveling company, in 1899, Ted Wharton had served as stage manager), the enormously popular jewel-heist melodrama had already enjoyed two runs in Manhattan before Greenwall selected it as the first play to open at his renovated American Theatre. As expected, the production, which premiered on September 1, 1900, was a great success. According to the *New York Times*, the "big theatre was fairly jammed," and the sensational staging was done "with fair skill and abundant spirit, and was applauded with great vehemence."[17]

Since his success in New York afforded him opportunities for better parts, Leo went back on the road again, this time touring as a principal player in *The Power behind the Throne* (1901). A "phenomenally successful romantic comedy" by Thomas Kremer based on Schiller's *Love and Intrigue* (*Kabale und Liebe*), the period piece was set in an eighteenth-century Austrian province, where rival factions in the court engage in intrigues to obtain ascendancy over the reigning prince.[18] Leo later recalled that his early career had been filled with many such roles; and in his later *Motion Picture Studio Directory and Trade Annual* biography, he enumerated some of the colorful personalities with whom he had been associated. They included many of the biggest names in the theater of his day: Olga Nethersole, an accomplished British actress and theater producer who appeared frequently on both the Broadway and London stages; Marie Wainwright, an American stage and sometime screen actress who was the leading lady for such notables as Edwin Booth (a relative of the Whartons by marriage); and Marc Klaw and A. L. Erlanger ("Klaw & Erlanger"), the famed theatrical producers who, as part of the Theatrical Syndicate, maintained a virtual monopoly on vaudeville talent and bookings during the early 1900s.[19] During these years, Leo was also professionally allied with the actor Creston Clarke, husband of Adelaide Prince (the stage name of the Whartons' cousin Lena Rubenstein), and with the stage and screen actor Maclyn Arbuckle, the cousin of Roscoe "Fatty" Arbuckle and brother of actor Andrew Arbuckle, whom he would eventually join in the San Antonio film company that Maclyn founded.

There were also a few even more curious involvements. As *Moving Picture World* reported, "To show his versatility, sandwiched in among these engagements was one where he took out his own company of black-face comedians."[20] Although little else is known about that particular venture, the formation of such a company would not have been unusual. Vaudeville, minstrel, and Tom shows were highly popular with audiences and often quite lucrative for producers. Widespread in the last years of the nineteenth century and into the early decades of the twentieth, they provided stage training for many early performers, from David Belasco and Ernst Lubitsch to Red Skelton, Fatty Arbuckle, and Pearl White.

By the turn of the century, Leo had remarried, to Bessie Emerick, a former showgirl, musical comedienne, and actress; together they had one child, Leo Richmond Wharton, who was born in Saint Louis in 1899 (and who, more than two decades later, would join his father in an unsuccessful attempt to form a new film company). For reasons not fully known—perhaps because he was ready to settle down as a family man, perhaps because he had grown tired by then of spending so many years on the road with different companies, perhaps because of his frustration over the vagaries of the stage—Leo took an eight-year hiatus from acting. During that time, according to Ed Hulse, he sold real estate.[21] But, like so many performers in live theater of that era, he became increasingly intrigued by the possibilities of the motion picture world and eventually decided to cast his lot with that rapidly evolving business, in which his brother Ted was already engaged.

The Lure of Moving Pictures

Leo's first known (and first credited) film appearance was in the title role of Lincoln in *Abraham Lincoln's Clemency* (1910), a photoplay produced by Ted Wharton for Pathé. Based on an actual event, the picture told the story of William Scott, a young soldier from Vermont who falls asleep while on watch, a transgression for which he is court-martialed. As Scott is being taken to the spot where he is to be executed, a coach pulls up in great haste, and out steps Lincoln, who—having received a letter from Mrs. Scott pleading for the pardon of her son—commutes his sentence. In a later scene, as Union soldiers are retreating in battle, Scott bravely picks up the color-bearer's banner and starts rallying the troops but is shot. Before falling dead, though, he has a vision of the president giving him a wreath of fame.

In the tableau that serves as the picture's climax, as "North" and "South" clasp hands, Lincoln takes the Union and Confederate flags—the "stars and stripes" and the "stars and bars"—from the respective color-bearers and rolls them together. When he unfurls them, they are transformed into the national flag, a symbol of postwar unity. *Moving Picture World* called *Abraham Lincoln's Clemency* "one of the strongest war plays ever produced" and predicted that it would be equally popular in all parts of the country. The poetic subtitles, the realistic scenes, and stirring action were "well calculated to advance the power and potency of the photoplay." And the climax tells "the whole story of the Civil War . . . in that little bit," so that "everyone who sees it is constrained to cheer."[22]

The picture surely gave Leo cause to cheer. The role not only garnered good reviews for his sympathetic performance and even for his resemblance to the revered figure whom he was portraying; it also led to an offer as a director for Pathé, the studio for which Ted was then working. There, Leo began directing similar shorts, such as the period historical drama *The Rival Brothers' Patriotism* (1911), in which Jim and Robert, two New England brothers, fall in love with the same woman. After the Civil War breaks out, both volunteer and win favor and promotion. But one day, when the mail arrives, Jim mistakenly opens and then hides a love letter that was intended for his brother. Sent on a dangerous mission and surrounded by Confederate soldiers, he finally gives Robert the letter, asks his forgiveness, and draws fire so that his brother can complete the mission. (The picture is extant, the only early Leo Wharton picture known to survive in an uncorrupted version.)

FIGURE 2.1 Leo Wharton's first known film appearance was in the title role of *Abraham Lincoln's Clemency*, a picture directed by his brother Ted for Pathé.

Program notes by film historian William K. Everson for a later showing of the picture—which, incidentally, listed the film's director as "unknown" (an indignity often suffered by the Whartons)—described the performances as "flamboyant [in their] over-acting," although the vigorous pace of direction created considerable interest. Everson also contextualized the picture within a larger cinematic tradition of films that treated the American Civil War as a theme. But, he underscored, whereas that war was usually examined from a "safer" and more neutral perspective, so as not to offend southern audiences, *The Rival Brothers' Patriotism* took a different and somewhat bolder approach, using the theme for dramatic purposes rather than for comedy or romantic adventure. Therefore, Everson concluded, the picture had its place in an exciting period of film history, and held the distinction of "having beaten D. W. [Griffith] to the punch with a very typical Griffith civil war story."[23]

Pleased with the performance of Charles Arling, the versatile Canadian-born star of *The Rival Brothers' Patriotism*, Leo continued to headline him in other of his Pathé productions. Many of them were sentimental dramas, such as *Memories* (1912), in which Arling portrayed a man in the twilight of his life who, "in fancy of his younger days," recalls "a heart that loved too well." Having left his bride-to-be in tears, he went to war; and when he returned, he found her married to someone else. Brokenhearted, he takes to drinking but cannot withstand "the pangs of regret" that memories bring.[24] And in the poignant *Anguished Hours* (1912), Arling played John Parsons, a man nearly driven to distraction by his noisy children. But after dreaming that his young daughter has locked herself in a chest during a game of hide-and-seek and died, he rushes to the children's rooms and is relieved to find them safe in their beds. Realizing how much he loves them, he resolves never to complain about their boisterousness again but instead to join them in their happy play.[25]

Leo also starred Arling in several of his comic romances, including *The Striped Bathing Suit* (1912), in which Mr. Peters buys his wife (Gwendoline, a.k.a. Gwendolyn, Pates) a swimsuit, which he sees her wearing as she engages in a seaside tryst with another man. Only after Peters, dressed in his best suit of clothes, wades out into the water to take a swing at the fellow does he discover that the woman is not his wife, merely a girl in the same striped swimsuit as hers.[26] And in *Locked Out of Wedlock* (1912), Arling starred as hapless Dudley Brown, who gets chained to a doghouse on his wedding day. After breaking free and taking with him a piece of the kennel, Brown is arrested by a policeman, who assumes that he is an escapee from an asylum. But all turns out well in the end.[27]

Another wedding-day calamity occurs in *An Exciting Honeymoon* (1913), a story of mistaken identities that involved the familiar blackface humor of the day, in which Leo again cast Arling opposite Pates.[28] When the nearsighted Lord Rowley loses his glasses just as he is about to leave to board a steamer for his honeymoon, some of the wedding guests decide to pull a prank on him: they persuade his new wife Gwendoline's African American maid to don the bride's travel suit, disguise her face with white powder, and pass for the bride. After learning of the trick, Lady Rowley rushes to the steamer but arrives too late: it has already sailed. Meanwhile, on board, the maid gets cold feet and scares off the bridegroom, who, in his rush to get away from her, falls into a coal bunker. After Lady Rowley engages a tugboat to take her to the steamer and after Lord Rowley conveniently finds his glasses, the newlyweds are reunited. But the maid, who must be lowered over the side by way of a derrick, is left hanging midair as the steamer resumes its journey—though, once safely in the tug, she is given a monetary reward for her part in the "exciting honeymoon." Pathé's advertisements ignored the racial implications and insisted that the picture was "the funniest, happiest, wholesome comedy in years! Two reels of screaming fun . . . the greatest laugh-getting film ever released."[29]

Since early movie audiences seemed especially fond of marital comedies, Leo produced several shorts in 1913 that revolved around wedding-day complications. In *An Itinerant Wedding*, when Widow Woods intercepts a note to her daughter Gwendoline (Pates) from Charley Arloss (Arling), she mistakenly believes it is her own hand in marriage he is seeking.[30] And in *The Elusive Kiss*, two bashful newlyweds are prevented from enjoying a first kiss, first by the presence of the company at their wedding reception and later by the train crew that tries to reunite the couple after the husband misses the train taking them on their honeymoon. Leo also starred Pates in *Baseball's Peerless Leader*, in which Ethel Norwood escapes the man her father wants her to marry and takes shelter in a bungalow owned by New York Yankees player-manager Frank Chance, who eventually helps her to reconcile with her angry parents. The photoplay, much of which was shot on the Yankees' home field at the Upper Manhattan Polo Grounds (a location Leo used again in an episode of the Whartons' 1916 *Beatrice Fairfax* serial), also featured actual Yankees players Ed Sweeney, Bert Daniels, and Roy Hartzell in cameo roles.[31]

While these and other short pictures that Leo produced for Pathé were often predictable in their plotting and formulaic in their execution, they were nonetheless popular with audiences and profitable for Pathé. And they established his reputation in the industry. As *Billboard* noted, Leo's long experience as an actor with the best companies, combined with "a mind fertile in

FIGURE 2.2   Several of Leo Wharton's short pictures for Pathé, including *The Elusive Kiss*, involved humorous complications for newlywed couples.

expedients, a sound judgment and a knowledge of what the public wants," made him a director second to none and earned him the nickname "the man who knows how."[32] He would put that significant expertise to good use at the Wharton Studios that he and Ted established in Ithaca in 1914. It was there that the Wharton brothers, known by locals as "the Wharton boys, " would make a real name for themselves—and there, with their sensational serial pictures, that they would find their greatest professional success.

CHAPTER 3

Bringing Essanay's "Special Eastern" to Ithaca

Ted Wharton could never have imagined that an ordinary football game would launch such an extraordinary film career.

The Whartons had relatives in Ludlowville, New York, a town not far from Ithaca. So when Ted arrived at Cornell University in October 1912 to film an intercollegiate football game between Cornell and Penn State, he was already acquainted with the diverse and remarkable scenery of rolling hills, placid waters, and deep gorges of New York's Finger Lakes. Both the town and the campus proved hospitable places. Centrally located, with convenient access to New York City, Ithaca offered unspoiled scenic beauty, a good economy, and a close-knit community. And the university—which, along with the Ithaca Gun Company, the Morse Chain Company, and the International Salt Company, was among the area's largest employers— boasted a distinguished faculty and an enrollment of just over forty-eight hundred students that included women and African Americans. For Cornellians, the "Big Red" football team was a source of great pride, and they flocked to the weekend games to support their home players and to cheer them to victory.[1]

Filmed with the hearty cooperation of the university's football team, the "corking good" footage that Ted shot at the game became a one-reel Essanay feature picture that was "as interesting a subject on college life as can be imagined."[2] It highlighted not just the prowess of the football team

ESSANAY
FIVE-A-WEEK

A WONDERFUL EDUCATIONAL PHOTOPLAY DE LUXE

"FOOTBALL DAYS AT CORNELL"
TAKEN AT CORNELL UNIVERSITY, ITHACA, N. Y.

BOOK THIS FEATURE AT ONCE!

Released Tuesday, December 3
"WESTERN GIRLS"
Depicting the bravery of two girls. A strong Western drama.

Released Wednesday, December 4
"ALMOST A MAN"
The sort of comedy that has made Essanay famous. A funny feature.

Released Thursday, December 5
"FOOTBALL DAYS AT CORNELL"
College life at Cornell University. An educational subject of more than extraordinary interest. Get it for your de luxe programme.

Released Friday, December 6
"THE SUPREME TEST"
A fine dramatic subject, teeming with gripping plot-strength.

Released Saturday, December 7
"BRONCHO BILLY'S LOVE AFFAIR"
Mr. G. M. Anderson in the role famous throughout the world. A vigorous Western drama.

NEXT WEEK:
"ALKALI" IKE'S MOTORCYCLE

Getting those catchy 3-SHEET POSTERS of all Essanay Saturday releases? Litho-graphed in full four colors, price 35 cents each. Order direct from your exchange or from Morgan Lithograph Co., Cleveland, O.

Photos of Essanay Players, size 8 x 10. Price $3.00 per dozen, can be secured from the Players' Photo Co., 177 N. State St., Chicago, Ill.

THESE MATTERS DEMAND YOUR IMMEDIATE ATTENTION!

ESSANAY FILM MANUFACTURING COMPANY
521 First National Bank Building, Chicago, Ill.
Factory and Studio, 1333 Argyle Street, Chicago
Branch Offices in LONDON, PARIS, BERLIN, BARCELONA

FIGURE 3.1 Filmed for Essanay, *Football Days at Cornell* was the first of many pictures that Ted Wharton would produce in Ithaca, New York.

but also the activities of the "hurrying throngs" of students on the campus, including the traditional game-day "snake dance" parade downtown and the humorous efforts of a freshman to become a member of the varsity squad.[3] Released on December 5, 1912, and shown at several of the university's alumni dinners that winter, *Football Days at Cornell* was touted as an "educational subject of more than extraordinary interest" and advertised as a wonderful "photoplay deluxe" that offered a close look at Cornell life. Although Ted did not realize it at the time, the picture would prove to be a turning point in his career.

After returning to company headquarters in Chicago in the fall of 1912 to edit the film, Ted busied himself making a number of new pictures for Essanay (none of which is extant). Sentimental and simply plotted, those pictures included *The Hero Coward*, about a policeman discharged for seeming cowardice who is reinstated after apprehending a notorious crook, and the similarly themed *Into the North*, in which a bank clerk is mistakenly accused of robbery and murder but later cleared by the real killer's confession.[4] Somewhat more ambitious was *Tapped Wires*, based on a story by Courtney Ryley Cooper (a former Denver newspaperman and highly successful short story writer who later became head of the Wharton Studio's publicity and scenario departments), in which the Coast News Service keeps scooping the Affiliated Press until office boy Mike discovers that Coast is tapping its rival's lines. The picture was praised for its depiction of "incidents—humorous, sympathetic and strenuous—that occur in the lives of plain people" and the "uniformly good photography and technique" that characterized Ted's work.[5]

Yet even as he was filming that winter and spring in Chicago, Ted fondly recalled his brief stay in Ithaca. Convinced that the town would be an ideal location for a full season of summer shooting, he pressed George K. Spoor, cofounder (with Gilbert M. "Broncho Billy" Anderson) of Essanay, to allow him to establish a temporary Ithaca studio facility where he could shoot pictures that made use of the architecture of the campus and the scenic wonders of the area.

Back to Ithaca

Spoor agreed to authorize the venture, and in May 1913 Ted—by then both director and general manager for Essanay—returned to Ithaca with the "Special Eastern," a complete company of some twenty crew members and photoplayers, including the studio's biggest star, Francis X. Bushman, and his frequent leading lady Beverly Bayne. Considered silent film's most glamorous and appealing couple, Bushman and Bayne (who, it would later be revealed, was his love interest off as well as on screen) were the "financial rock of the studio" and could be relied on to draw moviegoers into the theaters.[6] Ted, who planned to headline them in his Ithaca pictures, was well acquainted with the popular pair and had already starred them in earlier shorts such as *A Brother's Loyalty* and *The Power of Conscience*.[7] Bushman, in turn, admired Ted and credited him with keeping him in the business. "Theodore 'Pop' Wharton," he stated, "convinced me that the motion picture field held out more and larger opportunities, and I there and then determined to stay in it."[8]

Like Ted, the entire company looked forward to an exciting summer of shooting in Ithaca, where they would live and work in close proximity for the next few months. Bushman arrived first, on May 13, 1913, with his wife and five children in tow, and began waxing poetic about the locale. It "will form a splendid background for our pictures," he announced. "The beautiful hills, gorges and lake country are extremely adaptable to our plans."[9]

After a few nights in a local hotel, the Bushmans took up residence in a large home leased from prominent attorney and former city judge Paul K. Clymer, which they would share with the Whartons and their dog Buster. Located on Thurston Avenue in Cornell Heights at the edge of the university campus near the Fall Creek Gorge, the home offered easy trolley access to the town. Almost immediately after Ted's arrival, dressing rooms were created inside the house; a temporary carpenters' and scenic artists' area was established in the back; and an outdoor stage was set up adjacent to the property and draped with muslin sheets to shoot "exterior-interiors"—that is, scenes that could be filmed without artificial light—and to serve as a meeting point for actors traveling to location shots on any given day.

FIGURE 3.2   To maximize lighting, interior sets were often constructed in the open air.

The rest of the company quickly followed: actors Beverly Bayne, William Bailey, Frank Dayton, John Breslin, Helen Dunbar, Juanita Delmorez; Wharton's assistant director Archer (Archie) MacMackin; cameraman David Hargan; and property manager Al Tracy. They were joined a little later by Robin Townley, a former Ithacan who had been performing in stock companies in Canada, and Harry Carr, a native of Syracuse, New York, who had worked with Ted at Edison and Kalem. (For both Townley and Carr, the summer of 1913 marked the start of a long association with the Whartons. The two men would eventually follow Ted's brother and business partner Leo Wharton to Texas as part of Maclyn Arbuckle's San Antonio Motion Pictures.) The *Ithaca Journal* reported on the company's arrival and announced, optimistically, that Essanay will likely locate a permanent "special studio" in the city.[10]

As the members of the acting company settled into the community, Ted penned a quick scenario in preparation for the filming of *The Hermit of Lonely Gulch*, the first of the pictures the "Special Eastern" would produce that season. Hinting that he had some thirty other scenarios under consideration,[11] he assured concerned Cornell Heights residents that his filmmaking would be tasteful, not "in the form of a wild west show."[12] Securing locations, he constructed a picturesque cabin on an island—thereafter known to Ithacans as "Essanay Island"—just below the Fall Creek Falls, near the Lake Street Bridge and opposite the Fall Creek Milling Company.[13] Temporary quarters set up on the island allowed the cast to "make up" on site, and the island itself proved to be "ideal for the picture-taking," which proceeded efficiently once the last of the players had arrived from Chicago.[14]

With his customary rhetorical flourish, Ted described the plot of *The Hermit of Lonely Gulch* to the *Ithaca Journal*: "This is not a blood and thunder story" but "a beautiful story full of heart interest—and not mush."[15] A hermit who has lived wholly alone for fifteen years in Lonely Gulch is visited by his long-lost daughter Jean, who quickly endears herself to the townspeople and wins a proposal of marriage from Joe Bailey, "a splendid man." But the hermit also has romantic feelings for Jean, so he reveals his big secret: he is not really her father but rather an innocent man wrongly accused of a crime who had come to Lonely Gulch, cared for her ailing father during his illness, and assumed his identity after his death. Moved by his story, Jean admits that she reciprocates his affection and, learning that he has been exonerated of the crime, happily nestles in his arms.

The Hermit of Lonely Gulch proved to be an excellent start for the "Special Eastern." After seeing the finished print later that summer, the Chicago headquarters was so pleased that it instructed Wharton to keep making two-reel features, even though they required a full week to film, as opposed to one-reelers, which could be completed in as few as two to three days.[16] Moviegoers, too, responded favorably to the picture when it was released a few months later. Their interest was sustained by the publication of Felix Dodge's photoplay story in the *Motion Picture Story Magazine*, illustrated with stills from the Essanay picture, in another example of an early successful film and magazine cross-promotion.[17]

With the company working in a comfortable rhythm, Ted kept writing and producing pictures at a surprisingly steady pace, at times filming two pictures simultaneously. His next two-reel "human interest play," *Sunlight,* based on another of his scenarios, was shot largely in Ithaca but also included "unusually fine photo-scenes" and location shots of a country church in nearby Ludlowville.[18] It starred Bushman as Ben Grant, a young man who leaves the farm for the excitement of the big city, where he meets slum-dweller Mary Brown (Bayne). But after Mary is caught stealing coal, the two are forced to separate. Later, when Ben, disillusioned by the city, returns to the home he had earlier abandoned, he discovers that his parents have taken Mary in and become her foster parents. To the Grants' delight, the couple is happily reunited. The picture—described as "a good release . . . full of poetry and sunshine"—not only offered some excellent visual contrasts between the younger and the older, wiser Ben and between the slum and the farm scenes;[19] it also provided a pointed social comment on city life that Ted had examined at even greater length in his picture *From the Submerged* (1912), which highlighted the glaring disparity between the rich and the poor and the condescension of some of the privileged toward those less fortunate.

The first of his motion pictures to be shot using downtown locations, *Sunlight* drew considerable interest from locals, some of whom were initially unaware that the "thugs" and "coppers" running through Ithaca's streets and into the alleys were merely actors. Their confusion was understandable: the actors were wearing regulation police uniforms loaned by Ithaca's police chief Edward Buck, a relative of the Whartons by marriage (who, like so many Ithacans, began appearing in small roles in Ted's pictures).[20] The loan of the uniforms was part of the pattern of engagement and close cooperation that quickly developed among the town, college, and film communities and that continued throughout the Whartons' tenure in Ithaca; and it contributed to the very genial atmosphere that the entire company enjoyed.

Ted's two-reel poignant drama *For Old Time's Sake* generated much local interest as well. When Tess's former-boyfriend-turned-burglar Will (Bailey) breaks into her home, she protects him, "for old time's sake," by telling the police that he is a gentleman visitor. After her husband Charles (Bushman) mis-understands the situation and assumes the worst of Tess (Delmorez), "some latent spark of manhood" arises in Will, who calls back the police officer and gives himself up as a criminal.[21] The film required considerable planning: in addition to transforming a Cornell fraternity house into a gentleman's club, carpenters spent long hours on an outdoor set, constructing a "house" and a dining room that would serve as the scene of the all-important confrontation. The crew and cast (which included Police Chief Buck) reportedly worked smoothly together, with Delmorez "intensely earnest and interested in her work, . . . [laughing] a merry laugh 'between breaths,'" and Bushman "never let[ting] a chance go by to 'get off' a merry quib."[22]

Capitalizing on the appeal of his handsome star Francis X. Bushman, Ted introduced a variety of romantic themes into his pictures. The "burlesque-style" comedy *A Woman Scorned*, for example, featured a twelve-year-old girl (played by Bushman's daughter Josephine, billed under her mother's surname as "Josephine Duval") who is enthralled by the romantic stories she reads in novels. Convinced that an architect is in love with her, she begins writing him anonymous notes. But he misconstrues the situation, believing the notes to be from her older sister, whom he pursues and wins. Feeling scorned, the younger sister refuses to be pacified—at least not until the architect presents her with a life-size doll, which brings about their reconciliation.[23]

FIGURE 3.3   A woman tries to protect her former boyfriend, now a burglar, in *For Old Time's Sake*.

Tony the Fiddler, known alternatively as *Antoine the Fiddler*, employed a different sort of romantic twist. In the film, described by the studio as a "2 reel feature of the Canadian border in early days, containing many thrilling adventures,"[24] bank robber "Big Bill" (Bailey) has been terrorizing Valleyfield, yet no one seems able to catch him. That is because, in reality, Bill is Bill Carson, one of the community's best-known citizens. When Bill learns about a large shipment of silver, he holds up the stagecoach and orders Tony (Bushman), one of the passengers, to play the violin for him. Afterward, Tony comes to town, falls in love with the sheriff's daughter Sue, and determines to win her heart by earning the $1,000 reward for Bill's capture. Yet while he succeeds in apprehending Bill, he fails with Sue, who is already engaged to another man. Taking his violin in hand, Tony wanders off by himself, and "the soul of the musician soon finds relief and solace in his music."[25]

Like many of Ted's pictures, the filming of *Tony the Fiddler* had its perils: the popular actor William ("Blond Bill") Bailey, one of the picture's stars, was shooting the climactic scene of the stagecoach robbery when he became the latest member of the company's "casualty list."[26] Attired in cowboy gear, he had been riding down a stretch of road on Cornell Heights when his horse stumbled and fell, turning a complete somersault with Bailey underneath.

FIGURE 3.4 *Tony the Fiddler*, starring Francis X. Bushman, was the story of a musician who apprehends a robber and wins a reward but not the hand of the woman he loves.

Painfully bruised, the actor was sent home for a few days of rest and recuperation. But when Bailey returned two days later, believing himself sufficiently healed to try the scene again, the same thing happened. This time, though, Bailey was not badly injured. So Ted, who seemed unfazed by Bailey's earlier accident or by several similar incidents over the past few weeks, was able to finish his filming on schedule.[27]

Even more sentimental in its theme was *Dear Old Girl*, a two-reel love story that reworked Ted's Pathé melodrama *Waiting* (1911), in which a young rancher cannot escape the memory of his sweetheart who was killed in a train accident. *Dear Old Girl*, Wharton's most collegiate-oriented picture since *Football Days*, similarly featured two young lovers, Ted Warren (Bushman) and Dora Allen (Bayne), who plan to marry at his fraternity house on the day of his graduation from Cornell University, where the film was shot. As Ted arrives at the station to meet Dora's train, he hears the university's chimes playing the tune of "Dear Old Girl" and thinks immediately of her. But the train is delayed, and he soon learns that it has been involved in a high-speed accident, fatally injuring his beloved and the entire wedding party, including his father and his future in-laws. Grief-stricken, Ted loses his senses. Every day thereafter, when he hears the chimes ring out, he insists that his faithful servant "Old Jim" (played by African American Ithaca resident Robert Walker Sr.)[28] take him to the train station, where he believes that he will be meeting Dora. One morning, after Ted ventures out unattended, he hears the train engine, runs eagerly in its direction, and is struck. Before he dies, though, he has a vision of his bride "coming to greet him at the beginning of the long journey."[29]

Bushman, who released sheet music of the song "Dear Old Girl," engaged in some savvy self-promotion, insisting that he had seen the film over fifty times, and each time the whole audience was crying.[30] In "A Thrilling Parallel," a story that he wrote for *Photoplay Magazine* (May 1915), he recalled that he had learned of an interesting real-life parallel to the character he played in that film. According to a newspaper article, workmen razing a home in the small town of Heywood, Oklahoma, had unearthed a "time-worn, moth-eaten diary" that cleared up the mysterious life and death of aged recluse Henry Martin. Apparently, "a trick of death" had wrecked a train and killed the woman who was on her way to become Martin's wife. Every day after that, "rain or shine," Martin would make his way through town to meet the train and then hobble home again to his cabin. But the film story for which Bushman claimed some credit was not suggested "by any anecdote of fact. It occurred to me from an actual playing of 'Dear Old Girl' on a set of chimes, at sunset, in a college town in [Ithaca] New York last summer."[31]

Essanay's Special Eastern Company on the Campus of Cornell University, Ithaca, New York.

Back Row, Standing—Juanita Dalmorez, Helen Dunbar, Albert Tracey, Master Everly, Harry Carr, Theodore Wharton, David T. Hargan (Cameraman), Archer McMackin. Second Row—Otto Breslin, Virginia Duval, Francis X. Bushman, Josephine Duval, Frank Dayton. Sitting—Beverly Bayne, Bruce Duval, Frances Duval, Robin Tonley, Edna McClellan, William N. Bailey.

FIGURE 3.5   The Essanay "Special Eastern" Company gathered on the Cornell University campus.

The completion of that picture coincided with the visit of Ted's friend Hugh Hoffman, one of the editors of the influential *Moving Picture World*, who arrived from New York City to spend a short vacation in Ithaca. Hoffman later wrote that, having "hopped a rattler" (that is, boarded a train) from the city, he wished himself into the charmed circle of the Essanay company for the space of a couple of weeks.[32] After touring the town and the Cornell campus, he announced that he was extremely impressed with the wonderful scenery of Ithaca and particularly with the pictures that had been filmed there.[33] It was, to be sure, a valuable endorsement of Ted's vision for the Essanay Eastern Studio.[34]

Archer MacMackin

Just as Ted Wharton did, assistant director Archer MacMackin—working under Ted's close supervision—kept himself and the company busy throughout the summer with rehearsals and production. A former newspaperman, MacMackin had already achieved some small success as a play writer and producer for Essanay with pictures such as *Chains* (1912), about a woman who is "chained" by her vows to her degenerate convict husband, even though she has the prospect of real love with another man.[35] But *The*

Whip Hand, which Essanay advertised as "an exciting melodrama that will universally appeal," was the first of MacMackin's story ideas to be filmed in Ithaca. In the "beautiful [one-reel] love drama," wealthy Frank Burton (Dayton) carries off Nell Grant (Delmorez) the night before her wedding to Jim Dowling (Bushman). Years later, the couple returns to her old home, where Nell accidentally causes a dynamite explosion that kills several men, including her husband, and injures Dowling. The accident crazes her. After she recovers, she seeks out her former fiancé, who is still convalescing, with the intention of resuming their earlier courtship. Saddened to learn that he is married with children (played by Bushman's own children), she "takes this final blow stoically."[36]

Ithaca's Portland Cement Works, where part of the story was shot, afforded MacMackin "the benefit of real blasts in the quarry and the explosions," which he used to good advantage.[37] The local paper also reported on a humorous incident that occurred after a horse, hired from a local livery for use by Bushman, was brought by a "superstitious negro" to the site where the crew was filming but forgotten in the excitement of the picture taking. When it was later discovered that the man had waited patiently until 9 p.m. before riding the horse six miles back to town in the dark, Frank Dayton, the "poet laureate" of the group, penned an original poem that amused readers and reflected contemporary racial attitudes and stereotypes. Entitled "Sambo and 'The Whip Hand'" and published in full in the paper, it began "I's hiked aroun' de country an' I's been in foreign lan's, / I's trabbled wif a circus an' wif Pickaninny ban's; / I thought I knew de business but I reckon I must talk / About sat Moving Picture Life in Ithaca, New York."[38]

Another of MacMackin's pictures, the two-reel "character Southern play" *The Way Perilous* that starred Bushman as Frank Davenport, also incorporated Ithaca locales. To cover his debt after losing heavily at cards, Davenport changes the amount on his father's check from $200 to $2,200. Feeling that he has disgraced his family, he leaves for the West. Aware of what he has done, Virginia (Bayne) uses her small inheritance to pay off the bank. Later, learning that his father is dying, Frank returns home to ask forgiveness but is surprised to discover that his parents know nothing of his dishonesty. "Owing to Virginia, he is still their pride and joy."[39]

Since a number of the scenes were filmed in a large colonial home in Ithaca that passed for a southern manor, an actor was needed to play the part of the family's black retainer, whom property man Al Tracy "scoured the city" to secure. Although his first candidate declined at the last minute, Tracy soon found an even better prospect, Eugene Gladsby, who reportedly was "almost an image in appearance of the famous Uncle Tom" and therefore ideal for the "old darkey servant." Gladsby performed his part to perfection, to the delight of Ted, who noted that he could not have done better if he had been rehearsed for two weeks. In fact, Ted was so pleased with his performance that he intended to feature him in a special photoplay, but Gladsby died before filming of that new picture began.[40]

Bushman and Bayne also appeared together in MacMackin's film *The Right of Way*, in which young Rosemary subverts the attempts by a railway company to build an extension through a piece of property where her beloved mother is buried. Engineer Frank Robinson, en route to the site to mediate the impasse, is injured in an automobile accident.[41] Unaware of his identity, Rosemary dutifully attends to him—a kindness that he reciprocates by persuading the railroad office to implement a detour. The burial ground is preserved, and the two fall in love. The conflict that Frank experiences is reflected in the film's title, which suggests not just the actual right-of-way that he is sent to build but also the right way that he resolves the highly sensitive issue.

Several scenes were shot at a railroad construction site in the nearby town of Geneva, New York, and at a small old graveyard near Slaterville Springs where the forty Italian road workers who played the laborers "performed their dramatic duties very acceptably, acting the role of quitting to perfection."[42] The railroad settings were not only appropriate to the plot; they also added to the picture's popularity by highlighting what Ben Singer called "the marvels of the machine age."[43] In the train, as Christian Hale observed in "Phantom Rides," cinema had "found a technology to rival its own wonders, and early train films are often records of one modern technology marvelling at the other. It was a relationship that in a way began decades earlier; through the train carriage window, passengers were offered a cinematic experience years before the emergence of cinema itself. . . . These two technologies were fused together to produce an all-new cinema spectacle." *The Right of Way* thus became part of a tradition of railroad films, from "actualities" such the famous Lumière brothers' film *L'Arrivée d'un train* (1896) of engines entering and leaving stations,[44] to Edwin S. Porter's milestone *The Great Train Robbery* (1903).

The Right of Way was also memorable for a hair-raising stunt that was said to be one of the most thrilling scenes ever filmed, "sure to bring gasps" from those who witnessed it. As Frank makes the trip from the railway station to Rosemary's home, he gets into a fight with his drunken and speed-crazed chauffeur, who loses control of the vehicle. Although Frank is able to jump out, the car goes over an embankment and plunges two hundred feet into Taughannock Gorge, killing the driver. To be sure, the spectacular scene required considerable planning: the action had to be stopped at a critical point, a dummy chauffeur substituted, and the car pulled by means of an attached cable to the edge of the gorge. At great expense, two separate cameras were set up at different angles to capture the fall. Reportedly, it cost seventy-five dollars just to pay the extra cameraman, who spent a mere half hour filming the critical moment before he returned to the Essanay studio in Chicago.[45]

The fall, of course, was staged; but a related accident was quite real and almost claimed the life of a young Ithacan who was working with the company. As part of the filming, C. J. Evans was supposed to position himself near the wreckage at the bottom of the gorge. Rather than taking the time to climb carefully down the embankment—an "arduous labor in the boiling sunshine"—he decided instead to shinny down a rope that had been tied to a tree. Momentarily losing his grip, he started down the cliff but managed to hang on to the rope long enough to retard his fall. The result was a terrible case of rope burn—and surely a severe reprimand from Wharton and Mac-Mackin, both of whom were unaware of his perilous plan.[46]

Equally challenging to film was MacMackin's double-reel photoplay *The Love Lute of Romany*, a dramatic story with "many exciting and thrilling scenes of more than ordinary pulling power," "a splendid cast," and a theme that Essanay ads promised would be "new and one to be remembered long." Sybil (Delmorez), the daughter of Chief Castrous (Dayton), is in love with "Gypsy-poet" Raoul (Townley). But the Chief does not sanction the vagabond's attentions and, in a climactic scene, chases him to the edge of a cliff, where Raoul plummets into the gorge. Banished from the camp, Sybil is discovered by Frank, who had earlier visited a fortune-teller in the Roma camp. He brings her to his home to be cared for by his kindhearted mother. Recognizing, though, that she is causing strife between Frank and his sweetheart Constance (Bayne), Sybil takes to the road, where she encounters Raoul, who has miraculously survived the fall; and they walk together, hand in hand, into the woods.[47]

Like the planning of the car stunt in MacMackin's earlier *The Right of Way*, the preparations for *The Love Lute of Romany* were extremely complicated. Much of the underbrush had to be cleared so that the camera could get a sweep down the gorge and out toward the lake; a dummy had to be prepared; and the right tree had to be selected for the scene. The one that MacMackin originally wanted to use proved to be rotted; nonetheless, Townley gamely climbed out to test it. The tree that was ultimately chosen required considerable cutting away, which Townley did himself while attached to a rope held by the crew. And Frank Dayton, whose role as the Chief required him to stand at the very edge of the gorge, found himself nauseated and "affected when looking down from a great height" into the abyss. Each time he left the brink of the chasm, he sighed in relief. It was a trying ordeal all around. MacMackin admitted that he did not take as many feet of film as intended because he was "all-in" from the continual strain of half expecting at any moment to see one of his actors drop into the gorge.[48] And, of course, adding to his other difficulties, MacMackin had to secure real Roma, a band of whom he fortuitously found encamped at nearby Beebe Lake.[49]

The Toll of the Marshes, based on a scenario written and directed by Mac-Mackin, presented yet another kind of production challenge.[50] The two-reeler was a moving story about two men: John Rogers (Dayton), a crooked wealthy land agent, and John Hammond (Bushman), one of the people whom Rogers swindled in an investment in a southern "farm" that turned out to be nothing more than swampland. Despite having every reason to hate Rogers, Hammond tries not to lose faith or hope. When Rogers and his family travel south, and his daughter Josephine (played by twelve-year-old Josephine Bushman) is accidentally lost in the marshes, Hammond finds her clinging to the weeds and saves her life. Afterward, a grateful and penitent Rogers returns the money that he had fraudulently obtained from Hammond and other investors.[51] "This picture," one reviewer noted, "tells the story in true dramatic fashion, and is worth going to see,"[52] while another reviewer praised the "excellent bit of act-ing" by Bushman and his "splendid cast," which included Juanita Delmorez, Helen Dunbar, William Bailey, and Harry Carr.[53]

Most of the exterior filming on *The Toll of the Marshes* was conducted in the Montezuma swamp wastes at the north end of Cayuga Lake, where director MacMackin, camera operator Dave Hargan, and property man Al Tracy "secured some clever scenes." But Bushman, Josephine, Dunbar, Carr, and the other cast members who filmed on location were less than enthused about making the trip or braving the mosquitoes and gnats in the swamps. Clearly, the *Ithaca Journal* reported, their experience proved that "the life of the moving picture actor is arduous and far from pleasant at times."[54]

The Toll of the Marshes would be the last picture filmed by Ted's Essanay "Special Eastern." On August 23, 1913, the company of actors prepared to return to Chicago to resume work on some photoplays they had left unfinished before relocating for the summer to Ithaca. Only a few days earlier, *The Whip Hand* had premiered at the Star Theater to a large crowd that thronged the doors at both evening shows. Yet while the cast (which included Wharton crew member Al Tracy and other locals) was hailed for their performances, the film itself left the audience underwhelmed. According to the *Ithaca Journal*, "all the actors in the scenes did very capable

FIGURE 3.6 Although he has been swindled, John Hammond (Francis X. Bushman) saves the crook's daughter (played by Josephine Bushman) in *The Toll of the Marshes*.

work, although the scenario failed to arouse any enthusiasm [and] the plot did not seem over-strong."[55]

Even sadder was the news that Bushman's son "Baby Bruce" had fallen out of a second-story window at the Thurston Avenue home that served as Wharton's headquarters. Both the Wharton company and the Ithaca moviegoers who had just watched him in the final scenes of *The Whip Hand* were soon relieved to learn of Bruce's excellent prognosis for a full recovery.[56]

Returning to Chicago

After the company departed Ithaca, Ted remained in town a few days longer to attend to some final details of the pictures (none of which is extant). Even though he had reportedly lost almost twenty pounds over the summer from the stress of managing and directing the company, he felt buoyed by the success of his temporary Ithaca studio, the lease on which officially ended on the first of September. The production had been steady. The entire company had worked closely and cooperatively, filling in for each other as necessary, making the filming at times seem like a family affair and providing a model of collaboration that Ted would draw on in his later filmmaking. In fact, it really was a family affair, with Cornell professor Louis Agassiz Fuertes and his son Sumner, Bushman and his children, Leo's wife Bessie, and police chief and Wharton in-law Edward Buck all enacting roles in the pictures, and with many Ithaca residents serving as extras. So it is no wonder that Ted was already looking forward to returning, possibly as early as the fall, for more filming.

Essanay appeared to be just as enthusiastic as Ted about the prospect of his return to Ithaca. Only weeks before the summer's filming ended, Essanay cofounder George K. Spoor had traveled to New York to see for himself the scenic beauties of the town and vicinity.[57] Impressed by the quality of the pictures that had been produced there, as well as by the diverse offerings of Ithaca itself, he urged Ted to begin scouting possible locations as soon as possible. "Before he [Spoor] left," the *Ithaca Journal* happily announced, "it was pretty well understood that he would build a permanent studio here."[58]

For Ted, this was welcome news, and he was only too happy to oblige. According to the *Cornell Alumni News*, he stated that Ithaca was "so good a field for production" that he expected not only to find a suitable lot in town but also to film there the entire year round. "He says that every scenic setting that can be desired for a 'photoplay' can be found in the neighborhood of Ithaca," from the waterfalls, the gorges, the lake, the university buildings and fraternity houses to Wild West backdrops.[59]

The generosity and support of the locals made Ted doubly eager to lay down roots in the upstate community. After all, as *Moving Picture World* editor Hugh Hoffman had observed during his two-week visit, the Wharton studio and adjacent stage served both as a gathering place for the photoplayers, all of whom seemed genuinely fond of each other, and as a general rendezvous point for Ithacans "who could spare the time and for many who could not." Townspeople, moreover, were always anxious to assist, whether by lending their furnishings or by "holding themselves in readiness to appear [on screen] at any time" as extras. They also showed their hospitality by inviting the Essanay people to their dances and other social affairs—courtesies to which Ted and his company warmly responded.[60] And college boys donated their fraternity houses, carried their furniture to and from the studio, used their influence to get props from the Cornell Museum of Natural History, and performed as though the very honor of their alma mater depended on it.[61] It was therefore with some reluctance that Ted finally departed Ithaca, which he confessed to the local paper already felt like home to him.

Not long after his return to Essanay's headquarters in Chicago, however, Ted was unpleasantly surprised to learn that the company had reversed its thinking and decided against opening a permanent eastern studio. At that point, he made a momentous decision of his own. He determined that he would leave his position as general manager and director, terminate his contractual association with Essanay, and move to Ithaca to form his own independent production company. It was, to be sure, a risky move—but it was a risk that Ted believed was worth taking.

CHAPTER 4

Taming and Reframing Buffalo Bill

Only one thing now stood in the way of Ted's return to Ithaca: Buffalo Bill.

Before making the decision to terminate his contract with Essanay, Ted had committed to completing a final film for the studio: a historical epic, originally titled *The Indian Wars* and later released under various other titles, including *The Last Indian Battles from the Warpath to the Peace Pipe*, *Indian War Pictures*, *The Indian Wars Refought*, *The War of the Civilizations*, *The Wars for Civilization in America*, and *Buffalo Bill's Indian Wars*.[1] That film, one of the first to be made with historical preservation in mind, would reenact some of the major Indian battles and feature a series of "Frontier Celebrities [who would] Revive Days of Indian Wars."[2]

Few other producers were capable of managing such a massive and challenging project. Ted, however, had already demonstrated his ability to recreate a similar large-scale "splendid Historical Pageant." The previous year, he had served as assistant director to Harry McRae Webster, Essanay's "chief dramatic producer," on a mammoth production titled *The Fall of Montezuma*, which told the story of Spanish invader Hernando Cortés's conquest of the Mexican Empire. Starring Francis X. Bushman as Cortés and Frank Dayton as Montezuma, that three-reel epic "spared neither time nor money in making it as well-nigh perfect in every detail as possible," and it garnered much praise for its broad scope, dazzling costumes, and realistic scenes of military assaults, Aztec battles, and defiant opposition based on the most important incidents leading up to the final overthrow. Just before the film's release in September 1912, *Motography* announced that audiences would be able to "witness a marvel of artistic photoplay triumph that unquestionably will go down in picture history as a masterpiece."[3]

The Indian Wars promised to be even more spectacular. As *Moving Picture World* reported on October 25, 1913, "The executive brains of the big Essanay production of 'Life of Buffalo Bill' [one of several early working titles for the film] at Pine Ridge, South Dakota, are mainly under the hat of Theodore Wharton. To him has been entrusted the enormous undertaking of handling several thousand troops and Indians, and as many horses, to say nothing of handling the Colonel [Cody] himself, who is said to have all the ways of a prima donna." But, the journal accurately predicted, if Wharton "gets away with it, which he undoubtedly will, he will earn further glory for himself as a top notch producer."[4]

The film was largely the creation of the legendary William Cody, a colorful and iconic figure. Known worldwide by his public persona of "Buffalo Bill," Cody, as Nancy M. Peterson writes, "radiated derring-do, invited exaggeration. He was flamboyant, a spectacle, an idol, and he worked hard to maintain that stature."[5] As a young man, Cody had held many jobs: first as a cattle herder and wagon train driver on the Great Plains; then as a fur trapper, gold miner, and Pony Express rider; and later, after the Civil War, as a bison hunter and army scout. Capitalizing on the popular fascination with life in the West, he embarked on a new profession, transforming himself into a successful showman. He began his entertainment career in 1872, at the age of twenty-six, with *Scouts of the Prairie*, a stage drama created by dime novelist Ned Buntline (the pseudonym of Edward Zane Carroll Judson Sr.), who first coined the "Buffalo Bill" nickname. By the following season, Cody had organized his own troupe, the "Buffalo Bill Combination," whose *Scouts of the Plains* show featured himself and his fellow plainsmen John Burwell ("Texas Jack") Omohundro and James Butler ("Wild Bill") Hickok. Wild Bill and Texas Jack eventually left the show, but Cody continued staging a variety of plays until 1882, the year he conceived his new Wild West show. That outdoor spectacle, which was designed to educate as well as to entertain, employed a cast of hundreds, along with live buffalo, elk, and cattle.[6] As the show expanded, Cody incorporated new elements, including bronco riding, roping, and other skills that would later become part of public rodeos, and spotlighted such legends of the West as sharpshooter and crowd favorite Annie Oakley (billed as "Little Sure Shot") and trick rider and shooter Lillian Smith.

The show proved to be enormously popular, both nationally and internationally, especially as Cody kept adding features such as the "International Congress of Rough Riders" and the Lakota Ghost Dancers. But problems eventually arose. In particular, the 1906 settlement of the estate of circus promoter James A. Bailey, Cody's onetime collaborator who held half interest in the Wild West show, crippled him financially. As the William F. Cody Archive notes, he never completely recovered, leaving the show's fiscal status problematic from that point forward.[7] To survive, Cody sought various partnerships, including one with Major Gordon W. ("Pawnee Bill") Lillie in 1909; and he borrowed money from Denver businessman and *Denver Post* founder Harry Tammen, an unfortunate arrangement that ended in Cody's bankruptcy in 1913. Unable to make good on the debt, Cody had to liquidate all of the show's equipment and contents and even watched his beloved white horse Isham put up for auction.[8] After that, in a further humiliation, Cody was forced to work for Tammen's Sells-Floto Circus and later, briefly, for the Miller Brothers 101 Ranch "Real Wild West." He was never able to manage his own show again.

Cody's legacy had also been tarnished by another event: the divorce proceedings that he brought in 1904 against his wife Louisa, who he claimed had tried to poison him. Although his divorce petition was denied, the exposure in the press of Cody's drinking and extramarital affairs clearly diminished his heroic stature. So he welcomed any opportunity that might allow him to rehabilitate his image as well as to revive his career and his bank account.[9]

Buffalo Bill on Film

Recognizing the broad impact of film, Cody determined to use the new medium as a vehicle for writing—or, in some cases, rewriting—his own history and shaping his legacy. A consummate showman, Cody was no novice when it came to filmmaking: he had cooperated with Thomas Edison in the filming of his Wild West show at Edison's Black Maria studio in 1894, and he himself had filmed portions of the show in 1910 and 1911. He had also appeared in or served as the subject of other early shorts. But those pictures were little more than novelties that hinted at Cody's accomplishments. "I grow very tired of this sort of sham hero-worship sometimes," he had told a friend. What he wanted was to be real, "to present his West, as he knew it was, with no need for hyperbole" and thus to educate the public.[10]

It was not only his own history, however, that Cody was attempting to rewrite. Since most Americans knew little about the actual frontier that had been tamed and conquered in the late nineteenth century, their views were shaped by Cody's colorful tall-tale recollections and Wild West tableaux, which included exciting but historically inaccurate spectacles of savage Native Americans attacking innocent villagers, raping settlers' wives, and scalping cavalrymen. The war-whooping Indians whom his shows evoked not only became the way that Native Americans were perceived in that era but also, as David Burrell and others have demonstrated, laid the foundation for "the entire 'western' genre of books and movies in the twentieth century." Cody's public entertainments, coming as they did so near the end of the Indian Wars and building as they did on years of propaganda regarding war atrocities, stirred hatred and great resentment against Native Americans, which were spurred by contemporary "scientific and popular opinion" that allegedly confirmed the innate superiority of the white race and underscored Indians' lack of culture and sophistication.[11]

A 1912 film, *The Life of Buffalo Bill*, produced by the Buffalo Bill and Pawnee Bill Film Company, had attempted to highlight his achievements. It depicted him falling asleep near a stream and "Dream[ing] of the Days of His Youth," with flashbacks of some of his best-known adventures. But the picture was not the breakthrough opportunity that Cody was hoping for: he wanted something bigger, something better, something that might elevate his standing in the public eye and even restore him to financial solvency. That opportunity came after he approached Essanay Films in Chicago, which prided itself on its "genuine" westerns. The company seemed an ideal choice for the project. As Sandra K. Sagala writes, the *Denver Post* disclosed that Essanay cofounder George Spoor "taboos the vulgar and cheap grade of picture and leans to the educational, the patriotic and true to life." Spoor was also a longtime fan of Cody, who he believed had more to do with the remarkable progress and development of the West than any other person.[12]

Cody, in turn, was convinced that Spoor could help him realize his dream of faithfully preserving the country's western history through the new medium of moving pictures.[13] Fortunately for Cody, Sagala notes, he had "an uncanny knack for being in the right place at the right time." The year 1913 proved to be a watershed for him and for the entire movie industry: with the threat of war inhibiting production and import of European films, American movies proliferated in a growing market; interest in film stars fueled the appeal; and improved filming and production techniques enhanced the variety of topics that increasingly sophisticated audiences demanded. In short, as Sagala concludes, it was a good time for Cody to get more directly into the film business.[14] To that end, he formed the William

F. W. Cody ("Buffalo Bill") Historical Pictures Company, incorporated in Colorado, and named himself vice president.[15]

In conjunction with Cody's Historical Pictures (whose officers included Essanay founder Spoor and production manager Vernon R. Day), Essanay agreed to produce an "epic" eight-reel film titled *The Indian Wars*, which would present a historical account of the Indian wars on the Great Plains. The arrangement could not have been better for Cody: Essanay, as a full partner in the production, would "supply the technical assistance required of the film project, as well as the knowledge to market the finished project"; and Cody, without making any financial investment, would hold one-third interest in payment for his services and for the use of his name.[16] Showcasing his remarkable career and focusing on his role in the conflicts, the film would re-create a number of important battles fought between the U.S. Cavalry and various Sioux tribes and would reenact other related events.

Since Cody wanted the battles caught on camera to be fought on the original sites, he used his considerable influence to persuade Secretary of War Lindley M. Garrison to authorize the use of six hundred soldiers from the Twelfth Cavalry stationed at Fort Robinson, Nebraska. And he convinced Secretary of the Interior Franklin K. Lane to allow filming at the Pine Ridge Reservation in South Dakota, with as many as one thousand actual Sioux participating and Colonel H. C. Sickles, a lieutenant at the original battle at Wounded Knee, assuming command.[17] Scheduled to appear in the film alongside Cody were several of his friends: General Nelson A. Miles, who had fought with him at Wounded Knee; General Charles A. King, who was also credited with writing the film's screenplay; Generals Frank D. Baldwin and Jesse M. Lee; and Colonel Marion P. Maus. Cinematographer on the film was D. T. (David) Hargan, who had worked with Ted Wharton over the summer in Ithaca. Essanay's Vernon R. Day served as production manager. And Ted, tasked with coordinating the large and complex project that ultimately employed ten thousand people, was engaged to direct the spectacle.

Re-creating the Indian Wars

Anxious to begin production, Ted—accompanied by his wife, Day, and Hargan—left Chicago on September 26 for Pine Ridge, the site of Wounded Knee. By the time Cody arrived on October 2, Ted had already reviewed the script, plotted the scenes, and estimated the cost of production at about $100,000. He had also begun worrying about how best to manage the many unskilled amateurs who would be reenacting the events.[18] Perhaps he had heard about Thomas Ince's experiences with his Indian pictures, which forced Ince to pad the war clubs so that the Native Americans playing the vanquished in the battle scenes did not get carried away and cause any real harm to the white actors.[19]

On location, Wharton realized the magnitude of the undertaking. To his colleagues at *Moving Picture World*, he wrote,

> I am in the Bad Lands of South Dakota, hemmed in on one side by the U.S. Army and on the other side by the Sioux Nation. I will have to fight my way out, or in other words, reproduce the last Indian Wars, historically correct. I will be assisted in this way by Buffalo Bill . . . and all surviving officers of those wars, as well as hundreds of troops and Indians, and all surviving Scouts and Indians. A more wonderful sight you cannot imagine. As I look from my tent, I see hundreds of teepees stretched over the hills on one hand, and the camps of the soldiers on the other. To give you an idea of the magnitude of the production, I will say that we are using more than 1000 horses in the production, and that this is not a press agent's estimate either.[20]

As Essanay cameramen constructed the fifteen-foot-high wooden filming tower required for large-scale filming and prepared the wagon on which the tower would be placed, Ted worked closely with Cody and with General Miles, who served in a dual capacity as both actor and technical adviser. Once the scenes were set, the filming began. Shot at times out of chronological sequence, the footage included images of the ceremonial Ghost Dance,[21] an integral part of the Ghost Dance religion founded by the Paiute mystic and prophet Wovoka, who predicted that the Messiah would return to earth in the form of an Indian, after which white men would disappear from native lands, Indian believers would be reunited with their dead ancestors, and peace and prosperity would reign.

U.S. officials, intent on putting an end to the "Messianic craze" that the Ghost Dance inspired and aware that terrified settlers feared it was a call to attack, had tried to place Sitting Bull and other chiefs under arrest. During one of the confrontations, Sitting Bull was killed, thus exacerbating the hostilities that came to an even sorrier end in the battles that followed. The most horrific was the massacre at Wounded Knee, where the outnumbered Sioux fled into the ravine at Wounded Knee Creek as the artillery men on the hill lobbed exploding shells into their midst. On film as in fact, that was "a tragic, bloody business," which had deep resonance for the Native American performers, many of whom had lost relatives there.[22] "Squaws chanted their death song as they did years ago," reported the *Motion Picture News*,

FIGURE 4.1 Ted Wharton with General Nelson A. Miles in Pine Ridge, South Dakota, during the filming of *The Indian Wars*.

and "broke into tears as the vividness of the battle recalled that other time when lives were really lost and everything was actual." Chieftains, too, "now grown grey, and used to the sight of blood shed from the innumerable battles," became emotional, remembering the warfare that deprived them not just of power but "of brothers, wives and children" as well.[23] At the same time, according to Cody, during the filming "some braves were too excited to remain 'dead' until they were entirely out of ammunition; then they rolled over to watch the antics of their brothers," thus injecting some unintentional "comedy into an otherwise very serious affair."[24]

Since the Wounded Knee sequence was integral to his picture, Ted left little to chance. Using scene dissection during the filming—that is, three cameras in different locations—he planned to stitch the shots together in editing in order to create a greater illusion of reality in the finished product. "In complex spectacles such as this, with expansive sets, huge crowds, and enormous sweep of action," Sagala noted, "the benefit was a diversity viewers normally found only in studio films."[25]

Filming of the battle of the Mission at Pine Ridge, fought the day after Wounded Knee, was scheduled to follow immediately. But shooting was delayed first by bad weather and then by General Miles's insistence that the scenes be shot on location, a task that involved a fifty-five-mile trek for the Sioux families and the company of actors, along with the dispatch of wagons ferrying provisions and equipment. *Billboard* noted that such "adherence to official records . . . will not only aid in impressing upon the public those thrilling scenes and interesting subjects, but will please artistic circles by their clear sharpness and perfection of detail."[26]

Once the Pine Ridge Reservation scenes were completed, Ted turned his attention to the filming of two earlier battles: Summit Springs (1869), where a young Cody shot (but did not kill) Chief Tall Bull, and Warbonnet Creek (1876), the scene of Cody's legendary fight with Cheyenne Chief Yellow Hair and his claim of "the first scalp for Custer." Though he no longer cut the same dashing figure he did decades earlier, the white-haired Cody performed admirably in both.

Before breaking camp at the end of filming, Ted instructed the cameramen to record some images of modern-day life on the reservation at Pine Ridge, with farmers bringing in their crops and children attending school—a sharp contrast to their pre-reservation lives.[27] That footage would be used to conclude the picture and reveal "the transition of the Red Man from Warpath to Reservation Pursuits under the American Flag."[28] Afterward, by way of farewell, Ted, his crew, and the Sioux celebrated with a great feast, during which Ted was "adopted" into the Sioux Nation and given the name Waubli Wicasa (Eagle Man).[29]

On the way back to Chicago, the Whartons stopped briefly at Fort Robinson, where Ted shot still more footage. On his return to the Essanay Studios, he began reviewing all the raw film and started the protracted two-month-long process of editing, a task complicated by the fact that so many scenes had been filmed out of sequence. As Charles J. Ver Halen reported

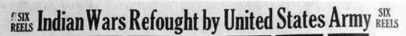

Indian Wars Refought by United States Army

SIX REELS

COL. WM. F. CODY
(Buffalo Bill)

Lieut-Gen. Nelson A. Miles

The last of the great Indian fighters are the leading players in this most realistic film of the age. Nothing more picturesque, more thrillingly entertaining was ever staged. Nothing to equal it will, perhaps, ever be done again. No boy, girl or grown-up should be allowed to miss this picture.

GREAT HISTORICAL EDUCATIONAL VALUE

OF MORE THAN ORDINARY INTEREST TO THE PUBLIC

Exhibitors:
These Pictures are what your patrons want Fifteen Different Styles of Posters, Heralds, Slides and Lobby Displays

Enacted Under the Direction of the War Department	Approved by the United States Government	Beautiful Photography and Realistic Scenes	All the Veterans Living of the Original Battles

One Thousand Indians, Many Famous Chiefs and 1000 U. S. Troops

The Col. Wm. F. Cody (Buffalo Bill) Historical Pictures Company
521 First National Bank Building, Chicago, Illinois

Write, wire or see, for bookings in below mentioned territories

F. W. REDFIELD, 67 Walton St., Atlanta Ga.—Ga., Tenn., Fla., Ala., N. & S. Carolina.
JOHN F. CONNOLLY, 203 Brooks Arcade, Salt Lake City, Utah.—Mont., Utah, Wyo., N. Mex., Colo., Nev.
ROBT. A. BRACKETT, 124 W. 4th St., Los Angeles, Cal.—California and Arizona.
W. T. NORTON, 206 National Theatre Bldg., Portland, Ore.—Wash., Oregon and Idaho.
E. H. PAINTER, 824 Columbia Bldg., Cleveland, Ohio.—Ohio.

FIGURE 4.2   The Ted Wharton–directed picture reenacting the Indian Wars was recut and retitled several times.

in *Motion Picture News*, Ted found himself "burdened with many thrilling experiences, none more so, however, than the actual scenes as they are registered by the camera."

Once the picture was finished, Ver Halen extolled its merits and affirmed that now there was a "history on record that has an inherent interest to all of us, and that will have an added charm when it flashes before our vision just as it happened."[30] *Moving Picture World* similarly praised the film, writing that it was "no five-cent novel of our boyhood days" but rather an exciting portrait of "the war dances of the Indians in the native costumes, the encircling of the camps of the settlers, the killing of settlers and Indians and the burning of tepees, horse rustling, scalping, real battles between red-skins and troops, wonderful rescues, and other hair-raising thrillers."[31] Cody, too, pronounced himself pleased that Wharton had been able "to preserve history by the aid of a camera, with the living participants who took an active part in the closing Indian wars of America."[32]

Sadly, Cody's high hopes for the picture were never realized. Although Secretaries Lane and Garrison endorsed the film and declared it historically correct in every detail, audiences responded with little enthusiasm.[33] Perhaps, as Nancy Peterson suggests, the quest for realism had reached too far; perhaps the desperate on-screen fighting proved too intense; perhaps the actions of the cavalry seemed too cruel and the plight of the victimized Sioux on the reservation too pitiful. Or perhaps, as Andrea I. Paul observes, the depiction of the Native Americans as savages who bore the blame for the battles in which they were so dramatically outnumbered and slaughtered by the "heroic" military was simply too controversial.[34] Whatever the reason, the picture proved a financial failure and was quickly withdrawn from distribution. Reedited by Essanay in 1917 and distributed by K-E-S-E (Klein-Edison-Selig-Essanay), a shorter five-reel version titled *The Adventures of Buffalo Bill* was released, largely as a pictorial tribute to Cody, who had died earlier that year.[35]

For Ted, though, the film (only a brief fragment of which survives) was both a major achievement and a critical transition. It marked the end of his association with Essanay. It confirmed his directorial abilities. And it prepared him for some of the challenges that he would face as an independent producer and director at his own studio. Most importantly, though, it freed him to move on to Ithaca.

CHAPTER 5

Going Independent

With the editing of *The Indian Wars* complete,
Ted was finally ready to cut his ties to Essanay and to begin scouting potential sites for his new Wharton studio. Almost immediately, a number of
cities started vying for his business—among them, Rochester, New York,
which was home to philanthropist and film pioneer George Eastman, and an
unnamed nearby "Canadian city" (likely Toronto). But, as Ted readily admitted, he had long been partial to Ithaca, both because he had a personal liking
for it and because he believed that the scenic beauty of the area was unsurpassed.[1] He saw little reason to look elsewhere, especially after the Ithaca
Men's Business Association, acting on behalf of the Industrial Commission,
approached him with a proposal.

Realizing that even a small business employing twenty or thirty well-paid
people would be a real boon to the local economy, the association members
determined to do all that they could to make Ithaca as attractive as possible
to him. As incentive to make the move, they offered him, free of charge, two
acres on Cayuga Heights and promised improvements on the property in
the approximate amount of $3,000, to be paid for by "mutual agreement"
between the Industrial Commission and the producers. At the same time,
Ithaca Light, Heat & Power Company pledged to extend its wires to the site.[2]

The recruitment efforts paid off: by mid-March of 1914, Ted announced
that he and his brother Leo, by then formally his business partner, would

base their new moving picture operation in Ithaca. Outlining his plan to the commission, Ted explained that the studio would be a project of some magnitude. Although he would initiate production with fifteen to twenty performers and crew, the number would gradually be increased to one hundred employees. Experience, he said, had taught him that salaries, property, and other considerations would cost approximately $1,000 a week simply for the operation of a single camera; but since he intended to use two cameras much of the time, the actual expenditures would be far greater. In fact, just the money invested in locating the studio in Ithaca would "be about $80,000."[3] As for the studio itself, Ted planned to invite local architects to bid on the building, projected to be a concrete, steel, and glass structure approximately sixty by one hundred feet, with two stories, a basement, and a glass roof that would allow natural light. The estimated construction cost would be $35,000. In consideration of the cooperation of the Industrial Commission, Ted agreed to place the label "Ithaca, N.Y." on every film to be released; given the broad international distribution of motion pictures, that advertising would be an excellent way to promote the city. He also informed the commission that he and his brother already had orders for films that would take them three years to fill.[4]

Distribution would be handled by the Eclectic Film Company, one of several releasing companies of Pathé Frères, with whom both brothers had earlier been affiliated. The Eclectic Film subsidiary, originally called Cosmopolitan Films, had been formed by Pathé as another means of getting its European- and American-made pictures into theaters after being "enjoined from releasing too much product through the [Edison] trust's distribution outlet [General Film Company]." Although Pathé, fearful of antagonizing the Edison Trust, did not publicize its ownership of the company,[5] Eclectic quickly gained a reputation for the high quality of its releases and became the distributor for Pathé's more ambitious films, such as the serial The Perils of Pauline.[6]

The establishment of the Wharton Studio, one of the first independent production studios in the United States, was in itself a remarkable venture—all the more, given its regional location. Although several major producers had briefly filmed in southern locales—Kalem, Biograph, Edison, Lubin, Thanhouser, Gaumont, Vitagraph, and Essanay in Jacksonville; Pathé Frères in St. Augustine; and the Star Film Company in San Antonio—few studios operated beyond the New York metropolitan area, Chicago, and Southern California, where most filmmaking of the time was clustered.[7] Nonetheless, the Whartons believed that, given the advantages of remarkable scenery and reasonable operating costs that Ithaca offered, they could make their studio a success. Adding to their confidence, as Aaron Pichel noted, was their extensive background in live theater and their years in the early silent movie industry, which they knew would enable them to draw on contacts from Broadway and from movies for story material and stars. After all, "professionals knew and trusted the Whartons."[8]

Making Preparations

Before any actual filming could begin, however, Ted needed to form an acting company. Based on his experience performing in and managing theater stock companies, he knew that a cadre of reliable and versatile actors would be critical to his studio's success. As he traveled to New York City to recruit players and select equipment, rumors began flying about which actors that company might include. He soon returned to Ithaca to announce the good news: the leading man would be Thurlow Bergen, a "well known actor with exceptional ability," and the leading lady would be Bergen's wife, Elsie Esmond, also a performer of some note. Both, the *Ithaca Journal* underscored, had been selected with great care by the Whartons, who vouched "that they made no mistake in choosing two principals of the highest histrionic calibre."[9] William ("Bill") Bailey, already known and popular among Ithacans from his work there the previous summer, would be joining the company as well. Since leaving Essanay, Bailey had played in winter stock but reportedly was ready to buckle down again to the "strenuous" life of a moving picture actor.[10] And former Pathé Company member Bessie Emerick (Mrs. Leo Wharton) was recruited to assume character parts and matronly roles. In addition, Al Tracy, the "peppery little fellow" who served as property man, and expert cameraman J. A. Dubray of Paris would lend the new company their skills.[11]

With his Essanay contract officially expiring on April 1, 1914, Ted readied himself for the move from Chicago. Ithaca, he declared, would become the new permanent home for him, his wife, and the latest "acquisition to his staff," a dog named Broker that he had purchased from a Wall Street broker.[12] While Leo remained in New York City a little longer to make the final arrangements for the assembly of the cast that would accompany him to Ithaca at the month's end, Ted set about locating a temporary site for the studio.[13] He also invited local writers who were interested in scenario writing to propose and submit samples of their work to him, so long as they were "of superlative quality," not "of the common variety."[14]

Given all the ongoing preparations, the pace of activity was dizzying. "The Whartons are as busy as two beavers," the local paper reported, such activity being "a Wharton characteristic."[15] By the first week in May, after having secured a temporary studio at 946 East State Street, Ted was already overseeing construction of a stage, which, at thirty by fifty feet, would be much larger than the stage he had used the previous summer. Bergen and Esmond, the star couple Ted had recruited in hopes of replicating the successful pairing of Bushman and Bayne, were scheduled to arrive within the next few days. The latest additions to the company included Harry Carr and Robin Townley, both of whom had been part of the Essanay "Special Eastern" company in Ithaca the previous year, and Ithacan R. A. ("Dick") Bennard. Also set to debut with Wharton were two attractive young local women, Frances White (no relation to serial queen Pearl White) and Mary Gilman, who were expected to play minor roles at first and progress to larger ones, as their dramatic talent developed.

Excitement, to be sure, was high. Although Ted kept secret the details of his proposed filming, he teased the press, saying that he would be introducing a number of sensational features in connection with his proposed scenarios, as well as several "Indian legend plays." "They will not be blood and thunder plays," he claimed, "but true Indian historic legends, in which real Indians will participate," among them several of the chiefs who had appeared in his recent *Indian Wars*.[16] He explained that he and his brother would work collaboratively but divide their labors: Ted would be "the originator and director of the scenic plays," while Leo would have charge of enacting the scenarios on a day-to-day basis.[17] And while the Whartons sometimes hewed to those more defined roles, over the next months and years the organizational structure of their company proved far more fluid, making distinctions such as "producer" and "director" interchangeable and blurring the line between creative and management responsibilities. Crew members would be pressed into service as extras or supporting actors in the pictures; occasionally even Leo himself would appear on screen. Actors, who also generated story ideas, would sometimes direct; property men served as acting scouts in the community; and a local businessman who played supporting roles eventually formed his own film company and hired the Whartons as his contracting producers. Yet it was precisely the collegiality and enthusiasm behind such grassroots efforts that gave the pictures their unique flavor and texture and that propelled the studio through its first season of filmmaking.

Production and set designer Archelaus ("Arch") D. Chadwick, who became a longtime crew member and trusted associate,[18] later described the experience of those early days during which "Ithaca was a center of the moving picture industry when Hollywood was nothing more than a barren cactus grove." As Chadwick recalled, "We had no traditions to fall back on. Believe me, it was a case of everlasting experiment." The films, he said, "were literally *built*. A rough idea was drawn up into a scenario. This was the plan. The actual scenes, the detailed continuity was created day by day, week by week."[19] Story lines often harked back to, or otherwise reworked, plots from the brothers' earlier films.

Once shot, the footage had to be sent off-site for development and processing. Since prints were expensive, only a limited number could be struck, which helps to explain why none of the pictures from the studio's first year of operation survives. Nevertheless, the feeling of camaraderie was high among the producers, actors, and crew, all of whom felt that they were in it together, creating something truly magical. Commenting on the "genuinely happy organization," *Motion Picture News* noted that "Everyone is ready to pitch in and help by doing anything needed in times of stress. All seem to take a real pleasure in their work—so much so that frequently the cashier finds on Saturday noon that a half dozen persons have neglected to call for their pay envelopes which sometimes lie in the safe for three or four days."[20]

Filming Begins

That camaraderie was evident as early as *The Boundary Rider*, the Whartons' first independently produced picture, which they began filming in early May 1914. Originally titled *The Line Rider* (with a working title of *In the Revenue Service*), it was advertised as an exceptional offering based on an unusually strong story. Although rain immediately delayed production, Ted remained confident about his progress. "We are not going to rush things," he insisted. "We are not here to grind out pictures by the wholesale, but we intend to produce high-grade photo-plays, taking our time, so that they will be of the highest grade of perfection."[21]

A four-reel adventure-drama that reportedly included forty persons in the cast,[22] *The Boundary Rider* starred Thurlow Bergen and Elsie Esmond; featured were William Bailey, Harry Carr, and F. W. Stewart, an Ithacan who eventually gave up his career as a broker to become a full-time actor.[23] In the film, after a smuggler refuses to handle any more opium because his customers are being closely watched by the police, Big Bill (Bailey), the supplier who ships the drug across the border, confronts him to demand an explanation. During the struggle that follows, the smuggler is killed. Bill attempts to make off with his cash box, and a clerk (Bergen) who arrives on the scene is mistakenly arrested by police on the charge of murder. But the clerk escapes, joins the border patrol, and becomes the means by which Bill is brought to justice. Afterward, Bill's Chinese helper (Esmond), who is actually a Secret Service agent in disguise, reveals herself and offers proof of the clerk's innocence.[24]

To create a realistic "Oriental" atmosphere, Leo Wharton ingeniously transformed Ithaca's streets and alleys, using signs in Chinese and decorating the scene with real Chinese lanterns, boxes, and other effects. To add further realism, he outfitted several members of the company in Chinese costumes and engaged three Chinese students from Cornell University to play the part of waiters in a Chinese restaurant.[25] It was an indisputably clever use of backdrops and budget, far more cost-effective than the $5,000 "Chinese village" that Universal created for its 1914 serial *Lucille Love* and used in only two scenes.[26]

Thrilled by the fact that the filming had proceeded without a hitch, the Whartons predicted that *The Boundary Rider* would be a tremendous success.[27] And indeed, on its release and exhibition in Ithaca in August, the picture was positively received—even though, because of an error on the part of Pathé, it did not bear the label "Ithaca, N.Y.," as promised.[28] The actors, who included Leo's wife Bessie Emerick as Chinatown beggar "Mary Ellen,"[29] were recognized for their contribution; and Thurlow Bergen was singled out in particular as "worthy of the highest of praise" in advancing a role that at first seemed a minor part into a commanding lead.[30]

The five-reel *The Pawn of Fortune* (originally titled *The Shanghai Man* and then *The Mechanic's Daughter*), the Wharton Studio's second film, told the story of John Hadley, who has been discharged from his job. Despondent, he jumps from a dock, is rescued by a group of criminals who hold him hostage on a yacht owned by gangster J. Harvey, and later put him off on the shore among savage Aztecs. Meanwhile, back home, after his wife collapses on the street from want and starvation, her baby Janet is taken to the home of the gangster Hall, who raises her as his own. When Hadley returns a rich man (having escaped the savages but still in possession of their priceless jewels), he locates his wife but not his child. Seventeen years later, Janet, having inherited her real father's mechanical talents, proves to be of great value to her foster father's band of crooks, who try to use her skill to crack safes. After a series of improbable events and chases around New York by a detective hot on the girl's trail, the family is finally reunited.

The film featured spectacular camera effects that employed several recent technological advances. "Leave it to 'Ted' Wharton to get hold of any new features in the moving picture industry," the *Ithaca Journal* observed, adding that he had "sprung a new one, . . . showing his resourcefulness and tact in selecting unique stunts for his scenarios," such as the filming of the Cornell-Princeton-Yale regatta on Cayuga Lake.[31] Ted also managed to create the appropriate maritime atmosphere by shooting several scenes on the yacht *Calypso* (owned by wealthy J. E. McIntosh of Auburn), where the thugs take Hadley, the bound-and-gagged clerk.[32] And in a later dramatic scene,

A LATE ECLECTIC FEATURE, "THE PAWN OF FORTUNE."
Produced in Five Parts by T. W. Wharton.

FIGURE 5.1 In *The Pawn of Fortune*, a man is eventually reunited with his lost child, who has been adopted by a gangster and forced to aid in his crimes.

Hadley fells an Indian drummer, knocks down the rest of his Aztec escort, and makes his escape by leaping from a bridge into the gorge, a stunt that required the use of a dummy.

But perhaps the most sensational effect of all was the Whartons' use of actual Onondagas to play the film's savage Aztecs. The "fifty 'heap big Injuns,'" as described in the local paper, had arrived on a special trolley car from Syracuse and then toiled all day in the hot sun in the Aztec village scenes, which were shot in the Fall Creek Gorge. By all reports, they performed well and seemed to revel in their time in Ithaca. Elderly Chief Harry Jacobs, in full regalia, even took a fifty-foot dive into the pool below Triphammer Falls, a daring act that "was greedily snapped by the camera" and brought much delight to onlookers.[33] Although one reviewer suggested that the finished film was "hardly in the spirit of a modern crook story" and that the savages (augmented in their number by Cornell University students looking "Injunlike" in full bronze makeup) appeared a bit out of place, others praised the production, particularly Ted's artistry in the arrangement of some of the scenes.[34]

The primary occupation of the Wharton company was, of course, picture making; but the actors also enjoyed participating in local events, which endeared them even more to the Ithaca community. While Ted refused a request to play a baseball game against the Pathé Roosters, explaining that his actors did not know the "difference between a baseball and a golf ball,"[35] they happily turned out for one of the fraternal nights at the Renwick Park Airdrome organized by Paul Clymer, whose home Ted had leased the previous year as the Eastern Essanay's base. For that occasion, the company—all of whom at one time had been involved in legitimate theater—worked up a presentation of vaudeville sketches to accompany the moving picture bill.[36] The actors also appeared at the local Lyceum Theater in *The Uplift*, a play written by James H. ("Morry") Morrison, then secretary and treasurer of the Wharton Company.[37] And during the downtime between pictures, they engaged in various activities in and around town. As the local paper reported, Bergen occupied himself with horseback riding, tending to the flower garden at his home, and writing short stories. Bailey took in movies and relaxed with a lemonade on the hot days. Townley helped cameraman Dubray with camera work, and Carr caught up on his reading.[38]

By the end of July, the Whartons were back at work on an ambitious four-reeler written by Ted, *A Prince of India* (originally titled *The Kiss of Blood*), about a Rajah (M. O. Penn) who arrives in America with his handsome son (Bergen) and brings with him his jewels, the most valuable of which is a large blood ruby. Although legend has it that anyone other than the Rajah's family who tries to possess the ruby will die, various opportunists try to acquire it; and it passes through many hands before being recovered.

The picture—a "meller" that, as *Variety* noted, played to near capacity audiences[39]—was filled with exciting action, including a wild motor chase. The high point, though, was the plunge of a real streetcar into the deep gorge below, a daring and technologically sophisticated stunt made possible "due to the ingenuity of Manager Ted Wharton" and witnessed by a crowd of more than a thousand onlookers.[40] As Chief of Police Buck and one of his officers blocked traffic and prohibited anyone from entering the Stewart Avenue Bridge, Car 305, retired from service in New York City, was given a trial run over the tracks and up to the throw-off switch on the bridge, after which it was towed back to its starting point some one hundred yards away. Then, with a dummy strapped in to represent the villain escaping with the jewels, as the power was turned on again, the car sped along the bridge tracks, turned abruptly to the right, and, with a ripping noise, crashed through the railing and into the creek bed below. The front of the car, noted the *Ithaca Journal*, "acted as a weight and the car shot down through the air

FIGURE 5.2   *A Prince of India* featured an exciting action scene that culminated in the plunge of a streetcar into a gorge.

like a rocket. It seemed but a second's interval when the car struck the rocks with a crash that sounded like the explosion of dynamite." The sensational stunt required several cameras to film, with one camera focused on the front of the streetcar and another on a ledge in the gorge. Luckily, it was a complete success, because a second attempt would have been impossible.[41]

Adding even more realism to the filming was the staging of the Rajah's apartment, which Ted claimed was outfitted with more than $50,000 worth of furniture at one time owned by "a sure-enough rajah." Learning that the potentate's elegant tapestries and other fineries were stored nearby, Ted—who recognized filmgoers' fascination with the exotic—had gone "gunning" for them. Fortunately, the current owner, the Rajah's former private secretary, was willing to lend the furnishings at no charge and opened his warehouse to the Whartons to select whatever they wanted for the picture. "We took up the offer, you may be sure," Ted reported.[42]

The summer had brought a few new additions to the cast and crew: Billy ("Smiling Billy") Mason, a former circus clown and vaudevillian who had previously been employed by Essanay; William Riley Hatch, an actor well known for playing "heavy" parts; and Ben Strutman, an expert camera operator whose earlier experience was at Pathé. But the filming of *A Prince of India*, for the most part, "looked like old home week" at the Wharton Studio, with many familiar faces.[43] Even Leo Wharton, who directed the picture, made a cameo appearance as a hotel clerk. Because of their familiarity and ease with each other, the cast was able to perform at a remarkably fast clip, enacting twenty-four scenes in a single day. That pace not only broke the work record for the Wharton players but also allowed Ted—who described himself as a man so tired that he likely "could go to sleep standing up"—to make up for two days' rain that had slowed the shooting.[44]

Reworking Familiar Themes

For the themes and characters of their Ithaca pictures, the Whartons often looked back to the stage melodramas in which they had performed and to the early films they had directed for Pathé and Essanay; and on occasion they even reworked entire earlier story lines. Leo's three-reel *The Warning*, for example, provided exactly what its title suggests: "a wholesome warning against drink on the part of the young" delivered by Reverend Goodrich (Penn) to his erring son Lester (Hale).[45] After the sermon, the drunken young man falls into a stupor and dreams a terrifying dream in which he steals the church contribution money, abducts a girl (White) who accidentally drowns, kills one of his pursuers, and is sentenced to and escapes from a prison camp. When his father forces him to return to the scene of his crime, the ghosts of his victims rise accusingly from the water. Waking with a start from the dream, the young man repents and is reunited with his family. The plot was strikingly similar to several of Ted's earlier Essanay films, including *The Voice of Conscience* (1912), in which a man who has accidentally killed his friend is prompted to confess his crime after seeing a drawing that depicts conscience rising from the grave of a victim and appearing before the murderer, and *The Power of Conscience* (1913), in which a preacher's sermon rouses the conscience of a man whose actions have accidentally caused the death of his rival.

Not only was *The Warning* replete with thrills and stunts such as those performed by White, who was thrown from the lighthouse pier into the waters of Cayuga Lake in what the local paper called a "wet day's work." It also, as the *Dramatic Mirror* noted, revealed a thorough mastery of drama psychology: the sermon was "direct and to the point, but so well disguised in the delivery" that it bore more power than an actual sermon delivered from the pulpit.[46] Even the members of the board of censorship praised its moral lesson and pronounced the picture to be "the finest they had seen in months."[47]

Ted's three-reel *The Fireman and the Girl*, based on a scenario written collaboratively with Leo, also recalled an earlier picture—Ted's *Napatia, the Greek Singer* (1912), in which a young fireman marries the woman he loves, despite her foster father's attempts to thwart their romance. In the similarly themed *The Fireman and the Girl*, Larry (Bergen), a popular member of a city fire company, goes to the country for a vacation, meets Sarah Jane (Esmond), and elopes with her over her foster father's objections.[48] Members of the Ithaca Fire Department appeared in several of the scenes, which included a dramatic fight between Larry and the other suitor competing for Sarah Jane's hand that resulted in a fall from a bridge. The fall, in actuality only about fifteen feet but filmed to look as if it were one hundred feet down, was precisely the kind of spectacular stunt that moviegoers had come to expect from the Whartons and that the brothers rarely failed to deliver.[49] Reviewer Clifford H. Pangburn offered perhaps the best assessment of the production, which he described in *Motion Picture News* as "an unusually fortunate combination of exciting and humorous incidents" that are used to tell an interesting story in an entertaining style.[50]

Like *The Warning* and *The Fireman and the Girl*, Ted's *The Stolen Birthright* reached back to earlier themes—in this case, mistaken identity and twins, which he had employed in pictures such *A Brother's Loyalty* (1913). Based on a scenario written by Ted, *The Stolen Birthright* was codirected by Louis J. Gasnier, director of the enormously successful *The Perils of Pauline*, whose Pathé Players, just the month before, had used the Wharton Studio to shoot several episodes of that serial.[51] The three-reel picture (whose working title was *The Two Sisters*) told the story of farmer Silas Haskins, whose wife, crazed by an eviction attempt by the sheriff, smothers their infant. When Silas takes the baby away to bury it, he finds a carriage that had fallen from a cliff; inside are twin newborns, one of whom he substitutes for his dead daughter. Years later, after the farmer and his wife have moved west and opened a saloon, an amiable gambler begins wooing the daughter. Vowing to reform, he goes east, where he meets the "twin," whom he mistakes for his sweetheart. The twin's husband likewise misconstrues the situation and suspects a romantic relationship between his wife and the gambler. Eventually, though, the truth is revealed and the mix-up resolved. Despite the numerous melodramatic coincidences, there was, according to the *Dramatic Mirror*, "a certain freshness" and appeal to the story, which was "undoubtedly of sufficient force and novelty to hold almost any audience."[52]

The two-reel *A Change of Heart* also had a plot that was noticeably similar to one of Ted's Essanay pictures. In that earlier film, *The Turning Point*, after bilking a widow out of her inheritance, a con man is reminded of his mother; regretting his swindle, he returns her money. In *A Change of Heart*, James Mason (Bergen), known as "Handsome Harry," is one of four grifters who defraud an old woman (Esmond) of $5,000. But, in an interesting use of double exposure, Harry remembers a happier time when he was his mother's honorable "boy" and is overcome by feelings of guilt, after which he fights his fellow crooks and refunds her money. In gratitude for his honesty, the widow slips a bill into his vest pocket, which he finds after he arrives at the train station. Instead of spending it, though, he puts it in an envelope to be returned to her, spends his last penny on a newspaper, and then—unable to afford a train ticket—starts the long walk back to his home. As *Variety* observed, the story was "as old as the hills but at the same time will appeal to the old and young alike," especially since the plot was "well connected" and had an unusual ending. Noting that the Wharton brothers have been "prominent in directing and acting of Pathé photoplays for a long time," the reviewer praised them for striking out on their own and predicted that they are bound to be "heard from" in the industry.[53]

The final feature that summer was *Slats*, a three-reel melodrama that included a revolver fight and a thrilling chase over a distance of three miles, with robbers speeding away in an automobile while the police, "clinging to the running-boards and firing at the fleeing machine," pursue them by trolley car. Elsie Esmond starred as Slats, a "Sis Hopkins"–style part (that is, as an unsophisticated country girl whose cleverness is underestimated by those around her), which allowed her to show off both her comic and serious acting talents.[54] Filmed in record time, "3½ reels in 3 days," *Slats* was ready

A **CHANGE** *of* **HEART**

Two-reel Wharton-made American Drama. In which an ex-convict, headed once more for the bottom is brought to himself through the memories stirred by a photograph. The story of a confidence gang who were a bit too confident—it gets a heart-hold at the beginning and keeps it to the finish. Featuring Thurlow Bergen. 1-3-6 sheet posters.

FIGURE 5.3   Overcome by guilt, a con man compensates a widow for her loss in *A Change of Heart*.

for exhibition by early November—although there is no record in the trade papers of its release, at least not under that title.[55]

The completion of *Slats* marked the end of the Whartons' production for the 1914 year. Since filming was not expected to resume until the following spring, the brothers made arrangements that would take them in different directions over the next few months. Leo and his wife scheduled a trip to Florida, where they intended to spend the winter. While there, according to the *Ithaca Journal*, Leo hoped to film a number of scenes for use once play-making in Ithaca resumed. Ted, on the other hand, planned to remain in town to shoot some exterior scenes, then go to New York City to undertake some work on a new production at the Pathé Studio there.[56]

Taking Stock

By all measures, the Whartons' first season as independent producers had been a success, and it reaffirmed Ted's confidence in what initially seemed a risky venture. Ted—by then affectionately known to his associates as "Pop"— acknowledged that he and Leo had been quite fortunate not only in finding excellent story material but also in attracting "splendid actors and camera-men" and "first-class carpenters, scenic artists, and property men," many of whom would stay with the brothers throughout their tenure in Ithaca.[57]

That first season, though, was not without its challenges, perhaps the greatest of which was the outbreak of war in Europe, which had broad impli-cations for all filmmakers, especially for Pathé Frères, the distributor of the Whartons' pictures. Countering the rumors printed in the local papers that "the European trouble might halt the production of pictures by the Whartons for some time," Ted insisted that "the enacting of photo-plays will be con-tinued with unabated activity." Yet the practical suspension of the European film industry inevitably affected American concerns as well; and although the Whartons did not have to suspend their productions entirely, they were forced to make some adaptations in their own operations, including a longer period of inactivity between pictures than they originally intended, a cut in their payroll, and a retention of only those actors and stage employees required in ongoing filming (on a "pay as you work" basis).[58]

At one point, Arch Chadwick and scenic painter Fred Haskins were tem-porarily released; four stagehands and mechanics were laid off; Billy Mason, a member of the acting company, concerned that the studio seemed at one point "practically at a stand-still," accepted employment in California and moved west; and actor Creighton Hale returned to New York City to await a call for further work.[59] The outbreak of war also resulted in the calling up for French military service of Wharton cameraman J. A. Dubray, who wrote from the front that he was "collecting great ideas for war stories" to enact after his return.[60] (Later, actor Moe Penn would be called up as well, and celebrated cameraman Ray June would leave the studio to serve in the Signal Corps.)[61]

The *Ithaca Journal* confirmed that "the foreign troubles, however, are not disheartening the Whartons to the extent that they are quitting work."[62] In fact, despite the very real wartime concerns, both Ted and Leo Wharton remained optimistic about the future of their studio. Recognizing that the slowdown in European film production actually presented some opportunities for American filmmakers, they continued to press forward with ambitious plans for spring production, more determined than ever to make their Ithaca studio a success.

CHAPTER 6

Exploiting *Elaine*

The fictional Elaine Dodge, an enterprising young woman who dedicates herself to solving the mystery of her father's death at the hands of an anonymous villain, would help to shape and advance the Wharton brothers' film career.

As Pathé-Hearst's *The Perils of Pauline* (1914) neared its conclusion, newspaper tycoon and movie producer William Randolph Hearst was determined to create a new serial that would afford his popular star Pearl White an exciting encore. That serial was *The Exploits of Elaine*. "Sparing no pains or expense to insure [its] artistic excellence," *Moving Picture World* reported in January 1915, "Pathé Freres [distributors, at the time, of both Hearst's productions and Whartons' pictures] have prevailed upon Theodore Wharton to set aside his other business interests and co-operate with his brother Leopold in the direction of the picture." Since "two such high-class directors from the same family on the same picture [made] an unusual combination," *The Exploits of Elaine* was expected to be a landmark venture for Hearst.[1] In turn, for the Whartons, the chance to be associated with Hearst's enterprise seemed an unparalleled opportunity, one that would allow them to move beyond short pictures and to make their own singular contribution to the increasingly popular serial genre.

By the mid-1910s, movies had become the locus of popular entertainment. Over a third of all Americans frequented them on a weekly basis; and serials, which could be produced quickly and profitably, satisfied the public's desire and demand for new films. They also had the benefit of expanding movie attendance by women, who began filling the theaters, where they discovered a visual imagery on the screen that was as uplifting as it was entertaining. Serials, as Shelley Stamp writes, "offered [them] novel, even radical, forms of viewing pleasure through the characters of their famously modern heroines, the 'plucky young women beset by harrowing adventures and blessed with unrivaled strength and bravado.'"[2]

Those serials typically highlighted aspects of the "New Woman" who, by the 1910s, had become ubiquitous in American popular culture and whose influence was widely felt, from magazines, periodicals, and illustration to fashion and social politics. As her name implied, she was a modern twentieth-century woman. Determined to reject Victorian-era proprieties and attitudes of female subservience, she challenged and then tried to redefine outmoded notions of her role in society by seeking some measure of personal, social, and economic agency. And she attempted to exert control over other aspects of her life, too, especially by rejecting conventional marriage as the sole and automatic expression of her womanhood. The social and technological advances of the early decades of the twentieth century gave her both the means and the opportunity for such expression, and her sphere of influence was further expanded by her role in shaping the production of goods—material, humanistic, literary, and artistic.[3]

In some ways, though, the "New Woman" was not entirely new. She had her genesis in the literature of the nineteenth century, in works such as Maria Edgeworth's *Belinda* (1801), which went beyond the traditional marriage plot in exploring the expanding potential for women in society, and Elizabeth Barrett's epic poem *Aurora Leigh* (1856), which depicted the plight of a woman in terms of the choice to be made between a conventional marriage and the unconventional possibility of independence as an artist. And many celebrated later writers, from George Bernard Shaw and Bram Stoker to Henry James and Kate Chopin, also integrated the figure of the free-thinking "New Woman" into their work.

With the so-called "Woman Question" dominating much of the social discussion of the late nineteenth century, the New Woman found her avatar in the turn-of-the century Gibson Girl, the athletic, fashion-forward, and increasingly liberated woman drawn by magazine illustrator Charles Dana Gibson, and was further popularized in newspapers and in many of the progressive journals and magazines published mainly for female readers in the early decades of the twentieth century. Even some of the turn-of-the-century stage melodramas introduced audacious heroines who demonstrated "climactic female agency" by rescuing the heroes from railroad tracks, buzz saws, decapitations by guillotine-like devices, waterfalls, and impending explosions.[4] In these various incarnations, the New Woman was depicted as the antithesis of the nineteenth-century woman, whose life was more passive, largely limited to the home, and restricted by her role as wife and mother.

The "New Woman" and Film

But it was in cinema, and especially in the serial picture, that the New Woman heroine found her fullest expression. Unlike many of the non-serial short films of that era that showcased male stars and celebrated traditionally masculine qualities of athleticism, ambition, and fearlessness, serials flipped the script and typically featured athletic, ambitious, and fearless females. That shift is confirmed by even the most cursory look at some of the titles, often alliteratively named for their lead characters: *Lucille Love*, *The Perils of Pauline*, *The Hazards of Helen*, *Dolly of the Dailies*. An extension of the popular motifs pervasive in the "10–20–30" plays and sensational stage melodramas, the serials reflected "both the excitement and the anxieties surrounding major transformations in the cultural construction of womanhood around the turn of the century."[5] By 1914, with virtually every major studio—Universal, Edison, Thanhouser, Kalem, Essanay, Mutual, Reliance, among them—engaged in or planning new serial productions, *Variety* observed that "there's hardly a big concern now that isn't getting out a melodramatic series in which a young woman is the heroine and the camera has her having hairbreadth escapes by the score."[6]

So when the Whartons took up the filming of the first of Elaine's exploits, they were able to draw on certain narrative patterns that earlier serial filmmakers had introduced. Primary among them was the nature of the heroine herself, whose independence was conspicuously marked by the loss of a father or guardian and whose subsequent serial adventure was in some way devoted to a search for his killer. That heroine's story, in fact, often began with her "release from familial bonds" as she is cut adrift from conventional family relationships, particularly from paternal control, a situation that frees her from the constraints under which many real women still lived, bound as they were "by the dictates of marriage and domesticity."

But while the heroine manifests progressive thinking, athletic talents, and a taste for adventure that belie outmoded notions of feminine behavior and societal roles, she eventually comes to realize that her life is nonetheless circumscribed by certain family ties; consequently, engagement or marriage, initially forsaken or rejected, often marks the conclusion of her escapades.[7] In the first episode of *The Perils of Pauline*, for example, Sanford Marvin dies, but not before designating his longtime servant Raymond Koerner as guardian to his ward Pauline, to manage her fortune until such time as she weds Marvin's son Harry—or to serve as her beneficiary, should she die before the marriage occurs. Only at the conclusion of the serial, which ends happily for both Pauline and Harry, does she learn that the treacherous Koerner was behind most of her perils. Similarly, after Captain Hare goes missing in *The Adventures of Kathlyn*, his daughter Kathlyn embarks on a journey to find him in India, where she faces numerous hair-raising threats. Once reunited with him, she returns home to wed the American hunter, John Bruce, who had assisted her in her search. As Shelley Stamp and other film historians have demonstrated, the serial heroines exhibit remarkable tenacity and bravery. But despite their initial break from home life, they realize that their lives are inevitably circumscribed "by familial ties in the end, since heredity and lineage come to assume central importance in virtually all the plots."[8]

Notably, in early serials, the heroine was almost always a person of means, usually the heir to a considerable family estate or trust. That wealth was not incidental. As Ben Singer observed, the "serial melodrama's utopian fantasy of female freedom concerned a liberation from ideologies of female passivity and weakness," in part by envisioning a "female liberation from conventional material or economic constraints." The notion of financial liberation was especially significant—and aspirational—in the context of the period, during which young female wage earners typically handed over their paycheck to the head of the family, more often than not to the father. Serials, therefore, divested the heroines of paternal power and control, and "with the assassination or abduction of the heroine's father—an absolutely essential generic element—[created] . . . a world fantastically free of direct patriarchal authority."[9]

Introducing *Elaine*

To make their own contribution to the serial, the Whartons knew they needed an interesting, independent heroine whose adventures would keep moviegoers returning week after week. The lead role was ideally suited to Pearl White, the reigning queen of serial pictures. Elaine Dodge, after all, was a "slip of a girl" much like White herself: "both the ingénue and the athlete—the thoroughly modern type of girl—equally at home with tennis and tango, table talk and tea. Vivacious eyes that hinted at a stunning amber brown. . . . Her pearly teeth, when she smiled, were marvelous. And she smiled often."[10]

The most iconic of the "serial sisters" of her day, White had already amassed a huge following, both nationally and internationally. A former child performer on the stage and in the circus, she had brought that experience to her early film work at various studios such as the Powers Company and the Lubin Manufacturing Company, where she acted in shorts that have been largely forgotten today. More memorable were her split-reels for the Crystal Film Company directed by Phillips Smalley (husband of the director and actress Lois Weber) and distributed by Universal Film Manufacturing Company, in which she achieved considerable popularity playing comedy parts. That led to her casting in multiple Crystal films, including *Pearl as a Detective, Pearl and the Tramp, Pearl and the Poet, Pearl's Mistake, Pearl's Dilemma,* and *Pearl's Hero* (all 1913), in which her characters were subsumed under a recurrent character name—her own. Her big breakthrough, though, came as Pauline in *The Perils of Pauline,* a serial that allowed her to distinguish herself as the new and versatile female type of protagonist within a sensational, action-packed serial framework.[11]

It was Ted Wharton who first brought White to the attention of his former Pathé colleague Louis J. Gasnier for the role of the plucky eponymous heroine in the *Perils* production.[12] In a later interview, White acknowledged the significance of Ted's mentorship. Speaking fondly of him, she recalled that he was both the first movie director whom she met in New York and the one director who "crossed her path at every turn" in her career and helped ensure her success; she considered him to be "her guiding star."[13] And indeed, in *The Exploits of Elaine,* he cemented her stardom and launched her even further on a serial career that proved to be phenomenally long and successful and that outlasted the Whartons' own.

With Hearst's powerful publicity machine solidly behind the new *Elaine* serial, White seemed to be everywhere. Her fashionable costumes, which set new trends, were widely imitated. Her face appeared almost daily in the Hearst press, splashed across the front pages of newspapers and magazines. Her name was known in virtually every quarter; and both her on-screen adventures and her off-screen escapades fascinated her many admirers worldwide. In short, White's Elaine became one of early cinema's most recognizable and iconic characters.

Costarring opposite White in the role of renowned "scientific detective" Professor Craig Kennedy was well-known actor, playwright, producer, and matinee idol Arnold Daly. His signing by Pathé not only promised to "do much to increase the popularity of the new serial."[14] It also suggested that *The Exploits of Elaine* would be a vastly different proposition from *The Perils of Pauline* insofar as the new story would require more artistic interpretation and depend less on sensational incidents for its interest.[15]

The character of Craig Kennedy had been created by Arthur B. Reeve (1880–1936), the popular American writer best known for his "Craig Kennedy, Scientific Detective" sequence, the most significant titles being the eighty-two short stories first published between 1910 and 1918 in monthly installments, beginning with "The Case of Helen Bond" in the December 1910 *Cosmopolitan*.[16] Often called the "American Sherlock Holmes," Kennedy solved challenging mysteries using both science and intuition. Walter Jameson, a young reporter at the *Star* newspaper, served as his Dr. Watson. In Reeve's stories, it was Jameson who narrated the adventures and recorded the numerous instances of Kennedy's investigative acumen. Almost every story—and later, almost every serial episode based on those stories—incorporated one or more technological devices that Kennedy invented or employed and that were vital to the resolution of the plot. While common today, those devices—which included wireless telephones, laser lights, and portable seismographs—were revolutionary more than a century ago when Reeve introduced them into his fiction and the Whartons brought them to the screen.[17] Quick to confirm that the marvelous mechanisms depicted in the serial were "not the product of the studio workshop, but the genuine article," Ted pointed specifically to the "telegraphone," which allows callers to leave long-distance phone messages in their own voices, and the "electric resuscitator," an invention of "Dr. Leduc of the Nantes École de Medicin" that is "truly almost supernatural in its power" to restore life. "We are not faking any scientific apparatus in 'The Exploits of Elaine,'" he insisted, "[because] we don't have to."[18]

Reeve's clever scientific detective proved to be even more popular on the screen than he was in print. In addition to his appearances in *The Exploits of Elaine* and its two sequels (the thirty-six episodes known collectively as *The Exploits of Elaine*), his character was central to the later silent serials *The Carter Case* (1919) and *The Radio Detective* (1926), to the sound picture *The Clutching Hand* (1936), and to the television series *Craig Kennedy, Criminologist* (1951). For Ted Wharton, though, Kennedy held a special appeal: Kennedy presented him with the opportunity to create a true mystery story, something he had long wanted to do.

Of course, a great detective required a worthy opponent. And the mysterious "Clutching Hand" offered just that. The first in the serial genre's "long parade of unknown menaces," the Clutching Hand established a new type of villain whom audiences reviled and filmmakers adored for years to come. "Masked by a handkerchief drawn tightly about his lower face, leaving only his eyes visible beneath the cap with visor pulled down over his forehead," he had, as Reeve described him, "a peculiar stoop of the shoulders and wore his coat collar pulled up. One hand, the right, seemed almost deformed," a condition that gave him his name in the criminal underworld.[19] Since his real identity was concealed until the final episode, the Clutching Hand added even more carryover mystery to the visual action and served as an excellent device for sustaining audience interest throughout the months in which the serial drama ran.[20] As a way of encouraging moviegoers to speculate about who he might actually be, all the episodes (except for the last) ended with a close-up of his tightly clenched fist followed by a large question mark. He even inspired a popular song, "That Clutching Hand," with music by Jean Schwartz and lyrics by Coleman Goetz.[21]

Observing that while, in terms of serial production, "some say there is nothing new under the sun," the trade journals lauded *The Exploits of Elaine* for successfully combining elements of plot and character in a manner so ingenious "as to appear actually novel" and "decidedly unusual."[22] Indeed, in comparison to its predecessor *The Perils of Pauline*, the *Elaine* serial proved to be a far more polished production, with a smoother and improved narrative and better production values in its fourteen weekly installments.[23] With Charles W. Goddard working in conjunction with Reeve to picturize the story, the writing was better. With Wharton regulars Creighton Hale and Bessie Wharton performing as part of the cast and Sheldon Lewis bringing a sinister charm to his role as the villain, the acting was stronger.[24] And with veteran scriptwriter George B. Seitz (who would go on to direct Pearl White in most of her later serials) and cinema pioneer Louis J. Gasnier sharing responsibilities with the Whartons, the direction was more impressive as well. As Raymond William Stedman observed in *The Serials, The Exploits of Elaine* became "the proving ground for suspenseful action *within four walls* [as opposed to the outdoor action of *Perils*] and the point of departure for the death ray, the hypnotic drug, the life-restoring machine," and other gimmicks introduced by the brothers and used by scriptwriters well into the sound era.[25] Consequently, it remains the prototype of the scientific mystery serial that gave much service to chapter-play makers over the years.

It was heroine Elaine Dodge as the emblematic "New Woman" who most immediately distinguished herself in the production. Despite the fact that she is often the object of various forms of surveillance that Kennedy employs to protect her from her "incessant exposure to harm," Elaine, as Margaret Hennefeld has observed, was nevertheless an undeniably adventurous young woman who defies traditional gender roles and social expectations.[26] Fearless yet feminine, determined but dutiful, she assumes an increasingly vital part in the action, which often finds her in alarming situations typical of the serial genre: she is kidnapped, held hostage, drugged, poisoned, physically overpowered, threatened, and repeatedly terrorized by a faceless villain and his confederates. Yet, in many ways, she is able to hold her own. Not so bold as to intimidate the men like Kennedy and Jameson who are devoted to protecting her (and thus not to alienate the male audience), she displays a sense of daring, defiance, and athleticism that elevates her above earlier non-serial damsels in distress and enables her to survive the predations of her antagonists. As comfortable in the outdoors as in the drawing room, the quick-thinking and quick-witted Elaine epitomized the modern woman celebrated in the literature and the cinema of the day and became the touchstone for later film heroines (whom other producers, in advertisements for their own films, invariably compared to the Whartons' "exciting" and "daring" Elaine).

At the same time, as Ben Singer argues, Elaine personified the profound cultural discontinuity of modern society, as "traditional ideologies of gender, essentially stagnant for centuries, became objects of cultural reflexivity, open to doubt and revision." Elaine's prowess, like that of other serial

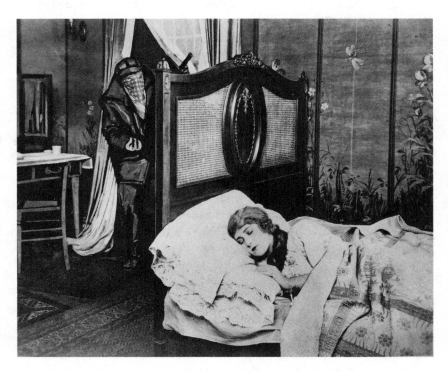

FIGURE 6.1   In *The Exploits of Elaine*, the unsuspecting heroine (Pearl White) becomes the victim of the Clutching Hand.

heroines, functioned as "a reflection of both real social change in gender ideologies and, paradoxically, of utopian fantasies of female power betraying the degree to which traditional constraints still prevailed."[27] Those constraints were apparent in the serials' sometimes sadistic spectacle of victimization, which coupled an "ideology of female power with an equally vivid exposition of female defenselessness and weakness" that demonstrated the conflict between the promotion and celebration of empowered women and the anxiety that such female empowerment and social transformation created.[28]

Plotting Elaine's *Exploits*

The first episode of *The Exploits of Elaine* ("The Clutching Hand," released on December 28, 1914) introduced the central characters of the serial: the eponymous heroine Elaine Dodge; her kindly Aunt Josephine; famed professor and scientific detective Craig Kennedy; his assistant, *Star* reporter Walter Jameson; the affable and handsome Dodge family lawyer Perry Bennett; and the masked villain known as the "Clutching Hand." As the episode begins, Taylor Dodge (William Riley Hatch), whose Consolidated Insurance Company has lost considerable money because of the diabolical robberies by the Clutching Hand, is visited by one-legged "Limpy Red" (Robin Townley), a criminal who wants to expose his old boss. Almost immediately afterward, the Clutching Hand has the traitor murdered. As Dodge retreats to his study, Jameson (played, in the opening episodes, by Raymond Owens, and later by Creighton Hale, who took over the role) overhears him tell Bennett that he knows how to find the villain. When Jameson calls Professor Kennedy to share the news, his friend warns him that Dodge's life is in danger.

The warning quickly comes true. As night falls, two masked men drag some wire to the basement of the Dodge home and attach it to the furnace. At that moment, Dodge decides to secrete the papers from Limpy in a hidden cavity in the study wall and substitute a fake envelope in the safe instead; but when he turns to answer his telephone, he steps on an iron register on the floor and is instantly electrocuted.[29] "The briskness with which the first two-reel instalment strikes the imagination," reviewer Margaret I. MacDonald noted, makes clear that the new Pathé-Hearst production bid "fair to surpass in popularity its predecessor." The audience receives "just enough daylight on the mysterious forms and happenings which characterize the story to arouse the most rabid interest as to what will follow."[30]

The second episode ("The Twilight Sleep") aroused that interest even more and established the pattern for the rest of the serial. As Kennedy searches for clues in the Dodge home, the villain drugs Elaine and forces her at gunpoint to discharge Kennedy from further service. But the next day, when Kennedy calls her, Elaine has no recollection of having communicated with him. Suspecting that she has been doped, Kennedy realizes that the only way for her to get back her memory is with another injection. As she comes out of her sleep, however, a note appears under the door, warning Kennedy to cease his investigation. Pocketing the note, he seems indifferent to the threat but clearly not to Elaine, whose pretty face "has begun to crowd against science in the mind of scientific Craig."[31]

Over the next few episodes, the Clutching Hand continues to menace Elaine, first by threatening her friends, the Martin family, whose jewelry shop he has looted ("The Vanishing Jewels"), then by rigging an "infernal" trap that will release a hail of bullets, killing anyone in their path ("The Frozen Safe").[32] When that fails, with the help of an associate who is posing as Elaine's servant Michael, he sprays Elaine's room with an invisible powder that contains arsenic ("The Poisoned Room"), nearly poisoning both Elaine and her dog Rusty. Frightened by the villain's diabolism, Elaine—whom one reviewer described in these episodes as "exploited rather than carrying out any exploits"—begs Kennedy to curtail his investigation; but he refuses to be deterred.[33]

FIGURE 6.2   When his other schemes fail, the Clutching Hand turns to arsenic to sicken both Elaine and her dog in "The Poisoned Room."

To this point in the serial, Elaine has played a rather passive role, serving primarily as the unwitting target of the Clutching Hand and his deadly associates and suffering their repeated assaults. As Ed Hulse notes, "the serial's first half largely restricts Elaine to distressed-damsel status, with the detective falling in love and rescuing the girl week after week." But apparently "someone realized that fans would want to see the daredevil star of *Perils of Pauline* take a more active role—Pathé was promoting her as 'the peerless Fearless Girl,' after all—and in the latter chapters she becomes [more] central to the proceedings."[34]

So when the next attack occurs, Elaine is ready. After Pitts Slim, another of the Clutching Hand's accomplices, tries to enter her bedroom window, she shoots him with the pistol that Kennedy had given her for protection—although afterward she is forced to offer the injured Slim her own blood for transfusion ("The Vampire").[35] And, in the next episode, after the Clutching Hand uses his confederate "Weeping Mary" to lure her to a church, it is Elaine who saves Kennedy after a hair-raising wrestling match with the villain leaves him clinging desperately to the church's steeple ("The Double Trap").[36]

Knowing that the Clutching Hand will retaliate, Kennedy deploys more of his trademark crime-detective devices. The "vocaphone" that connects his laboratory with the Dodge home scares off the criminals who try to assault Elaine ("The Hidden Voice"),[37] and his "Infra-Red Ray" ultimately alerts the police and prevents a fiery death ("The Death Ray").[38] A later attempt by the Clutching Hand to poison Elaine with a wristwatch that contains ricin also proves unsuccessful ("The Hour of Three"), thanks to Kennedy's "telegraphone," a recording device that allows him to overhear a call about a "trick [that] will be pulled off at three o'clock" and race madly, in time to rip the watch from Elaine's hand.[39]

To discredit the detective in Elaine's eyes, the Clutching Hand employs a new approach. Conspiring with "Flirty Florrie," who claims that she is in need of Kennedy's services, the villain obtains photographs of what appears to be Florrie and Kennedy caught in a passionate embrace, which Florrie then shares with Elaine ("The Life Current"). When Kennedy arrives bearing an engagement ring, Elaine angrily rebuffs him and goes to Florrie's house, where she is overpowered by the accomplice, dragged into an unused sewer, and left to die from asphyxiating gas. But once again Kennedy, in the familiar pattern of the serial, tracks her down and rescues her. Although she is pronounced dead by doctors, he uses his "ultra-modern science" and applies electrical resuscitation,[40] earning Elaine the distinction of being the only heroine in serial history to die and come back to life.

FIGURE 6.3   In an attempt to discredit him with Elaine, Flirty Florrie puts Craig Kennedy (Arnold Daly) in a compromising position in "The Life Current."

Unfortunately for Elaine, a new villain sets his sights on her as well. Chinese adventurer Long Sin (played by M. W. "Mike" Rale), "a mandarin with a drooping mustache,"[41] wants to recoup his lost fortune by playing on Elaine's credulity, so he lures her to his apartment, where she ends up stabbing him in self-defense ("The Blood Crystals"). But his "death" is just a trick. After his associate promises Elaine that, for $10,000 cash, the evidence of her crime will be destroyed, Kennedy analyzes the blood drops on her handkerchief, realizes they are actually canine, and uses his "detectascope" and "telautograph" to intercept the villain and defeat his plan.[42]

Naturally, there is another complication. Following a quarrel with Kennedy, Elaine receives a marriage proposal from Bennett. When she calls Kennedy with the news, he promptly hangs up on her—or so she thinks. (In fact, the discourtesy is the result of burned phone wires caused by Jameson's spilling of a bottle of nitro-hydrochloric acid.) Afterward, coaxed by pseudo-medium "Mme. Savetsky" into visiting a séance parlor, Elaine is confronted by the "ghost" of Long Sin, who is now in league with the Clutching Hand, and taken to the Temple of the Heathen God to be prepared as a sacrifice to the idol Ksing-Chau. But Kennedy, in disguise as one of the temple's old "heathens," saves her, promising Long Sin immunity if he betrays the Clutching Hand ("The Devil Worshippers").[43]

In the fourteenth and final episode, "The Reckoning," unaware that his coconspirator has been compromised, the Clutching Hand instructs Long Sin to deliver a chemical bomb to the professor's laboratory. Detected by Kennedy's X-ray machine and dismantled, the bomb reveals a scrap of paper-wrapping with a distinctive battered letter *T* in the type that conclusively proves Bennett is the villain. Confronted with the evidence, Bennett metamorphoses "from the Jekyll of a polished lawyer and lover of Elaine into an insanely jealous and revengeful Mr. Hyde."[44] After attacking Elaine and overcoming Jameson, he seeks out Long Sin, promising him a portion of his immense fortune in exchange for his help. Instead, Long Sin gives him a potion that puts him in suspended animation (a scene that anticipates the clamping of Myra's "pneumogastric nerve" in *The Mysteries of Myra*), which he agrees to reverse only if Bennett discloses the location of the fortune. Although Bennett complies, Long Sin reneges; so when Kennedy and Jameson arrive, they find Bennett dead from the poison. Free of him at last, Kennedy and Elaine enjoy a warm and overdue reconciliation.

The Impact of *Elaine*

While *The Exploits of Elaine* followed many of the conventions and narrative devices of its serial predecessors, it also distinguished itself in several significant ways. One was the level of danger that it created for the heroine, which often necessitated Kennedy's involvement and intervention. As Shelley Stamp observed, it was his methods of detection, foregrounded in most of the episodes, that created much of the excitement for the audience.[45] The reviewer for the *San Francisco Examiner*, in fact, went so far as to suggest that he was relieved to see that the plot did not revolve simply around the escapades of "pretty and attractive little Elaine, but of the wizards of science."[46] Unlike Harry Marvin, who stands on the sidelines throughout most of Pauline's trials, "either trying in vain to get her to stay home or ending up trapped along with her and only infrequently coming to her aid," Kennedy is indeed instrumental in virtually every installment of Elaine's story, particularly in revealing the identity of the Clutching Hand and resolving the mystery.[47]

Although Elaine becomes a more active and empowered player as the story progresses, her passivity in the early chapters is related in part to her physical entrapment, much of which occurs in the bedroom of her home. There, she is dosed with the "twilight sleep" drug scopolamine by the Clutching Hand, who has entered through the window as she sleeps; she is sickened by arsenic that the villain has sprayed on her bedroom walls and activated from the basement of her home; she must fend off an attack by his accomplice Pitts Slim, who has crept through her bedroom window; and she barely escapes harm after a rock that is thrown through the window lands next to her on her bed. That entrapment and imprisonment continue as Elaine watches in shock when the new safe in her home is mysteriously penetrated from the inside, leaving her literally "unsafe." She is also held hostage in a church; trapped in Kennedy's laboratory and made to witness the near-execution of her friends; overpowered and dragged to an unused sewer, where she is left to asphyxiate from the gas; kidnapped at a séance; and taken to a temple to be sacrificed.

These situations not only underscore Elaine's loss of bodily and psychological control; they also, as Stamp suggested, have strong reverberations of sexual violation. After Elaine's bedroom is "penetrated," she is awakened by a gun placed to her head, injected with a drug, and forced, while still in her nightgown, to perform certain "acts" that the villain demands (e.g., writing Kennedy to dismiss him from further service). The next day, when Kennedy tries to make her recall the events of the previous night, he injects her with the same drug, assuming it will help her reenact those events, in effect repeating the original assault. In another violation, Slim skulks just outside Elaine's bedroom; but after shooting and wounding him, she is knocked out by his associates, hidden inside a suit of armor, and taken, unconscious, to the Clutching Hand's hideout, where she is forced to donate her blood by way of a transfusion—and thus, literally, to exchange bodily fluids with Slim. Moreover, she must also endure the gaze of the villains, who peer at her prone body as the exchange occurs. And the wristwatch that she receives, altered by the addition of a small needle filled with deadly ricin, is set to "prick" her at the appointed hour.

The most dramatic violation occurs in "The Life Current" episode, in which Elaine not merely loses consciousness but actually dies. Using the resuscitator to pass an electrical current from his hands into her torso, Kennedy manipulates her body in singularly intimate ways. Throughout each of the ordeals, the mysterious potions and gases not only render Elaine unconscious, entranced, or delirious; they also ensure that "the specter of her body is repeatedly offered for display."[48] Yet it is precisely this oscillation between vulnerability and agency that expresses the paradoxes and ambiguities of Elaine's "New Womanhood" and that makes her representative "of women's new situation in urban modernity."[49]

To achieve their visual effects, the Whartons employed a number of different techniques. As the surviving episodes of the serial reveal, iris shots (fade-in or fade-out shots that contract and widen, like the iris of the eye) called attention to supporting characters such as Elaine's servant Michael, who is killed in his hotel room as he prepares to expose the Clutching Hand ("The Poisoned Room"), and the pedestrian who is murdered as he is walking down the street, an innocent victim of the Clutching Hand's revenge against Kennedy ("The Death Ray"). Close-ups similarly emphasized key moments or events, such as the clock that counts down the minutes before the noon-day robbery of the Martins' jewelry store ("The Vanishing Jewels") and the "clenched fist" signal that the criminals use to communicate with each other. And occasional flashbacks filled in plot details, revealing, for example, how the villain steals a vial of the therapeutic medicine scopolamine from the Hillside Sanitarium for Women in order to use it for a far more malicious purpose on Elaine ("The Twilight Sleep"). That same episode also made interesting use of superimposition (a technique that the Whartons would use more frequently and even more successfully in their later serial *The Mysteries of Myra*) when an image of Elaine's pretty face appears suddenly on the wall of the laboratory to suggest that she is in Kennedy's thoughts.[50]

Perhaps the most effective device of all was the manner in which the Whartons built up, and then sustained, a sense of suspense around the figure of the Clutching Hand for fourteen episodes. The cross-cutting between Kennedy in his lab, working on new inventions by which to trap the villain before he can inflict further injury on Elaine, and the villain, plotting new ways to harm Elaine before Kennedy can undermine him, created both momentum and tension. And the repeated close-ups of the Clutching Hand's deformed fist that ended every episode became a motif that added even more uncertainty to a genre already defined by its holdover suspense.

Maintaining the mystery of the villain's true identity, which was central to the premise of the serial, presented a special challenge. The Whartons met it in several ways, usually through clever editing (in "The Vampire" episode, for example, the camera cuts away just as the Clutching Hand turns his head to reveal his unmasked face) or misdirection (setting up any one of a number of possible criminals as the villain, from the accomplice who throws the rock through the Dodges' window in an early scene to the servant who keeps eavesdropping at the door on conversations). Thus the eventual exposure of Bennett, the handsome "lawyer and lover" of Elaine and devoted nephew of Taylor Dodge, as the masked and grotesque Clutching Hand comes as quite a surprise to the audience. According to the title card in the final episode, because Bennett is actually an "insane criminal" who possesses two distinct "Jekyll and Hyde" personalities, he has been able to metamorphose, both psychologically and physiologically, into a hunchbacked and deformed monster. Yet until he is tripped up by his own carelessness, no one harbors any suspicions about him or doubts his motives. His seeming affection for and proximity to Elaine throughout the serial enable him to stay one step ahead of Kennedy and Jameson and to undermine their plans for her safety. The revelation of Bennett's real identity therefore lends an unexpected twist to an already suspense-filled story.

Naturally, in a serial that highlighted Kennedy's forensic science skills, the Whartons made especially imaginative use of his inventions. "The Hidden Voice" episode, for example, demonstrates how his "vocaphone" frustrates the villain and serves to rescue Elaine. The episode opens with a bedroom scene—this time Jameson's, not Elaine's—as Kennedy's assistant is startled by a disembodied voice invoking him to "Wake up, Jameson." Whereas the typical method of conveying telephone or telegram messages on screen in early films and serials was through intertitles,[51] in this scene the Whartons employed an entirely different technique: a message, written out in cursive and superimposed on the frame. Emanating from the vocaphone in a V-like pattern that simulated sound waves, that message visually re-created the "sound" of a gramophone; and, by avoiding the interruption or distraction of a cutaway to the intertitle, it created an even greater sense of urgency.[52]

Satisfied that the vocaphone works, Kennedy packs up the device, a square metal box that looks like a small Geiger counter, and rushes to the Dodge home, where he installs it inside the helmet of a suit of armor in Elaine's hallway (the very same suit of armor that, in an earlier episode, the villain and his accomplices had used to spirit Elaine from her home). The vocaphone indeed serves its purpose by allowing Kennedy to overhear the Clutching Hand's assault on Elaine, to scream back at the villains and cause them to flee, and to ensure that Elaine is unharmed.

In another episode ("The Frozen Safe"), the seismograph that Kennedy installs outside his apartment door lets him detect and track any break-ins that might occur in his absence. So after the Clutching Hand sets a deadly trap in the apartment, Kennedy is literally able to retrace the villain's steps and evade the danger. And in "The Reckoning," using an X-ray machine in his laboratory to scan the package brought to him by Long Sin, he dismantles the bomb it contains—and discovers a vital clue to the villain's identity.

There is, of course, some irony in the fact that Kennedy at times becomes the victim rather than the master of such scientific technology. In the poisoned kiss episode, he finds himself entrapped by a device quite similar to one of his own, when the Clutching Hand's associate Flossie and her accomplice install a small camera into the glass eyeball of a stag's head mounted on the wall in order to catch him in an embrace that the pair has orchestrated. That camera, connected to a hidden wall switch, snaps incriminating photographs that Flossie, posing as Kennedy's fiancée, uses to convince Elaine that she has been betrayed. Similarly, in the "The Death Ray" episode, Kennedy is almost undone by the deadly "Uliva" ray that the Clutching Hand and his associates employ to force him to capitulate to their demands. Although Kennedy is able to wield his "Infra-Red Ray" shield to deflect the ray (whose powerful

FIGURE 6.4. The Clutching Hand paved the way for other masked menaces and even inspired a popular song.

"beam" was created by clever use of alternating bright and dark lighting that simulated a strobe effect), it sets on fire the ceiling of the basement room in which he and Jameson are being held and almost incinerates them along with Elaine, who is forced to watch helplessly from above. Only the intervention of the police, whom Kennedy had alerted earlier, saves them from certain death.

Despite such outlandish plot contrivances—and, arguably, because of them—*The Exploits of Elaine* proved to be a huge critical and financial success. Reviewers hailed it as "a serial of remarkable excellence" that kept "interest at the highest pitch," not "by smashing property" but by depicting "tense situations and marvelous achievements of science."[53] And audiences rushed back to the theaters every week to see how Elaine and Kennedy would hold off, and ultimately best, the villainous Clutching Hand. Business on the serial was so brisk that, as Ed Hulse notes, "Pathé executives at the firm's July 1915 sales-force convention reported it had [already] generated more than a million dollars in film rental"—an unprecedented amount for the time.[54] The passing of the million dollar mark was celebrated that same month with a large banquet in honor of the Whartons held at Rector's Restaurant on Broadway in New York, an event attended by Ted, Leo, and their brother-in-law J. Whitworth Buck.[55]

There could be no doubt: with the success of *The Exploits of Elaine*, the Wharton brothers had arrived.

CHAPTER 7

Extending *Elaine*

A good serial demanded a good sequel. So it is hardly surprising that, given *Elaine*'s enormous appeal, plans for an extension, or "extender," began even as the original serial was still in production or that the opening episode of *The New Exploits of Elaine* was released just one week after the first serial concluded. By picking up where *Exploits* left off, both Hearst and the Whartons hoped to maintain the keen interest in the adventures of Elaine Dodge and Craig Kennedy (and in Pearl White and Arnold Daly, the popular stars who played them).[1] As *Motion Picture News* observed, "It is with real satisfaction that we look forward to the "New Exploits of Elaine. . . . If the new series is half as good as the old, it will hold any audience spellbound. There seems every reason to expect that the forthcoming pictures will be even better."[2]

The production of serial-sequels, by then, had become an increasingly common practice among studios hoping to capitalize on their original successes. The popularity of the early twelve-part Edison production *What Happened to Mary* (1912) starring Mary Fuller had led, a year later, to the six-part sequel series *Who Will Marry Mary?* Thanhouser Film Corporation's twenty-three-part *The Million Dollar Mystery*, which starred another early screen favorite, Florence La Badie, spawned a twenty-episode sequel *Zudora* (1914). And Kalem's *The Hazards of Helen* (1914–1917) served, in some ways, as its own sequel, since its 119 installments stretched the heroine's adventures out over a period of more than two years with a succession of new "Helens." But even more than those earlier serials, Elaine, especially as enacted by the sensational Pearl White, promised an almost endless variety of new exploits to fascinate the movie public.

The cunning "Oriental" Long Sin who had been introduced in the final episodes of *The Exploits of Elaine* ensured some carryover to the plot of the next series, *The New Exploits of Elaine*, but the death of the Clutching Hand required a new primary antagonist. Fortunately, the filmmakers found an ideal cinematic adversary in Long Sin's master, the "inscrutable" Wu Fang, whose name was based on that of Washington-based Chinese diplomat Wu Ting Fang (author of *America, through the Spectacles of an Oriental Diplomat*). Dangerous and menacing, Wu Fang made Long Sin look like "a mere pigmy," effectively "his slave, his advance agent, as it were, a tentacle sent out to discover the most promising outlet for the nefarious talents of his master."[3]

The extreme racist representation of the villains added to the serial's topicality. According to Raymond William Stedman, by *The New Exploits*, "Pathé had recognized the growing commercial viability of the yellow peril and was going to make much more of it." "Orientals" (whom early filmmakers rarely differentiated by their actual nationalities) had, by the mid-1910s, become objects of race fear and hatred or, alternatively, victims of ridiculous stereotyping, with white actors made up in exaggerated "yellowface," a practice similar to the execrable but extensive use of "blackface" on the nineteenth-century stage and in early twentieth-century cinema. As detestable "heathens" who were part of the "Yellow Menace" said to threaten American society, Wu Fang and Long Sin—whose names had just the right ominously foreign ring to them—not only had a fearsome racial characterization that the Clutching Hand lacked. They also anticipated the more vicious character assassinations of Asians and other ethnics that would follow a few years later in the numerous so-called patriotic "preparedness"' features and serials, which included the Whartons' Hearst-backed production *Patria*.

The New Exploits of Elaine also introduced a new mystery, which involved the search for a ring that would unlock the vault where the Clutching Hand had hidden his millions. That mystery played out over ten two-reel installments and, like the earlier serial, was filmed at the Pathé Studios in Jersey City, New Jersey. Pearl White and Arnold Daly reprised their roles as wealthy socialite Elaine Dodge and scientific detective Professor Craig Kennedy, while Creighton Hale and Bessie Wharton returned as Walter Jameson and Aunt Josephine. And Edwin Arden, an actor, theater manager, and playwright of some renown, assumed the role of Wu Fang. As with the original serial, episodes of the sequel appeared regularly in story form in the Hearst publications and were later novelized by Arthur B. Reeve as *The Romance of Elaine: A Detective Novel Sequel to the "Exploits."* [4]

The New Exploits of Elaine

As *The New Exploits* opens, Aunt Josephine, now living in Bennett's former home, has reported hearing strange noises in the early hours of the morning, which are emanating from a secret passageway in the home's fireplace ("The Serpent Sign"). When Kennedy and Jameson decide to explore it, they are nearly murdered by Long Sin, who had entered by way of a cave in the woods, marked on the map that he had extracted from the Clutching Hand in the final episode of the original serial. After Elaine follows her friends into the passage, she too encounters Long Sin, who flees and, bearing a mystic ring, returns to his "master," the heathen Tong leader Wu Fang. [5]

Later, when Elaine innocently purchases that ring as a decoration for her "Oriental" party, she is unaware that it has been stolen from Long Sin or that Wu Fang, who knows that it holds the key to retrieving the late Bennett's fortune, is desperate to recover it by any means possible ("The Cryptic Ring"). On the pretext that Kennedy is ill, Long Sin lures Elaine to Wu Fang's rooms, but his murderous trap is interrupted by Kennedy, who has learned of the deception. Following a brief scuffle, "the Chinaman" escapes by way of a tightrope strung between two skyscrapers, cuts the cable behind him, and nearly kills Kennedy, who is in close pursuit. After Jameson comes to Kennedy's rescue, they realize that Elaine has been kidnapped, [6] an event that initiates the serial's ongoing pattern of deception, abduction, confrontation, rescue, and escape.

Believing that he can outsmart his opponents, Kennedy forges a copy of the real ring that Long Sin and Wu Fang demand as payment for Elaine's release ("The Watching Eye") and accidentally discovers what Wu Fang already knows—that the ring unlocks the box in the tunnel where Bennett hid his fortune. [7] Having been beaten to the gems, Wu Fang releases Elaine but announces his diabolic plan to kill off her friends as revenge ("The Vengeance of Wu Fang"). First, he plants a deadly African tick in a phone receiver to infect Kennedy and Jameson with a lethal and malicious fever. [8] When that fails, he engages an aviator to drop a bomb on what he believes to be Kennedy's home ("The Saving Circles"); but Kennedy outsmarts the aviator and brings down his plane. [9] Wu Fang's next attempt—to have another one of his confederates, who poses as a maid, rig a chair that will spontaneously combust and incinerate Elaine as soon as she sits in it—is similarly frustrated when Kennedy arrives in time to save her from a frightful death ("Spontaneous Combustion").[10] And the villain's sadistic plot to force Elaine to choose who will die first—Kennedy or Aunt Josephine—fails as well, thanks to Kennedy's opportune intervention, which results in the capture of Long Sin and several of Wu Fang's accomplices ("The Ear in the Wall," alternatively titled "The Listening Ear").[11]

A later effort, however, proves more successful. After substituting a henchman for her chauffeur, Wu Fang kidnaps Elaine and stows her away on a sloop to Shanghai, where he intends to sell her into white slavery ("The Opium Smugglers")—a fate, as reviewer Clifford H. Pangburn notes, that is "worse than anything that Wu Fang could devise at home."[12] Fortunately, a disguised Kennedy, who has gone searching for the villain in Chinatown, encounters Captain Brainerd of the U.S. Secret Service, and together they hop a revenue cutter in order to apprehend a band of opium smugglers who are operating from a sloop—conveniently, the same craft to which Wu Fang has taken Elaine. After communicating her location by way of a wireless telephone that Kennedy had given her, Elaine flashes a lantern from the porthole, climbs a rope ladder to the topmast in order to elude her guard, and makes a daring leap into the dark water, from which she is rescued. The danger,

The arrest of Long Sin.

FIGURE 7.1 In *The New Exploits of Elaine*, the villainous Long Sin, who terrorized Elaine in the earlier serial, is finally apprehended and arrested.

though, is not yet over for her. "Innocent Inez," another of Wu Fang's confederates, sends a Roma accomplice to read Elaine's fortune, instructing her to bind Elaine's eyes with a handkerchief that contains radium, which will blind her. Luckily, Kennedy saves her from harm and, using the "sphymograph" in his lab, persuades Inez to reveal Wu Fang's address in Chinatown ("The Telltale Heart").[13]

In the tenth and final episode ("Shadows of War"), Wu Fang determines to steal the model of the super-powered torpedo that Kennedy invented, which secret agents are anxious to purchase. Acting on the information from Inez, Kennedy and Jameson are able to capture him, but he quickly escapes their custody, heads to the Dodge home, and manages to gain possession of the device, which his associate hides in a large flowerpot. As Wu Fang and his men flee, Kennedy commandeers a car and chases them. Their "game of wits" ends with a big explosion in the waters off the wharf, after which the spy's corpse floats to the surface. Although Kennedy is presumed dead as well, Elaine discovers a note advising her to "trust" him, which gives her some hope.[14]

Since *The New Exploits of Elaine* is not extant, it is not possible to offer a close visual reading of it. But contemporary trade journal summaries of the episodes suggest that Elaine, though still largely reliant on Kennedy and his interventions, has gained a greater sense of agency. Drawing on her own bravery and athleticism, she confronts the villains, resists her captors, and engages in bold escapes, such as the leap from the schooner that is spiriting her away to China. And whereas in the original *Exploits of Elaine* a kidnapped Elaine is forced to transfuse her blood in an effort to save one of his accomplices, in *The New Exploits* it is she who helps save the lives of Kennedy and Jameson after they have been infected by a deadly tick. First, she exposes Wu Fang's associate "Weeping Mary" (a holdover from the original *Exploits*) who had been substituted for the surgeon's nurse in order to poison the medical instruments; then she steps in personally to assist in the life-saving procedure.

In addition to the pervasive xenophobia and distrust of Asians and the wartime intrigue, the serial also incorporated another timely topic, white slavery, which the Whartons would take up again a few years later in their first independently produced feature film, *The Great White Trail* (1917). As Lewis Jacobs demonstrated, such themes of wickedness and political corruption were surprisingly pervasive in early cinema. The feature film *Traffic in Souls* (1913) had created a sensation by depicting white slave conditions in New York, where gangsters were shown to recruit innocent victims from ships arriving with immigrants, from railroad stations, and from the slums;

and pictures such as *The Inside of the White Slave Traffic* (1913) simultaneously horrified and titillated curious movie audiences—particularly women, who found visual pleasure in them through an erotic voyeurism not normally associated with "a ladylike gentility" and seemingly at odds with more refined, highbrow entertainment.[15] Elaine's kidnapping by Wu Fang and his attempt to sell her into bondage in Shanghai not only exploited that theme. It also underscored the link between serials and popular white-slave narratives, both of which, as Shelley Stamp suggests, evoked "the peculiar mixture of liberation and trepidation many young women might have experienced when living away from home for the first time." And it revealed how new freedoms increasingly open to women were circumscribed within an aura of danger that was often explicitly sexualized.[16]

The Romance of Elaine

The unresolved-plot ending of *The New Exploits of Elaine* provided a natural segue into the third and final installment of the *Elaine* serial. On the one hand, *The Romance of Elaine* harked back to familiar elements of the serial formula, among them recurring threats from a mysterious villain, death-defying escapes, car chases, explosions, and romantic rescues. On the other, it celebrated Elaine's tenacity and reinforced the image of her as a new and increasingly independent female type of protagonist within a sensational, action-packed, typically male-oriented and male-dominated story line. As Marina Dahlquist suggests, especially for the women in the movie audience, *The Romance*'s Elaine offered "a template for negotiating gender stereotypes." Removed from "the confines of Victorian domestic femininity and familial obligations and the meek modesty expected of women," she acts in ways traditionally associated with masculine brawn and bravado—firing a pistol, handling a bomb, and demonstrating keen athletic agility—that help to destabilize traditional gender norms.[17]

The Romance of Elaine, whose purpose was more overtly political than the two earlier *Elaine* installments, was structured as a topical melodrama of wartime espionage, in which Kennedy is missing and his marvelous model torpedo has presumably been lost. The episodes, Ed Hulse writes, were inspired by actual historical events, particularly the sinking of the *Lusitania* by a German submarine off the coast in Ireland on May 7, 1915, an attack that the Hearst papers called "a deed of wholesale slaughter"[18] (and to which the Whartons returned in their later serials *Patria* and *The Eagle's Eye*). The fear of wartime foreign intrigues not only defined *The Romance*'s spy plot but also set the tone for most of the episodes, which anticipated the "preparedness"

FIGURE 7.2   To draw moviegoers into their theaters, exhibitors were urged to book *The Romance of Elaine*.

themes so integral to the many patriotic pictures that soon followed, including the Marie Walcamp serial *Liberty, Daughter of the U.S.A.* (1916) for Universal and the Pearl White serial *Pearl of the Army* (1916) for Pathé.

The Whartons had shot the first two *Elaine* serials at the Pathé Studios in New Jersey and in the New York City metropolitan area. For the filming of *The Romance*, however, they returned to Ithaca, bringing with them the entire *Elaine* cast and crew, an event that generated tremendous excitement in the upstate community. Departing from the Hoboken station with two carloads of scenery and props, the company clearly "look[ed] forward to their work" and to their new permanent address.[19] *Motion Picture News* noted that they asked each other the same question: "Won't it seem good to get those lake breezes again and breathe that fine air away from hot sidewalks and humidity?"[20]

Codirecting the episodes was George B. Seitz; the scenarios, based on the stories by Arthur B. Reeve, were written by Charles W. Goddard and his brother-in-law Basil Dickey.[21] Most of the original *Elaine* actors, including Pearl White, Creighton Hale, and Bessie Wharton, reprised their roles. But a clever accommodation had to be made for Arnold Daly, who, "though both willing and eager to continue in Craig Kennedy's shoes," was committed to starring in a revival of *Candida*, the role that had already brought him considerable fame. The revival, which began on May 18 in New York's Garrick Theater, made him unavailable for much of the filming.[22]

A new addition to the cast was Lionel Barrymore, a member of the distinguished theatrical Barrymore family, who brought a sinister energy to his role as the serial's villain. Barrymore had begun performing in his early twenties on Broadway, where he earned acclaim in several plays produced by the legendary Charles Frohman before taking a brief hiatus to pursue life as an artist in Paris. By 1910, though, he was back on Broadway; by the following year, he was on the silent screen as well, acting in films for D. W. Griffith at his Biograph Studios and for other producers, including Louis B. Mayer. Unfortunately, in the Wharton serial his appearance was brief. Barrymore, who reportedly cared little for Ithaca and even less for the Wharton brothers,[23] abruptly left the production midway and had to be replaced by Warner Oland, the Swedish-born actor who would go on to find fame as film's legendary detective Charlie Chan. Oland, who would appear again the next year as a villain in the Whartons' serial *Patria*, took over the role and played it with histrionic perfection.[24]

While *The Romance of Elaine* (which, like *The New Exploits of Elaine*, is not extant) carried over most of the principals from the two earlier serials, it also introduced a number of new characters, both major and minor. As the first episode opens, the wreckage of a submarine rises to the surface, and a mysterious figure, Marcius Del Mar, swims to the shore ("The Lost Torpedo"). Later that day, Del Mar, claiming to be a government agent, volunteers to assist Elaine and Jameson in their search for Kennedy and his model torpedo. Unknown to all of them, that torpedo has been moved by Elaine's dog Rusty from the potted palm where Wu Fang's man had placed it in the final episode of the previous serial to a new spot behind a trunk in the attic. Assuming that Elaine has deliberately concealed the device, Del Mar pledges to find it. At the same time, an unnamed old man who had witnessed Del Mar come out of the water warns Jameson to beware of the stranger—a warning that almost immediately comes true, when the old man is set upon by Del Mar's associates.[25]

When Elaine receives a mysterious note telling her that Kennedy is safe, she celebrates by throwing a masked party, during which Del Mar ransacks her home, a search that is observed by a guest disguised as a friar ("The Gray Friar"). Afterward, quite by accident, the model torpedo is discovered by a housemaid and passes through many hands in rather spectacular fashion before being returned to Elaine by a local farmer.[26] Having failed to secure it, Del Mar initiates a new plot to threaten American national security: he orders the destruction of the transatlantic communication cable and the mining of the harbor in preparation for a full-scale attack ("The Vanishing Man").

Later, out for a spin with Jameson, Elaine notices a group of workers, who, unknown to her, have received a signal to demolish the bridge she is about

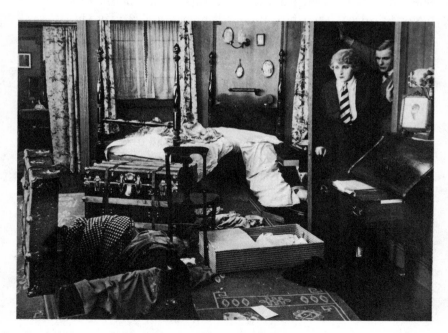

FIGURE 7.3   In "The Gray Friar" episode of *The Romance of Elaine*, Elaine (Pearl White) finds herself once again the target of a mysterious villain.

to cross. Fortunately, the farmer (who seems to find himself close by Elaine at times of her greatest peril) intercepts the message and, even though the bridge is blown, prevents any harm from befalling her.[27] "Elaine's sojourn in the country is not at all quiet and restful," reviewer Edward Weitzel observed with some understatement, "but just the reverse. Events move with the high-speed controlling the clutch. As usual, the photography and filming, under the direction of the Whartons, calls for unqualified commendation."[28]

Over the next few episodes, Elaine faces threats from a gunman she encounters near one of the bridge-wreckers' caves ("The Submarine Harbor") and then from Del Mar himself, who takes her hostage ("The Conspirators"). In the first instance, a naturalist who has been watching from a distance comes to Elaine's aid; in the second, Jameson, who observes her capture but is unable to prevent it, rushes to Fort Dale to seek assistance from Captain Burnside of the U.S. Aerial Corps.[29]

Despite such close calls, and having once again escaped her captors, Elaine persists in investigating the curious events that have been occurring near her home ("The Wireless Detective"). Disguising herself as a man (an act that critics like Ben Singer have noted is a further appropriation of masculine attributes by a "New Woman" heroine), she happens upon the entrance to Del Mar's secret cave; but she is swept away and nearly drowned after one of the spy's confederates spots her and opens the floodgates. Meanwhile, at Fort Hale, Elaine's new friends Lieutenant Woodward and Professor Arnold intercept a message confirming that the enemy is attempting to mine the harbor. But by the time the cavalry arrives, Del Mar has already dismantled the wireless station and escaped to his cave.[30]

Nonetheless, his assaults on Elaine continue. After she stumbles upon the contraband he has stored at the Wilkeshire Country Club, she is taken captive again and held prisoner alongside a mysterious tramp, who helps her escape ("The War Cloud," retitled "The Death Cloud" in Reeve's novelization).[31] Afterward, she finds a bomb that one of Del Mar's associates has placed in her home. With Jameson's help, she tries to bring it to Professor Arnold, but on the way, the pair is attacked. Although Jameson is able to hurl the bomb from their car and onto the roadway, where it tears a deep gash and kills Del Mar's chauffeur, the villain continues the chase. Using the highly accurate revolver that she has mysteriously received as a gift, Elaine kills one of her pursuers and wounds another ("The Searchlight Gun").[32]

More intent than ever to destroy her, Del Mar lures Elaine to the dress-making shop of his confederate "Mme. Lorenz" and then spirits her away to a house in the woods, where she escapes by hopping into a canoe; only the human chain formed by Jameson and the naturalist from an earlier episode prevent her from going over the falls ("The Life Chain").[33] Meanwhile, Professor Arnold locates some stolen defense plans, which he slips to Elaine. She in turn gives them for safekeeping to Jameson, who hides them in the Dodge home, where he rigs a flash to photograph anyone who might attempt to steal them ("The Flash"). A photo later reveals an image of the thief, whom Elaine instantly identifies by the distinctive ring on his finger.[34]

Despite the danger, Elaine and Jameson accept an invitation from Del Mar, who renders Jameson powerless, encases Elaine in a diver's suit, and drags her into the deep waters. Her abduction is witnessed by Arnold, who has uncovered Del Mar's actual criminal identity using a "telaphotograph" that transmits photographs over a wire ("The Disappearing Helmets").[35] The kidnapping, though, inadvertently discloses the whereabouts of Del Mar's secret underwater harbor site. In the twelfth and final episode, "The Triumph of Elaine," Arnold, curiously invested in Elaine's well-being and assisted by Lieutenant Woodward and his troops, is able to track the spy by means of an underwater telescope. Once Del Mar's submarine rises to the surface, a fierce confrontation ensues, during which Del Mar breaks free and makes a final attempt to sabotage the transatlantic cable. On Arnold's orders, Jameson and Woodward rush to Burnside's hangar, attach Kennedy's wireless torpedo to a

FIGURE 7.4 In the final episode of *The Romance of Elaine*, the identity of the stranger who has assisted Elaine (Pearl White) throughout the serial is revealed.

hydroaeroplane, and strike and sink the submarine, killing the perfidious spy. Del Mar's last message exposes his true allegiance: "Tell my emperor I failed only because Craig Kennedy was against me."

After a bound-and-gagged Elaine is discovered in the hillside hut where Del Mar had left her, Professor Arnold makes a stunning revelation. He is actually Craig Kennedy, who—in his various disguises, including old gentleman, gray friar, farmer, naturalist, and tramp—has been protecting her all along. With the nation secure, its foreign enemies dead, and Elaine safely back in his arms, he happily reports, "My work on the case is done."[36]

The Reception of the Serial

Advance advertisements for *The Romance of Elaine* had hinted that Elaine's "trials and tribulations" would be drawing to a close and that her "final triumph" was near: "After her desperate dangers, her narrow escapes from the highly intelligent and malevolent enemies who for months have beset her, she becomes Elaine the victorious." The ads also posed teasing questions: "Does she marry? Does society claim her? Do art and literature make her life? Or do home and children? ? ? ?"[37] Naturally, moviegoers packed the theaters to learn the exciting outcome of Elaine's story.

Hailed by *Motion Picture News* as a "production of the masterpiece class" and applauded for its ingenious story construction and other "points of excellence," *The Romance of Elaine* reaped real financial rewards for both the Whartons and Pathé.[38] It also set an important precedent by incorporating plot events that revolved around possession of a recently invented weapon of great power. As Ed Hulse observed, "Kennedy's super-charged torpedo was the first of innumerable death-dealing devices whose plans or prototypes were coveted by serial villains. . . . Over the course of the movie serial's five-decade history, plots of this type [many of which harked directly back to the Whartons] animated at least 200 chapter-plays."[39] *The Romance of Elaine* also solidified Elaine's status as a "New Woman" heroine who breaks from traditional gender roles and exhibits her daring and athleticism as she conducts her own investigation, in Kennedy's apparent absence, into the various mysteries.

After their months of filming at the Pathé Studios in New Jersey, the Whartons' return to Ithaca in May to shoot *The Romance* had been a cause of much excitement. Ithacans, who had long embraced the brothers and their film enterprise, were thrilled that their town would once again be the temporary residence for "a galaxy of brilliant moving picture stars."[40] And even if the plot of the final *Elaine* serial ultimately proved more disjointed and transparent than the first two, the stars themselves did not disappoint. Upon their arrival, they ingratiated themselves with the community. Pearl White became a particular favorite. Easily recognizable, even without the blond wig that she wore during filming (it seems that Hearst, who was deeply involved in the serial's production, had insisted that Elaine Dodge be a blond), White proved to be a free and lively spirit, every bit as independent as the serial heroines she played. Locals regaled each other with reports of her irrepressible behavior, which included wearing trousers, smoking in public, and using salty language. And they shared anecdotes about her brassiness, especially the time she drove her yellow Stutz Bearcat through the nearby town of Trumansburg at a speed that far exceeded the posted limit. Reportedly, when she appeared before the local magistrate, she was fined five dollars for the violation. Handing over a ten-dollar bill, she advised him that he had better keep the change, because she intended to drive out of the town "a hell of a lot quicker" than she had come in.[41] The story, by all accounts true, was also part of a publicity trope that performers like White cultivated and exploited to keep themselves in the public eye.

Taking both interest and pride in production, Ithacans gathered in Groton City to witness the bridge that Elaine and Jameson were crossing get blown up with twenty pounds of dynamite.[42] At the Taughannock Falls, they held their breath as they watched Elaine "going over" the falls in a canoe. Later, they cheered as Del Mar's submarine was finally sunk.[43] And, of course, they flocked to the local theaters every week to savor each new episode as it was released.[44]

Collectively titled *The Exploits of Elaine*, the *Elaine* serials proved to be a tremendous success at the box office. One hundred and fifty prints—far in excess of the usual thirty or so—were struck and sent to the exchanges for distribution to exhibitors.[45] The *Ithaca Journal* noted that, in total length alone, the three pictures, if "laid flat on the ground, would reach from Ithaca to Omaha, Nebraska, or a distance of 1,000 miles."[46] And indeed, from Ithaca to Omaha and well beyond, audiences queued up to follow Elaine's latest adventures. "Flattering attention from trade papers" and congratulatory telegrams and letters poured in.[47] At least one New York critic, in town to observe the production, arrived as a skeptic but left as an enthusiast. Having underestimated the Whartons, he admitted that the "City [of Ithaca] Will Gain Fame" because of their work.[48]

Elaine found an enthusiastic audience overseas as well. Almost immediately on the serial's completion, Pathé exported it to France, where its thirty-six episodes were condensed, recut, and rearranged into twenty-two episodes, each approximately twenty minutes long, by French writer and playwright Pierre Decourcelle. Retitled *Les Mystères de New-York*, it was serialized in *Le Matin*, published in a weekly booklet by La Renaissance du Livre, and eventually novelized. While the French version of the film roughly followed the American serial's order, Decourcelle, who relied heavily on the Reeve stories in his editing and rearranging, developed and expanded some of the

FIGURE 7.5   *The Exploits of Elaine*, recut in France and retitled *Les Mystères de New-York*, became a smashing success in Paris (1915).

characters, even the minor ones like Limpy Red ("Le Bancal Rouge").[49] He also transformed the central character of Craig Kennedy, from a resourceful American into the "famous and fearless Frenchman" Justin Clarel, who holds a double job as a crime detective and a professor at Columbia University. The timeline of the story was altered as well: rather than occurring during wartime, which gave historical immediacy to the torpedo that Kennedy had built and the Atlantic cable that Del Mar tries to cut, the French version was set entirely before the war, with the outbreak of that event merely hinted at in the final episode.[50]

By December 1915, *Les Mystères*, the best-known of the American productions that were sent to the French market, was playing weekly in almost fifty Parisian cinemas.[51] According to prominent film critic Louis Delluc, it instantly sparked a fashion trend in Paris, with White's costume as the chic and modern Elaine Dodge—"the black dress, sober skirt, white spats and the little hat"—widely imitated by fashionable French women.[52] And while the French were among the most dedicated of her many admirers, with the overseas distribution of *Elaine*, the "Pearl White craze" spread to other countries as well, including Russia and China. Nationally and internationally, the Whartons' first serial had proven to be an unqualified success.

CHAPTER 8

Establishing Roots in Renwick Park

The enormous popularity of *The Exploits of Elaine* was not the only good news for the Whartons. Another cause for celebration was the new Wharton Studio facility that they established at Renwick Park (now Stewart Park), at the southern tip of Cayuga Lake

After arriving in Ithaca to open their own production studio in May 1914, the brothers had operated out of cramped quarters on East State Street. Processing and developing, of necessity, were done out of town, in New York City or Chicago. In early 1915, however, when the former amusement park in Renwick Park went into foreclosure owing to various liens placed against it, they expressed interest in taking over the property.[1] With its lake frontage, gardens, bandstand, pavilions, open air theater, carousel, miniature steam railroad, and trolley connections, the site seemed ideal for their purposes. It even had "frontier settlement streets, log cabins—all the locations necessary to Western work."[2] Best of all, the new facility would give the brothers the space they sorely needed and the opportunity to expand their operation. By March, they had placed a lease offer for a period of five years, promising to spend approximately $20,000 in improvements, provided that they would have the option of buying the Renwick Park property at the expiration of the lease.[3] The terms on which they eventually settled stipulated that the annual rental would amount to $2,000, with a purchase option of $35,000 after five years.[4]

FIGURE 8.1 Originally the site of an amusement park in Renwick Park, the Wharton Studio brought the brothers new production opportunities.

With the Whartons still at Pathé's New Jersey studio wrapping the second *Elaine*, their brother-in-law and general manager J. Whitworth Buck concluded negotiations on their behalf.[5] Upon acceptance of the offer, Buck hired a local company, the Driscoll Brothers, to begin the necessary renovations. Over the next few months, terra cotta block walls were built between the original perimeter columns to enclose the exterior porches and create additional usable interior space for dressing rooms, property rooms, and an indoor stage. An open stage was constructed to the west. The water tower became offices on the first floor and wardrobe on the second. The pavilion to the east, once a café, was divided into carpentry and property shops, and small buildings were dedicated to developing, printing, title making, and editing. A bowling alley became a projection house. Separate small ironclad buildings were erected to store the highly combustible film materials.[6] And, for the next year, until a security fence was erected, the grounds stayed open to the public, who came by special trolley to picnic and to watch the stars in action. It was, as a visiting reporter from *Motography* raved, "a very complete equipment for the making of quality pictures."[7]

Buck, too, remained "busily engaged" in helping to get the studio into shape for production and readying it for the May arrival of the Whartons' *Elaine* company.[8] In addition to overseeing the construction, he hired a squad of stage carpenters and scenic artists. He also assured the *Ithaca Journal* that local talent would continue to be needed for roles in upcoming productions. And indeed, once the renovations at the new Renwick Park studio were almost complete and the filming of the third segment of the *Elaine* serial was finished, the Whartons began planning their next projects.[9] Several new pictures, they announced, would go into production simultaneously, with Ted and Leo sharing directorial responsibilities with James Gordon and Harry Mainhall (both of whom continued to assume small acting parts).[10] The most

FIGURE 8.2 Wharton actors and crew enjoy a ride on the studio's tiny train conducted by Pearl White (the Whartons are at the far right ahead of the locomotive).

ambitious was *Get-Rich-Quick-Wallingford*, later released under the title *The New Adventures of J. Rufus Wallingford.*

Introducing *Wallingford*

The fourteen-part serial comedy was based on the "Get-Rich-Quick-Wallingford" stories by popular author George Randolph Chester, originally published in *Cosmopolitan* magazine and later collected in the book *Get-Rich-Quick Wallingford: A Cheerful Account of the Rise and Fall of an American Business Buccaneer* (1907). Chester's fictional title character J. "Jim" Rufus Wallingford was a genial confidence man and promoter of various financial schemes. Usually accompanied by his equally affable partner-in-crime Blackie Daw, he "could sell a phonograph to a deaf man, opera glasses to a blind man, [and] running shoes to a cripple."[11] A familiar figure thanks to the popular Broadway production *Get-Rich-Quick-Wallingford* (1910) written and scored by George M. Cohan, he found his way back to the screen in several later films, including *Get-Rich-Quick Wallingford* (1916), directed by and starring Fred Niblo; *Get-Rich-Quick Wallingford* (1921), directed by Frank Borzage; and *New Adventures of Get Rich Quick Wallingford* (1931), starring William Haines as Wallingford and Jimmy Durante as his friend and partner. But perhaps no film version was more anticipated than the Wharton serial.

As the *Ithaca Journal* reported, production began the second week in July 1915. Based on scenarios prepared by Charles W. Goddard, adapted by George B. Seitz, and codirected by Ted Wharton, Leo Wharton, and James Gordon, the serial starred Burr McIntosh, who took over the title role from Frederic de Belleville after only three episodes. McIntosh, who had an interesting and eclectic career as an author, publisher, lecturer, and studio owner, was an early radio pioneer. Like so many of his contemporaries, he came to silent film by way of the legitimate stage, first in England and Austria, then in the United States.[12] Described by Mary Pickford as a "giant" (albeit a gentle one), he seemed the embodiment of Chester's mustachioed con man.

Costarring with McIntosh as Wallingford's pal and coconspirator Blackie Daw was Viennese-born Max Figman. A veteran stage actor who had performed in some of the same companies that Ted Wharton had (including those of Augustin Daly and Charles Frohman) and who was associated with John Cort and Mrs. Minnie Maddern Fiske (who crossed paths with Leo early in his career), Figman was one of the best-known actors of the day.[13] Also in the cast, as Violet Warden, was Figman's real-life wife Lolita Robertson, who often performed in films alongside him, and Wharton regular Frances White as Violet's sister, Fanny Warden. Appearing in minor roles were Harry Mainhall, Allan Murnane, Dick Bennard, and F. W. Stewart, most of whom had played in earlier Wharton productions. Among the most notable of the performers, though, was the young O. N. ("Babe") Hardy, who later found fame as part of the legendary comedy team of Laurel and Hardy.

The plot of the serial was relatively straightforward. The "Falls clique," a group of corrupt financiers, has swindled the late Mr. Warden and precipitated his untimely demise. When Warden's orphaned daughters Violet and Fanny meet Wallingford and Daw in the drawing-room car of a train, they invite the men to do their utmost to recover the lost fortune, a challenge they accept "with much gusto." The ensuing comedy, reviewer Margaret I. MacDonald wrote, "is, of course, all action; and in spite of the fact that a farcical element is introduced, there is a pleasing absence of slapstick play."[14]

Although Wallingford's adventures are told in a serial format, the individual episodes were, in many ways, self-contained, with every one telling a complete story. In each, Wallingford and Daw target one of the members of the clique, use their unique talents to extract the money owed to the late Mr. Warden, and then "cross off" another name from their list. In the first episode, "The Bungalow Bungle" (released October 4, 1915), for example, the con men invest in a portable house company owned by young Falls, son of the president of the O., Q., & T. Railroad Company. A large order comes in from a farmer, who stipulates that certain improvements to the product must be made. Wallingford immediately steps in to offer several solutions, which the company is forced to accept if they expect to ship. Just then Onion Jones appears, claiming that the inventions required to solve the problem actually belong to a client whom he represents. Threatening to sue for patent infringement, he demands that the entire output be turned over to him. Afterward, the scam is revealed: Jones is one of the members of Wallingford's firm, and Blackie had been posing as the farmer. The sisters get restitution; and Wallingford, with due ceremony, crosses off Falls's name and prepares to "land" the next one.[15]

The men continue their crusade of righteous revenge in "Three Rings and a Goat" by targeting Silas Bogger, another member of the corrupt clique, and selling him a circus, whose company of performers creates so many problems that Bogger is relieved to pay extra to release himself from the contract.[16] And "A Rheumatic Joint" finds the genial con man in Zwick's Sanitarium for treatment, where he meets Cornelius Rockewell, a millionaire who is willing to invest any amount to be rid of his ailments. So Wallingford and

FIGURE 8.3 Gentlemen con men Rufus Wallingford (Burr McIntosh) and Blackie Daw (Max Figman) open a phony sanitarium in order to trick a millionaire and right the wrong that he has caused.

Daw decide to offer him an "anti-old-age cure" at the bogus sanitarium that they establish, which Rockewell is anxious to buy. But Onion Jones feigns interest in the property and successfully pushes Rockewell to raise his bid, which allows Wallingford to cross off another man complicit in the ruin of Mr. Warden.[17]

The next name on the list is banker J. D. Prine, whose associates have $350,000 in bad loans for which they could be jailed. Wallingford threatens to expose the bankers unless they pay him to maintain his silence, which they gladly do ("The Master Stroke"). Then he goes even further: forcing them to "finance a campaign" against themselves, he speculates on a lot next to Prine's general store and, in "an excruciatingly funny scene," has thousands of skunks shipped to him for use in the chemical factory he says he is opening there.[18] The foul smell drives all Prine's customers away, giving him no alternative but to buy Wallingford out.[19]

A similarly unhappy fate awaits Perigourd, "a polished crook" who works in a modiste's shop and allows cheap dressmakers to copy the latest fashions ("The Lilac Splash"). After overhearing Wallingford and Daw in his shop discussing a lucrative scheme, he begs to be let in. The investment wipes him out but compensates the women for the loss he earlier helped to engineer.[20] Another member of the clique of the corrupt financiers, the "over-shrewd automobile dealer" Louis Trapp, is likewise played for a sucker ("A Trap for Trapp"). When a plan that Wallingford and Daw devise excites his cupidity, Trapp senses an opportunity for a quick profit and offers Wallingford $50,000 for what he believes is a thriving business. Wallingford accepts, but immediately alerts postal authorities to a mail fraud scheme, which sends the new owner into ruin.[21] And in another episode ("A Bang Sun Machine"), unscrupulous rural banker Dana Morley is fooled into thinking that a large factory is being built to manufacture inventor Edward Bang's sun engine; so he buys the Warden sisters' shares, only to discover that they are completely worthless and that he has been "stung."[22]

Much of the humor in the serial stems from the guises and disguises that Wallingford and Daw assume in the course of their campaign. Pretending to be the owner of a popular resort, Wallingford purchases "Pine Lake Hotel," an aged and dilapidated place on a swamp that is overrun with mosquitoes ("A Transaction in Summer Boarders"). After packing the place with a stranded burlesque company, he unloads it on the simpering newly wealthy Charles Algernon Swivel, who believes the land is rich with oil (which a Wallingford confederate put there precisely to attract his attention). "A very laughable bit of comedy" is provided by the "Prancing Pink Pretties," including Miss

Tottie Vorhies (one of the burlesque performers, who becomes Mrs. Swivel), and especially by Onion Jones, who pretends to contract "smallpox, cholera, and leprosy," all at the same time, which clears out the guests.[23] In another episode, in the "sordid little municipal-ownership town" of Spanglerville that was implicated in the ruin of Mr. Warden, Wallingford and Daw assume the identities of detectives "Mr. Scotland Yard" and "Mr. S. Holmes" ("Detective Blackie"). After exhibiting some of their latest detection devices, including a "sneakograph" and a "sleuthophone," they hoodwink the rubes into purchasing a new invention for a sum that covers the money stolen by them from Warden.[24] And later, posing as "business doctors, sick and dying enterprises cured while you wait," they assist both the sisters and a small-business operator, Mr. Pushman, who is heavily in debt to another clique member, the scheming country banker G. W. Slookum ("Apples and Eggbeaters"). Enticed into buying "Pushman, Inc. Kitchen Supplies," which he believes is a thriving enterprise, Slookum soon realizes it is a failing business whose books the "doctors" have cooked.[25]

Occasionally, the gentlemen con men get a taste of their own medicine, as in "A Stony Deal," when J. Squibble, the tight-fisted farmer whom they have scheduled for a "shakedown," begins assessing them in turn, by taxing the Warden girls ten cents for taking a drink from his well and charging Wallingford for driving an automobile across his property. An angry Wallingford buys the place before reselling it to Squibble for $35,000; but Squibble gets the last laugh by immediately reselling it for $50,000. Wallingford, though, does not really care, since he has already reclaimed the money that was due Mr. Warden.[26]

In Jinkinsville, home of clique member Benjamin F. Quirker, a man who "has a 'past' and maintains a present—with the ladies," the con men stir up even more trouble ("Buying a Bank with Bunk"). After exposing Quirker as a philanderer and sending the "hyena-like" Mrs. Quirker on the warpath, Wallingford writes a bad check in order to acquire Quirker's shares in the bank and uses them as collateral to borrow a like amount from the bank's directors.[27] And the duo entrap corrupt lawyer P. S. Hutch by renting a "Spirit Parlor" for the day to convince him that he is being haunted by Lundy, a man who wants his rightful compensation for the money that Hutch had embezzled ("The Missing Heir").[28]

In the final episode ("Lord Southpaugh"), after Wallingford and Daw persuade Oak Centre bank president Eli Spooger that the Bessemer Malleable Iron Foundry in which he is invested will be getting a million-dollar war order, they purchase shares of the company from the other townspeople, create a bidding war, and clean Spooger out. The serial ends on an even higher note, though, when Daw agrees to sell a lovely little cottage to Violet for only a dollar, provided that she takes the contents as well. The contents, she discovers, include Daw. As *Moving Picture World* reports, "We leave [Violet and Daw] in a state of rapture," as Wallingford moves on to a new con, selling bill-posting rights to the North Pole.[29]

Unlike the more technically innovative *Elaine* serial, *The New Adventures of J. Rufus Wallingford* (which survives only in fragments) was an entertaining comedy whose self-contained stories, straightforward narration, and clever plots ensured its broad appeal. According to advance publicity, even the early episodes were "radiantly indicative" that the picture would be an unprecedented success.[30] Later reviewers concurred, praising the Whartons for "the creditable style in which the series is being represented in pictures"; and they observed, with its good photography and strong attributes of direction and cast, *Wallingford* "bids fair for a large following in leading picture houses."[31] Promotional advertisements in major movie journals similarly touted the serial, observing that "all who have read these great stories will want to see the pictures[,] and the stories will be published simultaneously by the Hearst and other big newspapers all over the country." The occasional review, however, took issue with the "forced" and "broad" comedy. In particular, *Variety* alleged that the serial was too commercial and stated that it would have no appeal to women since they, "as a rule, have no head nor inclination for business."[32]

Most of the episodes were filmed in and around Ithaca, largely at the new Wharton studio in Renwick Park, and—as had become the Whartons' practice—featured a number of locals as extras called "supers" (short for supernumeraries). Prior to the shooting of the scenes featuring the Sig Sawtelle Circus that had been imported from nearby Homer and set up on the park grounds, the *Ithaca Journal* announced, "[The Whartons] will need large numbers of people. . . . The general public is welcome to participate, no histrionic ability needed." The response was enthusiastic. After the scenes were completed, the extras and the locals were rewarded by an actual day at the circus, with "Cupid" (Oliver) Hardy performing as a clown and leading men Burr McIntosh and Max Figman participating in the event.[33] The local paper also reported on other aspects of the serial production, from the problems experienced by McIntosh and Figman ("in false whiskers"), who nearly got arrested while enacting scenes in the commercial section of town after a local constable failed to recognize them, to the mayhem that resulted when the "polecats" (skunks) required for one of the scenes got loose and literally raised an enormous stink.[34] Later, on October 1, when the first episode of the serial premiered at Ithaca's Lyceum Theater to capacity audiences, it was clear that, once again, "Ithacans are with the Whartons heart and soul in their productions."[35]

Breaking into Feature Filmmaking

No doubt it was the success of their serial pictures that inspired the Whartons to try their hand at something new: the production of a feature film. As was commonplace among early filmmakers and producers, the brothers looked to stage plays that they could adapt to the screen. Adaptation of literature, both classic and popular, was, after all, an easy way to secure rich and varied source material; and the legitimacy of a literary source usually ensured a picture's immunity from the increasing threats of censorship. According to Lewis Jacobs, in addition to providing critics with little excuse for attacks, material "from decorous works" gave films a sense of purposefulness and familiarity, since movie audiences were already likely to be acquainted with the stories.[36]

So, at the same time that they were completing the final episodes of the *Wallingford* serial, the Whartons began production of a five-reel feature, *Hazel Kirke*, based on the four-act play of the same name. Written between 1878 and 1879 by playwright and theater manager Steele MacKaye expressly for Augustin Daly's company at New York City's Madison Square Theatre (a company with which Ted had performed and which he briefly stage-managed in the late 1890s), the play starred actress Effie Ellsler in the title role. Premiering on February 4, 1880, it ran for 486 consecutive performances, which set a record for its time.[37] Over the next two decades, the play was staged thousands of times on several continents and, at one point, was revamped to include a musical score, which in turn spawned sheet music for the "Hazel Kirke Waltz" and the "Hazel Kirke Polka."

By the time that the Whartons adapted the play to film, the story of Hazel was already a familiar one. The daughter of miller Dunstan Kirke, Hazel has been sent off by Squire Rodney to be educated, with the understanding that she will marry him upon her return. All of this is in repayment of the loan that Rodney advanced to save the town's old mill from the auction block. Despite renewing her promise to Rodney, at school Hazel falls in love with and marries wealthy Arthur Carringford. But Arthur's mother, desperate to save the family fortune, wants her son to wed her ward, Maude, who in turn is loved by Pittacus Greene. After Mrs. Carringford informs Hazel that her marriage to Arthur is invalid because it was performed by a fake minister whom she hired, a despondent Hazel returns home and tries to drown herself. Arthur, however, follows her, rescues her from the icy waters, and assures her that the marriage was real and that they are and will always be husband and wife.[38]

The Whartons were not the first to bring *Hazel Kirke* to the screen: Majestic Pictures had released a version of the drama-romance four years earlier. Directed by Oscar Apfel, Ted's former colleague at Edison, that short starred Mabel Trunnelle, Herbert Prior, and Edward P. Sullivan. But the Whartons' version had something that the earlier production lacked: the enduring and bankable appeal of its star, Pearl White, in the title role. Filming in Ithaca began in mid-November 1915, and the picture was released January 28, 1916, for distribution through the "Golden Rooster Plays," a prestige program that Pathé hoped would "become the signal mark for films that are absolutely good in every respect."[39] In addition to White—who, according to *Billboard*, gave a perfect portrayal of an ignorant mountain girl growing into "a full grown school graduate" and finally into a developed woman—it included Allan Murnane as Arthur Carringford, William Riley Hatch as Dunstan Kirke, Creighton Hale as Pittacus Greene, and Bruce McRae as Squire Rodney, all of whom "add[ed] strength to the story."[40]

FIGURE 8.4   A despondent Hazel (Pearl White) in *Hazel Kirke* is relieved to learn that her marriage is valid after all.

Reviews of the film (which is not extant) were positive. Glad that "poor dear old Hazel . . . has finally succumbed to the pictures," *Variety* praised all the performances, noting that the late Steele MacKaye would be proud of the cast selected for the "picturizing of what in those days of playwriting was a 'masterpiece.'" The play is still fine melodrama today, the review continued: "the direction is good, the photography adequate (barring a tendency to haziness when tinting is resorted to) and the photoplay, taken as a whole, and considering the full value of the name, is almost certain to prove a big winner."[41] *Billboard* concurred, calling the plot an old one, but handled in a way "to keep the interest up to the highest pitch." The direction and photography were "of the highest order, and the 'local color' could not be improved upon." Ultimately, *Billboard*'s reviewer found *Hazel Kirke* to be "a story so complete, interesting and entertaining that its success can safely be predicted."[42]

Contract Producing

Buoyed by the reception of *Hazel Kirke*, the brothers began production of film versions of two other popular plays, *The City* and *The Lottery Man*, both based on script adaptations by Ted. The melodrama *The City* was begun in October and released on January 17, 1916. "A modern play of American life in three acts," it was originally written in 1909 by Clyde Fitch, a New York–born dramatist who was one of the most popular Broadway playwrights of his day.[43] Although little known today and infrequently performed, *The City*, like all Fitch's plays, featured characters who were more complex than those in standard melodramas. Sophisticated in its psychology, the play challenged audiences to question their own values and practices.[44]

In the stage version of *The City*, the George Rand family has a "New York bee in their bonnets" and wants to relocate from the comfortable suburb of Middleburgh to the big city. But Rand Sr. prefers to stay in a town where they are "it" rather than relocate to a place where they will be "nit." Conveniently, he soon dies of a heart attack, though not before privately sharing some damaging personal secrets with his son. Once the family makes the move, many of their dreams start coming true: Mrs. Rand enjoys the city's society (including a better dressmaker); the daughters find good marital prospects; and George Jr. accumulates both money and power. But just as he is on the verge of being nominated for governor, a ghost from the past arises to haunt him. Fred Hannock, who knows about George Sr.'s shady dealings, blackmails George Jr. and threatens to expose his family's secrets. George must then decide whether to do the right thing, for which he will certainly suffer, or the wrong thing, which will ensure his continued success. "Fitch presents complicated individuals living in a self-interested age," and, as the play makes clear, there are no easy answers.[45]

The City (which, like *Hazel Kirke*, does not survive) was the first of two films produced on contract by the Whartons in the fall of 1915 for the F. Ray Comstock Photoplay Company. That company was owned by the New York–born Comstock (1878–1949), an American theater owner and theatrical producer whose productions included variety shows and musicals such as the first "Negro musical" *Bandana Land* (1908), as well as plays adapted from serious literature. The film starred Thurlow Bergen as George Rand Jr., Elsie Esmond as Emily Rand, and Allan Murnane as the shady Jim (changed from Fred in the play) Hannock Jr., with William Riley Hatch and Bessie Wharton as Mr. and Mrs. Rand Sr., and F. W. Stewart as Jim Hannock Sr. And while it altered a few of the play's elements— including the revelation of the drug-addicted illegitimate son, who is part of the "secret" that is ultimately exposed—the film was, "all told, a well-acted and well-directed picture, with an excellent selection of types and a number of 'big' scenes." Some reviewers, however, were disappointed by the ending, which they argued lacked a satisfying conclusion, much as the legitimate stage production had. The idea of a woman addressing a political convention and winning it over to a vote of acclamation, wrote *Variety*, "is still far-fetched—at least in New York State, where suffragism hasn't yet secured very strong foothold." Nonetheless, the reviewer acknowledged that *The City* taught a real moral.[46]

As was typical, the Whartons invited locals to serve as extras in the feature. The *Ithaca Journal* reported that for the final scene alone—of the convention filmed in the airdrome in the park ("the biggest scene of its kind" ever attempted in Ithaca)—actor and Ithaca resident Dick Stewart visited all of the area factories to get five hundred volunteers, and the "Whartons paid everybody's carfare."[47] Not surprisingly, when the finished film was previewed locally, the response was overwhelmingly enthusiastic, with moviegoers vouching that it had "great promise" and "excell[ed] anything" previously undertaken by the Whartons.[48]

The second of the films produced by the Whartons for Comstock was *The Lottery Man* (released June 26, 1916), based on the play of the same name that opened at the Bijou Theatre on Broadway on December 6, 1909, and ran until May 1910, for a total of two hundred performances.[49] The play was written by Rida Johnson Young (1875–1926), an American playwright, songwriter, and librettist with over thirty plays, musicals, and operettas such as *Naughty Marietta* and more than five hundred songs to her credit. *The Lottery*

FIGURE 8.5 Family secrets are exposed in *The City*, which ends with an elaborate political convention scene.

Man, her most enduring work, proved so popular with theatergoers that producers Lee and J. J. Shubert sent out four touring companies to perform it on the road.

In the play, Jack Wright, a young newspaperman who is down on his luck, lives with his mother. After he borrows money from his friend and boss Foxey Peyton for a speculative scheme that fails, he proposes to Foxey a plan that will not only sell more papers but also bring him some much-needed cash: he offers himself as the prize in a marriage lottery, which the paper would advertise and to which it would sell one-dollar tickets. The winner would then have the option of marrying Jack or splitting the lottery winnings with him. Naturally, the plan goes awry. Just after the first issue of the paper hits the streets, Jack meets and becomes enchanted by a young woman, Helen Heyer, who is Foxey's cousin. Despite his efforts, it is too late to stop the contest, which exceeds all expectations in sales. Unknown to him, in the hope of boosting Helen's chances, both Mrs. Wright and Mrs. Peyton buy up as many tickets as possible. But when the contest ends and hundreds of excited women gather to learn the outcome, the winning ticket is claimed by Mrs. Peyton's spinsterish assistant, Lizzie, who takes every advantage of the situation until it is revealed that she stole the ticket. Jack is then free to pursue Helen, the woman he really wants to marry.[50] After all, as Edward F. O'Day observed in *Town Talk*, "The whole plot of the play would go to pieces if The Lottery Man were [actually] won in the lottery."[51]

The Whartons recognized the genius of the play, which showcased likable characters and humorous incidents, and they knew that it would translate well to the screen. They even invited two of the stage actresses who originated roles in *The Lottery Man*, Ethel Winthrop and Mary Leslie Mayo, to reprise their roles on screen.[52] The lead parts went to the husband-and-wife team of Thurlow Bergen and Elsie Esmond, who had been members of the original company that the Whartons formed in Ithaca more than a year earlier. Other familiar faces in the cast included Allan Murnane (who would go on to play in several other Wharton productions, including *Beatrice Fairfax*, *The Mysteries of Myra*, *Patria*, and *The Eagle's Eye*) as well as Ithacans and Wharton regulars Louis A. Fuertes, F. W. Stewart, and Frances White. Most interesting, perhaps, was the casting of the twenty-three-year-old actor

FIGURE 8.6   The devotion of Jack Wright (Thurlow Bergen) to his impoverished mother leads him to offer himself as the prize in a marriage lottery in *The Lottery Man*.

Oliver Hardy in a key role that is pivotal to the resolution of the plot. By then Hardy had performed in numerous shorts, including several episodes of *The New Adventures of J. Rufus Wallingford* serial, but *The Lottery Man* was one of his first appearances in a feature film role.[53]

Filming began in September 1915 and was completed late the following month. Basing his script on the original play, Ted Wharton made a few changes, transforming Jack into a collegiate football hero, whose play on the field (filmed during an actual game at Cornell) wins him much renown and helps him secure a position at the local paper, thanks in part to his well-connected college chum Foxey. But unlike the play's Jack, who undertakes the lottery scheme as a way of redeeming his own bad debts, the film's Jack unselfishly wants to support his mother, whose investments have failed and who has accepted piecework at home to pay for his education. Perhaps the most interesting change, though, was the creation of the character of Maggie Murphy, the cook at the Peyton home, who purchases multiple tickets in the hopes of winning the lottery. Her loss—and eventual reclamation—of the winning ticket provides much of the plot action and the comedy in the picture. Ultimately, the ponderous Maggie decides to reject Jack, take half the money, and marry her boyfriend, the diminutive butler, instead. What makes Maggie even more comic, of course, is the fact that "she" was played by a young Oliver Hardy in drag.

The acting in the film was credible, and the relationships among the characters convincing, especially the friendship between Jack and his good friend Foxey and the affection between Jack and his elderly mother, on whose behalf he undertakes his scheme. That loving mother-son relationship stands in sharp contrast to the strained relationship between Foxey and his self-absorbed, fad-obsessed mother, whom the kindly Mrs. Wright helps to mend her ways and to reconcile with her son. Some of the strongest and most amusing scenes, however, were those that featured Lizzie (played by superb comedienne Carolyn Lee), a relative of the Peytons who, as a title card indicates, serves as Mrs. Peyton's "goat." The rail-thin and spinsterish Lizzie virtually steals the film with her antics, from her hilarious slips off Mrs. Peyton's weight-reducing machine to her schoolgirl-swooning at the sight of Jack, whom she contrives to claim in the lottery with a ticket not rightly hers. Shot largely at the new Wharton Studio in Renwick Park, *The Lottery Man* (which is extant) included many scenes at familiar local landmarks such as Cornell University's new Schoellkopf football field, the Ithaca Town Hall, and the office building of the *Ithaca Journal*, the paper that had given the Whartons so much positive publicity over the years. Reportedly, after the conclusion of the lottery scene in the film, an actual lottery was held with "real money" prizes (five, ten, and fifteen dollars), which cast member Lieutenant Theodore Tweston awarded to three lucky women.[54]

Crucial to the production was a climactic scene in which a large mob of women clamors to learn which of them has won the lottery. Through the *Ithaca Journal*, the Whartons issued a call for 250 extras who might be willing to appear.[55] Apparently, many heeded that call: "men, women, children, and dogs galore."[56] Film historian Aaron Pichel writes that, according to one Cornell alumnus, "Trains of open trolley cars left State and Tioga [downtown] every five minutes, loaded down with Ithaca girls." By early afternoon, nearly one hundred volunteers had registered at the Renwick Park studio, "young, medium-aged, old, one even on crutches," leaving Ted to observe wryly that "It certainly pays to advertise."[57]

But even that was not a large enough crowd to satisfy Ted, who proceeded to draft male extras, whom he "transformed by grease paint, eyebrow pencils, wigs and skirts into dashing brunettes, appealing blondes and other types of feminine beauty." Apparently no one was exempt: fifteen supers from the Wharton Company were added to the crowd.[58] Even actor and director Harry Mainhall was pressed into service as "a lovely blonde," although he destroyed the illusion by chain-smoking cigarettes.[59] In the end, though, the attention that the Whartons put into the details of the production paid off. "The direction and photography are well worthy of consideration," *Billboard* observed. "It is a clean comedy that is sure to be a winner."[60] Consequently, the trade journal ads promised, exhibitors who booked the film would not have to "take a chance," because it "was a capital prize for every box office."

The success of the Whartons' first feature films, following on the heels of their phenomenally popular and influential serials *The Exploits of Elaine* and *The New Adventures of J. Rufus Wallingford*, added to their renown and confirmed their ability to work innovatively in both dramatic and comic modes. And their ongoing association with William Randolph Hearst, which boded well for further collaborations on new serials and on feature films, created much excitement at the studio and in the town of Ithaca, which—thanks to their pioneering productions—was defying the odds and gaining a reputation as a center for filmmaking.

CHAPTER 9

Unraveling *Myra*'s Mysteries

Things were certainly looking good for the Whartons. In early February 1916, the *Ithaca Journal* announced that a "big deal" was imminent: an expanded collaboration with publishing magnate and producer William Randolph Hearst that the brothers anticipated would bring them numerous opportunities, paramount among them the prospect of "a huge new studio to be called 'Hearst-Wharton.'" After conferring for weeks with the Whartons, Hearst reportedly was ready to move forward on a proposal for a $1,000,000 company and a "great plant" to be built in Ithaca.[1]

Owner of a large interest in Hearst-Selig and Pathé, Hearst had already contracted the previous year with the Whartons for several popular serial films, including the thirty-six-episode *The Exploits of Elaine* and the *Wallingford* comedy, which were distributed through the Pathé Exchange. Anxious to build on his success, Hearst decided to expand his International Film Service (IFS), which he described as "the first producing and distributing organization to give the exhibitor the consideration and service that he justly deserves," by applying the power of the press directly to motion pictures.[2] Originally established in 1915 as an early film studio to capitalize on Hearst's newspaper comic strip properties, IFS quickly branched out into "live-action fiction film production," an expansion that meant all future films the Whartons produced in collaboration with Hearst would be marketed and distributed to the Pathé exchanges through Hearst's company.[3]

The Whartons, too, had ambitious plans for new productions. Although they apparently abandoned some of the shorter pictures that they had been considering, early in the new year they began preparations for *The Mysteries of Myra*.[4] That serial centered on "the occult forces of Good and Evil, show[ing] the puzzling phenomena of premonitions—prophetic dreams— and play[ing] upon the visions and communications with the spiritual world." Based on the efforts of modern science and technology to penetrate "the mysteries of our future life," it contained "an intensive love story, full of heart-throbbing interest, hatred, pathos, and intrigue, and touching the heart-strings of your every emotion."[5]

Pioneering in both subject and execution, *The Mysteries of Myra* aimed to avoid the hackneyed melodramatic lines of many early serials by offering instead what one contemporary reviewer called "a wonderful new theme that compels attention because of the puzzling thoughts regarding mental telepathy and spirits presented in a manner which follows authenticated scientific discoveries."[6] In other words, the serial purported to demonstrate the way that science had become powerful enough to "prove" the existence of the unscientific.[7] Leo himself attested that while "the average layman, and even the most rabid movie fan, does not seem to realize that every episode of the *Myra* series is authentic, . . . we have the word of dozens of good men and true" that they have witnessed astral projections and other similar events, precisely as the picture depicted.[8] And he may have had the word of a woman as well: his sister Genie Buck, reputed by locals to be an avid spiritualist.

Making *Myra*

The scenario for the serial was written by Charles W. Goddard, a veteran of serial pictures who had scripted *The Perils of Pauline* and whose association with the Whartons dated back to their first *Elaine* serial production in 1914. On the *Myra* scripts, Goddard collaborated closely with Hereward Carrington (1880–1958), who supplied most of the occult story lines. A well-known British-born American investigator of psychic phenomena, Carrington was the author of more than a hundred books and pamphlets on subjects ranging from parapsychology, spiritualism, and psychic phenomena to stage magic, alternative medicine, and fasting. His career, *Moving Picture World* observed, was almost as interesting as an episode from his own dramatic creation.[9]

As an amateur conjuror himself, Carrington—author of an astrology column in the Hearst newspapers[10]—was critical of certain paranormal phenomena. In his books, he exposed fraudulent mediums who used such tricks as table knockings, trumpet mediumship, spirit materializations, and sealed-letter readings. At the same time, consistent with his fervent belief that some mediumship was genuine, he supported "true" practitioners of the art. Through his passion for the subject, he became acquainted with prominent occultists in the field of astral projection and compiled a personal library that comprised more than four thousand volumes of psychic lore—or, as he called them, "spook books."[11] Yet, while Carrington was widely known, his reputation within the psychic community was uneven. Some lauded his research, while others felt that he allowed his personal relationships with his subjects to cloud his investigative judgment. Still others alleged that ultimately he was as much of a hoaxer as the mediums whom he exposed.

What is certain, though, is that Carrington introduced many of his unorthodox ideas into the Whartons' serial *The Mysteries of Myra*. Some of those ideas derived from his association with noted occultist, ceremonial magician, and novelist Aleister Crowley (1875–1947), who at one point visited the Wharton set during the filming, likely at Carrington's invitation.[12] The serial's Black Order was clearly modeled on the "Golden Dawn,"[13] of which Crowley was a member. That order—the "Hermetic Order of the Golden Dawn," in full—was devoted to the study and practice of metaphysics, paranormal activity, and the occult. Founded in Great Britain, it gained popularity in the late nineteenth and early twentieth centuries. The "magical" organization had both a hierarchy and a set of elaborate initiation rituals; its members—who included Sir Arthur Conan Doyle, Bram Stoker, and William Butler Yeats—passed through three distinct orders, which taught mystical skills such as astrology, divination, occult tarot, geomancy, scrying (foretelling, usually with a crystal ball), alchemy, astral travel, and, at the highest level, spiritual communication. Eventually, the organization founded "temples" in London and other cities, including Edinburgh and Paris. As internal disputes developed, however, the order began to splinter.

One such dispute involved Crowley, who was initially refused initiation into the "Adeptus Minor" (second order) grade by London officials who objected to his libertine lifestyle and constant feuding with other members. A few years later, he founded his own occult order based on the magico-religious doctrine "Thelema," which held that "Do what thou wilt shall be the whole of the Law." Central to the rituals of that order, conceived as a successor to the Golden Dawn, was the practice of "Magick" (as Crowley called it), which allowed individuals to communicate with others on a higher plane and which employed "Lesser and Higher Rituals of the Pentagram" and the ubiquitous NOX / "Night of Pan" "thumbs-up" sign that occurs so frequently in *Myra*. Sexuality, too, was part of the magical practices, as was Satanic imagery, which, Crowley believed, restored paganism to a purer form. His Thelema movement continued to spread even after his death, and it took root in the popular culture.[14] As late as the 1960s and 1970s he was hailed as an influence by the counterculture, including musicians such as the Rolling Stones, Led Zeppelin, and the Beatles, whose *Sgt. Pepper's Lonely Hearts Club Band* album cover featured his image.[15]

Both Crowley's influence and Carrington's enormous fascination with spiritualism were evident throughout *The Mysteries of Myra*, which drew directly on their ideas and practices. According to film historian Ed Hulse, the serial was originally titled *The Mysteries of Mona* and centered on Mona Mason, a nineteen-year-old with a "sensitive nature and latent psychic ability" that makes her susceptible to the predations of the members of the devil-worshipping Black Lodge, who wish to destroy her. The Lodge's Grand Master has already caused the demise of her two older sisters, and he intends to bring about Mona's death as well, knowing that if she dies before she reaches her twentieth birthday, her late father John Mason's fortune will revert to the Black Order that he leads. Scientist and psychic researcher Dr. Payson Alden, Mona's champion, devotes himself to protecting her from the ongoing interference of Arthur Bayliel, who pretends to be her friend but is secretly a member of the Lodge.

For reasons that are not known, in the final version, scenario writer Goddard changed the names of Mona Mason to Myra Maynard and Arthur Bayliel to Arthur Varney. He also lowered Myra's age from nineteen to seventeen, and the ages at which her sisters committed suicide from twenty to eighteen.[16] But the gist of the original story remained the same.

Chosen to play the lead was actress Jean Sothern, a former child star in vaudeville who had appeared in numerous pictures for Fox, IMP, and other studios. According to *Motography*, Sothern had been personally selected for the part by Goddard and Carrington, who believed that she possessed extraordinary mental powers and was "capable of performing the emotions of one subject to the compelling influences of a superior will" while maintaining "grace, poise and a personality which will actually reach out from the screen, [and] take possession of people." As if to prove correct the suspicions of her special powers, Sothern reportedly had an unusual experience: during one of the hypnotizing-wheel scenes, she actually became hypnotized. (Later, a woman in the audience was supposedly hypnotized, too.)[17]

Leo, though, had a somewhat different recollection of Sothern's casting. In an article titled "Where Only Youth and Beauty Can Triumph," he wrote: "I recognized the combined qualities of beauty and brains when I first met her. Miss Sothern had a friend who knew someone who had acted in one of my productions, and came one day to the studio to see us put on a scene. She watched the acting fascinated, and as she was going away began spontaneously imitating the leading woman. It was marvelous." Realizing she was a rare find, Leo immediately engaged her. He also noted that, after being in the picture business for fifteen years and seeing thousands of actresses, he had developed a knack for spotting talent, and "Miss Sothern more than fulfilled my expectations."[18]

Playing opposite Sothern as psychic investigator Payson Alden was Detroit-born Howard Estabrook, who began his career as a stage actor in New York before making his film debut in 1914. Although he left film acting soon after his role in *Myra*, he returned to the industry a few years later, first as a producer and then as a screenwriter for some of the most successful films of the 1930s. As Dr. Alden, he not only served as Myra's admirer and protector (making his character "human to the extreme and polished in mannerisms");[19] he also introduced into the story a variety of fantastic investigative devices like the hypnotizing wheel, the mystic mirrors, and the thought camera, all of which were reminiscent of Dr. Craig Kennedy's inventions in the *Elaine* serial.

FIGURE 9.1   Leo Wharton directs Jean Sothern in the opening episode of the supernatural thriller *The Mysteries of Myra*.

Cast as Myra's antagonists were several Wharton regulars. M. W. "Mike" Rale, who had appeared in *The Exploits* (and who would appear again in *Beatrice Fairfax* and *Patria*), played the sinister Grand Master of the Black Lodge, who is determined to destroy Myra and claim her fortune. Allan Murnane, a veteran of the Wharton films *The Lottery Man* and *The City*, was cast as Arthur Varney, a follower of the Master who is torn between his devotion to the Black Order and his affection for Myra.[20] And performing in small roles were a number of locals, whose participation helped ensure that the production was greeted with special enthusiasm in Ithaca, where most of the episodes were filmed.

The character of Mrs. Maynard (played by Leo's wife, Bessie Wharton) was an anomaly of sorts, since mother figures in early serials were rare. As Ben Singer explained, unlike the ubiquitous benevolent father or father figure, who is usually killed off in order to set up the central narrative conflict, the mother—"the very emblem of the [later] Hollywood woman's film"—is almost entirely banished, in large part because "the serial-queen melodrama sought to represent an antitraditional conception of womanhood, one appealing to a generation of young women eager to differentiate their worldview from that of their mothers."[21] The maternal absence thus allowed the heroine to make her own choices, free of maternal influence. Even in *Myra*, Mrs. Maynard— while present for some of the action—plays only a minor role, serving mostly as a foil to her more independent daughter.

The Mysteries Unfold

The opening chapter ("The Dagger of Dreams," released April 24, 1916, which is not extant but whose script is reprinted in full in appendix 1) established the serial's unorthodox premise and introduced the main characters: the late John Maynard, member of a mysterious organization that possesses occult powers; his daughter Myra, now approaching the age of her elder sisters' suicides; her concerned mother Mrs. Maynard; Arthur Varney, a frequent guest at the Maynard home and member of the Order that wants Myra dead; and Payson Alden, the young doctor who has given up the practice of medicine in order to pursue investigation of spirit phenomena.

Things admittedly look bleak for Myra. It appears that she is under some occult influence, a fact that is confirmed one morning at breakfast, when she unconsciously makes the Order's "thumbs-up" sign, and again on the night before her birthday, when she sleepwalks into her late father's secret crypt and nearly stabs herself with a dagger. Alden intervenes and takes her upstairs, where she starts to write a message from the other world; but she awakens before she finishes.[22]

The next day, both Alden and Varney call at the Maynard house—Alden, to tell Myra what happened; Varney, to find out what failed. As Varney eavesdrops, Alden hypnotizes Myra, who begins writing: "Your father wishes to warn you against the Black—" But Varney's mind control triumphs over Alden's, and she is unable to complete the message. Meanwhile, the malevolent Grand Master poisons a plant, which two flower sellers bring to Myra's home ("The Poisoned Flower"); but Alden intercepts it, saving Myra from another disaster.[23]

Later, when Alden explains how science has proved the existence of spirits, Myra begs him to try one of his experiments on her ("The Mystic Mirrors"). The experiment releases her astral body, which appears at the Lodge where the members are in session. Sensing opportunity, the Master instructs Varney to cut the astral thread so Myra will not awaken. At that same moment, Alden, unable to bring the unconscious girl back, drops to his knees and offers a prayer, which succeeds where his science had failed. Afterward, apart from the curious "thumbs-up" sign, Myra recalls little about her experience.[24]

When Alden and his Hindu colleague Professor Haji plot to infiltrate the Lodge ("The Wheel of Spirit"), the Master retaliates with his own scheme: he poisons balloons to be delivered to Myra, casts an "electric" spell that paralyzes Alden, and buries him alive in a coffin. After Haji digs him out, Alden hurries to the Maynard home and discovers the balloons, their gases now dissipated. But in Myra's room, they find confirmation of Alden's fears: her canary lying lifeless in its cage.[25]

Over the next few episodes, the Master continues to subvert Alden's plans, first by causing the Lodge to burst into flames and preventing the police from investigating ("The Fumes of Fear"), and then by allowing himself to be hypnotized so that he can "absorb" Myra's astral body into his own. When Alden tries to reverse the hypnosis, the two astral forms get confused and go back into the wrong natural bodies ("The Hypnotic Clue"). Eventually, Myra resumes her proper state but almost immediately faces new danger, from floodwaters that have been unleashed and that almost sweep her and Alden away.[26]

After proposing a truce that the Master rejects, Alden realizes that their fight will be to the finish ("The Mystery Mind"). So when the Master sends Varney's spirit—and then his own—to kill Myra as she sleeps, Alden is ready with a mercury vapor lamp that makes the Master's astral body dematerialize in agony.[27] And with a decoy mirror that he sets up in her bedroom, Alden frustrates another attempt on her life ("The Nether World").[28]

Myra, though, is not safe for long, especially after the members of the Lodge begin a chant that causes her heart to fail. To counter their hypnotic suggestion, Alden creates an "electroscope" to condense thought waves and collect them in a jar; then he instructs Myra to gaze into a crystal ball and call up the person who is hurting her. As she catches a glimpse of the Master in the orb, Alden touches the electroscope, which starts to spark. In that same instant, the Master recoils and falls to the floor of his chamber with a pain in his heart ("The Invisible Destroyer"). "Again, it seems, Alden's science has outwitted the Black Arts."[29] Another of Alden's inventions, an astral alarm, detects several astral intruders. So when Varney extracts the astral bodies of two of his companions and orders them to levitate Myra out of her bedroom window, Alden is there to catch her and to carry her inside to waken in safety ("Levitation").[30]

The Master responds with new measures of his own. From the dead, he summons a "Fire-Elemental" to set ablaze the barge where Myra is hiding and burn her alive; but Alden, working from his lab, manages to trap the creature, who later returns to confront the Master and demand the blood sacrifice he is due ("The Fire-Elemental").[31] The Master then promises an elixir of youth to an ugly, elderly couple possessed by demon spirits if they agree to destroy Myra ("The Elixir of Youth"), but that effort fails as well.[32] So does another attempt by the Black Order to trap and incinerate her in a small cabin belonging to a witch.[33]

Still more dangers follow, as Myra is kidnapped, almost poisoned, and then placed in a state of suspended animation (in "Suspended Animation," an episode reminiscent of episodes in *The Exploits of Elaine* when Long Sin places Bennett in suspended animation, and later when Elaine "dies" and is resuscitated by Kennedy).[34] Frustrated by his repeated failures to kill her, the Master creates a more reliable accomplice—a "Thought Monster," a frightening black-eyed, buck-toothed, otherworldly creature whom he sends to Alden's lab. There, a séance is being conducted that materializes Myra's father and exposes Varney. When the Monster, a kind of "Psychic Frankenstein," gets distracted by the hypnotizing wheel, Alden is able to take control and turn it against the Master ("The Thought Monster").

Back at the Black Order's Lodge, the Master and Varney prepare to destroy the Thought Monster once its work is done. The Monster, though, overhears its death sentence and pounces on Varney, stripping him of his weapon. Then, wearing Varney's protective clothing, it engages the Master in a bitter duel but momentarily gets careless, just long enough to be struck in the face by a deadly ray. Nonetheless, before it dies, the Monster deals a final and fatal blow to the Master, ensuring that Myra and Alden are at last free of the villain—and, presumably, free to live happily ever afterward.

While the finished serial comprised fifteen episodes, it appears that an additional two episodes were planned but never theatrically released. As film historian and preservationist Eric Stedman writes, one of those episodes, "Voodoo," featured Haitian priests who visit the Master and booby-trap Myra's house with cursed fetish objects; in the second, "Asylum," Myra is kidnapped and held captive in an asylum for the insane. Both were scrapped at some point between the scripting and the release stages. The most likely explanation, Stedman suggests, "is that executive producer W. R. Hearst, apparently near the end of March, 1916, visited Ithaca during shooting, sat down and viewed what had been completed up to that point of *The Mysteries of Myra* and rejected the content of both episodes, registering his complaints directly with scriptwriter Charles Goddard."[35] To the Whartons' dismay, such intrusions would become more frequent over the next few months, especially as Hearst expanded his "picture organization," the International Film Service, which began operating its own exchanges in all of the large cities in the United States.[36]

Already "in the can at the time of Hearst's creative assault, [Voodoo] likely never saw the light of day because the sight of blacks with magic powers sneaking into private parlors in the dark and placing fetishes capable of mind-controlling unwary subjects under couch cushions was just too shocking for [Hearst's] sensibilities." Similarly, the second missing episode, in which Myra escapes the asylum by way of an abandoned mine shaft, was at least partially filmed before being dropped. The deletion, according to Stedman, "was not necessarily a bad thing, in that the story includes descriptions of inmates engaging in preposterous, silly activities such as crawling under a bed and pretending to work on it as one would an automobile." But a portion of the episode was repurposed, if somewhat hastily, as the opening of the fourteenth episode, which became "simply standard cliff-hanger serial damsel-in-distress fare whipped up to fill in the blank space left by Hearst's episode-deletion."[37] Notes preserved in Goddard's original shooting script show that Hearst had other objections as well: to Mike Rale's acting as the Grand Master; to Rale's costume, especially his Chinese-style hat; and to the lack of "richness" in the Black Order's sanctum, which was subsequently redecorated with velvet curtains and wall coverings.[38]

Interestingly, the last episode of the finished serial may not have been intended to be final at all; in fact, it left open the possibility of additional chapters, perhaps even an entire sequel, that would continue Myra and

FIGURE 9.2   At the Black Order's Lodge, the Master (M. W. Rale) plots Myra's downfall in the hope of acquiring her father's fortune.

Alden's adventures. In that episode, before he dies, the Master pulls a switch and summons his followers. They carry him to a chamber adjacent to the ornately decorated cell of a veiled mystery woman, whom he has held prisoner because she would not yield to his love (and who, to this point, has not played a role in the story). Although her first impulse is to attack him, he begs for her forgiveness before he goes to his "punishment" and instructs his followers to pledge their loyalty to her: "I make this woman the heir to all my power. To hear her is to obey!" His dying words are an exhortation: "Now each one of you in turn shall avenge my death or die in the attempt." Both the introduction of the veiled woman and the call for revenge suggest that the Whartons were laying the basis for a sequel and that they entertained the prospect of further episodes and forays for Myra into the otherworld.[39] But, whatever the reason, they never returned to her story.

Structurally, *The Mysteries of Myra* (which survives only in a few random reels and fragments) employed a familiar serial framework: a young, attractive heroine, supported by a devoted admirer with considerable sleuthing skills, who protects her from a powerful antagonist who wants to do her harm and steal her money. In the wake of the passing of her beloved father, she must resolve the mystery of his death—and the early deaths of her two sisters—in order to ensure that she does not meet the same fate. To claim and to maintain the Maynard fortune (which, curiously, passes to Myra's siblings, then to Myra herself, but not to her mother), she must fight off the predations of the Master of the Black Lodge, who serves the function of the evil guardian figure and who stands to inherit the fortune should Myra die before reaching her age of majority. Only by uncovering and confronting the secrets of her father's occultism and involvement with the Order can Myra complete the transition from adolescent dependence to womanly independence and free herself of the Master's menacing presence.

Complicating that transition is her relationship with trusted family friend Arthur Varney. Although he is in love with Myra and wants to marry her, at the same time, as a member of the Order, Varney is pledged to bringing about her destruction—a situation reminiscent of that of Perry Bennett (a.k.a. "the Clutching Hand" in *The Exploits of Elaine*), who loves Elaine but is ready to kill her, if necessary, to achieve his evil ends. Varney's ambivalent emotions and divided loyalties place Myra in extreme jeopardy. For example, he accommodates her request to be hypnotized with the hypnotizing wheel so that her astral body can be released to go to the aid of Alden, whom she believes to be in great danger; but once she resumes her true form, Varney follows the Master's instruction and tries to precipitate her death and Alden's by unleashing floodwaters that will sweep both of them away.[40] Later, when the Master sends Varney's spirit to the Maynard home to asphyxiate Myra as she sleeps, he hesitates, unable to fulfill the instruction, forcing the Master to return the next night to try to finish Myra off himself. And when Alden shows Varney the powerful "electroscope" that he has invented to collect the malevolent thought waves that are causing Myra's illness, Varney recognizes that the device could save Myra's life; nonetheless, he informs the Master that Alden is planning to defeat him by hurling his own thoughts back at him, thus endangering Myra even further by his disclosure.

Yet, at other times, Varney comes to Myra's defense and saves her from harm. For example, when she is set upon by the Black Order on the way to the witch's house, he helps her make it inside, where, despite the fire that her pursuers start, she is able to save herself by telepathically sending a message to Alden for help. And when Myra is kidnapped, he refuses to enact the Master's murderous plan and substitutes another body for hers.

Varney's ambivalence is mirrored by Myra's own. She accepts his proposal of marriage (although, notably, after she has exchanged astral bodies with the Master and is not speaking in her true voice). Afterward, she bristles at the prospect of a romantic attachment and returns his ring. Only after he pleads for her to save him, claiming that without marriage to a woman like her he will turn into a soulless "elemental," does she reluctantly reconsider the engagement. But it is obvious that her true affection is already for Alden. And ultimately, like her "serial sisters" who initially reject convention in favor of independence, Myra finds happiness with the man who has been at her side, supporting and protecting her throughout her various ordeals.

Yet, while its basic story line was consistent with the pattern of *The Exploits of Elaine* and other early serials, *The Mysteries of Myra* departed radically from its predecessors in other ways. Nowhere was that departure more evident than in the use of occult elements, evoked by a series of special effects that the Whartons, working in concert with skilled set designer Arch Chadwick and electrician Leroy Baker, created through unusual angles, lighting, and superior technical work. "Dissolves, double exposures, and fades were abundant," Kalton C. Lahue observed, "as was a two-color treatment in many scenes, which served to intensify the mood of mysticism."[41]

Especially well executed were the supernatural effects, among them the apparition of Mr. Maynard that Alden meets in the secret chamber of Myra's home, the ghost of Haji and the other spirits who are resurrected during the séances, and the various mystical materializations of the Master (in the crystal ball that Alden gives Myra, in which the Master's face regularly appears; on the stone balustrade at the Maynard home, where Myra glimpses the Master's image in a "thumbs-up" attitude; and again, in the "thought photo" that Alden takes of the sleeping gardener who is acting as the Master's accomplice, which produces a negative with a blurred image of the Master in his usual provocative posture). A similarly sensational effect, a combination of time lapse, double exposure, and other trick photography, occurs in "The Elixir of Youth" episode (a fragment of which is extant), in which the Master transforms an aged couple into a beautiful woman and a handsome young man; later, when the potion's effect is reversed, they are transformed again and returned to their original unfortunate selves. And the dancing fairies Myra encounters near the witch's cabin, who are more charming than menacing, hark back to the trick films and *féeries* of film pioneer Georges Méliès.[42]

Most memorable of all, though, were the scenes of the astral bodies leaping or flying out of their natural bodies, merging with other astral bodies, and dissolving again, as in "The Mystic Mirrors" episode, when the Master, unable to cut the astral thread to prevent Myra from reawakening, leaves her astral body swaying in the vapor until Alden brings her back through his prayers. Usually brightly lit and tinted in reddish tones to make them seem otherworldly, sometimes deliberately overexposed to evoke a sense of their ethereality, the spirit manifestations assume a truly spectral quality.

To be sure, such unusual effects were advanced for the time and quite complicated to film. Once the cameramen had the first scenarios in hand, they spent two solid weeks experimenting with lighting and double exposures prior to the commencement of principal photography. That meant relying heavily on photographic trickery to convince viewers that they were witnessing actual supernatural phenomena. Ed Hulse writes that the "eerie atmospheres were further enhanced by extensive tinting," as in the scene where the Master turns on the gas in Myra's room to asphyxiate her but instead is dematerialized by the violet light that Alden installed to thwart him. That violet light was produced by strategically placed Cooper-Hewitt lights, which created a brightly exposed image tinted in lavender on release prints.[43]

Leo Wharton acknowledged that creating the double exposures by running the film through the camera twice was a real challenge. "It's almost like producing two pictures at once, only it's a lot more trouble."[44] There

FIGURE 9.3 Among the most memorable special effects in *The Mysteries of Myra* was the disintegration of the Master's astral body, which was achieved by the use of special lighting.

were other technical challenges as well, such as maneuvering the ropes and the derrick that were required to lift Myra out of her bed and through the window in the levitation scene. According to Hulse, positioning the derrick, blocking the scene to conceal its presence, lighting the set, rehearsing the actors, and getting a usable take consumed an entire day and taxed the patience of both cast and crew.[45]

Reviewers were nearly unanimous in their praise of these and other appeals to a fear of the supernatural, which established a convincing atmosphere of impending tragedy. *Moving Picture World*, for example, commented on the originality of the conception and treatment of the "wonderfully produced" picture and observed that, just "as an expert fiction writer uses colorful words to create a setting for his characters, so the Whartons have used weird and strange effects in lighting and staging," along with "every [other] process known to modern photography . . . to make the audience feel the unspeakable horror of the Black Order."[46] *Motography* concurred that the effects were outstanding, adding that the wealth of material presented by the unusual story was splendidly utilized,[47] while *Motion Picture News* observed that the technical achievement was of the highest order, with the Wharton brothers supplying "some of the most novel camera work so far seen on the screen."[48] *Variety*, too, praised the Whartons' ingenuity in their use of double exposure and other trick photography and suggested that *The Mysteries of Myra* would prove to be "THE serial of the year."[49]

Promoting *Myra*

Such a nontraditional production demanded a vigorous and nontraditional promotion, and that is precisely what Hearst's publicity machine provided with its "million dollar campaign." In advance of the serial's release, Hearst placed full-page advertisements in the trade journals promising exhibitors that "Twenty Million People Daily Will Read About *The Mysteries of Myra*" in some of the biggest publications of the world, including the *New York American*, the *Chicago Examiner*, the *Boston American*, the *San Francisco Examiner*, the *Los Angeles Examiner*, the *Philadelphia North American*, the *Washington Times*, and the *St. Louis Globe Democrat*. Several of those ads reprinted endorsements from prominent theater owners such as Marcus Loew, who wrote that the serial was the "first real departure from the stereotype" that he had ever witnessed and who also praised International Film Service for having "the greatest publicity in the world."[50] To whet interest even further in the "spirit drama," Hearst peppered the journals with one- and two-page teaser ads that were striking in their graphics and exceedingly bold in their color. The promotion apparently worked: as *Motography* reported, "on release day it was stated to be thirty thousand dollars ahead of any previous photoplay series."[51]

Not only could people read about the serial; in Hearst's publications, they could read a novelization of it written by author and director Eustace Hale Ball. They could also enjoy various promotional novelty items, such as the small metal advertising buttons and the cardboard masks (now highly collectible) that featured the Master's distinctive "thumbs-up" sign. But the most interesting of the giveaways was the "Crolette," a cardboard planchette used for automatic writing that purportedly could be manipulated in order to contact the spirit world, much like a mini–Ouija board. Users were urged to ask questions, though not "of a frivolous nature," which would be answered, usually with a YES or NO response. According to the instructions, the best results were obtained by two persons, preferably of opposite sex, sitting by themselves in a dimly lit room. Moreover, "under the influence of certain people of particularly nervous temperament, the Crolette will be found to work to greater advantage."[52] The Crolette had another even more significant purpose: by explicitly encouraging such interactivity, it blurred the lines of identification between the movie audience and the serial's stars.[53]

Hearst's robust promotion of *The Mysteries of Myra* paid off. The *Ithaca Journal* reported that a showing of several of the serial's early episodes elicited a highly favorable reaction from exhibitors and journalists, with some newspapers proclaiming it among the best serials ever produced. After another such early showing, *Moving Picture World* reviewer Lynde Denig wrote that the Wharton brothers "scored so obviously, so decisively that to speak of their success is not expressing an opinion, but reporting a fact."[54] That impression seemed to be confirmed by the 703 bookings that Hearst's International Film Service secured after an advance showing in the greater New York territory.[55] A subsequent showing in Chicago evoked a similarly positive response.[56] And the *Atlanta Constitution* commented on the "unstinted praise without limitation" that had been heaped on *Myra* and noted that the Whartons, not content to rest on the laurels they had won "in their many years of catering to an exacting amusement public," will be "crowned" again by their latest brilliant achievement.[57]

The acclaim, however, was not universal. Future screenwriter Alfred A. Cohn, in an article for the February 1917 issue of fan magazine *Photoplay*, insisted that although *Myra* had plenty of thrills, it was "too much impregnated with mysticism to win great popularity."[58] The otherworldly monsters indeed proved disagreeable, even offensive, to some viewers, while the occult practices the picture highlighted were offputting to those who disdained the spiritualist movement that had taken such a firm hold throughout much of the country. Additionally, there were reports that *Myra*'s explicit devil-worshipping theme "alienated small-town exhibitors in culturally conservative areas, where local religious institutions wielded more influence than big-city journalists."[59]

Naturally, the serial generated much excitement in Ithaca, which enthusiastically embraced the actors and welcomed them into the community; and the actors returned the kindness. Howard Estabrook, for instance, became a real hero with the college men at Cornell University, especially after he helped them organize a benefit entertainment for the athletic fund and sponsored a big prize contest for an amateur one-act play.[60] On another occasion, pretending to use the "mental telepathy and scientific work" he had acquired while making *Myra*, Estabrook picked Cornell to win the spring regatta, a prediction that further endeared him to the locals.[61]

As the first serial to incorporate actual occult elements and practices, *The Mysteries of Myra* had a significant impact on the films that followed. According to Eric Stedman, some of its images and scenes, from "black-hooded cult members to hypnotist heroes, were habitually copied wholesale for use in subsequent serial productions," including *The Mystery of 13* (1919), Ben Wilson's *The Trail of the Octopus* (also from 1919), and *The Mystery Mind* (1920). That legacy continued in serials, features, and television programs, from 1934's *The Return of Chandu* to *The X-Files*,[62] and in blockbuster horror films such as *Rosemary's Baby* (1968).

Awakening Sexuality

Myra had other cultural reverberations as well. In addition to reflecting the unconventional "New Woman" type that had come into vogue in the 1910s, Myra Maynard was also emblematic of another early twentieth-century type in America popular culture: the adolescent girl as a liminal figure who, as she comes of age, uncannily mediates between the living and the dead. According to Diana Anselmo-Sequeira, characters such as Myra were part of a deep-seated cultural tradition that equated young femininity with mysticism. "A symbol of ephemerality, the growing girl was defined by her mysterious shape-shifting transformation from young child into young woman."[63] In the Whartons' "spiritual drama," the eponymous protagonist moves from an unaware, innocent girl to a more mature adult heiress via her "mediumnic awakening," a transformation that takes place on her eighteenth birthday and coincides with two other awakenings: her falling under the influence of the Black Order and her falling in love with the paranormal researcher Dr. Payson Alden.

By depending so completely on the adolescent Myra's psychic vulnerability to the supernatural, the serial, according to Anselmo-Sequeira, visualized a vital link between girlhood and mystic spirituality, a link that had been culturally forged in the mid-to-late 1800s with such adolescent medium-figures as Kate and Margaret Fox, who fascinated other early filmmakers. D. W. Griffith, in *What the Daisy Said* (1910), for example, directly explored the association of girlhood with the occult. In that film, adolescent sisters (played by Mary Pickford and Gertrude Robinson) compete for the attentions of a crooked fortune teller but ultimately abandon charlatanic spirituality and fanciful magical thinking for a sense of mature responsibility that includes marriage to honest farmhands.[64] Thanhouser's *The Portrait of Lady Anne* (1912) depicted an awakening similar to Myra's as Anne, an eighteenth-century beauty (played by Florence La Badie), time-travels to 1912 to warn her descendant, also named Anne, not to repeat her mistakes and thus enables the modern Anne's proper entrance into womanhood.[65] And in the megahit supernatural thriller *The Exorcist* (1973), Regan, a girl on the cusp of adolescence, occupies a powerful and frightening liminal position between childhood and adult sexuality that threatens everyone around her and must therefore be controlled.

Not surprisingly, Myra's liminality had sexual implications as well. The hypnotic trances that render her both vulnerable and suggestible correlate directly to the transitional but precarious position that she occupies, on the cusp between virginal adolescence and womanly maturity. Bereft of the usual paternal protection, more acted upon than acting, Myra seems largely powerless at first to fend off the advances and predations of the Master and Varney. The assaults on her begin at the Maynard home, whose confined spaces reinforce the sense of her entrapment and stress her lack of control over visual and narrative space.[66] It is these tight, typically dark interior spaces that the Master invades as he attempts to weaken her body and control her mind.

The assaults soon escalate to actual victimization of her body, which routinely gets moved, lifted, lowered, or otherwise manipulated, usually when Myra is unconscious or otherwise unable to respond or object. In her father's secret basement chamber, she is bewitched into picking up his dagger in order to inflict injury upon herself—the first of many occult and blood rituals to which she is subjected, all of which are orchestrated by the exclusively male members of the Black Order. Her heart is slowed in order to lessen her resistance; her astral body is forced to collide and merge with the Master's; her image in the decoy mirror in her bedroom is literally shattered by a bullet fired by the Master's accomplice; and her pneumogastric nerve is "clamped," putting her into a state of suspended animation. She is placed at the mercy of a demon lover, who has been rejuvenated by the Master's elixir; "beglamoured" and transformed into an insentient birch log; and nearly poisoned and drowned as the Master alternates between trying to possess her and plotting to kill her.

Myra's bedroom, in particular, becomes the site of numerous unwelcome and ongoing intrusions and assaults, not least of which is the attempt to levitate her body through the open window and into the waiting hands of the Black Order members below. That attempt, however, is frustrated by the appearance of Alden, who intervenes, catches her, and carries her to safety. Alden's ministrations, especially his efforts to remove her from the confines of her home and into the out-of-doors (where existing fragmentary footage shows them playing a lively game of tennis, running playfully through a field of lilacs, and enjoying a horseback ride), are instrumental in countering the Order's dark magic and in breaking Myra out of the trances by which the Master controls her.

Myra's awakening sexuality is clearly allied to her experience of the occult. Nowhere is this connection made clearer than in "The Poisoned Flower" episode, in which a magical flower created by the Master is delivered to her home by two flower sellers. Assuming that Myra will bring the flower into her bedroom, the Master ensures that it will unfold its deadly blossom and release its toxic white powder at the midnight hour, when she is asleep. Varney, too, is complicit in the event: he knows the grave danger that the flower presents but gives it to Myra anyway. The scheme, however, fails because a prescient Alden, who happens to be spending the night at the Maynard home, insists on taking the flower into his room instead. Although he is overcome by its poisonous vapors, he survives—and, more importantly, he preserves Myra's "purity" and prevents her from harm (just as he does a few episodes later, when he rescues her from the Master's poisoned balloons).

A less active and less hardy screen heroine than her predecessor Elaine, Myra was nevertheless "a charmingly fresh, seemingly normal young girl" who unconsciously keeps falling under the spell of the occult but who ultimately survives her ordeal.[67] Many filmgoers, especially female filmgoers, took a vicarious pleasure each week in being horrified yet titillated by her otherworldly encounters.

In bringing those encounters to the screen, the Whartons not only introduced fascinating plot devices and advanced techniques to create supernatural effects such as astral projection, levitation, and thought photography. They also demonstrated that they knew how to intrigue and excite their audiences, reconfirming their reputation as the most innovative serial producers of their day.

CHAPTER 10

Asking Beatrice

Soon after completing *The Mysteries of Myra*, the brothers undertook a new production, *Beatrice Fairfax*, financed once again by William Randolph Hearst and distributed by his International Film Service through the Pathé Exchange. Originally titled *Letters to Beatrice*, it capitalized on the recent trend of real-life female reporters, who, as Ben Singer writes, "became familiar, consistent personalities, much like serial queens" and who sought out "'novel and thrilling experiences' that extended the experiential sphere of women" by vivifying places and activities that were typically "out of reach to women, restricted by virtue of either their danger or their indelicacy."[1] The Whartons' serial, which reflected the strong real-life collaboration with newspapers that had made the serial genre so popular, was based on Fairfax's widely read "Advice to the Lovelorn" column syndicated by Hearst.

But, in fact, there was no actual Beatrice Fairfax. That was a pseudonym used by Hearst employee Marie Manning, who invented it by combining the name of Dante's guide Beatrice in *The Divine Comedy* with the Virginia county of Fairfax, where Manning's family owned property.[2] According to Cynthia Crossen in the *Wall Street Journal*, Manning, just twenty years old when she originated the column in the spring of 1898,[3] was part of the "hen coop"—slang for the women's department—of the *New York Evening Journal* when she was approached by her editor, Arthur Brisbane, who was holding three letters from readers seeking personal advice. He wondered if Manning would have any use for such letters on the women's page. She perused them and conceived an idea that would dramatically change newspapers' relationship with their readers. "I suggested a department where people could write about their personal troubles and receive unbiased opinions," Manning recalled. "If I had been 10 years older, I might have hesitated over the Frankenstein I was invoking. But 20 is a fearless age."[4]

By 1898, the *New York Evening Journal*, which Hearst had acquired only three years earlier, was engaged in a ferocious circulation battle with rival newspaper *New York World*, published by Joseph Pulitzer. Hearst had already poached much of Pulitzer's staff, including Richard F. Outcault, the inventor of color comics, and top editors Solomon Carvalho, Arthur Brisbane, and Morrill Goddard (brother of screenwriter Charles W. Goddard). The competition between the two papers—and particularly between the two men—was fierce, and their often bitter race for new ideas and new readers gave rise to an era of sensational yellow journalism. Among the most successful of Hearst's new features was the Beatrice Fairfax column. Within just a matter of months, Manning, under her pseudonym, was receiving more than a thousand letters a day from readers wanting advice on everything from philandering husbands, interfering in-laws, and nosy neighbors to suffrage, smoking, and "suppressed desires." As Crossen suggests, whereas people had once consulted friends, family, or clergy on such matters, by the turn of the century more of them were living alone in big cities and found themselves in need of impartial, anonymous advice. "At the time," Manning later said, "there were no generally accepted common-sense solutions to eternally familiar problems such as the deserted wife, abandoned children or the girl who had loved well and unwisely."[5]

Although the women's page typically covered cooking, etiquette, and beauty hints, Manning pitied "the lonely souls who filled two, three, even five sheets of pastel stationery with accounts of emotional dilemmas." And so she began dispensing pragmatic answers full of large doses of common sense to both the men and the women who wrote to her. Among those letters, she recalled, were "genuine tragedies and comedies aplenty."[6] Manning continued writing the column until 1905, when she left the paper to marry and raise a family. But she returned a few decades later, after the stock market crash of 1929 wiped out her investments, and kept sharing her wisdom with readers until her death in 1945. By then, Beatrice had many competitors, including the widely syndicated Dorothy Dix (pseudonym of

Elizabeth Meriwether Gilmer). Nevertheless, Manning remained a pioneer in the advice business.

Serializing *Beatrice*

The Whartons' *Beatrice Fairfax* serial unfolded in fifteen episodes. The scene was set in the first episode's prologue, in which Beatrice outlined her proposition for her milestone "Advice to the Lovelorn" column to *New York Evening Journal* editor Arthur Brisbane (played by Brisbane himself).[7] Each of the subsequent episodes was largely self-contained; and, as with the earlier *Wallingford* serial, each followed a well-defined pattern: "at the beginning of each episode Miss Fairfax receives a letter from some trusting reader and behind each letter is an exciting story. . . . Then Miss Fairfax, herself, is always ready to leave her desk for personal investigations of interesting cases."[8] The receipt of the letters by Beatrice, moreover, usually coincides with a story that her beau Jimmy has been assigned to investigate. An admitted amateur sleuth, he gladly assists her, often donning one of the costumes he conveniently pulls from a trunk in his apartment or borrows from others. Most of the episodes end with the pair returning to the newsroom to write up the story for the paper's midnight edition.

The serial, for which records show the Whartons were paid $4,500 per episode, was said to be "a pet idea" of William Randolph Hearst.[9] As *Moving Picture World* observed, that meant that it "receive[d] his personal attention and [would] be given every possible lattitude [sic]."[10] The coveted role of Beatrice went to the promising young actress Grace Darling, who "lent an attractive personality and a generous supply of good looks" to her sincere performance.[11] Her colleague, intrepid reporter Jimmy Barton, was played by Harry Fox, a vaudevillian, dancer, comedian, and actor who gave his name to the popular dance step the fox-trot.[12] The two made an appealing team. Reviewers noted that "in beauty and charm, Miss Darling will fulfill the Journal reader's idea of Miss Fairfax, whereas Mr. Fox is what all reporters should be but seldom are."[13] Appearing alongside the main characters were a number of other fine actors, many of their faces familiar to Wharton viewers: Bessie Wharton, Allan Murnane, Mike Rale, Dick Bennard, Olive Thomas, Warner Oland, Bruce McRae, and Frances White. And there were a few less-familiar faces as well, such as Wharton cameraman Levi Bacon, who appeared briefly before the camera as a soda jerk who is actually part of a criminal conspiracy.[14]

The episodes were directed by Robin Townley, a Wharton regular, and James Gordon, another Wharton associate, both of whom also appeared in minor roles in the serial; William Bradley codirected. The screenplay was written by Basil Dickey, brother-in-law of serial-picture veteran Charles W. Goddard. Dickey, who wrote for almost 150 films over his long career, had already worked with the Whartons on *The Romance of Elaine* and collaborated with Goddard on several earlier *Exploits of Elaine* episodes. His script for *Beatrice Fairfax* took the eponymous heroine all over New York City, from a high-society masquerade ball to the home field of the New York Yankees, from the county fair to the racetrack; but given the chase-and-escape nature of the serial, those stories occasionally became a bit convoluted in their plotting and overly reliant on incredible coincidences. So, in the end, their stirring quality depended on "the ability of the spectator to credit what he sees without asking for explanations that satisfy the mind."[15]

Apart from the missing first episode, in which Hearst is reputed to have made a cameo appearance, *Beatrice Fairfax* is the rare silent serial that survives virtually intact. "It's an interesting story of why these films were saved," film historian Aaron Pichel observed. "These episodes of 'Beatrice Fairfax' were at the Library of Congress, in the collection of Marion Davies, who was Hearst's mistress. Hearst did not like the films and intended to remake them starring Davies as Beatrice Fairfax, so he saved the films and gave them to Marion to show her what he didn't want the movies to be like. It's the rare case of someone saving movies because they didn't like them rather than because they loved them."[16]

The most common plot device in the serial, as in advice columns, was love, either unfulfilled or gone awry. (Accordingly, the tag line in trade ads was "Beatrice Fairfax: Big Sister to True Lovers.") In the first episode, "The Missing Watchman" (released August 7, 1916), for example, a woman writes to Beatrice because her fiancé, a watchman, has grown cold in his affections.[17] Beatrice realizes that his behavior is somehow linked to a recent bank robbery, so she and Jimmy decide to investigate. It turns out that the fiancé had been enticed by a woman who drew him into the crime and left him, bound and gagged, in one of the robber's basements. When Beatrice and Mary follow that woman to her home, they are nearly killed by deadly gas. But they survive, the bank's money is restored, and Beatrice and Jimmy snag a great story for the midnight extra edition.[18]

The second episode, "The Adventure of the Jealous Wife," had a similar theme. When Black Handers threaten to harm his wife Marie (Elsie Baker), newlywed Arturo Bocetti (Maurice Bond), a violinist and orchestra leader at the Venetian Theatre, is ready to pay them the $200 they demand. But after Marie discovers that the money is missing, she assumes the worst of her husband and writes Beatrice for help. The letter coincides with Jimmy's

FIGURE 10.1   In the opening episode of *Beatrice Fairfax*, advice columnist Beatrice (Grace Darling) looks into the case of "The Missing Watchman."

undercover investigation and infiltration of the criminal group. After the Black Handers are caught and the truth is revealed, a relieved Marie declares that without Beatrice's advice, her life might have been ruined.[19] And in another episode, "At the Ainsley Ball," Beatrice reunites two lovers, Robert Wells (Allan Murnane) and his fiancée Martha (May Hopkins), after a foreigner tries to come between them in order to gain Martha's fortune.[20]

Even a fourteen-year-old messenger boy seeks romantic advice from Beatrice. After young Billie delivers a message to the home of Judge Merton warning of the escape of convict Peter Raven, he meets the judge's twelve-year-old daughter Jean, falls instantly in love, and becomes caught up in a kidnap attempt orchestrated by the girl's governess, who turns out to be Raven's wife ("Billie's Romance"). After Jean's captors try to drown her in a stream, Billie jumps in to save her, while Jimmy, who has been working on the case of the missing criminal, arrives with two detectives to rescue Beatrice and apprehend Raven. Apprised of the boy's bravery, Judge Merton promises that one day, when Billie and Jean are older, he will entertain the proposition that they wed. The episode ends as many episodes do, with Jimmy and Beatrice hurrying back to the office with another scoop.[21]

When Beatrice is not helping young lovers, often she is battling criminals such as the Indian prince who wants to avenge the theft of an idol in "The Stone God." After Shara Ali (M. W. "Mike" Rale) stabs to death Christopher McRay (James Gordon), the man in possession of the idol, suspicion falls on Donald Jordan (Nigel Barrie), fiancé of McRay's daughter Dorothy, who had earlier written Beatrice for advice about resolving a bitter argument between Donald and her father. With Jimmy's help, Beatrice discovers the rendezvous point of the thieves, overhears their conversations, and uncovers the body of Ali in the vault, where he has been killed by a pistol cleverly rigged to kill any intruder who enters. That revelation solves the murder and exonerates Donald.

In "Outside the Law," Beatrice must contend with another criminal, extortionist Simeon Gold, editor of the weekly scandal magazine *The Vampire*, who tries to blackmail Madeline Grey (May Hopkins) over some scandalous letters that she wrote to another man before her marriage. Unable to pay his demand and unwilling to yield to his advances, Madeline turns to Beatrice, who, together with Jimmy, breaks into Gold's home and, after some shrewd maneuvering, locates the letters and returns them to Mrs. Grey, who immediately burns them.[22] And in "Play Ball," Beatrice helps to expose crooked gambler Martin O'Day, who plans to incapacitate Giants pitcher Bert Kerrigan (Nigel Barrie) and then to wager heavily on the opposing New York Yankees in the big benefit ballgame. To ensure his bet, O'Day arranges to kidnap both Kerrigan and his fiancée Rita Malone (Olive Thomas). Beatrice and Jimmy manage not only to rescue the lovers but also to get the pitcher on the field in time to save the game, which the Giants come from behind to win (a plot in many ways reminiscent of Leo's early film for Pathé, *Baseball's Peerless Leader*).

Beatrice solves not just one mystery but two in "The Ringer." Black Joe, a prize-winning racehorse, has been stolen from his locked stall, while nearby, at the county fair, a sideshow dwarf has gone missing. Alarmed by the dwarf's disappearance, his fiancée Cutie, "the Stout Lady," approaches Beatrice, who immediately connects the two incidents. After Jimmy disguises himself as a sideshow trickster in order to solicit information from the other performers, Beatrice discovers that the dwarf had broken into the horse's stall through a tiny door near the floor, stolen Black Joe, and conspired with a bookie to fix the big race by entering "White Stockings" (actually Black Joe, with white "socks" painted on his legs) as a ringer. The scheme is exposed; the bookie and his gang, including the dwarf, are arrested; and Beatrice is left to console Cutie.[23] As reviewer Edward Weitzel observed, "The scenes shift from the sideshow to the racetrack, and a lively rate of speed is kept up. The way in which the villains are exposed and the horse is restored to his

FIGURE 10.2   Beatrice consoles Cutie, "the Stout Lady," after it is revealed that her fiancé, a side-show dwarf, has been implicated in a crime.

owner makes an entertaining two-reel picture. Grace Darling and Harry Fox, assisted by several genuine 'freaks,' give a good account of the acting."[24]

An even more heinous crime, baby-napping, occurs in "A Name for Baby." Madge Minturn (Mary Cranston) contacts Beatrice because she wants her out-of-wedlock baby with Waldo Conley (Allan Murnane) to have a name—certainly a daring and controversial topic for the time. Conley, who is getting married to Margaret Wilson (Betty Howe), a woman of high social standing, is fearful that his secret might jeopardize the wedding; so he arranges to have the mother and child kidnapped. But with Jimmy at her side, Beatrice visits Margaret to reveal Waldo's duplicity, then tracks the kidnapper (Robin Townley) and rescues Madge and her child. The next day, the ceremony occurs as originally planned—at least until Waldo discovers that the heavily veiled bride he has just wed is actually Madge, a trick in which Margaret has been complicit.

The criminals in "The Wages of Sin" resort to an even more devious scheme: using a "ghost" to scare Jane Hamlin (Betty Howe) into giving up the "perfect infernal machine" created by her late father, an inventor named Cyrus. After Jane expresses doubts to Beatrice about her fiancé Clayton Boyd

(Nigel Barrie), he confirms her suspicions by selling out to a group of anarchists. Pretending to be Cyrus's ghost, he tries to persuade her to give up the device. Although in the end Jane is forced at gunpoint to relinquish it, she cleverly pushes a button on the machine that triggers the release of a poison gas that she knows will prove fatal to the thieves.[25] In a similar scheme, in "The Hidden Menace," Mr. Harvey tries to convince his ward, orphaned heiress Alice Masters (Betty Howe), that she, like her late mother, is going insane. Alice writes Beatrice to seek counsel about her engagement, which Harvey strenuously opposes, and about the delusions she has been suffering since the death of her other guardian, the sympathetic James Wells (F. W. Stewart). Meanwhile, Jimmy has been assigned by the paper to investigate Wells's death, and soon discovers that Harvey had murdered his partner to avoid having to give an accounting of Alice's inheritance. Harvey also tried to make Alice doubt her own sanity, since, under those circumstances, her fortune would revert to him (one of the most familiar plot devices in early serials) and cover the funds he lost through his careless speculation. Not only do Beatrice and Jimmy ensure that Alice's money is restored; they also learn that her mother's illness was actually the result of a fall suffered later in life, proving that Alice's fears of inherited insanity are unjustified.[26]

At times, the criminal activity that Beatrice investigates and exposes takes a political turn, as in "Mimosa San," in which Japanese government agent Hako Satsu (Frank Honda) conspires with Anna Cortes (Elsie Baker) to steal plans for a valuable rifle sight. Mimosa San (Yumiko Nagahara), the woman who loves Satsu, is initially jealous of his attentions to Cortes and writes Beatrice for advice, but eventually she pledges her allegiance to Satsu and aids in the theft. When the lovers try to escape, though, they are killed in an automobile accident; and Beatrice and Jimmy are able to retrieve the plans.[27] (In the original version, Satsu and Mimosa San do not die but instead make a successful escape by boat. From the dock, Jimmy is ready to fire at them, but Beatrice says, "Let her have him. We have the plans." As Ted Wharton explained to Hearst's International Film Service, the new ending was added in order "to cover the censorship proposition," since "a strict rule of all censorship boards, is that criminals must be punished.")[28]

The "Mimosa San" episode was especially timely since it capitalized on Americans' fear of the "Yellow Menace," or "Yellow Peril." The distrust of Asians, which had increased after the rise of Chinese immigration in the late nineteenth century, was reinforced by racist pogroms in California and elsewhere and strengthened by legislation such as the Immigration Act of 1917 that created an "Asian Barred Zone" and instigated other nativist efforts. The episode not only harked back to the racial characterizations of

Long Sin and Wu Fang in *The Exploits of Elaine*; it also anticipated themes that the Whartons treated more comprehensively in the preparedness picture *Patria* that followed a few months later and also in their ultrapatriotic *The Eagle's Eye* serial released in 1918, which, like so many productions of that period, used fear of foreigners and minorities to provoke and to stoke public sentiment.

In another politically themed episode, "Curiosity," Beatrice assists newlywed wife Gladys (Evelyn Fariss), who suspects her husband Henry Hanson (Nigel Barrie) of disreputable and criminal activity. Hanson, however, turns out to be the chief of the Secret Service, and his clandestine efforts prevent the explosion of a bomb that has been hidden in a coffin and placed on a steamship.[29] The Secret Service also plays an integral part in "The Forbidden Room," in which Jean Moore (Betty Howe), a young woman who works for "Mme. Gaillard," accidentally discovers the room where a gang of counterfeiters is making fake bills. To silence her, Mme. Gaillard, head of the gang, takes Jean hostage. But after her fiancé writes for help finding her, Beatrice and Jimmy expose Gaillard, who is actually a man (Dick Bennard), and call in the Secret Service to bust the criminal ring.[30] And in "Wrist Watches," the final episode of the serial, another government agent, U.S. Revenue Service agent Clinton Harding (Wellington Playter), is sleuthing for smugglers. After following fisherman Donald Dane down a well into a smuggler's cove, he is captured but rescued by Jimmy, who has used a "sphymograph" to get Dane to reveal his complicity with the criminals.[31] Afterward, Harding is reunited with Dane's niece, Dorothy (Evelyn Fariss), the object of his newfound affection.

Interference by Hearst

Two additional episodes of *Beatrice Fairfax* were suppressed and never produced. The first, "The Opal Ring" (the script of which is reproduced in full in an appendix to this volume), was reportedly too extreme in its depiction of the violence committed by Chinese villains. According to a billing sent to Hearst's International Film Service, the Whartons were prepared to start work on the scenario, but "at the last minute, we were informed that Mr. Hearst did not want this episode made and should replace it with the episode entitled At the Ainsley Ball." They estimated the loss of time in production along with salaries and studio expenses to be $2,854.50.[32] The second suppressed episode, "Grey Wolves," about spies, was also considered too immoderate in its politics and therefore, like "The Opal Ring," deemed unsuitable for theatrical release.[33]

Such major last-minute changes by Hearst were hardly unusual, and it was not just the Whartons who found his demands oppressive. As screenwriter

Basil Dickey observed in his correspondence with Edward A. MacManus at the International Film Service, the discussions "with Mr. Hearst made no impression upon him as to the difficulties under which the Whartons and I are working." As an example, Dickey explained that it took Hearst seventeen days to decide that he did not want a dream episode and then expected Dickey to substitute a new two-reel episode within two days. "I do not believe there is another scenario man in the country who can do it and make a good story of it," Dickey wrote, but he pledged to do the best he could. Dickey also cited other problems that resulted from Hearst's fickleness, including the order to rewrite an episode that Hearst found "lurid and sensational" long after it was in his hands, and the need to rework other scenes because of Hearst's delay in approving them. "Mr. Wharton is unable to do the twelfth episode written by Mr. Goddard," Dickey noted, "because it requires an ocean liner, therefore, I will have to rewrite part of this episode."[34]

Although *Beatrice Fairfax* lacked some of the novelty of its predecessors *Elaine* and *Myra*, it nonetheless made good use of conventional techniques. Working with stationary cameras, Wharton head cameraman John Holbrook, along with Levi Bacon, Ray June, Bill Pyles, and Lew Tree, used multiple angles in their filming, from long shots of the car chases in the "Mimosa San" episode to close-ups of characters such as the sweetly sympathetic circus fat lady "Cutie," who is desperate to understand her dwarf fiancé's disappearance in "The Ringer." Iris-in and iris-out shots directed the audience's attention to the principal characters in the various episodes, many of which opened on Beatrice and Jimmy at the *New York Evening Journal* office as they embark on their latest adventure and closed as they celebrate the outcome by preparing to write up the story for the midnight edition. And sometimes they reinforced the characters' oppositionality, as in the paired shots of Simeon Gold, editor of the scandalous *Vampire*, and Madeline Grey, the intended victim of Gold, who is threatening to publish some of her old love letters to a man she loved before she married her husband ("Outside the Law"). Iris shots also served to frame the flashback scenes—as in "The Stone God" episode, in which both Ali and McRay recall the circumstances of the theft from the Indian temple of the Buddha idol (who, in one of the special effects, comes to life and commands Ali to retrieve and restore it) or in "The Ringer," in which the manner of Black Joe's theft is revealed—and to introduce the fantasy sequences, in which Jimmy imagines himself marrying Beatrice ("The Wages of Sin") or Billie daydreams about being the dashing cowboy who saves young Jean from the band of Onondagas that is holding her captive ("Billie's Romance").[35]

Most important to filmgoers, however, was the solid entertainment that the serial offered. Beatrice, a modern, independent woman with a

FIGURE 10.3 Even the advertisements for *Beatrice Fairfax* portrayed the heroine as an aspirational figure for the women of her day.

challenging job in the largely male newspaper business, was both an engaging lead character and an excellent example of the "New Woman" type that had become so prominent in the popular literature and films of the 1910s. Her name boldly emblazoned on the glass door of her private office made clear that she was on equal footing with, or even superior to, her male counterparts, who worked out of the adjacent press pool—no mean achievement in any era, much less a century ago; and it suggested to women that they deserved parity in the workplace as well as in the home. (Reinforcing the point about women's equality is a conversation that explicitly references the issue of suffrage.)[36] And although her colleague and admirer Jimmy at times had the flashier role in the serial—in disguises such as the clumsy waiter who eavesdrops on the conversations of an Indian prince, a vegetable man who seeks favor with a housemaid in order to gain entrance to the home of an extortionist, a trickster in a sideshow who elicits secrets from his fellow performers, a trinket peddler who purports to be selling smuggled goods, a pigtailed "strong woman" who is hired to clean the hideout of a group of criminals, and even a white-sheeted ghost—it was Beatrice who always found herself in the midst of the action as she answered her readers' calls for help.

The influence of *Beatrice Fairfax* was broad: the serial not only spawned a popular song, "Beatrice Fairfax, Tell Me What to Do," and a later comic book series. It also initiated a genre of similarly themed productions, such as Mutual's *The Perils of Our Girl Reporters* (1916), which used the news world as its background,[37] and helped to pave the way for numerous later "girl reporter" pictures such as *Big News* (1929), *Dance, Fools, Dance* (1931), *Front Page Woman* (1935), *Nancy Drew, Reporter* (1939), and *Brenda Starr, Reporter* (1945).

With *Beatrice Fairfax*, the Whartons had once again struck a note that resonated with audiences and filmmakers alike.

CHAPTER 11

Preparing for War

The Whartons knew that it would take a powerful voice to make Americans feel the urgency of military preparedness, and they found it in Patria Channing.

Before undertaking *Patria*, the brothers, working at an almost unprecedented pace, had produced three serials in two years that featured strong modern heroines.[1] But unlike the adventures of her "serial sisters," which were intended to entertain rather than to provoke, Patria's story was conceived with a distinctly topical and political aim. According to *Moving Picture World*, it was created "for the dual purpose of furnishing the highest quality of photoplay possible and of instilling into the American public the deep obligation of preparing the country against invasion. Nothing has been left undone to accomplish these purposes."[2]

Although America had managed to stay out of the conflict that had raged in Europe since 1914, aloofness from affairs abroad was becoming more difficult, and some level of engagement seemed inevitable. American policies of neutrality and attitudes of peaceful idealism began shifting to a more violent war passion; and, as Lewis Jacobs observed, nowhere was "that transition revealed more patently than in the newly found language of the movies," with pro-war propaganda "subtly and astutely" being injected even into satires, comedies, dramas, and romances.[3] In particular, serials such as *Patria* sought to brace the American public for the possibility of entry into the conflict, typically by sensationalizing the threat to American national security.[4]

While *Patria* proved to be the best of the preparedness serials, it was not the first. Arriving in theaters almost a year earlier was *The Secret of the Submarine* (May 1916), a fifteen-episode thriller released by Mutual, in which Cleo Burke (Juanita Hansen), together with Lieutenant Jarvis Hope (Tom Chatterton), foils the efforts by agents of the Japanese and Russian governments to steal plans for a new submarine that can remain underwater indefinitely by means of an apparatus that operates like the gills of a fish.[5] Following just a few months later was Universal's twenty-part *Liberty, a Daughter of the U.S.A.* (August 1916), in which seventeen-year-old Liberty (Marie Walcamp), the sole heir to her late father's estate, is apparently beset from all sides: Mexican Juan Lopez plots to have her kidnapped and held for ransom in order to secure funds to finance a revolution against the legal government of Mexico, while one of her guardians has a similarly nefarious plan involving marriage to his son Manuel, who is in league with the rebels fighting border battles against the Texas Rangers. With the help of Captain Bob Rutledge of the Rangers (Jack Holt), Liberty is able to prevail. And *The Yellow Menace* (released September 4, 1916), a sixteen-part thriller produced by Unity, was just as xenophobic, even though its villain was not a Mexican but rather a mysterious Mongolian, Ali Singh, who wishes to exalt the yellow race at the expense of whites. While focused more on race issues than on preparedness, the serial was another important link in the chain of serials that "warned the public of the dangers of neutrality and apathy over what might well be going on inside the borders of the United States at the very moment they were watching their theater screens."[6]

Another preparedness serial—the one in most direct competition with *Patria*, which was released just a month later—was Pathé's *Pearl of the Army* (released December 1916), a twenty-part picture directed by former Wharton associate George B. Seitz and starring Pearl White in one of her finest screen performances. The plot concerned the "Silent Menace," an enemy who has stolen secret defense plans of the Panama Canal that Pearl is determined to recover. Her finest moment occurs during a rooftop confrontation as the shadowy figure of the Menace attempts to lower the Stars and Stripes, in a signal to his followers to begin the uprising. But she fights valiantly to keep the flag waving and finally knocks the Menace off the building. The film ends in a spectacle of patriotic fervor as Pearl is honored for her efforts with a full dress parade of American troops.[7]

Advertising for *Pearl of the Army* emphasized that it was a serial "the whole country will be talking about," with a star who was the greatest drawing card in motion pictures. Exhibitors were advised that patrons would flock to the exciting patriotic picture to see America's secret foes unmasked.[8] Yet for the Whartons, the casting of their former star Pearl White in a preparedness serial so closely themed to their own production must have come as an unpleasant surprise, especially since *Pearl of the Army* beat *Patria* to the theaters and was still in its early episodes when their own preparedness serial, filmed almost a half year earlier, finally appeared in theaters.

The Genesis of *Patria*

According to early film historian Terry Ramsaye, it was Edward A. MacManus, the head of both Hearst's International News Service and International Film Service (and, earlier, the force behind the landmark *What Happened to Mary* series), who first proposed the idea for *Patria*. After studying the war situation and looking for ways to capitalize on it, he hit on the notion of a modern-day Joan of Arc in glittering armor and mounted on a white horse, saving her countrymen from a powerful enemy—"the first flowering of an idea of preparedness for women." The idea evolved into an outline of a serial that conflated the patriotic wave with the new interest in feminism. *Patria* was, Ramsaye affirmed, "a motion picture written to a prescription."[9]

The chapter synopses, later serialized in the Hearst papers, were written by popular novelist Louis Joseph Vance,[10] with scenarios by Charles Goddard and John Blanchard Clymer. Loosely based on the history of the du Pont family of Delaware, famous munition makers for generations,[11] *Patria* arrived at a time when the country was "especially imbued with the spirit of nationalism and patriotism, and when every city and village has been stirred with the departure or return of troops, [and] every city has had its training camp."[12] It was also a time when certain historical events, such as the punitive expedition into Mexico, with its pursuit of Pancho Villa, were fresh in people's minds—especially in the mind of Hearst, whose ranch in Chihuahua Province had been seized and looted by Villa's raiders, to the indifference of the government and to Hearst's outrage.[13] Vance recalled the genesis of *Patria*: an employee of Hearst's International Film Company contacted him to inform him of his boss's plans for a new serial of national preparedness. "We're in no hurry," the employee announced, "but we'd like to have the first six or seven episodes in detailed continuity by tomorrow morning at the latest."[14] In this instance, as in so many others, the powerful Hearst's request would not be denied.

Following the *Myra* serial, Hearst had started taking an even more active role in the production of the pictures that he financed and distributed through his International Film Service. And because he could afford to underwrite films that reflected his own ideas, he determined to see such motion pictures made, especially when they allowed him to redress perceived wrongs. Opposed to involvement in the war in Europe—and to President Woodrow Wilson, who considered American entry into that war inevitable (and whom he regularly excoriated in his newspapers and publications)—pro-German Hearst was convinced that the true enemy of the United States was much closer at hand. Specifically, he embraced the conspiracy theory that Japan, "interested in subjugating America to further its domination of the Pacific," was secretly working with revolution-plagued Mexico to invade the United States from the south. Mexico, he concluded, posed the greatest and most immediate threat to this country's security.[15]

The Hearst papers had already "taken many belligerent slaps at the Japanese, Mexicans, and other sundry items related to American defense over the previous few years." As the possibility that President Wilson would not be able to keep the United States out of war became more apparent, Hearst felt an even greater urgency to put *Patria*, his most blatant argument that the American public should ready themselves for the worst, on the screen. Thus the heroine Patria "went before the cameras to face an allied army of Japanese and Mexicans," a construct that—while inherently racialist—was reflective of the American dominant culture of that period.[16]

Inimitable Irene

Apart from its preparedness theme, the most distinctive feature of the Whartons' serial was its star, Irene Castle, who was hailed as "the Best Known Woman in America."[17] The daughter of a physician, Castle had studied dancing and performed in amateur theatricals before meeting Vernon Castle, a stage dancer, in 1910. After their marriage in 1911, she joined him in various stage productions and traveled with him to Paris, where their act turned them into an international sensation. After bringing that act back to New York, they became fixtures on the social scene as well as staples of the vaudeville and Broadway stages. As their popularity increased, they found themselves in great demand as dance instructors and even published a book, *Modern Dancing*. Yet their influence was not limited to dance; it extended to the world of fashion as well. Irene's elegant but modern clothing set new trends; "her slim athletic figure caused millions of women to throw away their corsets"; and her short bobbed hair "was the windfall of beauty parlors the world over." To her, Hillary Rettig wrote, "must go the credit (or blame) for reshaping the American girl."[18] Frequently photographed, widely admired, and often imitated, Castle soon established herself as the model of the "new ideal woman." At times, her celebrity seemed to rival that of perennial audience favorite Pearl White.

According to Ed Hulse, when Hearst first envisioned the story of a fashionable debutante—the last of a patriotic family with roots going back to the American Revolution, who abandons her high-society life in order to fight the Japanese and Mexican conspirators bent on waging war against the United States—he already had Irene Castle in mind to play the lead. His relationship with the Castles dated back to 1913, when he first invited the renowned dancers to dinner at his New York apartment in the hope that they would teach him and his wife Millicent some of their latest dance steps. Since Hearst and Irene also shared other interests, including a love of dogs, the two remained friendly over the next few years, even after Vernon returned to England to join the wartime effort as a pilot in the Royal Flying Corps. By then, Castle had already appeared in several pictures, both alone and with her husband, and Hearst believed her perfectly suited to play the heroine of his chapter play. She agreed to take the role and committed to twenty weeks of work at a salary of $1,500 per week, which made her the highest-paid performer on the Ithaca lot. (By comparison, the otherwise princely salary of $500 per week that the brothers received seemed downright meager.)[19]

When Castle arrived in Ithaca in mid-July to begin filming, she made an entrance befitting her celebrity status. To the home she had rented in Cayuga Heights from Professor Alfred Hayes, she brought twenty trunks, fifteen hatboxes, two servants, two cars, and an entire menagerie of animals, including her three dogs, two horses named Minto and Lightnin', and two monkeys, Virginia and Rastus (the latter being an unfortunate allusion to a familiar black stereotype on stage and in early cinema).[20] Ithacans welcomed her into the community; and they embraced her even more warmly after the tragic death of her husband Vernon in a plane crash in 1918 and her marriage to local businessman Robert Treman.

Costarring with Castle was Milton Sills, the veteran stage actor who had already won fame as a leading man in film and who would become one of the biggest motion-picture matinee idols of the 1920s. The other performers included Dorothy Green, an actress famous for her "'vampire' characterizations," and Warner Oland, "a finished actor" who had started his career playing "heavies" on stage and who would gain even greater renown as one of film's best and most reliable villains.[21]

In the opening episode ("The Last of the Fighting Channings," released January 14, 1917), heiress Patria Channing is celebrating her coming of age in Newport. There, she meets and quickly develops a romantic attachment to Captain Donald Parr of the Secret Service (Sills), who is on the trail of Baron Huroki (Oland) and Juan De Lima (George Majeroni), representatives of a Mexican-Japanese alliance against the United States.[22] The two men, who hope to purchase a large supply of munitions to be sent secretly to Mexico, have been blocked by the Channings' policy of selling only to the government. After Patria receives an urgent message from estate trustee Peter Ripley, she and Parr set off for New York but are impeded by the conspirators, who continue to plot a way to get access to the Channing munitions plant.[23]

When Patria and Parr finally arrive in New York, they find Ripley dead and the body of his killer, a Japanese spy, nearby; they also find a letter informing Patria that she has inherited $100,000,000, much of it in gold, which one of her ancestors had specifically designated as a fund for national defense ("Treasure"). Although Huroki, in close pursuit, sets fire to the Channing mansion and traps Patria and Parr in the basement vault where the gold is hidden, they use a secret passageway to escape out to the garden.[24]

After tracking the plotters to a steamer, Parr is discovered and taken prisoner. Nonetheless, he manages to send a wireless message disclosing his

FIGURE 11.1   Patria (Irene Castle) is surprised to discover that one of her ancestors had bequeathed her $100,000,000 to be used as a fund for national defense.

whereabouts to Patria, who climbs into a motorboat, overtakes the steamer, and comes to his aid. With the help of the Naval Reserves, she rescues him just moments before a torpedo strikes and sinks the boat where he is being held. Huroki, De Lima, and the Japanese crew, however, evade detection and make their way to the Jersey shore ("Winged Millions").[25]

Frustrated in his attempt to steal the defense fund, Huroki redirects his attentions to destroying Patria and gaining control of her family fortune. Learning that a "Midnight Frolic" dancer named Elaine is virtually her double, he schemes to eliminate Patria and install the impostor in her place ("Double Crossed"). After conveniently ensuring that Parr misses the steamer heading for Newport, he smuggles Elaine on board and throws Patria overboard, thus setting his evil plot into motion.[26]

Patria, though, stays afloat and swims to the shore of an island on which a colony of spies is storing munitions. After another attempt to escape, she is again plunged into the sea ("The Island That God Forgot"). When a suspicious communication leads him to the same island, Parr hears Patria's cries for help and rescues her. In the fight that follows, the spy commander Haku's plane is hit with a can of nitroglycerin and downed, causing an explosion that destroys the storehouse of munitions.[27]

At the Channing home, the false Patria hosts a masked ball to celebrate her engagement to De Lima ("Alias Nemesis"). Accompanied by Parr, the real Patria slips in unnoticed, forces Elaine to change clothes with her, and then—after the impostor is inadvertently shot by her drunken and jealous manager—makes Huroki believe that she is actually Elaine and that the murdered girl was Patria.[28]

Realizing that he has been duped, Huroki initiates a strike that he knows will disrupt Patria's factory; then, to add to the chaos, he uncouples a freight car full of dynamite and sends it barreling toward the plant—a "mission of death" that Patria averts by placing her vehicle in the freight car's path to absorb the explosion ("Red Dawn").[29] Afterward, she confronts the strikers and promises to accede to their demands if they consent to undergo military training and break all ties with Huroki and De Lima. Then she and Parr return to New York, initially unaware that the conspirators have arranged to set fire to the docks at Black Tom in New Jersey, where millions of dollars of Channing munitions await shipment (a fictionalized version of an actual historical event that occurred on July 30, 1916, in Jersey City, New Jersey). Huroki is certain that, in their effort to prevent the ensuing explosion, the pair will be killed; but they narrowly escape, first by taking refuge on the topmast of a burning schooner and then by clinging to the wreckage until the police patrol arrives ("Red Night").[30] Although the strike scenes are not extant, according to the *Ithaca Journal* they were some of the most sensational in the picture: "250 extras worked from 9 AM to 7 PM on the scene," and in the climactic explosion "flames illuminated the sky for miles." In fact, the paper noted, "not since the Whartons sent a trolley car plunging over the Cornell Heights Bridge into Fall Creek Gorge several years ago has the local concern produced such a spectacular scene."[31]

Following Patria's rescue from the Black Tom disaster, Huroki conspires with her former suitor to compromise Parr, who evades the trap and secures warrants for the conspirators ("Cat's Paw and Scapegoat"). But before the warrants can be executed, De Lima is killed and Huroki escapes to a new hideout, from which he deploys the various military units of foreign employees whom he has assembled and trained ("War in the Dooryard").[32]

Under Parr's leadership, however, the well-organized and well-drilled men in Patria's military organization are prepared to rout the rioters. (In a masterly bit of camera work, as the workers file out of the Channing factory, they are transformed into uniformed troops.) As Patria rushes to the scene, the train in which she is riding is sabotaged by Huroki. But she is saved in a

FIGURE 11.2 In a valiant attempt to stop a freight car loaded with dynamite, Patria drives her car onto the tracks.

thrilling rescue by Parr, and together they chase Huroki, who ends up driving his car off a cliff into the water below.[33]

In the final episodes, the scene shifts as Patria and Parr leave New York to look after her interests on the Rio Grande ("Sunset Falls"). Her arrival is immediately communicated to Huroki, who, in true serial fashion, has survived the earlier fall and is now living as an outlaw on the other side of the border. With help from his new associate General Nogi, he assembles troops to invade the United States; but Patria, once again, is prepared with her own men, whom she has organized and outfitted through the Channing "Preparation" fund ("Peace Which Passeth All Understanding"). A raid on the property of one of her aides, local rancher Bess Morgan, confirms that rampage and looting are already occurring along the border, a prelude to the full-scale invasion that Huroki and Pancho Villa (Wallace Beery) are plotting.[34]

When Patria is forced at gunpoint to fly Nogi back to his lines across the border, she goes into a controlled dive and jettisons him from the plane ("Wings of Death").[35] Seeing Nogi's corpse, Huroki orders the invasion, and his well-trained Japanese forces follow the Mexican cavalry toward the border. For a while, a gallant band of Patria's troops is able to hold them off ("The Border Peril"). But the invaders prove too much for them, leaving Patria to rely on the men who are entrenched in the rear. Ascending in her plane, she signals the enemy's movements to Parr; then, in an exciting midair battle, she shoots down an enemy aircraft. As the invasion settles into an artillery duel, Patria and Parr gird themselves for the next assault.[36] The episode, while not extant, reportedly offered some of the amazing special effects for which the Whartons were well known. According to one reviewer, the sets fell "but little short of the real thing," with a line of trenches that resembled "the genuine article," while the size of the force on both sides and the skill with which they performed kept "the supply of thrills undiminished."[37]

Unable to take Patria's second line, Huroki launches a surprise night attack in which Parr is injured. Patria, in response, musters all her resources, including the "Caterpillar," a tank that is able to travel over any terrain and move into the midst of the enemy ("For the Flag"). Following on foot and on horseback, her men bring the battle to an end and at last defeat the enemy, after which the victorious Patria, reunited with Parr, receives the compliments of the Army and the gratitude of a nation.[38] In a spectacular finale, in which the glare of liquid fire lights up the night sky like "a grand display of fireworks that winds up a Fourth of July celebration," *Patria* "continues to show that the new woman is fit to command, even on the field of battle," a fact that the Army officers in the picture are forced to concede.[39]

FIGURE 11.3 Irene Castle played a dual role, as the heiress Patria and as a look-alike dancer (pictured here) who is impersonating her.

Only four episodes (none of them complete from main to end title) survive, so it is not possible to offer a close visual analysis of the entire serial. Yet even those few extant episodes seem to validate contemporary critics' praise of *Patria*'s first-rate production values and first-rate direction and editing.[40] They also clearly establish Patria as a modern independent heroine who demonstrates her daring behind the wheel of a car, at the helm of a motorboat, and in the cockpit of a plane, all of which she expertly maneuvers. The serial's excellent photography—especially the multiple iris shots, the interesting use of side-by-side split images (of Patria and Parr) and triple images (of Patria in full uniform), and the same-frame shot of the true and the false Patria (both played by Castle)—gives prominence to her character, while the binocular shots create a sense of immediacy by allowing the audience to see the enemy action through her eyes.

A Distinctive Heroine

Unlike earlier serial heroines such as Elaine or Myra, who are sometimes left in the shadows of their bolder male counterparts, Patria is indisputably in charge.

Hers is not a purely personal cause but rather a higher calling: to prepare the nation for war against the enemies who threaten its sovereignty. In the second episode, as the title card announces, she recognizes the gravity of the "sacred trust" that she must administer. By wielding tight control of her private army and air force, she does precisely that, refusing to let anything compromise her mission, not even her love for Parr (who—as another intertitle makes clear—plays a supporting role as her second in command).[41]

Many early serials, Ben Singer observed, stopped at the level of simply recounting the thrills and dangers of exploring worlds usually out of bounds to women, affording their heroines "vivacity and curiosity," which actually increased their vulnerability and necessitated a male rescue that posed a certain ambiguity about the ultimate nature of the heroine's independence. But *Patria* went far beyond, signaling the heroine as powerful in the public sphere and granting her "social power in terms of conventionally male positions of professional authority." That power was not diminished at all by *Patria*'s "fashion interest" (something on which Hearst insisted); in fact, the emphasis on her exquisite costuming actually added to her character. As Singer writes, it played on the fantasy of female glamour, situating her as "the passive center of attention, the decorative and charming magnet of admiration, while the fantasy of female power situated her as the active center of the narrative, the heroic agent in a male environment."

The glamorous but empowered Patria thus offered viewers the best of both worlds: "a representational structure that indulged conventionally 'feminine' forms of vanity and exhibitionism while it refused the constraints of decorative femininity through an action-packed depiction of female prowess."[42] As one New Jersey theater manager confirmed, the serial's appeal to fashion definitely helped to attract a class of patrons not usually drawn to motion pictures: "I can safely say," he noted, that "there are hundreds of women who have not missed an episode of 'Patria' simply because they wish to see the gowns worn by Mrs. Castle . . . the best dressed woman in New York."[43]

Promoting *Patria*

To promote *Patria*, which was billed as a "Serial Supreme," Hearst sent his publicity machine into high gear, promising and delivering nothing short of a media blitz. As advance advertisements in the major trade papers proclaimed, with *Patria*, the International Film Service was mounting "the most stupendous advertising and publicity campaign ever launched in connection with a motion picture serial." Part of that campaign included massive newspaper advertising in thirty of the largest cities in the United States, with full-page, half-page, and quarter-page promotional copy. On the Sunday preceding the release, three full pages in all the Hearst newspapers, for a combined circulation of more than two million, were devoted to the serial; and to ensure that every city, town, and hamlet was reached, over two hundred small papers carried the message of *Patria* as well. Moreover, Hearst bragged, *Patria* announcements would appear in *Hearst's Magazine*, *Harper's Bazaar*, *Good Housekeeping*, *Motor*, and *Cosmopolitan*, the magazine with the highest circulation in the world. Papers clamored for the privilege of publishing the story in serial form, and a novelization of the episodes under the title *Patria—the Last of the Fighting Channings* followed in a timely manner.[44] With typically inflated rhetoric, Hearst explained the rationale for his marketing blitz: "International knows *Patria* is the greatest serial ever produced. It is backing this knowledge with the greatest advertising campaign ever known."[45]

Hearst also ensured that the reception of the serial was as spectacular as his promotion. Determined to do it "big," he arranged to have the first episodes advance-screened on November 20, 1916, in the grand ballroom of the Ritz-Carlton in New York City, an event that highlighted both the rapid growth of the entertainment market and the highly effective publicity machine that fueled it.[46] In keeping with its patriotic theme, the film was projected from a flag-draped booth. So many prominent guests, including the ambassador to Germany, were in attendance that it was necessary to run the picture twice.[47] Several days later, the serial was shown at the Strand, where more than a thousand exhibitors assembled at the theater—"men not only from the Metropolitan district, but also from Philadelphia, Washington, Boston, Hartford, Springfield and Pittsburgh."[48] Their response, too, was overwhelmingly positive.

Early showings of the serial in other cities generated a favorable reaction as well. One theater, the Broadway in Portland, Oregon, saw "astonishing results" simply from local publicity. Declaring the opening week of the picture to be "Patria Week," the theater's president Edwin F. James invited the city's merchants to enter a friendly competition for first honors in decorating their store windows and "co-operatively stimulating a holiday spirit in connection with the showing of the famous serial." The winner was the Eastern Outfitting Company, whose display featured a life-size portrait of Castle as Patria in the background, with two full-size figures in the foreground, as well as "many small stickers bearing the likeness of Mrs. Castle," which were part of the giveaway.[49]

Theaters throughout the country developed similar schemes to promote *Patria*, which many exhibitors hailed for resurrecting the serial. As William

E. Madden, manager of Proctor's Broad Street Playhouse in Elizabeth, New Jersey, observed, movie houses in his area had abandoned serials as part of their programs, since "those shown in the immediate past had won little favor with their audiences" and were hardly missed. "I had begun to think that the serial belonged to history," Madden stated. But evidently *Patria* awakened producers to the fact that the serial "may be made to include features never before dreamed of."[50] Its appealing star and its wealth of action and dramatic force exerted such drawing power that, as one of Hearst's advertisements boasted, it was being "exhibited by leading vaudeville houses in seventy-five of the important cities of the country, many of them showing *a serial for the first time*."[51] Those houses included Keith's Palace as well as the other Keith Houses in greater New York—"the first time they have shown a motion picture serial."

Walter Hoff Seely, manager of the Picadilly Theatre in Rochester, New York, likely spoke for many exhibitors when he wrote Pathé, asking humorously: "We find it necessary to cancel Patria or enlarge our house. Playing to more than capacity. What do you advise?" Such commendatory reports on the attractiveness of box office receipts and satisfied audiences guaranteed continued heavy bookings, some of which were spurred by the "present hysteria of spy scares and plots throughout the country."[52]

FIGURE 11.4   In a massive publicity campaign, William Randolph Hearst touted *Patria* star Irene Castle as the best-known woman in America.

Not surprisingly, some of the biggest supporters of the serial were women such as prominent society matron Mrs. George J. Gould, who screened an episode of *Patria* as part of an elaborate evening entertainment at her home in Lakewood, New Jersey. Similar entertainments were hosted by other New York socialites as well.[53] In Philadelphia, a private showing attended by the ex-governor and his wife reportedly elicited delight from Mrs. George Urquhart, "one of the most active of Philadelphia women in the national preparedness movement." And a special showing organized by William Randolph Hearst in San Francisco for the "social register of the city" was replete with "a wonderful display of gowns and jewels" worn by the influential women in attendance, a "brilliant gathering" that was capped off with scores of dinner and dance parties.[54]

More Intrusions by Hearst

The celebrations, while massive, belied the behind-the-scenes problems that plagued the serial. Hearst's increasing insistence on being personally involved in the production had proven to be an incredible nuisance to the Whartons. "I like movies," Hearst admitted. "I like being on sets. I like picking casts. I like interfering with direction."[55] His criticisms, usually unwarranted, were constant. In one letter, for example, Hearst urged the Whartons to improve the lighting in their studio "to avoid the halation that made the figures seem vague and out of focus," a suggestion, he said rather condescendingly, that was intended merely to help the brothers "build a reputation" and to strive for "perfection in pictures."[56]

Even more annoying—and more costly—than Hearst's so-called technical advice was his interference over script content, which, as surviving Wharton correspondence and business records reveal, was unprecedented. His intrusions often necessitated extensive script changes, reshooting of scenes, and even elimination of entire episodes that had already been filmed.[57] To limit his meddling, the Whartons insisted that they be reimbursed for any retakes that resulted from his often capricious demands, since those retakes amounted to thousands of dollars per episode in film and crew costs, as well as in supplemental pay for the actors. Hearst, though, generally refused to recognize or honor those debts. Acting on Hearst's behalf and at his behest, International Film Service's manager Edward A. MacManus typically challenged the billings that the Whartons submitted and neglected to make the reimbursements promptly; sometimes he failed to pay them at all.[58] At one point, the Whartons were forced to sue for $39,000 in additional unreimbursed expenses that they had incurred during reshoots.[59] But, as Wharton attorney Howard Cobb soon discovered, "Hearst is an elusive person and it is no easy matter to get personal service of any paper upon him."[60]

For some time, the brothers had felt great dissatisfaction with these and other Hearst practices, such as the repeated failure by his International Film Service to acknowledge or credit them appropriately on the serials and films that they coproduced. In a letter to MacManus, Ted expressed his frustration. "I beg to call your attention to the fact that at no time during our business relations," he wrote, "has Wharton, Inc. been given the proper credit due them as producers of the various film subjects we have been making for the International Film Service. It is true that their [sic] is nothing in our contracts to cover such publicity, but we have on several occasions taken up the matter with you personally and have been given every assurance that the right thing would be done, but each and every press notice or advertisement sent out that has ever mentioned this concern, has relegated [sic] us to the background." Worse still, in many cases, "the name of this corporation has been entirely eliminated," with International being credited as the sole producer.[61]

As the filming of *Patria* progressed, the tensions between the Wharton brothers and Hearst created an unbridgeable rift.[62] The upshot was that the final five episodes of the serial were filmed not at the Wharton Studios in Ithaca but in Los Angeles, under the direction and immediate supervision of Jacques Jaccard, who had recently finished shooting his own preparedness serial, *Liberty, a Daughter of the U.S.A.*, for Universal; and Louis Joseph Vance was given oversight responsibilities for the production. The ostensible purpose of the move was to make use of California scenery that was consistent with the Mexican border scenes.[63] But clearly more was at play than just the locales.

In mid-November, the Whartons left Ithaca in order to make advance preparations for the West Coast filming of *Patria*, a trip that the *Ithaca Journal* reported cost several thousand dollars.[64] By December 30, 1916, two days before the first episode of the serial was originally set for release in the theaters, they were already in Los Angeles, along with Irene Castle and her entourage. Hearst planned to arrive shortly to "inspect the work of the company," which was scheduled to begin shooting the final scenes on the site of the old Universal ranch in the hills behind Hollywood.[65]

Unknown to the Whartons, director Jaccard had already invited several of his *Liberty* performers to appear in the picture, which further delayed the filming. Among Jaccard's "cast of 'stunt-makers' and daredevils" was Marie Walcamp, the star of the *Liberty* serial.[66] Her casting in the newly created role of Bess Morgan, the rancher who assists Patria and Parr in battling the foreign conspirators, required even more rewriting and additions to the script. That, in turn, created other complications, especially with Castle, who believed that Jaccard was devoting too much attention and screen time to Walcamp. Castle then demanded extra compensation from Hearst in order to cover the extensions on her contract, which had expired shortly before Christmas, in order to accommodate the shooting of new scenes.[67] Her request merely exacerbated the tensions over the budget on a picture in which Hearst had already invested $90,000.

The overages were not Hearst's only concern. Both Japan and Mexico were understandably displeased with many of the scenes in the serial, especially the depiction of the heinous crimes such as the Black Tom disaster that Hearst unabashedly blamed on the two countries. And there was backlash as well from film exhibitors and moviegoers in the United States, with pressure mounting nationwide to ban the film from being screened. Censors in Pennsylvania, Ohio, and Oregon had insisted that cuts be made to scenes depicting Japan as America's enemy, because the country had since become an ally in the war.[68] Ultimately, and perhaps most importantly, President Wilson found himself "very much disturbed" by the nature of the story and requested certain alterations and deletions. "It would seem desirable," Wilson wrote, "to omit all those scenes in which anything Japanese appears, particularly those showing the Japanese and Mexican armies invading the United States, pillaging homes, kidnapping women and committing all sorts of other offenses. I trust this will be found possible, and if not, I again venture to ask whether you are not prepared to withdraw the film entirely from circulation."[69] Hearst agreed to make some changes, but even after the recut prints were recirculated, the serial never "pick[ed] up the necessary steam to become the hit which he had envisioned."[70]

A Philadelphia case highlighted the censorship concerns. As *Moving Picture World* reported in May 1917, *Patria* was originally banned in that city on the charge of discouraging recruiting and enlistment of young men of military age by suggesting the country's unpreparedness for war. In particular, Secretary of State Robert Lansing and Pennsylvania State Attorney Francis Shunk Brown objected to the portrayal of the Japanese conspiring with the Mexicans against the United States, which seemingly ignored the country's new diplomatic relations with Japan as an ally in the war against Germany. After a conference in Washington, DC, with Pathé general manager J. A. Berst, a compromise was reached to eliminate all intertitles that reflected the Japanese as enemies of the country and to substitute other intertitles that emphasized the fact that the film told "an imaginary story." But the Whartons' reworking—most of it cosmetic rather than substantive—made for some ridiculous moments, as Huroki became "Señor Manuel Morales," despite the fact that he was repeatedly shown wearing a kimono, drinking tea, and living in an apartment decorated with plainly Japanese items.[71] Apparently, the concessions were enough to lift the ban and to allow the revised film to hurry out to local exchanges. On learning of the decision, Berst reconfirmed that it was Pathé's policy to cooperate with all departments of the government and to aid recruiting through patriotic production,[72] a statement that was echoed by the Motion Picture Industry and the Associated Motion Picture Advertisers. The incident, however, was a reminder of the way that the Whartons, who on the one hand advocated against censor boards (especially at the state level), deliberately courted controversy by the inclusion of sensitive or even incendiary subject matter in their serials and feature films.

Hearst-controlled publications nonetheless continued to extol *Patria*'s merits, as did a number of other papers and trade journals.[73] Reviewers like the one from the *New York Telegraph* remarked on Castle's charm and grace and praised her for playing "a Pearl White part" with a fascinating mixture of daintiness and fearlessness.[74] Others, though, were less keen on the production. Ben H. Grimm, in *Moving Picture World*, for example, suggested that audiences might enjoy it—but only if they were "willing to forego the seasoning of logicality in their dramatic food."[75] Castle, too, received mixed reviews for her performance, with some critics suggesting that her talents were better suited to dancing than to acting.[76] *Photoplay* was even blunter: "Mrs. Castle reminds us painfully of a dressmaker's mannikin."[77]

To her credit, Castle liked the excitement of the movies and tried to do most of her own stunts in the serial, even against the advice of her husband Vernon.[78] Gamely, she drove her car onto the railroad tracks and stalled it just as an actual train approached and stopped only a few feet from her vehicle; and she clung to the mast of a ship as it went up in flames. She even dove forty feet off the deck of a freighter into Cayuga Lake, into water so icy that she passed out, required rescue, and later had to be treated for pneumonia.[79] After the serial was complete, she assessed her own performance rather honestly: "Fortunately, I wasn't called on for any acting except to look terrified occasionally, and on those occasions I didn't need to act. I was."[80] She recalled that her costar Milton Sills, who played her ally and love interest Captain Parr, "kissed my hand when he felt affectionate, pounded assorted villains into jelly when he felt belligerent[,] and looked painfully mysterious over everything anybody said."[81] Sills, who also performed most of his own stunts, had a less generous memory of the filming. "For my many sins," he recalled, "I did penance for nine months of my life in *Patria*."[82]

The experience on the serial proved even more challenging for the Whartons than it did for the stars. Yet, while it often taxed their ingenuity as producers and directors, they managed to rise to the occasion. For instance, as local author and historian Arch Merrill observed, when the script called for the sinking of a battleship by an enemy submarine, they cleverly constructed the man-of-war out of wood, tin, and papier-mâché; and they covered a rowboat with a metal shell and transformed it into a submarine. "The torpedo, however, was real, for it contained 50 pounds of dynamite and it performed its mission spectacularly."[83] The brothers also created an entire village in miniature, which was subsequently blown up and destroyed,[84] and they gave the strike scenes a real authenticity with sensational special effects, such as the hand-colored red-tinted fires that rose from the buildings that were set ablaze.

There is no denying that the production was fraught with difficulties for the Whartons. The resulting break with Hearst nevertheless came as a real blow to them and to their studio—all the more so, given the economic realities of the time. The support of Hearst, after all, had been integral to their productions, beginning with their first serial *The Exploits of Elaine*. And they recognized that the severing of the relationship quashed all hope for a major Hearst-financed expansion of their Ithaca production facility. That expansion would have made the existing studio fireproof, permitted the installation of special lighting and other necessary features, and added several new buildings to the property—improvements that, in turn, would have allowed the Whartons to broaden their operation and take on new and bigger film projects.[85] But given the strain in their relationship with the tycoon, it was clear that the

FIGURE 11.5   The Whartons were known for their spectacular stunt effects, including the construction and destruction of entire miniature villages.

"huge new studio to be called Hearst-Wharton" that the *Ithaca Journal* had exulted in only a few months before would never materialize.[86]

A New Direction

An even more significant development, and one that would have the single most profound consequence for the Whartons as filmmakers, was their decision to curtail their activity as contracting producers. Years earlier, after opening their Renwick Park studio, the brothers had offered their services to other filmmakers and urged them to "let us relieve you of the heavy responsibility of producing your pictures." And for the next few years, they often acted in that contractual capacity, most notably and most profitably with Hearst. But in February 1917, *Moving Picture World* announced that the Whartons are "spring[ing] a real surprise": their "Wharton, Inc., will henceforth operate independently, marketing all of its productions as well as maintaining unhampered supervision in the filming of every picture." Without explicitly referencing Hearst, Ted explained the company's new direction. By making their own pictures in their own way, he stated, they could avoid outside interests, especially "influences that have more or less affected our work in the past." In the future, all Wharton productions would be handled by a separate company, the Wharton Releasing Corporation. The brothers insisted that they would be the sole stockholders in both companies and that no outside capital would be involved. And although they expected to establish important and far-reaching affiliations throughout the United States and Europe, "Wharton, Inc., would be essentially an independent corporation" with no working connection with other interests.[87] To handle local concerns, branch offices were planned in New York City and Chicago.[88]

While there is no record of a Chicago branch ever being founded, by July the Whartons had opened a New York City office at 130 West Forty-Sixth Street, which, according to its advertisements, provided salesrooms, projection rooms, and all other conveniences for buyers and exhibitors. Staffing that office were Charles S. Goetz, who reportedly had been "in the selling end of the picture game practically since pictures were pictures," and Edward Small, who had previously been associated with theater magnate Marcus Loew and who would go on to form Reliance Pictures. The plan was for the two men to oversee most of the marketing end of the business, while Leo, officially president of the corporation, would be "largely occupied in working with his brother on production in Ithaca."[89]

The Whartons claimed that by operating from that midtown location, the releasing company could afford better facilities for marketing their products, in large part by engaging directly with exhibitors in the critical New York and northern New Jersey markets and "state-righting" the rest—that is, selling the rights to agents who would then exploit the films in their given territories.[90] It was, to be sure, a bold move to make, especially for contracting producers who had long enjoyed a certain security thanks to the backing of a sponsor as powerful and influential as Hearst.

At the same time, it was also a move that required a considerable change in their business model. In terms of structure, the Whartons already had an efficient and largely self-contained organization in place for filmmaking, with everything from outdoor stages, editing facilities, and film labs to set designers, skilled cameramen, and construction and special-effects crews on site at the Renwick Park studio (which, according to the *Ithaca Journal*, employed sixty people).[91] But as independent producers working outside the mainstream studio system and without major financial backing, they were forced to tend more directly and more immediately to the business end of production as well. That meant organizing their operation more strictly, with separate departments, including scenario, photography, developing, mechanical, set design, production, and publicity.[92] And it also meant making their own arrangements to finance, write, direct, produce—and, perhaps even more importantly, to distribute and promote—their features, serials, and comedies. As Aaron Pichel writes, the brothers believed that, by leveraging their enormous experience in the movie industry and their very solid reputations, they could "transform their studio from a contract producer to a real independent movie studio that could control its own productions and control its destiny."[93] But while they were savvy filmmakers, the Whartons were largely inexperienced businessmen. They would soon discover just how seriously they had miscalculated by underestimating the effect that the combined loss of Pathé's international distribution and Hearst's media juggernaut would have on them and on their operation.

Yet, even as they made the transition, the Whartons' confidence in their signature production remained strong. In an essay titled "What of the Serial?" in *Wid's*, Ted Wharton opined on "The Serial and the Future." "Way back in the days when the motion picture was a novelty," he wrote, the serial, or continued story, became "a novelty within a novelty." Presented in two-reel chapters, its principal characters were taken through a series of connected adventures, "working always against the power of the villain." Since thrills predominated, dramatic situations were necessarily sacrificed for physical action, with logic and credulity discounted as well. But, he observed, a change had come about in the business of the serial, so long and so unjustly called the "dime novel" of the screen. "Long ago," he wrote, "[I] ceased to make serials as they are commonly known," with sensational incidents strung together by the thinnest of plots; and "in the future I shall make continued stories with the accent on the story," since the story is the thing. The serial era in motion pictures, he concluded, was just beginning, and the field had "limitless possibilities."[94]

In a separate article, "New Art of the Motion Picture," in *Moving Picture World*, Leo Wharton made a similar observation. "The man who makes a good picture in these days, must first of all have a good story, well knit, well told, well figured out in advance. That story must be more than possible. That story must tell something besides mere action. The story must be the type of story that will make the world a little better, a little happier, a little cleaner and purer for having been told." It must also have good characters, good lighting, and good photography. With all those elements in place, "one can readily see that the motion picture business is a business no longer—it is an Art."[95]

As always, the Whartons' faith in themselves and in their work remained high. But that faith would soon be tested as they faced new artistic and financial challenges.

CHAPTER 12

Moving into Feature Filmmaking

The Whartons were rarely reluctant to court controversy in their filmmaking. The release of their long-awaited preparedness serial *Patria* on January 14, 1917, was followed just weeks later by an even more controversial release: *The Black Stork*, a five-reel feature that they had filmed more than a half year earlier. That film told a fictionalized story based on the actual 1915 "Bollinger Case," in which Dr. Harry J. Haiselden, the chief surgeon at the German-American Hospital in Chicago, refused to perform a life-saving surgery on a severely disabled infant, "Baby [John] Bollinger." Haiselden justified his action by arguing that his decision was actually more ethical and humane, since the operation would offer at best a temporary benefit; and even in the unlikely event that the baby survived beyond infancy, he would suffer a horrible life as a "cripple." Subsequently Haiselden revealed that, during the decade before 1915, he had secretly permitted many other infants he had diagnosed as "defective" to die. And, as Martin Pernick, in his comprehensive study of eugenic policies, practices, and films, observed, "over the next three years he withheld treatment from, or actively speeded the deaths of, at least five more abnormal babies."[1]

While some were horrified by Haiselden's actions, others hailed him as a hero. Parents of children with severe handicaps wrote beseeching him to help terminate their children's lives. Haiselden, in turn, used their painful plights to publicize and promote his own campaign against the treatment of "defective" newborns. Garnering attention at every turn, he wrote articles for Hearst's *Chicago American*, delivered lectures on the subject, and appeared in countless newsreels. He even displayed dying infants and permitted reporters to photograph and interview their unfortunate mothers. At times, the sensational newspaper stories about Haiselden and the Bollinger case pushed coverage of the world war to second billing.[2]

The Black Stork

After being tried for his refusal to treat "Baby Bollinger," Haiselden was exonerated in court, although afterward he was expelled from the Chicago Medical Society—not because he allowed his youngest and most vulnerable patients to die, but because he publicized their cases.[3] Hoping to clear himself before the American public, he decided to participate, and even to star, in *The Black Stork*, the Wharton film based on the notorious Bollinger incident, which he felt would give credence to his practices. Collaborating with Hearst journalist John Lait, who had earlier written an important exposé about the horrors of institutionalizing the "retarded," Haiselden crafted a moving story about Claude Leffingwell, a man with "tainted blood" (a euphemism for a sexually transmitted disease), who, despite numerous unequivocal warnings from his physician Dr. Dickey, marries his sweetheart Anne Schultz (whose name, in later versions of the film, was Americanized to Smith). The baby who results from their union is born severely disabled, but Dickey refuses to operate on the "wretched bundle of bones."[4] Although Anne is distraught, after experiencing a vision of the misery that the child is likely to suffer as a misshapen social outcast and the crimes that he is likely to commit as a result of his anger and congenital madness, she accepts the wisdom of the doctor's decision. After all, Dickey proclaims, "There are times when saving a life is a greater crime than taking one." Anne's faith in the doctor is vindicated when the child's soul leaps into the waiting arms of Jesus.

In a heavy-handed subplot, the couple's close friends Tom Watson and Miriam Fontaine also wish to marry. Fearing, however, that they too might carry a hereditary taint because of the epileptic fit that killed Miriam's mother, they refrain from acting on their desire and are soon compensated for their prudence by the discovery that they are both healthy, allowing them to wed after all. The subplot clearly contained an implicit warning that Claude and Anne ignore and an explicit "reward" that Tom and Miriam earn for what the film defines as their socially conscious and morally appropriate conduct.

FIGURE 12.1   In *The Black Stork*, two couples react in opposite ways to the possibility that they might carry a hereditary "taint."

Advertised as a "eugenics love story," the film starred British-born Hamilton Revelle as Claude, Elsie Esmond as Anne, Allan Murnane as Tom, Jane Fearnley as Miriam, Bessie Emerick as Miriam's mother, and, of course, Dr. Haiselden as Dr. Dickey, the physician at the moral center of the drama. (Dickey, incidentally, was the maiden name of Haiselden's mother Elizabeth.) It also featured numerous actual disabled children and young adults, all of whom were labeled on the title cards as "defective," "subnormal," "mentally warped," or "hopelessly crippled" and depicted as "polluting the blood stream of the nation." That notion of pollution was also underscored in the promotions for the film. One full-page ad showed a confused black stork with a bundle in its beak being turned away from a house; a huge sign on the chimney warns: "Black Stork Stay Off!" The same ad proudly explained that "Dr. Haiselden's photoplay 'The Black Stork' will drive deformed babies from the country."

Although *The Black Stork* was filmed in the summer of 1916 while the Whartons were completing *The Mysteries of Myra* and beginning their new serial *Patria*, its official release was delayed because of concerns by the National Board of Review of Motion Pictures, which insisted on a number of changes and modifications before granting conditional approval. Yet even after its commercial release in movie theaters in 1917, the picture continued to spur a furious reaction, especially over the inclusion of real-life persons with disabilities who were presented as socially undesirable. The film's exposition of such sensitive issues resulted in an unusual exhibition practice at many theaters: women were admitted only into the morning and afternoon showings; men could attend only the evening performances; and children were prohibited from attending altogether.[5]

Not all of the national attention and comment that the film attracted, however, was negative. S. E. Conybeare, associate editor of the *New England Homestead*, praised Haiselden for "doing splendid work" and commended him on his "courage to do the humane thing" by spreading his convictions. Yale professor Irving Fisher concurred, applauding the doctor's stand on "the defective baby questions" and noting that "the custom you started will do good." Well-known Washington, DC, theater man Aaron Brylawski wrote Haiselden directly: "Your decision is appreciated by everyone who has had experience in defective cases. I don't believe you will find one among those who have criticized you that would undertake the burden of raising such a child." M. E. Mazur, general manager of the Sherriot Pictures Corporation of Chicago (which served as distributor of the film), claimed that since it was self-evident that moral and mental malformations "should not form a part of human existence," *The Black Stork* was actually "a living document calculated to teach as great a lesson as that preached in the churches—moral cleanliness."[6] Even trade publications such as *Motion Picture News* insisted that the film contained "nothing objectionable" and would, in fact, "serve to open the eyes of the general public to harsh realities."[7]

Although business on the film was strong in large cities throughout the country, it was especially brisk in Cleveland, Cincinnati, and Chicago, where Dr. Haiselden often appeared beforehand to deliver a ten-minute address in which he told of the "abuses" he was seeking to correct and "show[ed] how heredity will affect the nation in the present day crisis." He professed that he had seen more than two hundred men and women "herded together, rushing for marriage licenses." Yet many of them were evidently suffering from "dissipation and various resulting diseases" and would surely go on to infect their wives and to "propagate tainted and deformed children, who will be a burden to a nation about to undergo the hardships of war."[8] That, he suggested, was the best argument for the measures he so strongly advocated.

In a reflection of the eugenic marriage laws that were passed in 1918 and that the film helped to promote, *The Black Stork* was retitled and exhibited as *Are You Fit to Marry?* And in 1927, it was rereleased, in an expanded version, under that later title—although the Whartons' name was unaccountably omitted from the credits. The expanded version (which survives only in a corrupted form) preserved the original film but created a kind of frame around it, with a prologue and epilogue in which the fictitious Professor Robert Worth, an "eminent writer and authority on heredity," tries to persuade his future son-in-law Jack Gaynor of the necessity of premarital testing by telling him the story of his "chum," Claude Leffingwell. Even though Worth uses the example of thoroughbred horses and cattle to illustrate the merits of selective breeding—a practice that he contends ensures health, fine form, and promise—Gaynor resists. But after hearing the cautionary tale of Leffingwell, the young man complies in order to avoid a similar tragedy.[9]

Ted Wharton defended the original picture, saying that it "deals with a most remarkable subject—eugenics—a vital issue to every thinking man and woman. The subject is handled in a masterful way and with such a cast the feature is certain to cause a stir in filmdom when it is released."[10] And cause a stir it did, igniting a national debate that continued for years. Many prominent early twentieth-century Americans supported Haiselden's position, including renowned lawyer Clarence Darrow, Baltimore's Cardinal James Gibbons, and, perhaps most curious of all, disability advocate Helen Keller. Major newspapers and other publications offered Haiselden their editorial endorsement, among them the *Herald*, the *Tribune*, and the *American* in Chicago; the *News* and the *Free Press* in Detroit; the *Baltimore American*; the *Philadelphia Ledger*; the *New York American*; the *Washington Herald*; and the *New Republic*. Not surprisingly, a number of those papers were part of the holdings of Hearst, whose International Film Service had financed *The Black Stork*'s production.

In addition to its central premise that it is necessary, even laudable, to ensure the integrity of society by terminating the lives of "defectives," the film drew a further direct and unfortunate link between hereditary defects and ethnicity, class, and race. In the original version of the film, it was Claude's grandfather's liaison with a slave (played by Wharton regular Frances White)—"a vile filthy creature who was suffering from a loathsome disease"—that originated the "tainted blood" that Claude's infant son inherits. The grandfather's ghost, his face a gruesome "mass of sores" contracted from his intimate contact with the diseased slave, was evoked through flashbacks created by clever use of backlighting and superimposition, which generated an eerie double exposure.[11] That same special effect was used just as effectively near the end of the picture, to depict the hapless child being taken into the embrace of a waiting Jesus. Those two scenes—of the libidinous

FIGURE 12.2 Ted Wharton directing a scene showing disabled youngsters in the eugenics film *The Black Stork*.

progenitor and the sinless savior—served as bookend shots that implied that God's grace can redeem the original "sin" and right the social order.

As Martin Pernick observed, "The film industry, still reeling from the massive protests triggered by D. W. Griffith's offensive portrayal of blacks in *Birth of a Nation* [1915], demanded this [the depiction of sex with a slave woman] be deleted." Movie trade spokesmen feared that any mention of race could be inflammatory, while any depiction of miscegenation would outrage southern whites.[12] *Moving Picture World* similarly argued that "show[ing] the source of the stain to be a black woman . . . means [that] the contamination is of a double character."[13] And indeed, probably as a concession to reviewers or censors, the scene was later reshot using a white servant girl rather than a black slave. Nevertheless, as Pernick concluded, "The studio that produced *The Black Stork* was no stranger to racial fear-mongering; in fact, it was simultaneously shooting the notorious Hearst serial *Patria*, utilizing some of the same cast for both pictures."[14]

By the 1910s, eugenics films had become a familiar genre. Exploring themes similar to those in the Wharton production, pictures such as *Damaged Goods* (1914) and *S.O.S.: A Message to Humanity* (1917) proposed eugenics as a solution to cases of congenital syphilis, while *Parentage* (1917) touted the benefits of premarital medical examinations as an antidote to potential genetic problems. *Where Are My Children?* (1916) and *The Hand That Rocks the Cradle* (1917) offered eugenic arguments in favor of contraception. And features such as *For Those Unborn* (1914) and *Married in Name Only* (1917) championed selective marriage restrictions on the grounds of eugenics.[15] The eugenics films, moreover, spawned a related genre of anti-eugenics films, among them the fourteen-episode serial *The Red Circle* (1915), which countered Haiselden's radicalism by featuring a woman whose inherited tendencies are overcome by a good environment, and *The Regeneration of Margaret* (1916), in which a baby girl abandoned by one doctor and raised by another grows up to be a nurse. Of the films, especially the feature films, that tackled the eugenics issue, however, *The Black Stork* was one of the earliest and likely the most memorable; and it is one of the few to survive, albeit only in its later version.

The Great White Trail

The first new Wharton production of 1917, *The Great White Trail*, was less controversial than *The Black Stork*, though its subplot of white slavery and prostitution also elicited some concerns. With a working title of "A Tragedy of the Snows," the film, Aaron Pichel observed, was a "complex melodrama set during the excitement of the 1898 Klondike Gold Rush in the Yukon."[16] Originally released in eight reels and subtitled "An Epic of the Arctic," the "super-feature" was promoted as a sentimental family affair in which a man, his wife, and their child are torn apart by a misunderstanding and then estranged for fourteen years. Directed by the Whartons and assistant-directed by James Gordon, the film was written by Leo Wharton and Gardner Hunting, the head of the Whartons' scenario department (and later manager of Cayuga Pictures, the company that leased the Renwick Park studio after the brothers' forced bankruptcy in 1919).[17] Doris Kenyon, a singer and popular silent film actress (and future wife of *Patria* star Milton Sills), Paul Gordon, and Thomas Holding played the starring roles. Featured were Ithacans and Wharton regulars Dick Bennard, F. W. Stewart, Bessie Wharton, and Louise Hotaling, along with Hans Roberts and Edgar L. Davenport.

As the film opens, Prudence (Kenyon) and George Ware (Gordon) enjoy a comfortable life in their well-appointed home, where they are seen doting on their adorable infant daughter. But after George discovers a note from a man written in secret to Prudence—and after he spies that same mysterious man escaping through the window of her bedroom—he experiences what *Billboard* called "an asinine bit of jealousy."[18] Accusing his wife of infidelity, he denies the paternity of her "brat" and expels both of them from his home. Later, he is ashamed to learn that Prudence's clandestine meeting was not with a lover but rather with her brother, Charles Carrington, who had come to her in humiliation seeking a loan of money so that he could reimburse George for some bad investments he had made on his behalf. By then, though, Prudence has lost her senses over her husband's rejection and her subsequent impoverishment, a madness that is illustrated in a series of very effective double exposures that contrast her happy former life with her current desperation. One afternoon, she runs away with the baby, whom she hides in an old tree stump. When she returns, the baby is gone, carried away by a dog to the home of her former suitor Reverend Arthur Dean (Holding) and his mother (Bessie Wharton), who raise "little Marie" as a member of their own family.

More than thirteen years pass. Prudence, now a hardworking nurse living under the surname "Martling," decides to venture to Alaska. There, she believes, she can escape the painful memories of her lost child by bringing solace and comfort to others. Unknown to her, traveling north on the same ship is Reverend Dean, who, according to the intertitle, has experienced a similar calling to "seek fields of greater activity."

After discovering his wife's whereabouts, a remorseful George follows her north to beg forgiveness. But soon after his arrival in Alaska, he is struck and robbed by an unscrupulous local known as "the Vulture." The amnesia George suffers as a result of the Vulture's blow renders him a "mental derelict." A series of coincidences ensues, as Prudence, George, and Reverend Dean keep crossing paths, quite literally, and often saving each other from further harm at the Vulture's hands. Their intersections only increase after the Reverend's mother dies and his adopted sister Marie (the Wares' lost daughter) travels to Alaska to be with him.

Suddenly rich from the money he stole from George, the Vulture continues his predations, most notably when he kidnaps the newly arrived Marie and attempts to sell her into prostitution at the local saloon. But she is rescued by Prudence, who realizes that the girl is her beloved long-lost child. Both, in turn, are later rescued by George, who engages in a fight during which the Vulture is killed. During that fight, after sustaining a blow identical to the one that injured him in the first place, George regains his memory. In a poignant scene toward the end of the film, as Prudence and Marie tend to his injuries, the estranged husband and wife finally recognize each other.

The film's controlling motif and the device that precipitates the reunion is a pair of Marie's baby shoes. In the opening scenes, Prudence and George

FIGURE 12.3   In *The Great White Trail*, the villainous "Vulture" tries to kidnap young Marie and sell her into prostitution at the local saloon.

lovingly inscribe those shoes with the sweet sentiments "Mother's Darling" and "Papa's Dumpling." After Prudence flees with the baby, George finds one of the shoes left behind in the crib. For the next fourteen years, he clings to it, as a symbol of his hasty misjudgment in the past and as a promise of his hope for the future. Marie, who was wearing the other shoe when she was brought to the Dean home, treasures it because it is her only link to the parents she never knew. When Marie brings that shoe with her to Alaska, Prudence recognizes it—and consequently recognizes her daughter. Thus begins the reconciliation of the lost family. And when George reveals the mate to the precious shoe, that reconciliation is complete. In a kind of Cinderella moment, as the two shoes are once again paired, the estranged family is finally, and happily, reunited.[19]

The sentimental main plot was augmented by an amusing comic subplot, in which young Jimmie (Bennard), the butcher's boy who delivers groceries to Reverend Dean's home, becomes infatuated with Marie. After giving her a litter of puppies and a boxful of baby chicks as tokens of his affection, he makes an even more dramatic gesture: he pledges to follow her to Alaska.

Unable to afford the fare, he stows away on the ship on which she is traveling. But after being discovered, he is kicked off at the first northern stop, forcing him to make the rest of the hazardous Yukon journey on foot. In the final scene, unaware that by then the Ware family has left Alaska, he sets out on the Great White Trail in the hope of being reunited with Marie.

A second more serious and even more timely subplot concerned the kidnapping and intended forced prostitution of young Marie, who, recently orphaned by the death of her foster mother and bereft of parental protection, is susceptible to the predations of villains such as the Vulture and his associates. The sex-and-slavery theme, introduced earlier by the Whartons in an episode of their *Exploits of Elaine*, had become increasingly common in serials and feature films, going back to the widely viewed and widely imitated *The Traffic in Souls* (1913), one of many "white slave" or vice pictures that sparked controversy and nationwide panic over the safety of young girls, especially those who were leaving their homes and rural surroundings for better opportunities in the big cities. Those pictures often had conflicting purposes. On the one hand, they served as a response to progressive sentiments that prompted movie producers to take up current social problems in their pictures and give "movies better reason than ever to warn girls against the lures of the city."[20] But, at the same time, they sensationalized the very vices against which they railed by including scenes inside brothels, gambling halls, and other disreputable establishments to pique the curiosities of moviegoers and arouse their prurient interests, which in turn led to bigger ticket sales at the box office. According to Shelley Stamp, the distillation and negotiation of such unsettling aspects of prewar culture revealed a great deal about the new role that socially conscious films were playing in urban culture "and about the struggle over motion picture exhibition in cities across the country as film became the nation's premiere entertainment form."[21]

By the time that the Whartons incorporated the subplot into their film, white slavery was no longer the source of the widespread hysteria that had swept the country just a few years earlier. But their inclusion of the theme reflected their recognition of the pervasive social anxiety felt by men and women alike about "the consequences of woman's emancipation and independence in the heterosocial public sphere."[22] It also showed the tension in their own filmmaking: the conflict between their desire to attract attention by courting controversy as a way of playing on audience interests and their simultaneous attempt to downplay controversy to avoid censorship, which was becoming a growing threat to all filmmakers in the transitional era as cinema's social function was being reframed.

In an interview with *Motography*, Ted Wharton—who had set *Into the North*, one of his early pictures for Essanay, in the Northwest Territory—extolled the merits of the film and observed that he and Leo liked to include a lot of "little touches" of history or geography to educate as well as entertain moviegoers. That did not mean turning their "super-features" into "news pictorials" but rather "injecting into the action an atmosphere which is away from the ordinary and yet which sticks to the facts." In *The Great White Trail*, one of those touches was a scene that showed the method that the miners used to get their heavy packs over the road by carrying some of them up the hill and then sliding "like schoolboys" back to the bottom, to repeat the process all over again with the rest. According to Ted, that scene "made a good bit of action for the picture, but it also told a story of the gold rush that is not generally known."[23]

New Challenges

The typically snowy town of Ithaca seemed an ideal place to shoot the Alaskan adventure. But the relatively snow-free winter of 1917 forced the Whartons to seek a different filming locale. Consequently, as the *Ithaca Journal* reported, in early March, Leo and several members of his company headed to Saranac Lake, New York, where they established themselves at the camp of "Caribou Bill," a former employee of the Whartons who provided them with "a complete arctic village" to be used in the picture.[24] That village (called "Arctic City"), a permanent filming location that Bill rented out to Eastern movie companies, contained every accessory and property needed to create "Far North" scenes, including a dance hall, mining office, gambling hall, church, and hotel. Even malamute dogs, specially bred and trained for dog-sledding, were available for hire.[25]

Additional scenes featuring Kenyon were filmed at Lake Placid, while James Gordon took other members of the company to several sites closer to Ithaca, in Ludlowville, Enfield, and Taughannock Falls.[26] The undertaking was considerable and costly. One scene alone, filmed at the entrance to the Enfield Falls gorge, required 142 extras, some of them Cornell students, to play Gold Rush miners crossing Chilkoot Pass. According to the *Ithaca Daily News*, "The big crowd was transported to and from the city in automobiles and carry-alls," and the Whartons, who had a reputation for treating their extras well, dispatched an automobile to bring 150 lunches to Enfield for their staff and for "the mob."[27]

Filming of the feature, though, was not without some personal incident. Mary L. "Mame" Hennessy, who played the madam in the Alaskan saloon and who appeared in numerous bit parts in other Ithaca productions, recalled that the building used for that set (created by the Whartons' longtime set designer Arch Chadwick) burned down in a real-life accident. Although no one was injured, destroyed in that blaze was Ted Wharton's wife's mink coat, which Hennessy had worn as her costume.[28]

The Alaskan scenes were quite convincing in their depiction of the challenges of everyday life in the rugged Klondike, from the rigors of dogsledding and snowshoeing to the hazards of hiking the Great White Trail. Just as effective, though, were several scenes earlier in the film that used matching shots and irises to build sympathy for the characters. For example, when the grief-stricken and half-mad Prudence believes herself to be in imminent danger, she flees into the woods and hides her baby, only to discover on her return that the baby has been stolen. Her sadness over her missing child is palpable, as the close-ups of her beautiful but cheerless face reveal. Prudence's sorrow is mirrored by the misery of her husband George when he realizes his grievous error and hasty misjudgment of her fidelity. Especially after George is brutally assaulted by the Vulture, his face, too, reads like a virtual map of the pains he has endured over the past fourteen years. When he is rescued by Reverend Dean, who nurses him back to health after the initial attack by the Vulture, and later by Prudence, who scares off the Gold Rushers who taunt him and pelt him with snowballs, he demonstrates such sincere and unvarnished gratitude that it redeems his earlier unkindness. (The interrelationship among Prudence, George, and Dean was established as early as the opening shot, in which the two men stand at opposite sides of an oversize portrait of Prudence, which suddenly comes to life.)

Matching shots also evoked the parallels between Prudence and Dean. Each is filmed, separately, standing on the deck of the northbound steamer, seeking fresh hope and redemption—seemingly two strangers, unaware of just how closely their fates are actually intertwined. They are filmed again as they simultaneously leave their respective Alaskan boardinghouses, to embark on the same arduous journey along the Great White Trail, and again, in the Klondike, as they pass only minutes apart, after Prudence leaves the cabin of an injured man she has nursed and Dean arrives to minister to his spirit.[29]

Among the best and most sophisticated effects were the flashback sequences, expertly shot by cinematographers Levi Bacon and Ray June. Evicted from her home, the paternity of her baby denied, Prudence is haunted by visions of her once-happy family and of George's angry recriminations and baseless accusations. Later, on board the steamer, she has a similarly painful vision of her former life. Like the supernatural effects in the

Whartons' occult series *The Mysteries of Myra* and the resurrected ghost of the grandfather in *The Black Stork*, those poignant flashbacks were camera tricks created by superimposing images, resulting in a double exposure.

After the editing and titling of the film were completed at their Renwick Park studio, the Whartons organized a gala preview for potential exhibitors and buyers in New York City. For the big event, which was held on June 1, they rented the Broadway Theater, hired a full orchestra to accompany the screening, and personally hand-carried the finished print. As Aaron Pichel writes, "It was a big splash . . . and the brothers' emotions ran high."[30] Other prerelease screenings followed, including one less than two weeks later at the Crescent Theater in Ithaca.

Yet, while the Whartons promoted *The Great White Trail* as "one of the most elaborate pictures ever screened by any company,"[31] some early reviews were quick to note its faults. Although Kenyon was praised for her "dash, verve, and sparkle" and her dramatic ability and "rare courage,"[32] *Variety* observed that writer and producer Leo Wharton "must have thought that he was directing one of the serials for which the Wharton brothers were justly famous" because he "tried to deliver simply too much film in one order." Overly long, the film was "tiresome," with its thrills separated too widely by location shots of pretty snow scenes. A few changes, though—among them a substantial cutting of the "continual mushers passing over the Alaska trail," a retitling in a number of places, and a skillful editing for continuity—could, *Variety* believed, make the film a "corker."[33] *Moving Picture World* reviewer Edward Weitzel agreed that some tightening of the story was desirable, particularly so that the main characters do not simply "take turns at losing their wits." Moreover, he wrote, "certain fundamental laws of dramatic construction must be observed and the motives that actuate the characters must stand the test of being born of common sense." Weitzel concluded, however, that the photoplay is fairly well acted and the "general impression is favorable to the picture."[34] The Whartons took heed of some of the criticism and recut the picture, excising the equivalent of one of the original eight reels. But the film was still slowed by long and repetitive mushing scenes across the snow, which only confirmed the fact that "switching gears from producing serial movies was not as easy as anticipated" for the Whartons, who had not yet mastered the particular rhythm and pacing required in feature-length storytelling.[35]

To be sure, the Whartons hoped that *The Great White Trail*, the first film released under their new banner as independent producers, would be the start of many successes for them and for their studio. To that end, they tried to promote the film as extensively as possible, both locally and nationally, through newspapers and trade publications. Full-page advertisements of ambitious Gold Rushers braving the deep snows romanticized the challenges of taming the "unknown" and mysterious Yukon Territory. One ad even cleverly suggested that the wintry picture was ideal viewing on a warm summer's

FIGURE 12.4 In their advertisements for *The Great White Trail*, the Whartons emphasized their Ithaca connections.

day: "The Treat to Beat the Summer Heat."[36] But the promotional efforts fell disappointingly short of the massive publicity campaigns the brothers had enjoyed under Hearst, whose magazine and newspaper empire reached a far wider audience of readers, shaping their tastes and influencing their film choices. By contrast, the newly formed "Wharton Releasing" distribution company performed modestly, at best.

Of even greater concern were the operational changes that the Whartons were forced to enact following the termination of their long-standing affiliation with Hearst. As independent producers and marketers, they could no longer simply ship the final negatives and count on Pathé to do the rest, as they had done for the past few years. Film marketing and sales, they quickly discovered, were a "complex and costly part of the movie business." As Aaron Pichel writes, "What Hearst and Pathé once handled after the Whartons' cameras stopped cranking and editing was complete, now the Whartons had to arrange for themselves at their own expense."[37]

Distribution of *The Great White Trail*, they decided, would be handled largely on a state-rights basis. Although they retained the rights for the most lucrative market—the New York metropolitan area—for themselves, they contracted "for a very satisfactory sum" with M. H. Hoffman, giving his Hoffman-Foursquare Exchange all other exploitation rights. Hoffman, as *Moving Picture World* reported, in turn sold Canadian and Alaskan territorial rights to John C. Green, who acquired a "ton of advertising stuff" as part of the transaction and insisted that he would be "calling for three or four times as much" once the picture went into distribution through Regal Films of Toronto. Green's predictions proved correct: in November 1917, he reported that the picture had surpassed all previous attendance numbers at local theaters and "made the best record of any picture he [had] ever shown."[38] And indeed, wherever it played, *The Great White Trail* reportedly was well received, even if the revenue it ultimately generated was less than what Ted and Leo had hoped.[39]

Comic Relief

While their ambitious plan to produce and release one feature film each month was quickly scrapped, the brothers nonetheless proceeded with great optimism to explore new opportunities, one of which was a series of short comedies. Begun even as they were still filming their Arctic adventure, those comedies starred J. Edward ("Eddie") Vogt and featured several actors from *The Great White Trail*'s cast.[40] Vogt, a Brooklyn-born vaudevillian and comedian, had already appeared in a variety of comedy venues, among them the

Figure 12.5 Outdoor filming often presented numerous challenges. Pictured are Leo Wharton, John Holbrook, Robin Townley, Harry Smith, James Gordon, and Dick Bennard.

headline act of Field and Lewis, in which he performed in costume as the front part of a horse.[41]

The first of the comedies, *Below Zero* (completed in late May 1917, released the following July, and advertised in the trade papers alongside *The Great White Trail*), was a two-reel short based on a story by longtime Wharton associate Robin Townley. Directed by Leo Wharton and starring Vogt, it featured Dick Bennard, Harry Robinson, F. W. Stewart, Bessie Wharton, and Frances White. The *Library of Congress Catalogue of Copyright Entries* recorded other similar two-reel shorts that followed over the next few months in 1917–1918. Among them was *The Missionary* (advertised in late June for "early release"), which was written and directed by Ted Wharton and starred Bessie Wharton, Vogt, and White as well as Malcolm Head, Violet Palmer, Harry Robinson, Theodore Tweston, and Carolyn Lee, the comedienne who had provided many hearty laughs a year earlier in *The Lottery Man*.[42] Two other shorts, *Kute Kids vs. Kupid* and *April Fool*, based on stories by Leo Wharton, were directed by another Wharton associate, head cameraman John K. Holbrook. The latter involved a joke that Walter Halmer, a "young man about town," intends to play on his sweetheart, Elsie Milburn, on the eve of April Fools' Day; but instead he himself becomes the victim of a prank, a "stink pot" that results in his being ostracized by all his and Elsie's friends.[43] Another short, *The Candidate*, was directed by Robin Townley, who around the same time also wrote and directed *Marriage à la Mode*.[44]

Existing records show that on occasion the Whartons offered all six of the comedic pictures as a package to exhibitors, who found it a profitable practice to pair a comedy with a feature.[45] Such comic shorts had become increasingly popular with movie audiences, perhaps as a welcome and necessary palliative to the serious wartime concerns and preparedness propaganda. Not surprisingly, numerous studios, from Mack Sennett–Keystone to Fox Sunshine, produced similarly light fare, which was promoted as "a life preserver that saves a poor picture from giving your patrons a bad night."[46]

The comedies apparently inspired the Whartons to contemplate a new project that they believed would have an even wider appeal: the filming of the "Shoestring Charlie" circus adventure stories, originally published in 1916 in *Redbook* (then *Red Book*) magazine by Courtney Ryley Cooper, a fiction

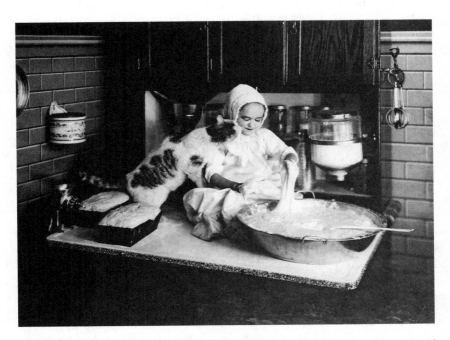

FIGURE 12.6 *Kute Kids vs. Kupid*, directed by head cameraman John K. Holbrook, was one of several short comedies that the Whartons produced in 1917–1918.

writer who was the head of the Wharton Studio's publicity and scenario departments and who later provided the novelization and print serialization of their serial *The Eagle's Eye*.[47] "Charlie" was a well-known circus character, and all the stories had "the atmosphere of the circus," a setting that seemed to engage moviegoers and that the Whartons had effectively employed in episodes of *Beatrice Fairfax* and *Wallingford*. To capitalize on the fascination stoked by such pictures as *Circus Mary*, *Polly of the Circus*, *Alice of the Sawdust*, *Peg o' the Ring*, and *Her Circus Knight* and to boost interest in their own production, they conceived a novel cross-promotion, in which they would not only film the stories but also persuade one of the big circuses to accompany the finished pictures across the country.[48] Interesting as that idea was, nothing ever came of it.

Around the same time, the brothers also became involved in the production of a six-reel feature *The Crusher*, which was filmed at their Renwick Park studio for the F. W. Stewart Company.[49] Produced by F. W. Stewart, John Holbrook, and Ted Wharton, the film was codirected by Stewart (who also assumed a minor acting role), Robin Townley, and the Whartons. It starred Derwent Hall Caine, son of the British novelist Hall Caine, and Valda Valkyrien (the stage name of the Icelandic-born Danish Baroness von Dewitz), a nineteen-year-old former ballerina with the Danish Royal Ballet and a renowned beauty.[50] Townley appeared as the "heavy"; Howard Cody (in blackface) as Big Little Jim, the "colored servant" of the "'darky' body servant" type; Harry Robinson as an old Virginia colonel; and Bessie Wharton as "a Virginia seeress" and one of the hostile plotters. A number of Ithacans also figured as supers.[51]

The *Ithaca Journal* observed that *The Crusher* (which is not extant) featured some of the finest photography ever seen in Ithaca; and it praised the excellent acting and the succession of strong, interest-sustaining scenes, including the sinking by a submarine of a transatlantic liner and a "real honest-to-goodness fight in a Chinatown 'hop joint'" (an establishment where opium is smoked), both of which were settings that the Whartons had used to good effect in earlier serials and short pictures. In the plot, which combined love and intrigue and anticipated elements of the Wharton patriotic serial *The Eagle's Eye*, ambitious young Virginian Arthur Morgan is working on a submarine engine that he hopes will revolutionize undersea science. But, beset by the financial troubles of his family and tired of life on the farm, he goes to New York City, where he falls in with a group of alien spies who conspire to acquire his invention (a plot point similar to the theft of Kennedy's model torpedo in *The Exploits of Elaine*). Fortunately, the fiancée whom he left behind in Virginia comes to his timely rescue.[52]

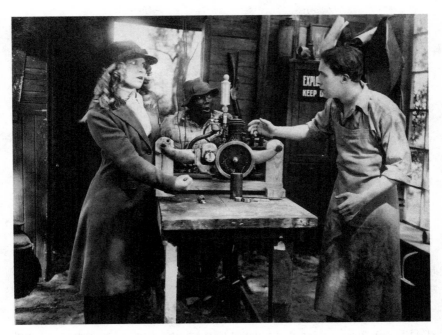

FIGURE 12.7 *The Crusher*, produced for the F. W. Stewart Company in 1917, was filmed at the Wharton Studio in Renwick Park.

The film's theme was certainly unique. According to the *Ithaca Journal*, it drew on the process of extracting gold from quartz: Arthur Morgan was the quartz; New York City was "The Crusher"; and the fiancée was the amalgam that extracts the gold from quartz and makes it of value. But perhaps the best part of the film, the paper suggested, was the fact that moviegoers would recognize many of their Ithaca friends and some of the beautiful scenery in and about the town.[53]

Pressures Mount

The Crusher was the only film made by the F. W. Stewart Film Company. But the Whartons' involvement in that production and in the Eddie Vogt comedies—and not exclusively in their own features or serials, as they had earlier announced—hinted at the financial problems that were becoming increasingly evident. Over the next two years, in fact, the studio would face debts that required several financial reorganizations to forestall bankruptcy (including a "chattel mortgage" secured by loans in the form of notes from a number of Ithacans and overseen by attorney Howard Cobb, with Jacob

Rothschild as trustee)[54] and that would dim, and ultimately extinguish, their hopes for long-term success in the industry.

In hindsight, those concerns were already apparent as early as January 1917, the month before the official split with Hearst and his International Film Service, which closed not long afterward. In previous years, even as the Whartons were at work on a picture, they enthusiastically discussed their forthcoming projects, and the daily and trade papers abounded with titles of pictures that they were preparing to film. But, as the *Ithaca Journal* reported on January 11, while the Whartons predicted that the year ahead would be the busiest ever for their studio, they offered few specifics.[55] Even after returning from Los Angeles, where they were completing the filming of *Patria*, "Mr. [Leo] Wharton," the paper noted, "is still not ready to announce future plans."[56]

Yet, while there were no firm plans to announce, other significant changes were already afoot for the filmmakers. In mid-January, the Whartons' brother-in-law and investor J. Whitworth Buck, who had served for two years as general manager, secretary, and treasurer, quit the company. After acclaiming a "Bright Future" for the Whartons' enterprise, Buck—who reportedly had "always had harmonious relations with the Whartons and [had] won many friends with his unfailing courtesy"—sold his stock to Ted and Leo and left Ithaca to go into business for himself in New York City.[57] His departure, while a wise move for him personally, was a keen loss to the brothers, who relied on his business acumen and family loyalty; and it was clearly a sign of their impending troubles. As Aaron Pichel observed, Buck had a close working knowledge of the company's books and a good understanding of the business, and, unlike Ted and Leo, neither of whom was particularly adept with finances, he surely "saw the writing on the wall."[58]

Meanwhile, the Whartons—still engaged, albeit less directly, in the completion of the final episodes of *Patria*, which by then was under the immediate direction of Jacques Jaccard in Los Angeles—became involved in an industry-wide action against new censorship legislation and film taxes. As members of the National Association of the Motion Picture Industry (NAMPI, the predecessor of the Motion Picture Producers and Distributors of America), they responded to an urgent telegram from D. W. Griffith and traveled to New York City to participate in an important meeting to protest the subjecting of movies to a state tax that would assess the cost of producing films rather than the profits from them and to raise funds to combat the unfair and discriminating legislation. To the *Ithaca Journal*, the Whartons confirmed that they were definitely opposed to the imposition of such taxes as well as to state boards of censorship, particularly since NAMPI had already established standards that most producers were voluntarily observing.[59] Their position seemed consistent with that of many in the industry, especially Marcus Loew, operator of one of the largest chains of theaters, who explained that he did not condone state censorship because "Every exhibitor should be his own censor."[60] Accordingly, when the Whartons returned the following week from New York, they announced a specific plan to set up their own censorship of their films—though, in truth, they continued to be as likely to court controversy as to avoid it.[61]

A few weeks later, Ted Wharton traveled again to New York City, this time to testify at a legislative committee on the issue of production costs, which he alleged were out of proportion to profits.[62] Like other witnesses before the committee, he had been given a "quiz sheet" with a variety of questions on which he was expected to report. In response to one of those questions, he testified that the net profits of Wharton Inc. for the year that ended on December 31, 1916, had been $45,229, most of it earned because the Whartons were contracting producers on the serials *The Mysteries of Myra*, *Beatrice Fairfax*, and *Patria*. To a question regarding his belief about prevailing conditions, he replied that the industry was definitely "financially weaker" than it had been for some time, and he reiterated his concern over the disproportionally high production costs that were driving many competitors out of the business. Even the International Film Service, he alleged (no doubt with some bitter feelings toward his former backer), had not been successful the previous year. In describing the kinds of challenges that he and other filmmakers faced in calculating costs to accommodate for unforeseen circumstances, Ted gave as an example the need to rebuild a whole town and to hire five hundred extras for his recent production *Patria* because the film exposed on the town's destruction the first time had been defective. Other witnesses that day corroborated his impressions of the difficulty producers faced, especially with "censorship, licenses, fire laws, and all manner of things."[63]

The difficulties for the Whartons, however, were just beginning.[64] Almost immediately after the critical announcement that they would cease acting as contracting producers and instead proceed exclusively as independent producers and marketers, they established their own distribution company, which they insisted had been formed without any outside capital (though the actual source of their funding is unclear). According to Ted, that company, Wharton Releasing, had already developed working connections with other film interests, which seemed to bode well for the future. But new financial problems soon arose, and the company's independence proved short-lived: before the year's end, it requested and received authorization to increase its capital stock with a sale of three thousand shares at fifty dollars each. Reportedly, the initiative, supported by existing stockholders Ted Wharton and attorneys Howard Cobb and A. W. Feinberg, would allow the filmmakers to operate on a larger scale. More likely, it was another unsuccessful attempt simply to stay solvent.

Replacing Buck as the new general manager of the Wharton studio was R. H. Hadfield of Chicago, who had worked on the production of *The Black Stork* (and later served as the film's Chicago distributor) and who was said to be well known in Ithaca.[65] But Hadfield's appointment was not the only news. The brothers also announced ambitious plans for new features: three tales from *The Arabian Nights* (*Aladdin and the Wonderful Lamp*, *Ali Baba*, and *The Fisherman and the Genji*),[66] each of which they claimed would cost $50,000 to $75,000 to produce and all of which would be released on a state-rights basis for local agents to purchase and then to exploit in their assigned territories. Other forthcoming Wharton productions, they said, would include *Red Robin*, an "amazing story of a secondary personality" by popular novelist Fred Jackson, and *The Burma Pearl* (both of which had originally been announced more than a year earlier but never begun), along with *The Pseudo-Prince* and an as-yet untitled serial. And several "Five to Ten Reel productions from well-known books and plays interpreted by prominent screen and stage stars, not merely supervised but "personally directed by Leopold and Theodore Wharton," would be announced "later."[67]

From Bad to Worse

The *Ithaca Journal*, too, reported on the Whartons' upcoming program of films, promising that it would be "versatile" and that director James Gordon would have a major involvement in it. But, in fact, Gordon resigned from the Wharton enterprise just two months later,[68] and the only evidence of film activity at the studio was the ongoing work on *The Great White Trail*, which ultimately proved to be the sole film of consequence that the Whartons completed that year. Over the next few months, as financial concerns became even more pressing and bankruptcy seemed imminent, the Whartons were forced back into contracting production work. They also started renting studio space to other companies, such as the En L'Air Cinema, which produced the aviation adventure and spy story *A Romance of the Air* (1917), suggested by the book *En L'Air* by Lieutenant Bert Hall, who also starred in the picture. The studio was also leased to the Metro Film Corporation, which shot *The Adopted Son* (1917) with former Wharton stars Francis X. Bushman and Beverly Bayne, and to the Norma Talmadge Film Corporation, which filmed *The Secret of the Storm Country* (1917), based on a story of life around Cayuga Lake by Ithaca native Grace Miller White.

The war further exacerbated the Whartons' problems. Production costs increased and movie attendance declined. In addition to the loss of several members of their company who had been called up for service, their films were subject to the imposition of war taxes; and, like their fellow producers, the Whartons received appeals from certain government agencies to refrain from the manufacture of any pictures that might be perceived as being anti-war. NAMPI responded to the appeals by forming a "War Co-operation Committee," which consisted of an executive committee as well as a committee of the whole, to which Leo Wharton was appointed. Among other actions, the War Co-operation Committee took out full-page ads in publications such as *Motion Picture News* to announce that it would "work in conjunction with George Creel [the head of the Committee on Public Information] and other heads of government's [sic] departments to arouse America's patriotism through films, and whose second duty [would be] to stifle poisonous German propaganda in neutral countries."[69]

An even more direct appeal was issued by President Wilson. In a letter to William A. Brady, president of NAMPI, Wilson observed that the film industry, by offering the most effective contact with the nation's needs, had "come to rank as the very high medium for the dissemination of public intelligence, and since it speaks a universal language it lends itself importantly to the presentation of America's plans and purposes"; he also praised the industry's "patriotic service." Brady had replied that "the devoted men and women of the motion picture world had already shown their eager loyalty to the country's cause"[70] and would continue to do so, a pledge that Ted Wharton explicitly stated his company would honor.[71] As late as November, returning from a NAMPI conference attended by more than thirty producers including Brady, Carl Anderson, and Samuel Goldfish (later Goldwyn), Ted reaffirmed his pledge to suppress photoplays contrary to the aims of the United States in wartime.[72]

In the autumn of 1917, the Whartons—in the wake of another reorganization to save the company from bankruptcy—joined thirteen other well-known independent producers who merged interests in a body incorporated in New York State under the title of "The Producers' Protective Association Inc." As one of the officers, Ted helped to define guidelines for systematizing the association's business, especially in relation to state-rights production and distribution.[73] Association president William I. Sherrill described the group's purpose: "We intend encouraging the states rights buyer to assist him in the operation of a legitimate business"; and he stipulated that "where any given territory is without any buyer with whom we can deal we intend ultimately to open our own producers' exchange in that territory."[74] The association, which included W. R. Rothacker and the Frohman Amusement Corporation, expected to grow and to be joined by other state-rights producers.

By then, though, it was already a matter of too little, too late for the Whartons. Their business was clearly suffering, their financial problems steadily increasing, and their bright hope for a million-dollar expansion of their studio frustrated. Without Hearst's money backing their productions, the entire studio and salary costs had fallen squarely on their own shoulders. Already overextended, they had few resources on which to draw. Without Hearst's publicity machine supporting their pictures and seeding the Hearst papers and magazine publications with positive reviews, promotion was difficult and costly. And without Hearst's International Film Service as distributor of their pictures, the brothers found few alternative sources apart from state-righting, which afforded them at best a slim margin of profit.

It seemed that the Whartons had exhausted all their options.

CHAPTER 13

Staring into *The Eagle's Eye*

Despite serious financial woes and impending bankruptcy, the Whartons pressed forward with a new serial. Using the profits from their feature *The Great White Trail*, they entered into a contract with the recently retired chief of the United States Secret Service William J. Flynn and, with much ado, began making preparations for the filming of a multipart patriotic picture, *The Eagle's Eye* (the Secret Service's nickname for itself).[1] Their first serial production since the Hearst-backed *Patria*, it had a similarly nationalistic theme, and it would, they believed, restore them to prominence and solvency.

Whereas *Patria* indulged Hearst's conspiracy theories about a Mexican-Japanese alliance intent on invading the United States at its western border, *The Eagle's Eye* was based on actual German spy plots that Flynn had discovered and thwarted.[2] Written by Flynn and his staff, it was arranged for the screen by scenarist and fiction writer Courtney Ryley Cooper, who also provided a later novelization and print serialization of the episodes. "For obvious reasons," the *Ithaca Journal* noted, "the methods of the secret service in frustrating the enemy's plans and averting the disaster which might have crippled the country had these plans been consummated are fictionized, and imaginary characters and situations have been introduced to sustain the romantic and sentimental interest of the drama."[3]

Still, *The Eagle's Eye* (which is not extant) claimed to be "the true story of the machinations of Germany, the intrigues, the plots, the counter-plots and the devilish ingenuity by which the German government, through its American officials, spies and ploters [*sic*], sought to put America into a position where it would be helpless under the mailed fist of kaiserdom," with "famous Imperial German agents shown doing the very reprehensible acts they were detected of doing by secret agents of this government."[4] The objectives of the serial were therefore many-fold: to aid the government in the fight against Germany, to muster support for the fighting men, and to explain the reason for the purchase of Liberty loans and bonds. (Each episode included a bond trailer.)[5] Flynn predicted that after seeing the serial, only the "mighty poor American" would be unwilling to jump with every possible strength into the winning of the war. Ted heartily agreed, adding that he had seen a good number of serials, including those he himself had made, but all of them were imaginary. "Beside the truth of the German espionage and plotting system in this country" revealed in *The Eagle's Eye*, those other serials "are nothing."[6]

The story centered on the Criminology Club of New York City, whose president, Harrison Grant, volunteers the assistance of his members to the Secret Service in order to foil the operations of the Germans working undercover to undermine the safety and security of the United States, an offer that Chief Flynn (impressively played by Flynn himself) accepts. Flynn's investigation soon reveals that the master spy in the intrigue is Count Johann Heinrich von Bernstorff, German politician and ambassador to the United States from 1908 to 1917, whose coconspirators include several other high-ranking Germans: statesman and diplomat Franz von Papen, embassy naval attaché Karl Boy-Ed, civil servant and commercial attaché Dr. Heinrich Albert, and New York-based agent Heinrich von Lertz.

Released in twenty weekly episodes beginning March 27, 1918, *The Eagle's Eye* was directed by former actor and prominent silent-era film director George A. Lessey and British-born actor Wellington Playter, who had earlier appeared in several episodes of the Wharton serial *Beatrice Fairfax*. Cast in the lead role of Harrison Grant was international film star King Baggot, known as "King of the Movies." Baggot had returned to act in the picture after a self-imposed retirement of one year not only because he was a personal friend of Chief Flynn but also because he could not resist the story. "My greatest admiration," he affirmed, "has always been for the secret service."[7]

Playing opposite Baggot as Dixie Mason of the Secret Service (changed from "Betty Lee" in the original script, the first episode of which appears in full in the appendix) was former child actress Marguerite Snow, then-wife of Famous Players–Lasky director and former actor James Cruze. The daughter

HARRISON GRANT AND SECRET SERVICE OPERATIVES LEARN
THAT DISLOYALTY EXISTS IN A FIFTH AVENUE N. Y. MANSION

FIGURE 13.1   Criminology Club president Harrison Grant (King Baggot) offers the services of his members to aid the Secret Service in foiling German spy operations in the U.S.

of a vaudeville minstrel comedian, Snow had appeared on Broadway and in several traveling theater stock companies before being discovered, quite accidentally, by a studio head at Thanhouser while she was visiting a girl-friend on the set of a film. Given their experience and their screen appeal, "the Snow-Baggot combination," predicted the *Ithaca Journal*, "will be a strong one."[8] Also cast in the serial were William Bailey, who had been part of the Wharton company in its early years, along with Florence Short, Bertram Marburgh, Paul Everton, John W. Wade, and Fred Jones. Appearing in minor roles were Wharton regulars Bessie Wharton, Robin Townley, Frances White, and F. W. Stewart. Reportedly, great care had been taken to select actors who bore a resemblance to the real-life German officers and agents, with the government providing photographs to help ensure as much authenticity as possible.[9]

Filming *The Eagle's Eye*

The first episode of *The Eagle's Eye* revealed the German conspiracies to prevent shipments to the Allies and the plot to destroy the *Lusitania*, a British ocean liner that was sunk by a German submarine on May 7, 1915, an incident central to the earlier Wharton serial *The Romance of Elaine*. According to one reviewer, "the excellent picturization of that ghastly affair held everyone breathless, for one seemed to actually be on that ill-fated vessel, and, as the torpedo approached it, one involuntarily shuddered with fear."[10] (Unlike other episodes of the serial that integrated actual newsreel footage, the *Lusitania* scenes were filmed on Cayuga Lake, with rowboats cleverly reconstructed to replicate both the submarine and the vessel involved in the incident.)[11] A particularly startling detail was the close-up and intertitle translation of a medal that had been cast and distributed in Germany to commemorate that "victory" two days before it actually occurred.[12]

Subsequent episodes exposed other sensational German plots of "alien-spy outlawry,"[13] including an attempt to blow up the Ansonia Hotel in New York City, the site of an elaborate naval ball that concluded President Wilson's review of the Atlantic fleet, which was prevented by Flynn and his assistants ("The Naval Ball Conspiracy"), and a spectacular near-successful torpedo attack on the flagship of the U.S. Navy in New York Harbor that would have blocked the channel and bottled up the rest of the fleet ("The Plot against the Fleet"). But that danger is averted at the eleventh hour, when the wireless controller regulating the torpedo launched from Staten Island is reversed by the joint efforts of Grant's club members, the harbor police, and the men of the Secret Service, who overpower the plotters.[14] A plan by German spies to destroy large numbers of horses and motor ambulances to be shipped to Europe ("Von Rintelin, the Destroyer") is similarly frustrated. All these early episodes, reviewers noted, "are simply great and will do much to educate America as to the intrigues and despicable ramifications of Imperial Germany's spy system," whose authenticity, endorsed by Chief Flynn, could not be doubted.[15]

Each succeeding episode created suspense, added to the mounting intrigue, and provided "a splendid stimulus to patriotism and physical and financial support" of the government and its work in crushing the country guilty of these outrageous acts.[16] "The Brown Portfolio," for example, depicted the events that result when the Secret Service gains possession of the portfolio in which Dr. Heinrich Albert, German propaganda chief and spy, carries correspondence and reports from spies all over the country. The papers, which include plans for the purchase of controlling interests in the "aeroplane industry," document the methods used to direct ships to Germany by agreement with their captains and the schemes for stopping the exportation of liquid chlorine; and they also explain the scarcities of sugar, a result of the burning of the *Craigside*, a sugar ship that lost its entire cargo due to German firebombing. (In real life, Albert lost his portfolio on a Sixth Avenue elevated train—the same train that Leo Wharton used to shoot the scene.)[17] The faithfulness to detail in the filming of such scenes created enormous excitement, "the best part being that they are reproductions of real life."[18]

A similar attempt at verisimilitude was evident in a later episode, "The Kaiser's Death Messenger," which was based on the actual confession of Robert Fay to Chief Flynn. Fay, who came to the United States as the kaiser's "special envoy of death," brought with him plans for a bomb so powerful that it could blow apart the largest ship afloat. Its strange clockwork device fastened to the ship in such a way as to ensure that the movement of the rudder would wind the clockwork and explode the bomb. Fay intended to attach the device to a munitions ship in the harbor, in the hope that the bomb would go off later, once the ship was at sea. But he knew that even if detonated before leaving port, it would explode that ship's combustibles. The resulting wreckage would be spectacular—dwarfing the death and destruction in the "Halifax Explosion," a maritime disaster in Halifax, Nova Scotia, on December 6, 1917, that caused a French cargo ship, the SS *Mont Blanc*, to ignite her cargo of explosives, killing over two thousand people and injuring another nine thousand.[19]

Of course, in the serial, New York Harbor is saved from that dreaded fate, and the German denials of involvement in the affair are shown to be lies when it is revealed that both von Papen and Boy-Ed aided Fay, while Bernstorff too was fully cognizant of the nefarious scheme. To add further realism to the scene, Flynn reportedly made an arrangement with the Secret Service to use the actual bomb case that Fay created in his boathouse in Weehawken, New Jersey. Such "thrills happen in plenty during the telling of the story," the *Ithaca Journal* stated, and gave "all of the Wharton actors plenty of opportunity for good work."[20]

In depicting the numerous German intrigues, the serial's chapters assumed a familiar pattern, with King Baggot chasing "a hundred or more aliens" through "The Plot against Organized Labor," "The Munitions Campaign," "The Invasion of Canada," "The Burning of Hopewell," "The Reign of Terror," "The Infantile Paralysis Epidemic," "The Campaign against Cotton," "The Raid of the U-53," "Germany's U-Base in America," "The Great Hindu Conspiracy," and "The Menace of the I.W.W." In fact, as Raymond William Stedman observed, "Evidently Baggot's adversaries left absolutely no stone, germ, or phobia unturned in attempting to destroy America."[21]

The Secret Service, which was instrumental in preventing the numerous attacks, had long fascinated filmmakers, as evidenced by such early shorts as *Secret Service Woman* (1909), *Secret Service* (1911), *Lieutenant Daring, R.N. and the Secret Service Agents* (1911), *Secret Service Sam* (1913), *A Debut in the*

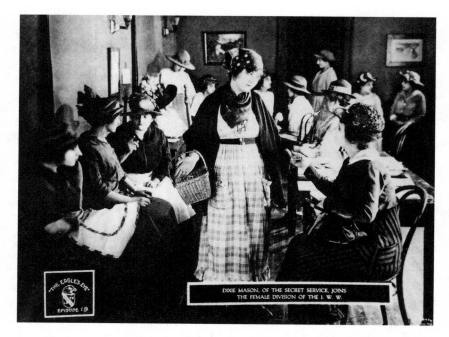

DIXIE MASON, OF THE SECRET SERVICE, JOINS
THE FEMALE DIVISION OF THE I. W. W.

FIGURE 13.2   Dixie Mason (Marguerite Snow) infiltrates the I.W.W. labor union in order to uncover German conspiracies.

Secret Service (1914), *Kate Waters of the Secret Service* (1914), *Secret Service Snitz* (1914), and *The Long Arm of the Secret Service* (1915). And it had figured in several earlier Wharton productions as well, including Ted's early Essanay picture *The Eye That Never Sleeps* (1912) and episodes of *The New Exploits of Elaine*, *Beatrice Fairfax*, and *Patria*.

With the onset of war, however, the Secret Service's clandestine operations became a topic of even more intense popular and cinematic interest. The year 1917 alone saw the release of such films as Pathé's *The Hidden Hand*, written by *Exploits of Elaine* novelist Arthur Reeve and Charles Logue and starring Doris Kenyon, who had appeared in the Whartons' *The Great White Trail*; Astra Film's feature *Sylvia of the Secret Service*, starring Irene Castle, in which a secret agent tries to stop a group of German saboteurs from blowing up an ammunition dump in New York City; and the nine-episode IMP serial *The Perils of the Secret Service*. But, unlike *The Eagle's Eye*, none could claim to have the "personal sanction" of President Woodrow Wilson,[22] or to be drawn directly from the archives of former Secret Service chief Flynn—even if the serial's story lines admittedly were "not completely historical . . . and tempered with a touch of romance."[23]

Much of *The Eagle's Eye* was filmed at the Whartons' studio in Ithaca, where unusual security precautions were inaugurated to guard against harm or injury by anyone who might try to prevent or delay the production. Reportedly, guards patrolled the grounds day and night, and no one was permitted to enter the premises without a pass.[24] As with other Wharton films, large numbers of extras volunteered their services and came to Renwick Park ready to appear before the cameras. In keeping with the wartime effort, the *Ithaca Journal* announced that the former supers, now called "thrift-stampers," would receive their pay in thrift stamps, "a new way for the promotion of patriots in the studios of Wharton, Inc."[25]

Several scenes, though, were shot in locations outside Ithaca, secured only through Flynn's influence.[26] The Ansonia Naval Ball, for instance, was filmed in the actual ballroom of the Ansonia Hotel in New York City, where the Whartons' "electrical wizard" Leroy Baker arrived early, accompanied by cameraman John Holbrook and art designer E. Douglas Bingham, to make preparations for the photography and stage settings. Baker, who had the intricate task of wiring the huge room for brilliant illumination befitting such a grand cinematic event, succeeded admirably by utilizing lighting that amounted to "over 450,000 candle-power."[27] The effect was so extraordinary that even John McE. Bowman, president of the company operating the Ansonia, wrote to extend his praises of a production that would "bring the spectators from their seats into a loud declaration of loyalty for this great country."[28]

Baker also received much attention for another of his innovations: the discovery of a new method of manufacturing paper bullets that was said to revolutionize "the science of sham warfare" by making it possible to achieve realistic effects never before attained on film—effects that were vouched for by experts in the employ of the Remington Arms Company.[29] Doing "something he was told could not be done," Baker invented a rifle shell of mixed black and smokeless powder, "the two kinds of explosives being separated in bullet and shell containers, of hard paper." The result was a peculiar kind of combustion that caused the paper bullet to disappear entirely within a space of fifteen feet while the black powder created a highly credible smoke effect.[30] The new ammunition, which proved suitable for use in both rifles and machine guns, was soon copied by other filmmakers.

At times, the location shots presented some unpleasant surprises. As *Motion Picture News* reported, Leo "learned something of Uncle Sam's protective system" when he brought the entire company to the New York City steamer piers. Despite having the paperwork that permitted him to film at the site, he was approached by four different authorities demanding to see his credentials. Each authority in turn had to telephone his individual head-quarters for confirmation. It took fully three hours in subzero temperature, with gale force winds, before Leo was permitted to proceed with his work.[31] The experience, though, was just another reminder of the precautions that wartime filming demanded.

Promoting and Exhibiting *The Eagle's Eye*

Claiming that it was the Whartons' best work, Leo believed *The Eagle's Eye* would be "the greatest success of any serial we have produced."[32] And indeed, even before production was completed, the serial began generating excitement. In mid-December, M. H. Hoffman, whose Hoffmann-Foursquare Pictures served as its distributor, took to the road in order to visit exchanges "in every city of importance in the United States" to whet the interest of exhibitors. "There is every indication that nothing of a serial nature ever created even a fraction of the interest now being aroused by 'The Eagle's Eye,'" Hoffman boasted to *Motion Picture News*. And "in light of all that it is only natural that exhibitors from everywhere are eager to learn, by word of mouth, of the many important matters relating to the serial."[33]

Advance bookings seemed to confirm Hoffmann's confidence. By the end of December, Hoffmann-Foursquare reported receipt of an unprecedented number of booking applications, with "hosts of contracts being signed—even in advance of the trade showing."[34] And new applications kept pouring into branch exchanges across the country. Samuel Rubenstein, Hoffmann-Foursquare Boston manager, predicted that the volume of business in New England would likely surpass all previous booking records. Managers Frank J. Flaherty in Chicago and Sidney J. Baker in Saint Louis reported that exhibitors in their territories were "appreciative of the qualities of this serial" and enthusiastic to begin screening it. Hoffmann, too, while visiting exchanges in the Middle West, had found especially big demand in Detroit, Cincinnati, and Cleveland.[35]

In January 1918, early episodes were screened to the press, which gave it highly favorable coverage. Following a private exhibition in New York City, Frances Agnew in the *Morning Telegraph* wrote that the serial, directed by such "master directors of chapter pictures," was bound to win nationwide approbation.[36] "Hilliar," *Billboard*'s reviewer, affirmed that it was the first time he had heard applause from the blasé critics at a private showing of any motion picture.[37] And the *Ithaca Journal* pronounced the serial an "epochal success."[38]

But that approbation was not universal. Marcus Loew, prominent New York City moving picture theater magnate, refused to book the film into his movie houses on the grounds that it might offend his German patronage.[39] Although Loew's refusal caused a sensation in motion picture circles and throughout the metropolitan area, the Whartons claimed not to be worried and countered that they had already received numerous bookings from "patriotic theater owners."

The same week that Loew turned down the picture, *The Eagle's Eye* was shown at a private exhibition before the Committee on Public Information in Washington, where committee head George Creel and the senators, congressmen, and other attendees were unanimous in warm praise of the picture.[40] An exhibition was also held before the National Press Club at the Capitol, where the newspapermen overwhelmingly agreed that *The Eagle's Eye*, based as it was on fact, not fiction, "will be of vital historical importance."[41] Another special showing held later at the Hotel Biltmore—for the American Defense Society, the American Flag Association, the American Legion, the Colonial Dames of America, the Guardians of American Liberty, the Daughters and Sons of the American Revolution, and representatives of other patriotic societies of New York—elicited a similar reaction.[42] For that event, the *Ithaca Journal* reported, the Biltmore ballroom was crowded to capacity with eighteen hundred guests, while another thousand had to be turned away.[43] A special screening of the first three episodes in the lodge rooms of the New York metropolitan Masonic Lodges on West Twenty-Third Street likewise proved to be an "unqualified success"; and even the city's Paulist Fathers promised to turn the serial into "a regular attraction."[44]

Given the positive reception, the Whartons made plans to show all twenty episodes of the picture "in every town and city in the United States regardless of its alien population."[45] Underscoring the fact that nothing had yet been produced to equal the startling detail of *The Eagle's Eye*, they determined to mount a nationwide publicity campaign. Full-page advertisements with provocative teasers soon began appearing in the trade papers. One such teaser noted the presence of "furtive, non-uniformed armies whose weapons are spying, sabotage, bomb-planting, incendiarism, murder and a hundred forms of insidious and demoralizing propaganda" and asked "What are we going to do about it?"[46] Striking in their color and bold graphics, the ads emphasized the patriotic theme by picturing Flynn literally in the eye of an American eagle, designed and drawn by Cornell University professor Louis Agassiz Fuertes, a renowned bird artist who had appeared in Ted Wharton's early Ithaca pictures. Additionally, a series of specially illustrated articles and stories relating to the history and the evolution of the German government's system of "industrial, diplomatic, military and naval" espionage was published to coincide with the release of the episodes.[47]

FIGURE 13.3 The bold advertisements for *The Eagle's Eye* underscored its patriotic theme and its connection to former Secret Service chief William Flynn.

Exhibitors, too, found original ways to promote and advertise the serial. Perhaps the most inventive was William O'Hare, manager of the Majestic Theater in Des Moines, Iowa, who fashioned a huge submarine—"52 feet long and 15 feet wide"—over a motor truck. In addition, he procured a real torpedo from the Des Moines Naval Recruiting Station and, for three days prior to the showing of the first episode, drove the submarine and torpedo through the city's business section. At each stop, the sailors who accompanied the sub explained its workings, solicited enlistments, and boosted the production, which ensured a big turnout at the theater on the opening day.[48]

A showing of the serial's first episode definitely made an indelible impression on residents near Covington, Kentucky, where several cavalry horses had recently been poisoned. "At a meeting on the matter," Craig W. Campbell wrote, "a number of the people who had seen the film declared that the poisoning was a typical Hun action. The next day a vigilance committee was formed in the town, and all persons were to pledge allegiance to the American government. Those failing to take the pledge were threatened with prosecution and sentencing to an internment camp." Newspapers followed the story, giving *The Eagle's Eye* additional, if unintended, publicity.[49]

A major purpose of the "Serial Supreme" was indeed its value as propaganda. Passed by the Committee on Public Information and ultimately approved by the Treasury Department itself, *The Eagle's Eye* was sanctioned for foreign use precisely for that reason.[50] As part of an effort to "combat the serpent of German intrigue and propaganda in Mexico" and prevent the "dissatisfaction and disaffection" that Imperial German spy agents had sown in the United States, the U.S. government, acting in concert with the Mexican government, arranged showings throughout the Mexican republic. The serial was reportedly sent out to "every [Mexican] motion picture house that possesse[d] a screen and projection machine."[51]

According to *The Canadian Moving Picture Digest*, that effort was a success. Used "quite extensively . . . to give the utmost publicity to the harmful effects of German propaganda," *The Eagle's Eye* was vigorously promoted in Mexico, with assistance from the British government, which also had heavy interests in that country.[52] By the following year, the serial was being shown for propaganda purposes in places as distant as China and Siberia.[53] And, as company records confirm, soon other unspecified "foreign countries," mostly "small countries," began expressing interest in acquiring prints, too.[54]

The Eagle's Eye was notable not only for its subject matter and propaganda value but also for its photographic effects. Among the new features in the serial was something the Whartons called the "triple iris": three diaphragms that opened at once to disclose three characters, then faded into a scene showing those characters in action. By underscoring the relationships among the characters, that particular feature helped to create both a visual and a narrative continuity. Another of Ted's innovations was a new form of close-up—a lingering camera shot, in extreme close-up, which seemed to reveal what a character was feeling or thinking. Reputed to be "of great value" to the film and to the industry, it was later imitated by other producers.[55]

All these factors—along with the exciting on-screen romance that develops between Criminology Club president Harrison Grant and Chief Flynn's aide Dixie Mason, who skillfully infiltrates the circle of German plotters (and whom Grant initially, but mistakenly, suspects of being a spy)—seemed to suggest that the first serial produced by the Whartons as independent producers would be a financial success. But, as Kalton Lahue noted, while *The Eagle's Eye* was indeed a preparedness picture of the first order and a first-class propaganda piece, ultimately it "aroused much pro and con but little coin."[56] Its disappointing box office was due in part to the influenza epidemic that was sweeping the country, creating, among other concerns, a steep decline in attendance at movie houses nationwide. And it was due as well to the fact that, by the time the serial was completed and ready for release, the war in Europe had ended and people no longer flocked to the theaters to see war films, no matter how well produced they were.

As one of the Whartons' state-rights distributors in the Michigan territory reported, his "investigation" into the matter revealed just that: the failure of *The Eagle's Eye* was attributable to the "unusual conditions which have prevailed," including the Armistice and the closing for cleaning of all picture houses for three to eight weeks in the wake of the flu pandemic. In addition, despite being offered rentals at a radically reduced rate, more than twenty exhibitors across the state declared propaganda pictures to be "dead" and "could not see [renting] it at any price. [And] the Exchange men report the same conditions here and all of the War pictures are on the shelves."[57] Consequently, the monies that the Whartons had invested in expanding the studio to accommodate production of *The Eagle's Eye*, compounded by the already precarious state of their finances, plunged them into even deeper debt and effectively destroyed their dream of independent filmmaking success.

Another Significant *Mission*

While *The Eagle's Eye* was the only feature picture that the brothers produced in 1918, they completed another short propaganda film of considerable merit. That one-reeler, which they wrote, directed, and produced as part of a patriotic charity effort for "the aid of the soldiers of the war," was *The Mission of the War Chest*.[58] Curtailing production of *The Eagle's Eye* for an entire week, they devoted their full attention to the project. Stars King Baggot and Marguerite Snow and every member of the Wharton staff, including John Holbrook, Levi Bacon, Leroy Baker, and Marshall Francisco, volunteered their services as well.[59] Also appearing were members of the Red Cross and the New York State National Guard, along with Alphonse Notebaart, a distinguished Catholic priest and former representative of the Belgian government.[60]

The picture had originally been commissioned by George Eastman, the successful Rochester businessman, film pioneer, and civic-minded philanthropist who was among the first to embrace the notion of a "Community Chest" (later the United Way). In a letter to one of his colleagues in which he discussed his forthcoming Red Cross campaign, Eastman outlined his plan for a "welfare or patriotic fund for the city to take in all the charities and the war charitable activities." An important component of that fund-raising project was the Whartons' film, whose profits Eastman intended to donate to the war effort.[61] He hoped that the "Red Cross motion picture," which was designed to show some of the horrors of war and the consequent necessity of liberal contributions, would help raise as much as a million dollars for the drive.[62] But, as *Moving Picture World* reported, it did far better than imagined. "With the aid of the picture, instead of getting a million, the Rochester workers got a million and a half."

The intention of the picture was to demonstrate what would happen if any of the organizations working for the welfare or comfort of "the boys over there" should have to cease operations owing to lack of funds. Specifically, it would illustrate "the fate of the wounded soldiers in case the Red Cross was handicapped, the diversions the soldiers would have to seek if denied the Y.M.C.A., the discomforts which would follow the withdrawal of the Salvation Army from the war field, and all the other activities which are dependent upon the generosity of Americans."[63] Initially, the plan was to make the film as a straight commercial product, with Eastman paying the Whartons directly for their work.[64] The brothers, however, refused to accept any compensation. Using a screenplay that had been written by Leo, they began production on what they expected would be a project to help the Rochester Chamber of Commerce raise funds locally and across New York State. The picture, though, quickly garnered wider attention. After requests began coming to the Whartons for exhibition in other parts of the country, it was turned over in its entirety to Evan Evans, chief of the motion picture division of the Red Cross, so that it could be given the broadest distribution in theaters nationwide.[65]

The Mission of the War Chest told the story of two men: a wealthy father, who is unwilling to contribute any funds to the War Chest, and his son Ralph, who is willing to sacrifice everything for the patriotic cause. The father remains obdurate, even after the son enlists in the service, and he continues to resist the entreaties for his financial assistance. Only after Ralph's mother begins receiving the son's letters from the front, in which he describes the brave sacrifice of his friend Joe Smith and the work of the relief organizations funded largely by the War Chest does the father recognize the error of his judgment and become a subscriber. In a moment of conscience, he realizes that while his son has been sacrificing overseas, he has been doing nothing but hampering the soldiers' efforts and endangering the nation. After pledging a donation of $5,000 per month, he even invites the poor widowed mother of Ralph's friend Joe to live in their home with him and his wife.

The picture (which is extant) was an extremely effective parable, delivered with a deceptive simplicity. From the title image—a nurse and a priest on one side, a young soldier and a Red Cross volunteer on the other, all of them gazing upward as money pours down into the war chest positioned between them—it moved quickly into a series of short alternating shots. As Ralph's father sits in his opulent office, smugly certain that he has no cause for personal investment in the war, Ralph is determined to enlist. Rejected at first as underweight, he swallows prodigious amounts of water until he gains just enough weight to pass the physical and qualify for service, after which he returns, in uniform, to bid farewell to his surprised parents. The picture then intercuts scenes of the comforts of Ralph's parents' home with various realistic battle scenes, in which the brave young enlistees mount dangerous assaults, and the injured and dying young men call out for help.

In a letter to his mother from the front, Ralph describes the horror of war and the charity of the aid workers, who risk their own lives to provide relief to the soldiers. In another series of alternating shots, the picture cuts from Ralph's letter saying he is enjoying a brief rest in the Y.M.C.A. tent, "the only place we boys have over here," to a tent full of exhausted but grateful young men; back to Ralph's letter praising the Red Cross for "keeping our army supplied with bandages," to an iris shot of volunteers rolling bandages for the wounded; back to the letter lauding the Salvation Army members who are "doing their best, God Bless Them," with minimal resources, to a scene of volunteers passing out food and drink to the injured in the field; back to Ralph's letter, in which he describes his friend Joe's death from a bayonet wound, to a shot of a priest administering the last rites to the young man in a trench; and finally back again to Ralph's letter, in which he reiterates his confidence that men like his father "will keep the War Chest filled." The quick cuts create a sense not just of the chaos of war but also of the urgency of the relief efforts.

As expertly staged as the elaborate battle scenes and the gas attacks were, the film's most poignant and enduring image was the final one, that of a single young soldier surrounded by battle carnage and clinging to a large cross. Harking back to the crucifix that the priest held above the dying Joe's head, that cross—hand-tinted red—serves as a symbol of the blood shed on the battlefield and the hope that agencies such as the Red Cross provide to the servicemen in combat overseas.

Although it was both affecting and effective, *The Mission of the War Chest* was not unique in its subject or theme. A 1917 article on "Patriotic and Red Cross Films" had urged theater owners and exhibitors "to place before [their] patrons patriotic inspiration." According to *Moving Picture World*, "[one] has only to look about him among the various news weeklies which are at the present teeming with pictures of this form . . . bearing on what is happening in the way of patriotic demonstrations or current military events." Pictures such as *How Uncle Sam Prepares* (Pioneer Films), *Uncle Sam, Awake* (Rogson Films), *A Daughter of Uncle Sam* (Jaxon), and *Mobilizing the Red Cross* (Paramount-Bray-Pictograph) presented those events in a stirring manner and "doubtless aid[ed] materially in inspiring the youth of the country to action."[66]

The work of the Red Cross was, in fact, celebrated by all branches of the film industry. Screenwriters as distinguished as Frances Marion incorporated

FIGURE 13.4   *The Mission of the War Chest* was part of a "war charity" effort to raise funds for organizations like the Red Cross.

it into their story lines. Marion's *The Beloved Adventuress* (1917), a feature film directed by William A. Brady, for example, portrayed a heroine who joins the Red Cross in France and dies bravely in an attempt to rescue a wounded woman.[67] Numerous other films, from *The Countess Charming* (1917) and *Jerry's Big Deal* (1917) to short comedies such as *Help Wanted* (1918) and *Red Crossed* (1918), also wove the Red Cross into their plots.[68] In a different kind of promotion, *Photoplay Magazine Screen Supplement* offered a special opportunity to state-rights exhibitors: twelve "single-reel journeys" to the homes of the players, including Douglas Fairbanks and Charlie Chaplin, showing how they "live, frolic, and indulge their pet hobbies when away from the studios—with All the Profits to the Red Cross!"[69]

Support for the cause was nationwide. Director William Christy Cabanne produced a seven-reel feature based on a spectacular Red Cross pageant "to be shown in every city and town."[70] "Preparation parades," membership drives, benefit concerts, Red Cross movie charity balls, and other fund-raisers became increasingly common.[71] Theaters across the country sponsored "cigarette drives" for the soldiers overseas, screened films such as *The Red Cross Nurse* and *American Ambulance Field Service in France*, and took up collections that realized handsome sums. Movie houses in Seattle and elsewhere outfitted their doors in red crosses and conducted "Mercy

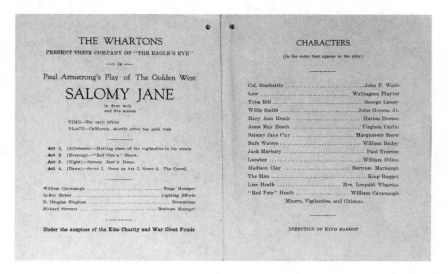

FIGURE 13.5   In another effort to help the war cause, the Whartons' *Eagle's Eye* company staged a performance of *Salomy Jane*.

Mondays," during which the salaries of all employees were donated to the Red Cross.[72]

The Mission of the War Chest was not the Whartons' only contribution to the war effort. In addition to donating their services for the picture, *The Eagle's Eye* actors and company members volunteered to perform at another similar event: a well-received benefit production of *Salomy Jane* under the auspices of the Elks Charity and War Chest Funds. The "Play of the Golden West," written by Paul Armstrong and based on Bret Harte's novella, was directed by King Baggot, who had appeared in an earlier staging of the play in New York City. Highly anticipated, the performance was held on April 5 and 6 at the Lyceum Theater in Ithaca and generated "large ticket sales." The company even considered the possibility of touring the play "in principal cities of the country" at the conclusion of *The Eagle's Eye*.[73]

A New *Peril*

Unlike the favorable response to the performance of *Salomy Jane*, however, the reception of *The Eagle's Eye* was quite disappointing, and the revenue was poor. Although both the influenza epidemic and the signing of the Armistice had "cut its career short . . . [and] caused the cancellation of nearly a half million dollars' worth of contracts," the following year the serial was given a second life in movie houses. Financed by a syndicate of Ithaca businessmen headed by longtime Wharton attorney and trustee Howard Cobb and edited down to a feature-length film retitled *The Red Peril*, it was reworked to emphasize the dangers of Bolshevism rather than of German militarism (a radical shift in focus, possible only in silent film).[74] Yet the scenes, composed largely of existing footage from *The Eagle's Eye*, were "so cleverly modified, retitled and interwoven" that viewers, unaware of its resemblance to its predecessor, would assume that the "revitalized production" was actually a new motion picture entirely.[75] In Ted's words, the "straight from the shoulder" depiction of "the attempt to start Bolshevism in America" offered some startling revelations about the influential movement. "The locale of the story is America," he stated, "[because] I wouldn't be at all surprised if the Bolsheviki attempted to blow us up."[76]

Apart from the profuse praise heaped on *The Red Peril* by Senator Clayton R. Lusk, a Cornell graduate who hailed it as a powerful weapon with which to fight the perils of Red activities, the film received little press.[77] Although the film does not survive, Charles V. Henkel, then-manager of the Wharton Releasing Company in New York City who worked closely with Ted Wharton on the editing, provided important insights into its rerelease. Describing the often fractious attempts at collaboration, Henkel detailed some of their disagreements, among them Ted's "crude and amateurish" work in the final scenes, his reluctance to delegate responsibilities for assembling the picture and making duplicates, and his unfortunate "blowing [bragging] about the wonderful production" that he believed could have a big run in New York before being placed on the market for wider distribution.

As Henkel wrote at some length to Wharton attorney Howard Cobb, he was shocked that "anyone who claims the ability that Ted claims" would be willing to let such sloppy work "go by." Confessing that he was "sick and tired of [Ted's] supercilious manner and actions regarding the production," Henkel stated that he had taken it on himself to resolve some of the production and distribution issues "in a satisfactory manner." At the same time, he admitted that "no matter what changes are [ultimately] made, Ted is bound to blame the no-success of the production (if it turns out that we cannot do anything with it) on these changes."[78]

The feature, which Henkel initially proposed calling *The Menace of the Red Rag*, attempted to chronicle the development and growth of Bolshevism and possible anarchy in the United States. In the picture, the defeated Germans of the aristocratic party are incensed by the American intervention in the world war that brought victory to the Allies, and they hope to get retaliation and revenge by involving the U.S. in the horrors of bloodshed.[79] Since German money, influence, and propaganda had inspired Bolshevism in Russia and other countries, they believe that similar conditions can be spread in America by the scores of German agents, who presumably went undetected during the war. The International Workers of the World, "already subsidized and in sympathy with the devilish plans[,] are valuable tools, particularly because they [the German agents] are distributed all over the country and in addition are posing as loyal members of various labor organizations." Thus, the disruptions resulting from the strikes the agents initiate and the destruction of property they cause will be blamed on the unions.

By exposing the scheme "to create strife between Capital and Labor" and by depicting the subtle propaganda that such agents use to create dissension and win sympathizers to their side, the film, Henkel insisted, would be invaluable. In correspondence and memos preserved as part of the Wharton Collection at Cornell University in Ithaca, he outlined his specific and cost-efficient suggestions for the revising of the story line and the recutting of *The Eagle's Eye*, most of which apparently were incorporated into the final version. He synopsized his version of the film as follows:

The Secy. of the Dept. of Labor is in session with several of his assistants. Newspaper headlines suggest the spread of Bolshevism to this country.

General discussion follows which leads to showing of headline news article to the effect that Labor demands continuance of war wages. Discussion leads to title suggesting that Bolshevism is possible only through stirring up trouble between Capital and Labor. This leads to the decision to instruct the departments secret service to watch for trouble breeders.

Bolsheviki leaders are in session (Marburgh and other Germans), they discuss plans and show by overlap dissolve, scene of mass meetings (Library Film), also destruction of bridge and train.

The first three scenes will, with titles, and inserts, serve to establish the general plot. The first, (or NEW SCENE), can be used—with diversified action—for cutbacks throughout the story.

The Secret Service of the Dept. of Labor, (the Criminology Club), receives word to watch for Bolsheviki agents who are attempting to influence Labor organizations to start strikes, etc.

Baggot is Chief of the Dept. of Labor Secret Service. Snow is one of his operatives, but unknown to the other operatives.

Grant notifies Dixie (by letter—omit code) to ingratiate herself with Bolsheviki agents.

She is introduced to Bailey [who played von Lertz] to hotel girl (omit typewriter signals—this can be done by cutting in another scene).

The harbor workers threaten to strike and there is general unrest among union labor.

The burning of the stock yards takes place (episode #4). Other calamities happen.

Hopewell is burned. (Use exteriors of ammunition plants, etc. for cutbacks showing close-ups of destruction.)

Baggot is at wits end when papers are found (Dr. Albert's) disclosing evidence of plans. These cause Baggot to become longshoreman leading up to happenings at docks.

The quarrel between [Florence] Short and Campbell to be used. Also Short betraying her confederates. Her death and Bailey losing life in vessel.

The President is appealed to meanwhile to end the strike. He writes and his message is received. The strikers receive message with great enthusiasm. The Capitalists agree to accept arbitration.

FINAL. President Wilson shaking hands with soldier and sailor. This dissolves into Capital (President) Farmer (Sailor) Laborer (Soldier).

Notably, Henkel's re-editing accomplished several things: it maximized existing footage from the serial *The Eagle's Eye*, minimized the need to shoot additional scenes, and inserted newspapers and library film "of outdoor labor meetings, parades, and socialistic gatherings" to good advantage as cutbacks. A few new scenes provided the necessary transitions and included labor meetings, "staged to purpose," with scenes of "Capitalists" and "ship-owners" illustrating the wealth and character of these substantial men of affairs, while the activities of the Bolshevik agents created the false impression that Capital and Labor were at loggerheads.

In keeping with the spirit of the original serial, *The Red Peril* emphasized patriotism. During the labor meeting, for example, speakers "call[ed] attention to the sacrifices made by the boys who went into the army, showing the sacrifices they endured while the workingmen at home lived in comfort and plenty. Also showing scenes of wounded and other boys returning, to suggest 'What will these boys say when they learn you have surrendered to Bolshevism, when they lost lives, sight and limbs to protect you and your families.'"[80]

Although Ted Wharton generally agreed with Henkel's cuts and edits, King Baggot, who had starred in the serial, raised objections. After hearing Ted brag about "the wonderful picture," he argued that the reedited film was in fact a new and separate production, and he insisted that he should be compensated for his performance, even though no additional acting on his part was required. It is unlikely that Baggot's request was honored, particularly since, by the time *The Red Peril* was released as a seven-reel feature film in 1919, the Wharton Studio was crippled with debt and on the verge of dissolution.

The disappointing box office of *The Eagle's Eye* and the lack of viable prospects for new productions totally dashed the Whartons' hopes for success as independent producers; and this time there would be no coming back. The brothers would soon be forced into another—and final—bankruptcy that required them to sell off most of their equipment and to vacate the Renwick Park location that had served as the site of so many excellent and pioneering serials and other productions. Even more significantly, they would soon terminate their long-standing partnership and go their separate ways to pursue their filmmaking plans in new and distant locations—Leo in Texas, Ted in California.

CHAPTER 14

Leaving Ithaca

The time that Ted and Leo spent in Ithaca (1913–1919) was the most prolific and sustained period of filmmaking in their careers.

After leaving New York, both tried to pursue new film ventures in the West. But neither was able to recapture the heady excitement of their years as independent film producers at the Wharton Studio in Renwick Park or to re-create the success that they achieved as masters of the serial motion picture. During the Whartons' time in Ithaca, the landscape of filmmaking had literally changed. In the early years of the twentieth century, production had been concentrated largely in the New York and New Jersey metropolitan area. By 1919, however, much of the film industry had moved west to Los Angeles. As film historian Robert Sklar noted in *Movie-Made America*, "within an hour or two of downtown Los Angeles one could find a location resembling almost any conceivable scene one might want to use—factory or farm, jungle or snowy peak."[1] The successful antitrust suit instigated by William Fox, founder of the Fox Film Corporation, had terminated the Motion Picture Patents Company (Edison) Trust and ended the dominance of the East Coast studios. Attracted by the mild and sunny weather that made year-round outdoor filming possible and by the cheap nonunion labor, a score of movie production companies—Universal, Famous Players–Lasky, Goldwyn, Louis B. Mayer, and Fox among them—established offices in Los

Angeles or relocated operations there. By the mid-1910s, more than 60 percent of American motion pictures were being filmed in Hollywood.

The changes at Renwick Park were just as dramatic. The once-bustling Wharton Studio was, by 1919, a film studio in name only. With its debt increasing and prospects for new production slowing correspondingly, it was facing an uncertain future. A reorganization to avoid bankruptcy in 1917 had brought the company some much-needed funding. A number of Ithacans had loaned money in the form of notes, securing "a chattel mortgage" of which Jacob Rothschild was the trustee; and with the cooperation of the Board of Commerce, attorney Howard Cobb was placed in charge.[2]

Over the next few months, however, the Whartons' debt continued to mount. The break with Hearst had curtailed most of the plans to improve and expand the studio, but preparations for filming of their last serial, *The Eagle's Eye*, in 1918 had necessitated a large new storage building with floor space of more than twenty-five hundred square feet. These and other production expenses were aggravated by the cost of establishing and maintaining a suite of offices in New York City for the Wharton Releasing Company, which was formed to handle distribution of their independent productions.[3] Furthermore, the rapidly rising cost of film production since the outset of the world war and the falling receipts at motion picture theater box offices only exacerbated the bad situation, as did the flu pandemic of 1918, which created enormous panic and ultimately killed more Americans than the war had.

Simply put, the Whartons were far better filmmakers than financiers.[4] Their casual organizational structure and fiscal mismanagement reportedly led to "lavish spending on serials and feature productions," which in turn necessitated many recapitalizations.[5] By some accounts, the problems worsened significantly after their brother-in-law and business manager J. Whitworth Buck left the operation.[6]

To deflect attention from their difficulties, the Whartons tried to shift the focus from their finances to their productions, which they continued to promote as energetically and as widely as possible. Prior to the release of *The Eagle's Eye*, for example, in a by-then familiar example of a film and newspaper cross-promotion, the three hundred thousand readers of *Photoplay* were advised to look forward to a serialization written by Courtney Ryley Cooper, who had already prepared the screenplay for the serial picture. That serialization began with the April 1 issue of the magazine, with four episodes included in each installment. Another novelization, starting on May 1 in the *Gentlewoman*, was expected to reach an even larger audience—about 1.5 million, according to the *Ithaca Journal*. Additionally, a novelization in five hundred of the country's leading newspapers had been arranged, with one installment appearing daily beginning about April 10.[7] (Written "in three different styles," all three serializations and novelizations had been penned by Cooper.) Such publicity, along with the striking full- and double-page graphic ads in the major trade journals, not only generated excitement about the serial but also helped to quell some of the gossip about the solvency of the studio.

Still, the rumors persisted, especially after the Whartons resigned from the National Association of the Motion Picture Industry, the regulatory body created by the studios in 1916 to answer demands of censorship. Claiming that the association "did not cooperate either with us or themselves," they argued instead for a proper organization that would represent all members by bringing about "salvation" of the movie business. Moreover, even though new production at the Whartons' studio had ceased, Ted insisted that several of their pictures were still going through the exchanges; and he continued to maintain that the current inactivity was entirely voluntary. "Our plant is idle now," he told an interviewer from *Moving Picture World* in January 1919. "We are not producing and don't intend to until conditions change in the industry. We don't know when that will be, but our plant is, meanwhile, ready and equipped to handle any kind of picture that can be reduced to film."[8]

In fact, the situation was far more serious than the brothers let on. By May 1919, their long-standing money troubles had become too big to hide or ignore. Under a headline reading "Sell Wharton Property to Satisfy Claims," the *Ithaca Journal* reported that although the Whartons had struggled bravely after their 1917 recapitalization, the debts kept accumulating, to the point that the "odds [now] were too formidable," and, given the inflated cost of picture production and general decline in patronage during the influenza epidemic, "claims against the firm again predominate in its financial situation."[9]

New Financial Woes

The Whartons found themselves facing bankruptcy once again. But this time, with their creditors pushing for foreclosure proceedings, they were forced to sell off the contents of the studio in order to pay off some of the debts. The sale, however, netted a mere $12,000, which local attorney A. W. Feinberg, acting on behalf of the mortgage trustee Jacob Rothschild and other local creditors, disbursed among his clients. Conducted by Constable Shaw, agent for the mortgagees, the sale consisted of "scenery, lighting equipment, furniture and other interior effects, and general motion picture paraphernalia," the disposal of which foreclosed the mortgage amount of $10,000 that had been advanced by local businessmen to the Whartons but left numerous other debts unpaid.[10]

Afterward, when Rothschild was asked about future operations at the studio, he stated that he had nothing to announce. But the *Ithaca Journal*, which had long been supportive of the Whartons and their film efforts, expressed its hope that "the foreclosure will not necessitate an absolute termination of the motion picture industry here."[11] (The bankruptcy would not be resolved for years. As late as the end of 1923, the finances were still being litigated, with Ted questioning the final settlement, in which, according to attorney Howard Cobb, creditors had "closed the affairs of Wharton, Inc." and "received five cents on the dollar," leaving "a deficiency of about $29,000." Ted admitted to being puzzled by the value of the assets that Cobb had enumerated, suggesting that even if they "had been sold to a junk man," they should have yielded more. He also called for return of, or payment on, his and his wife's shares of both Wharton Inc. and Wharton Releasing Company stock, which Cobb replied were, by then, of "absolutely no value."[12] Cobb in turn noted that creditors and attorneys had thoroughly investigated the books, leaving "little doubt for you to raise any question that things were not properly handled."[13] Leo, too, after writing separately to Cobb in early 1923 to request clarification of various foreclosure and lien settlements, was surprised to learn that the closing accounts administered by trustee Jacob Rothschild showed such a large deficiency and that, even with "the proceeds from the Great White Trail and the comedies" serving as collateral for some investors, the "boys" who loaned Wharton Inc. money to prevent bankruptcy in 1917 had "lost the whole principal [and] were unable to get their pay."[14] Complicating matters even further, the hundreds of films that Cobb had been storing in a shed behind his house as part of the protracted litigation over the finances were destroyed in a fire.[15])

To be sure, the Whartons' prospects in the industry looked grim. Yet surprisingly, within just days of the sale of the studio contents, reports surfaced of a new Wharton film venture. A headline in the *Ithaca Journal* of May 17, 1919, declared that "Whartons Form New Company in San Antonio." The brothers, the paper stated, "are to enter business at San Antonio Texas, on an extensive scale[,] and citizens of that city have subscribed for $150,000 worth of preferred stock for that purpose." Specifically, sixty San Antonians were said to have invested $1,000 each or more in the new enterprise.[16]

The president of that new corporation was actor and producer Maclyn Arbuckle, with whom Leo had been briefly associated years earlier when both performed on stage together. Leo was appointed manager and vice president, with Ted as supervising director. The other officers were all wealthy local businessmen (who no had doubt been made even wealthier by oil money and the recent boom in the stock market), with the board of directors composed exclusively of San Antonians as well. Reportedly, a new studio had been constructed and was nearly ready for "the initial output,"[17] with scripts for the photoplays being furnished by Irvin S. Cobb, Holman Day, Harry Leon Wilson, George V. Hobart, and other American writers.

According to the same article, Ted Wharton, just back from New York City, had "sprung another surprise": he announced that he had signed a contract for three motion picture serials for the Pathé Company, which he intended to produce at the Renwick Park studio over the summer. Telling reporters that he did not anticipate that the recent foreclosure would interfere with those plans in any way, he added that he would remain in Ithaca, traveling only occasionally to San Antonio "to supervise the picture production there." He also indicated that he had contracted with George Eastman, the Rochester philanthropist and magnate whose advances in film development allied him closely to the movie industry, to produce another picture in Rochester for the Monroe County War Chest. "Mr. Wharton," the article concluded, "has in the past two years produced similar pictures for Mr. Eastman in behalf of the Rochester Red Cross and War Chest organizations."[18] (In fact, the Whartons had produced only a single Red Cross film; and no new picture would ever be made.)

The rosy forecasts about the new projects obscured one significant detail: the relationship between the Whartons had deteriorated, both personally and professionally. Leo had long felt himself to be in his brother's shadow, an unequal partner in the Ithaca studio that Ted had established after he left Essanay's employ. Over the years, Ted often assumed the more exciting and glamorous role in the Whartons' production partnership, generating story ideas (many of which he wrote himself) and promoting the company. Much of the day-to-day operation of the studio and the implementation of those story ideas—and the problems that came with those responsibilities—fell to Leo, who, though widely admired as a director, was reportedly "nervous," quick to "go all to pieces," and prone to worry.[19] The production of *The Eagle's Eye* had further complicated relations between the brothers. Under Leo's direction, the serial had failed to return financial solvency to the studio, by then already devastated both by the break with Hearst and by the postwar social and economic changes that reverberated throughout the industry and challenged even larger, more established production companies.

And so, perhaps as a result of tensions over the multiple liens and lawsuits brought against them, perhaps because of family issues related to their mother Fanny's year-long illness (from which she died in early August 1919), perhaps out of a desire to start fresh in a new location, the Whartons—after a decade-long pioneering and profitable partnership—decided to part ways.

Sadly, they would never work together again.[20] And, by at least one account, after the summer of 1919 they rarely if ever crossed paths.[21]

A New Ithaca Studio

By late June, Leo had already left—alone—for Texas to join Maclyn Arbuckle's film company, which had been incorporated on March 22, 1919, with capital stock in the amount of $450,000.[22] But despite the earlier and much-heralded announcement of his seminal role in that company (an announcement that he later curiously denied), Ted's only involvement would be ownership of some stock shares. Instead, he remained full time in Ithaca to pursue his new and now-solitary projects such as the proposed serial *The Crooked Dagger*.[23] Frustrated in his hope of returning to shoot in his former studio in Renwick Park, the establishment of which had been the fulfillment of his longtime dream, Ted moved to a cheaper and smaller property in town, an abandoned skating rink that he leased on West State Street. Promising that work on a "full season of motion picture production" would begin shortly, he projected that each film, to be released directly through the Wharton Releasing Company, would be budgeted at $50,000 to $75,000.[24]

By July 1919, the former skating rink was already in the process of conversion to turn it into what, according to Ted, would be one of the finest and most modernly equipped motion picture production plants of its kind. A rotary converter was being installed to supply direct current to the studio; steel beams would replace the wooden ones, raising the roof by ten feet. The new site would also have a new name: the "Theodore Wharton Studio."[25]

Plans for *The Crooked Dagger* seemed to be proceeding smoothly, too. The picture, adapted from stories by popular author Fred Jackson, whose work both brothers long favored, was publicized as the antithesis of the usual "knock-'em-on-the-head-and-drag-'em-out" type of serial. Rather, it would "show how a master criminologist is able to beat expert criminals at their own game." Written "along intelligent lines with elements of honest mystery in them," the ten-part serial was said to be so exciting that it would draw President Wilson himself each week to see the succeeding chapter.[26]

Filming was originally scheduled to begin August 18, with Ted personally directing, and Jack Norworth, vaudevillian, songwriter, and "best all-around entertainer in the business," starring as detective Lloyd Demarest.[27] On summer hiatus from his vaudeville engagements, Norworth arrived in Ithaca and immediately ingratiated himself with the community by participating in local events. At the weekly trapshoot at the Lakeside Gun Club, for instance, he showed off his shooting skills.[28] And at the "Elks' feed," he "scored a direct hit" with a repertoire of original songs, which "went over big" with the two hundred Elks and their guests who were in attendance.[29]

Set to appear in the serial with Norworth were May Hopkins, who had been featured in a "vamp" role in *Beatrice Fairfax*; Bertram Marburgh and William Cavanaugh, both veterans of the serial *The Eagle's Eye*; George Goldsmith, the "heavy" from the Wharton picture *The City*; Helen Ferguson, a popular actress who would later become a Hollywood publicist; Janet Adair, a musical comedy performer; and well-known character actor Phineas W. Nares, who had worked with Ted years earlier at the old Edison Studios.[30] The company of actors was expected to reside in Ithaca for some time in order to complete the picture. And although several other producers were also in town filming, Ted professed to feel no rivalry toward them. Since dozens of other motion picture-producing companies had worked together harmoniously in the past, he said, he saw no reason why similar cordial relations would not prevail in Ithaca. "After all," he claimed, "the more the merrier."[31]

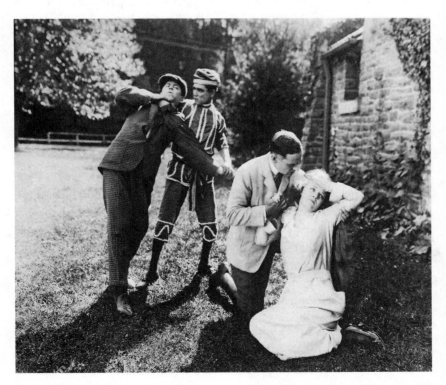

FIGURE 14.1 Jack Norworth starred as detective Lloyd Demarest in *The Crooked Dagger*, the final film produced (but never completed) by Ted Wharton in Ithaca.

In August, Frederic Chapin, playwright, scenario editor for Pathé, and author of the scenario for *The Crooked Dagger*, arrived in Ithaca to acquaint himself with the community and to finalize details of the picture. Expressing his faith in the continuing popularity of the serial, he stated that he believed that *The Crooked Dagger* would not only pique moviegoers' interest and draw them into the theaters; it would also raise the form to the same high standard as a feature photoplay. Chapin added that the public would marvel if they realized the complexity of the work involved in the serial's planning and production, particularly "the days and nights of countless hours of long and painstaking effort on the part of authors and producers."[32]

Chapin's words about the challenges of serial filmmaking may have been prophetic. Almost immediately, problems arose with the production. By the time that interior shooting was supposed to begin on September 4, the studio renovations were still incomplete, forcing Ted to travel with a small complement of his actors to Sayre, Pennsylvania, to film a few exterior scenes on a five-car train leased from the Lehigh Valley Railroad Company. Then leading woman May Hopkins, who was playing the vamp part, was injured in a car accident and could not fulfill her contract. She had to be replaced by local actress Frances White, who had served as a stand-in for Pearl White and who had appeared in several earlier Wharton productions, including *The New Adventures of J. Rufus Wallingford* and *The Black Stork*. Actress Janet Adair was also forced to resign, after the powerful lighting required for interior shots proved injurious to her eyes. And arrangements for the sensational stunts such as the aerial bombing of a dirigible over Cayuga Lake that Ted had planned were proving increasingly complicated and prohibitively expensive, only adding to his frustration.[33]

But the biggest blow of all came from Pathé, which abruptly canceled the contract for the serial, causing work at the studio to cease entirely. With no guarantee of when, or even if, production would resume, Jack Norworth and a number of other cast members returned to New York. Furious over Pathé's action, Ted Wharton instructed his attorneys to file a lawsuit against the company to recover $80,000 for breach of contract. Although, under the circumstances, resumption of filming seemed unlikely, Ted refused to admit that the interruption might be permanent. Publicly, he remained upbeat, quoting the manager of the New York Giants, who had told him that "the game is never over until the last man is out."[34]

As it turns out, though, the last man was already out—or, at the very least, on the way out. Between the problems with Pathé and the loss of the serial's leading man and other actors, Ted found himself unable to move forward with the production. Consequently, although a number of filmographies list

The Crooked Dagger as a completed picture, the serial, as Kalton C. Lahue confirms in *Continued Next Week*, "never saw the light of day."[35]

Leasing Renwick Park

When Ted was forced to move to his new West State Street location in Ithaca to undertake the filming of *The Crooked Dagger*, the Whartons' original lease on Renwick Park had not yet expired. So the former Wharton Studio, which the brothers had occasionally leased on short term to other filmmakers such as F. W. Stewart and Norma Talmadge, was sublet to Grossman Pictures Company of New York on a six-month lease, beginning April 1, 1919. Almost immediately, two large Grossman trucks started ferrying "scenic effects, studio equipment, and other picture-making paraphernalia" from New York City to Ithaca. Harry Grossman, the head of the corporation, arrived soon afterward and began extolling the town's merits. In all of his long experience in motion pictures, he remarked, he had never seen a community so ideally located and scenically endowed for film work.[36]

By July, director George A. Lessey, a veteran of several Wharton productions (including *Patria*, in which he appeared, and *The Eagle's Eye*, which he directed), was also in town, in preparation for the start of a new Grossman serial for Pathé the following week. And E. Douglas Bingham, former technical director for the Whartons and current business manager for Grossman, was back in Ithaca, too, "to make preliminary arrangements for an extensive producing season" that would include twenty two-reel feature films with such popular stars as Mae Marsh and Norma Talmadge, both of whom had earlier been associated with the Whartons. The Ithacans who had previously appeared as extras in earlier Wharton pictures would, Bingham affirmed, be employed by Grossman productions in similar scenes that were being "contemplated on an elaborate scale." Bingham seemed to take special pride in the fact that it was he who had been responsible for inducing Grossman to come to Ithaca, which, as he said, offered "the real advantages of unexcelled exterior scenery."[37]

Harry Grossman had high hopes, too. Serial pictures, he insisted, were in higher demand and playing in a better class of movie houses than ever before, so they needed to be constructed more thoughtfully and intelligently. To that end, he pledged to produce serials with fewer "impossible impossibilities" and more "probable probabilities."[38] Yet despite Grossman's good intentions, his company fared little better at Renwick Park than the Whartons had in their final years there. According to the *Cornell Daily Sun*, by early 1920, less than a year after relocating to Ithaca, the company decided to return to New York City.[39]

During its tenure at the former Wharton studio, Grossman Pictures completed only a single project: *The $1,000,000 Reward*, a fifteen-part serial that starred Lillian Walker and Coit Albertson and featured George A. Lessey and Charles Middleton, a reliable character actor who would go on to play many film heavies and villains, including Ming the Merciless in the Flash Gordon serials in the 1930s. Unfortunately, Pathé rejected the picture, which, as Colleen M. Kaplin writes, "ended up being anything but a million dollar reward for its producers."[40] The fact that the serial was not more successful is perhaps surprising, given that its story was written by Arthur B. Reeve, the mystery writer best known for his creation of the popular forensic detective Craig Kennedy, who became a central character in the Whartons' highly successful 1914 serial *The Exploits of Elaine* and its two sequels (for which Reeve had authored the screenplays) and whose character would be revived in several 1920s and 1930s films by other producers. The trade papers had hailed the signing of the contract between Grossman and Reeve as "one of the biggest deals ever arranged between an author and a producer" and predicted that the collaboration would be a huge success.[41]

In an interview with the local paper, Harry Grossman estimated that, during its brief stay in Ithaca, his company had expended $180,000 in production costs. Anticipating that the move to New York City would allow the company greater productivity, he announced that he expected to begin filming twelve features and four serials there over the next year. But even in its new metropolitan location, Grossman Pictures did not have much better luck. The company's only other picture, *Wits vs. Wits*, a five-reel detective drama in which the heroine, out to avenge her father's death, entraps a gangster as he attempts to perpetrate a large bank fraud, was released in June 1920.[42] In Ithaca, though, Grossman was remembered less for his pictures than for the trail of unpaid debts that his company left in its wake before leaving town.

The Wharton Studio site did not remain vacant for long after the departure of Grossman Pictures. As reported in the *Cornell Alumni News*, a new company for the production and sale of moving pictures organized in Ithaca under the name Cayuga Pictures Inc., with a capitalization of $525,000. The company leased the studio and fixtures at Renwick Park, securing control of about forty acres of woods and some twelve hundred feet of lake frontage, including boathouses and docks. Managers Gardner Hunting, who had earlier worked as a screenwriter for the Whartons' feature film *The Great White Trail*, and James N. Naulty were put under exclusive contract for a period of five years. They anticipated producing six feature pictures during the first year, with filming set to begin in early summer.[43] Pledging "to produce the very finest element of human interest" in their stories "rather than the hectic or flamboyant type of narrative," they "hope[d] to photograph Ithaca's beautiful scenery as it has never been photographed before."[44]

Cayuga's ambitions, however, evidently outstripped its means, and the company produced only a single feature film, the six-part *If Women Only Knew*, before moving its operations from Ithaca to New York, just as Grossman had done. Loosely based on Balzac's meditations in *The Physiology of Marriage*, the film (whose working title was *The Three Women Who Loved Him*) began shooting in June and was in release by late August 1921. Its plot involved a young man, a senior at the famed Colburn University, who is seduced and betrayed by the wealthy daughter of one of the university's trustees; but he eventually finds his way back home to the kind and unselfish woman who has loved him all along and who cared for his ailing and widowed mother in his absence. Shot at Cornell University, which doubled for Colburn, and at other locations in and around Ithaca, *If Women Only Knew* featured some spectacular scenes, such as the burning of a fraternity house especially erected for that purpose at the former Wharton Studio, a stunt that attracted much local attention.[45]

The first and only picture made by Cayuga Pictures at Renwick Park, *If Women Only Knew* marked both an end to the company itself and the end of an exciting era of filmmaking in Ithaca.

But the legacy of the Whartons endured, particularly among the locals who had encouraged and supported the brothers' filmmaking and performed bit parts in their pictures. During the heyday of production, the *Ithaca Journal* had teased that "You'd Better Watch Out or the Whartons'll Get You [into their pictures]."[46] And Ithaca resident Mrs. James J. "Mame" Hennessy recalled, "Good Lord, the whole town worked down there."[47]

The upstate town of Ithaca where the Wharton brothers had produced numerous landmark pictures throughout the 1910s would never be a center of filmmaking again.

CHAPTER 15

Heading West

The once close relationship between the Wharton brothers had irreparably broken. In late spring of 1919, after he and Ted parted ways, Leo Wharton left New York and headed west—not to Los Angeles but to Texas, which he hoped would become part of a film community that might rival Hollywood. At San Antonio Motion Pictures, he believed that he would have the opportunity to produce the kinds of feature films that he had long wanted to make.

Leo was not the first filmmaker to have that particular dream. Almost a decade earlier, in 1910, the Star Film Company established a studio in San Antonio to serve as the winter headquarters for producer Gaston Méliès, one of cinema's pioneering Méliès brothers. The city's sunny weather was conducive to the shooting of outdoor scenes. "The land of sunshine," as Star Film director Wallace McCutcheon had called it, "would afford us a great deal of scope for our operations." McCutcheon was certainly right about the city's promise. At once frontier and metropolis, San Antonio was "no stranger to the movies." There were, historian Frank T. Thompson writes, at least seventeen moving pictures showing around town by 1910, which drew thousands of moviegoers every day.[1]

Accompanied by McCutcheon, Gaston's son Paul located and leased twenty acres across the San Antonio River near the famed Hot Sulphur Wells Hotel, a large resort that had entertained such prominent guests as

Will Rogers, Teddy Roosevelt, Tom Mix, and Sarah Bernhardt. The property contained a plain two-story farmhouse, quickly dubbed the Star Film Ranch, and a large barn that served as storage for props and costumes and an area for film development. Star's company of actors included Francis Ford, actor, director, and older brother of director-to-be John Ford; Ann Nichols, who later wrote the Broadway hit *Abie's Irish Rose*; William Clifford, a noted Shakespearean actor; and Edith Storey, a lively teenager whose expert horsemanship was featured in many of the company's films.[2] Between 1910 and early 1911, the company turned out some seventy one-reel films, mainly westerns with Mexicans or Indians cast as the villains. The most memorable of those films was *The Immortal Alamo* (1911), many scenes of which were shot on site at the Alamo, with cadets from the Peacock Military Academy acting as Santa Anna's army. By April 1911, however, the Star Film Company pulled up stakes in San Antonio and moved to California, where they continued filmmaking for a few more years.[3]

Around the same time that Méliès was producing his pictures, Paul and W. Hope Tilley, brothers from Illinois who had moved to Texas around the turn of the century, began filming "actualities" (newsreel footage). Although their company, Satex—its name derived from the initials of San Antonio, Texas—was forced out of San Antonio in 1911 because of pressure by the Motion Picture Patents Corporation, they relocated their operation to their new home in Austin.[4] In 1913, two San Antonians, J. O. Taylor and H. O. Grigg, established their Taylor Movie Picture Manufacturing Company near Mission San José but had little success, while in 1916, Gotham Pictures Company, headed by Marshall W. Taggart, purchased the Hot Wells property and considered building a production facility to be called Gotham City. Taggart's plan to produce "fifty-two features and three serials per year" never materialized,[5] though the company eventually released a few minor films a decade later. A much larger and better-known company, Vitagraph, never opened a studio in Texas but, in February 1917, sent a troupe to San Antonio to make two films, *Westwind* and *His Bunkie*. And in 1918, the newly formed San Antonio Photo-Plays, located on the site of the former Star Film Ranch, made a single five-reel drama there.

Partnering with Arbuckle

Though similarly named, San Antonio Photo-Plays had no relation to the San Antonio Motion Pictures Corporation with which Leo Wharton became affiliated in 1919. In his capacity as vice president, manager, and director, Leo worked in close cooperation with San Antonio–born Maclyn Arbuckle, who founded the company and served as its head. A popular stage actor who, like many performers of his day, was anxious to make the transition to the screen, Maclyn was the brother of actor Andrew Arbuckle and a cousin of comedian Roscoe "Fatty" Arbuckle. Already in his thirties when he began his stage career, Maclyn appeared in a number of Broadway productions, including classic works such as *The Rivals* and *She Stoops to Conquer* and more contemporary offerings such as *The County Chairman* (a 1903 stage play by George Ade that Maclyn filmed in 1914) and *The Round-Up* (which Fatty Arbuckle filmed in 1920). And, like the Whartons, he too had a Hearst connection, albeit a far more tangential one: he appeared with Marion Davies, Hearst's mistress, in several elaborate costume dramas that Hearst had financed.

Like the producers before him, Arbuckle realized that the city of San Antonio offered filmmakers many advantages. "Companies can work from early morning until 8 o'clock at night," he noted. "The quaint scenery, varying from Spanish mission to that of the sagebrush, hills and cactus suitable for Western films is ideal for film production. The coast is only a few hours' distance, where marine views can be secured if wanted."[6] Even more important, Arbuckle had numerous local connections on which he could capitalize.

Leo, who had been raised in Hempstead, Texas, and who as a young man had worked in Dallas, also had some connections in the state. And, like Arbuckle, he extolled the merits of San Antonio, which he called "ideal picture country. Climate, light, everything combine to make a producer happy." As *Motion Picture News* observed, "the 'other member' [Leo] of the Wharton team is just as enthusiastic about San Antonio as both Whartons—Leo and Theo—have always been about Ithaca, NY."[7] Making the move to Texas with Leo were several members of the original Wharton company, including Robin Townley, the longtime Wharton associate who would serve as manager and head director of the new studio; Howard Cody, property man; Lew Tree, cameraman; and Antoinette de Francisco, head of the negatives department.[8]

San Antonio Motion Pictures set up shop on South Presa Street, across the street from Hot Wells and slightly north of the Southwest Insane Asylum, on the grounds of the Exposition Amusement Park, which had recently closed after nearly a decade of popularity.[9] Arbuckle assured the press that he had an ambitious program scheduled. The company's initial project, though, got off to a rocky start. The illness and death of Leo's mother Fanny, who was then living just outside New York City, postponed plans to begin filming.[10] And that was not the only delay. No sooner had Leo returned to San Antonio from New York than Arbuckle fell ill and production on their first feature comedy was canceled. As reported in *Moving Picture World*, "Mr. Arbuckle was stricken with double pneumonia while in Texas and confined to his bed for two months, compelling Mr. Wharton to abandon the comedy and hasten Mr. Arbuckle to his home in the Thousand Islands [of New York], where he is now convalescing."[11] (Notably, such reports of actors going to the country to recuperate became, during this time, a common public relations trope that helped to normalize and humanize movie personalities and to keep their names in the news.)

Fortunately for the company, its subsequent efforts proved more successful. Over the course of the next two years, in fact, San Antonio Motion Pictures produced four pictures (none of which is extant), all of them starring Arbuckle and distributed by Producers Security Corp. The first was *Squire Phin*, a five-reel comedy released on October 10, 1921. Based on the novel of the same name by Holman Francis Day, the film—advertised as "A Three-Ply Combination: Famous Star, Famous Story, Famous Actor"—was directed by Leo Wharton and Robin Townley; the scenario was prepared by Lee Royal.[12]

In the picture, Phineas Look (played by Arbuckle), the "Squire Phin" of the title, has endeared himself to the residents of the town of Palermo for his ability to settle disputes. His brother Hiram, who has lately returned from a ten-year absence, however, is well remembered and much disliked for being the town bully. After Hiram learns that Judge Willard is using the town treasury for his own purposes, he seeks to defeat him in an election. Hiram's campaign, though, is complicated by the fact that Squire Phin, who is in love with Willard's sister, supports the judge. Happily, Phin persuades

FIGURE 15.1 As "director general," Leo Wharton had ambitious plans for the San Antonio Motion Pictures Corporation.

the judge to return the money, a resolution that appeases Hiram and wins the peacemaking Phin permission to marry after all.[13]

Another film, *Welcome to Our City*, followed a few months later. Released on February 1, 1922, the five-reel comedy was once again directed by Leo Wharton and Robin Townley, with a scenario by Basil Dickey, who had earlier scripted the serials *The Romance of Elaine* and *Beatrice Fairfax* for the Whartons. In addition to Maclyn Arbuckle, the cast included Leo's wife Bessie (billed as "Besse Emerick"), Fred Dalton, Jack Crosby, Gertrude Robinson, and Charles Holleman. The film was based on a three-act farce of the same name by George V. Hobart, which had been designed to give Arbuckle a stellar stage role. But, according to *Theatre Magazine Advertiser*, the play was "a misfit part and a dire bad farce," and the production itself was "a criminal waste of space."[14] Although the film version was not much better, it allowed Arbuckle the opportunity to reprise his role as Jim Scott, a southern colonel who was always finding trouble and drawing everyone around him into it as well.

The third San Antonio Motion Pictures production, *Mr. Potter of Texas* (released on June 15, 1922), was based on a novel of the same name by Archibald Clavering Gunter that was said to be one of the most popular works of its day. Directed by Leo, with a scenario by George Rader, the five-reel comedy-drama starred Arbuckle as Sam Potter and featured, among others, Harry Carr, who had worked with both Whartons in Ithaca. The character of Potter, Leo believed, fit Maclyn perfectly and "would bring the Arbuckle name fame in the screen world equal to that it enjoyed on the stage."[15] According to a summary of the plot in the *American Film Institute Catalog*, Potter arrives in Texas with only a few dollars but eventually becomes an oil millionaire. After being widowed, he accepts an invitation from boyhood friends to visit England; from there, in the company of his daughter, he continues his journey to Egypt, where he gets involved in a revolution. Falsely accused of a crime, he is cleared by the deathbed confession of Lord Annerly, after which "Lady Annerly ends Potter's life as a widower," thus giving the story a happy ending.

Although two other pictures—*The High Sheriff* and *Red Robbin* [sic] (based on works by Irvin S. Cobb and Fred Jackson, respectively)—were advertised, *Mr. Bingle* (released on August 22, 1922) proved to be the company's fourth and final film. A melodramatic five-reeler, it centered on a poor but faithful bookkeeper who has difficulty supporting his family. His cousin's children, on the other hand, have every luxury, yet are greedy and unscrupulous. When their father returns home, apparently penniless, they turn him away. But the bookkeeper takes the man in and later inherits his million-dollar fortune, putting it to good use by establishing an orphanage. After a court ruling strips him of the money, "he loses [the] orphans but [a] child of his own arrives, and he again finds complete happiness."[16]

When Leo traveled to New York in late 1922 to market his Texas productions, the trade papers, which jokingly wondered "if he had forgotten pictures to go after oil," headlined his return: "Wharton Here with Features" and "Veteran Producer Expects to Fill a Long Felt Want with New Productions."[17] *Motion Picture News* predicted that his films "should find a ready market, since New York is always hungry for good pictures and since the Whartons know how to turn out this brand."[18] But sadly for Leo, the pictures garnered little attention, and the success that he so zealously sought continued to elude him. Nothing, moreover, came of the work that his assistant director Robin Townley was reportedly conducting in Texas in his absence. Soon thereafter, the company went out of business.[19]

Like so many smaller and independent companies, San Antonio Motion Pictures had begun with great expectations that were ultimately dashed by a lack of funding and by the centralization of the film industry in Hollywood. Its demise also effectively marked the end of Leo's film career. Although he reincorporated his film company under his own name and that of his son Leo R. Wharton (who had moved with his father to San Antonio, where he worked for a time as the assistant treasurer at the Majestic Theater, and who later followed him to New York),[20] apart from the occasional advertising short for local companies, he never made another film, either serial or feature.

A Questionable Business

While Leo's name remained in the trade papers over the next few years, it was not in connection with new film productions but rather in conjunction with a major fraud case in which he was implicated. As one of four producers associated with the Bristol Photoplay Studios, Wharton was indicted by a grand jury in New York and charged with "the solicitation of funds from those seeking advancement in the arts" and the use of the mails in a scheme to defraud.[21] Specifically, the four producers falsely claimed that they "represent[ed] well-known authors, that many of the most successful scenarios now being presented had passed through their hands, and [that] the success of them had been due to the editing and touching up by the defendants."[22]

By the late 1910s, a number of companies on both coasts had begun to capitalize on the glamour of the burgeoning film industry by pitching their services to aspiring writers who were eager to break into the business. Those writers were invited to enroll in courses or programs that would afford them access to actual film studios, which purportedly were willing to purchase their scenarios. While Bristol Photoplay Studios Inc. of New York City was only one of many such enterprises, apparently it was among the least reputable. According to its own literature, the company not only offered to put the writer's manuscript in a "photoplay form" suitable for studio consideration but also guaranteed a payment of "not more than $100" if the photoplay did not sell within thirty days. The proverbial fine print, however, stipulated that there was absolutely no assurance of the photoplay's acceptance by the studios, only Bristol's promise of submission, and that the payment from Bristol to the writer if his or her photoplay was rejected would be a mere one dollar.

Founded in 1921 by William E. Hallamore, the Bristol Photoplay Company was soon sold to Phillip Kunzinger, who became sole proprietor in 1923.[23] Editor-in-chief Vernon Hoagland was featured as "Author, Critic, Photoplaywright [sic], and Scenario Editor"; but his "lengthy pedigree, including positions with leading producers," proved to be his finest example of creative writing. It was soon revealed to be every bit as false as the numerous laudatory statements extolling his successes and his services. Yet even after Hoagland severed his relationship with the company, Bristol continued to exploit him as an "ace" among scenario writers and to claim that he would offer individual attention to every manuscript received. Of course, that in itself was "a highly improbable and physically impossible task for one man to live up to," given the number of stories submitted—by some accounts, as many as five hundred pieces of mail per day. As the new editor-in-chief, Leo Wharton "fell heir to the toga" of Hoagland in September 1924 and evidently inherited the company's problems as well.[24]

The indictment against Bristol Photoplay came about in part as the result of a case brought by Mary K. Sweeney, a young woman in Plattsburgh, New York, who was the daughter of police officer John E. Sweeney. Concerned about the fate of her photoplay "Romance," Mary wrote to Bristol Photoplay, to whom she had earlier submitted it. Leo Wharton replied, telling her that the play had not yet been accepted by any producing company. But, Mary alleged, she later learned from a friend in Troy, who had a brother on the Pacific coast in the moving picture business, that that a film company was at work on a photoplay bearing the same name and plot as hers. The case resulted in a charge of participating in a scheme to defraud that was brought against Leo and another Bristol official, both of whom were released "on heavy bail."[25]

That incident, and apparently other similar ones, led to a broader federal indictment in November 1924. According to one report, "1,800 amateur scenario writers had paid [a total of] $52,000 to the Bristol Photoplay Studio. . . . Federal officials told the court victims of the concern paid from $12 to $36 [each] for 'expert advice' and editorial revision and that, contrary to the claims of the concern in its mailed advertising, not one scenario had ever been produced through its efforts." While Bristol had promised writers that, with the company's assistance, their stories would be acceptable for photoplay use, no such market for the works existed. And even though Bristol billed itself as a studio, it had no ties to any producing companies and had never made a single film. In fact, as the indictment alleged, the company was nothing more than "a dyed-in-the-wool fake school, operated to dupe uninformed amateur playwrights."[26]

Unfortunately, Leo—by then, the head of the company—found himself in the thick of the scandal; and he was indicted along with Hallamore, Kunzinger, and Hoagland. Although the disposition of the case is unclear, it was a sad postscript and a rather ignominious end to an otherwise illustrious career.

California Dreaming

Ted Wharton, who left Ithaca less than a year after his brother Leo did, also traveled west. But whereas Leo had sought fame and success in Texas, Ted moved to Hollywood, which, especially in the wake of the dissolution of the Motion Picture Patents Company, was rapidly evolving into the film capital of the United States. As *Moving Picture World* reported, he arrived in California in early 1920 "looking for studio accommodations to produce a spectacular feature from the story 'Tangled Flags,' based on the Boxer Rebellion,"[27] whose film rights he had purchased. Written by Archibald Clavering Gunter and published in 1900, *Tangled Flags* was a popular novel that featured a Japanese officer educated at West Point who attempts to purchase artillery equipment for his government from a Connecticut arms manufactory. (Apparently, Gunter's work appealed to both Whartons: Gunter's novel *Mr. Potter of Texas* was the basis of one of the films that Leo directed for San Antonio Motion Pictures in 1922.) Although the "Tangled Flags" project never materialized, Ted found a number of studios eager to make use of his talents in other ways.

Almost immediately, Universal—by then well known for its popular westerns—hired him to work on the production of *The Moon Riders* (1920), an eighteen-part western serial that he cowrote with a team of writers that included Albert Russell and George Hively, and codirected with B. Reeves ("Breezy") Eason, a former actor and director of low-budget westerns and serial pictures. *The Moon Riders* starred Art Acord, a popular performer and stuntman in western silent films.[28] Acord had gotten his start as a cowboy and ranch hand, which is how he acquired the skills that made him a rodeo star and a two-time winner of the World Championship in Steer Wrestling at the famed Pendleton Round-Up. For a time, around 1909–1910, Acord worked with Dick Stanley's Congress of Rough Riders, a Wild West show. Later he performed alongside other cowboys from the Miller Brothers' 101 Ranch, a proving ground for the western actors who were in great demand in Hollywood.

Few rodeo stars, however, had a longer or more successful film career than Acord, who starred in over one hundred film shorts with various stock companies and movie studios. *Dramatic Mirror* described him as "the genuine cowboy: slowness of speech and unconscious drollery, the easy, graceful walk, the gentlemanly seriousness. His type is rapidly passing, and one who is able to conserve it on the screen is contributing in no mean degree to native art."[29]

In *The Moon Riders*, whose working title was *The Man Hunter*, Acord played Ranger Buck Ravelle. His costar was Mildred Moore, a former Ziegfield girl who had been featured as an ingénue in the Irene Castle melodrama *The Firing Line* (1919) and who appeared in five two-reel westerns as Hoot Gibson's leading lady before landing the coveted role opposite Acord. Billed as "an astounding Superserial of brain, brawn and bravery of catacombed cliffs and Devilmen's desperate deeds," *The Moon Riders* consisted of eighteen chapters whose titles such as "Over the Precipice," "The Death Trap," "Caves of Mystery," "At the Rope's End," and "Death's Door" suggested its holdover suspense.

In the serial (whose first episode was released on April 26, 1920), after Buck is bequeathed a large sum of money by a distant relative, he resigns his position as a ranger and sets out to collect his inheritance.[30] On the way, he rescues Anna Baldwin (Moore) from the unwelcome advances of Egbert (George Field), who is the secret leader of an outlaw gang called the Moon Riders, also known as the Devilmen. Posing as a respectable rancher, Egbert is in fact the financial backer of a group that attempts to claim title to local ranches under an old Spanish land grant. Persuaded by Anna to accompany her to her family ranch, Buck frees her father "Arizona" Baldwin (Charles Newton) from the clutches of the villain and even offers to lend Baldwin money from his inheritance so that he can settle accounts with Warpee (Tote Du Crow), an old Indian who is the chief land grant claimant. But before

FIGURE 15.2 Soon after arriving in Hollywood, Ted Wharton was engaged as a scriptwriter and codirector for the serial western *The Moon Riders* (1920).

Buck can reach Los Angeles to secure the funds, he is attacked by the Moon Riders, who steal the papers validating his inheritance. Ultimately, after passing through many hands, the money is recovered, Warpee is compensated, and the claim is settled.

In a subplot, Egbert continues his villainy. Although he has promised to marry his housekeeper's daughter Rosa, he is actually in love with Anna, whom he forces into a secret marriage. After making several attempts to eliminate her rival, Rosa eventually induces Egbert to marry her; but when he attacks and fatally wounds her, she reveals all of his deceptions before she dies. The forced marriage having been proven illegal, Anna weds Buck, who then exacts punishment on Egbert for the harm and injury he had inflicted.

The Moon Riders (which is not extant) was a true cliffhanger, "A Cyclonic Western Serial" with one or more of the principals in mortal danger at the close of each episode; and it allowed Ted to put his vast experience in serial writing and producing to good use. As Moving Picture World confirmed, "for sheer, irresistible fascination and genuine, deep-rooted interest, . . . for absolute NOVELTY, ingenious conception and gripping interest," no chapter play compares to The Moon Riders. It "grips you and holds you" and puts it over "like a Blast of T.N.T." Exhibitors were encouraged to book immediately and "to make your summer money REAL."[31]

As one of the most popular serials turned out by any studio in the silent era, The Moon Riders not only enhanced Acord's reputation as a star; it also increased Ted's foothold in the Hollywood film community. Over the next few years, he would go on to work with a number of different studios and producers. For Oliver Morosco Productions, for instance, he was signed to direct a screen version of "Slippery McGee."[32] But while Morosco found success as a theater producer on Broadway, his eponymous film company quickly folded, and the proposed film was never made. For Zenith Features Inc., Ted secured noted Greek actor George Rigas to star in a feature film based on Leota Morgan's story "The Besetting Sin," to be shot at the Louis B. Mayer studios.[33] Zenith, formed as Wharton's own production unit, had reportedly been funded by "local capital," and The Besetting Sin was scheduled to be the first film made by the company, which planned to complete four pictures a year.[34] But ultimately nothing came of that venture, either—although Ted continued for a while to maintain an office on the Mayer studio lot. For Universal, he served as part of the "Scenario staff" on pictures such as The Hunchback of Notre Dame and was credited as a writer on the studio's fifteen-part serial The Eagle's Talons.[35] Released on April 30, 1923, that serial was directed by Duke Worne and starred Fred Thomson, Ann Little, and Al Wilson; Ted shared the writing credit with Anthony Coldeway, Bertram Millhauser, Jefferson Moffitt, and Frances Marion, the most renowned female screenwriter of the twentieth century. And for the Midnite Frolic of the Ad Club in Los Angeles, a professional organization for the advertising industry, Ted directed an amateur feature written by Nick Harris, "the local Burns-Pinkerton" (security professional) who also starred in it.[36]

For the Palmer Photoplay Corporation, Ted performed a somewhat different type of service. Formed in the 1910s by Frederick Palmer, Palmer

Photoplay was a clearinghouse for story materials to be considered for film production. The company also operated the "Palmer Story Service," which synopsized new novels and stage plays as well as "worthy" original stories that were sent to the company for possible submission to the various studios. Through its "Palmer Institute of Authorship," Palmer Photoplay also offered extensive courses in photoplay writing, short-story writing, and dramatic criticism.[37] Students were encouraged to sign up for a series of correspondence studies that would develop their self-expression and self-mastery, hone their writing technique, and sharpen their "personality," all of which could lead to sales of their material to the film industry.[38] The executives on the institute's staff included industry professionals "Theodore Wharton, Studio Representative," and former Wharton screenwriter Basil Dickey, who was listed as the sole member of the "Reading Committee." The Advisory Council boasted such notables as Cecil B. DeMille, Lois Weber, and Thomas Ince, while various producers, directors, and authors/scenarists including Bess Meredith, Marion Fairfax, and Clarence Badger comprised the institute's "Contributing Instructors."

Whereas many such schools misrepresented their ties to major Hollywood studios in order to bilk aspiring and tuition-paying scenario writers, Palmer Photoplay actually functioned, at least briefly, as a studio (although, by most accounts, only at the most rudimentary level). It produced three pictures (none of which is extant), all of them made in 1924 at the Thomas Ince Studio. *Judgment of the Storm*, directed by Del Andrews and later novelized, was based on a script by one of the institute's students, Ethel Styles Middleton. The convoluted melodrama centered on the love between a young ingénue and a campus hero, whose wealthy widowed mother secretly runs an illegal gambling den, which becomes the scene of a murder that alters the lives of all the characters. *The White Sin*, another melodrama, was directed by William A. Seiter and starred Madge Bellamy as Hattie Lou, an innocent woman who is tricked into a sham marriage, abandoned by a wealthy young man, but eventually finds both legitimacy for her child and true love with that man's brother, an injured war veteran. The third and final Palmer Photoplay film, the six-reel *His Forgotten Wife*, was directed by William A. Seiter and starred Warren Baxter as soldier "John Rolfe," who suffers amnesia during the war, Madge Bellamy as the wartime nurse whom Rolfe has married and whom he loves, and Maude Waye as the woman who was affianced to "Donald Allen" (Rolfe's real name) and who inherited all his property when he was reported dead. The amnesia and the many coincidences, as one review observed, were "the ancient hokum of the film business," and the picture itself was dismissed as little more than a yarn produced by the

Palmer Photoplay School as an inducement to show those who took scenario courses that there was a production chance for the work they turned out after paying to learn how it was done.[39]

Although Palmer Photoplay never found itself embroiled in major scandal or under indictment as other similar "schools" did, it is doubtful that many—if any—of its students went on to achieve real success as scenarists, writers, or critics. And while Ted's affiliation with Palmer never compromised or tarnished his reputation the way Leo's involvement with Bristol Photoplay did, it likely did little to enhance it, either.

A Fresh Start in Santa Cruz

Ted Wharton's most ambitious cinematic effort in California, however, was not the work he did for other studios; rather, it was his attempt to launch Wharton Film Studio Inc., the company he hoped to establish in Santa Cruz and to model on the original Wharton Studio in Renwick Park. As Ted explained in his promotional materials for the project, while Los Angeles and Hollywood were among the best known and best advertised cities in the world, Santa Cruz was "off the beaten path." Yet it was, in every sense, a hidden paradise, a locality endowed with both the beauties of nature and "climatic ideality." Its scenic locations could serve as backdrops from "the wide stretches of the sands of the Sahara to the deep blue waters of the Mediterranean, or from the South Sea Islands to the snow-clad peaks of Alaska, as well as metropolitan cities and rock-bound, storm-swept coasts," all of which could be "brought within range of the camera" within just a few hours' ride.[40]

Wharton was just one of many filmmakers who attempted to capitalize on the possibilities that Santa Cruz offered. As early as 1915, the California Motion Picture Corporation created "Poverty Flat," a gold-rush village in Santa Cruz's Boulder Creek that became a set for its first picture, which was based on Bret Harte's poems.[41] The following year, 1916, another entrepreneur, Edward Ferguson, who was associated with the Universal Film Company, and his partner W. D. Dalton expressed a strong interest in establishing a permanent studio in Santa Cruz; but nothing came of their "Fer Dal Motion Picture Company" venture.[42] And in 1917, in Santa Cruz, Cecil B. DeMille filmed the drama *A Romance of the Redwoods*, which starred "America's Sweetheart" Mary Pickford as a young girl who moves west to live with her uncle, an honest prospector, only to discover that he has been killed by Indians and his identity assumed by an impostor.

A few years later, in 1923, Santa Cruz businessman and mayor-to-be Fred Swanton succeeded in drawing two other studios to the city's Boardwalk.[43]

The first was Tracy Productions, "an unassuming, yet energetic and progressive, newly-formed moving picture producing company" headed by Bert Tracy, who planned to employ a crew of Hollywood-experienced technicians and players to create a series of comedies to be released under the brand name "Lightening Comedies."[44] Tracy, who knew Santa Cruz well and who in turn was well known in the community, had an extensive background in comedy that included acting, writing, and directing, all of which seemed to work in favor of the new enterprise. But his company produced only one film, *His Weekend*, directed by Glen Lambert and starring comic actor Vernon Dent as the heavy.[45] The second studio, simply called Santa Cruz Productions, was also located on the Boardwalk. And while it attracted much attention from locals for the elaborate Tahitian village set built for its production of the picture *Hands across the Sea*, it too proved to be short-lived.[46]

Santa Cruz, however, welcomed the prospect of a permanent studio that would bring jobs and attention to the city. And that is precisely what Ted Wharton hoped to deliver. Capitalized with $1 million, consisting of one million shares of stock valued at a dollar each, Wharton Film Classics Inc., Ted boasted, would not only fill the void left by those other studios; it would also offer opportunities for the advancement and general welfare of the entire community through proposed activities "of everlasting benefit to every person." After all, "where there is an active motion picture company in their midst, there must be a considerable portion of its prosperity and success in the community."[47]

When outdoor pictures were the vogue, the consistent climate of the southern part of the state was essential to filming. But, Ted recognized, while modern lighting equipment could compensate for sunlight, there remained an "insufficient variety of natural and architectural backgrounds for the needs of the producing organizations." Consequently, up to 65 percent of California-made pictures had to be "laid in backgrounds that are from 300 to 500 miles from the many Hollywood studios," forcing producers to move their equipment great distances and then later to "reproduce in the studios the interior settings of such architectural structures as may have been used while on such locations." Retakes, moreover, necessitated a second costly and inconvenient trip.[48]

A permanent Wharton studio, Ted argued, would minimize the time and money lost in transporting actors, technical staff, and extra people. And Santa Cruz would be an ideal site, since it offered wonderful new scenic locations that had never been screened and that would prove a "revelation" when used for photoplays. The studio he proposed to build would be fully equipped, with facilities for a minimum of four producing units. The most up-to-date lighting, generators, wind machines, laboratory equipment, and a complete property and costume department would be available, along with facilities for the viewing of dailies and for the requisite post-production work. In short, Wharton Studio Services would "be all that their name implies— SERVICE," both for Wharton companies and for others at a fair price.[49]

In terms of entertainment value, Ted explained, the studio would not attempt to revolutionize motion picture production methods or to outrival the spectacular accomplishments of Griffith or DeMille. Rather, it would "cater to the masses, and not to 'the classes'" by enacting splendid stories that would not offend more delicate sensibilities. The goal for the first year would be a minimum of four feature productions, with the possibility of a serial to follow, since "distributing interests in the industry have frequently urged Mr. Wharton to produce a high-class serial of the type made famous by him in the past; it being a matter of record in the industry that the Wharton Serials are the only pictures of this type that have ever been shown in the 'first-run' theatres." The projected costs, including promotion and allowance for delays caused by illness or weather, would range from $25,000 to $50,000 for the feature pictures and $100,000 for the serial. Above all, as "an influence for good," the Wharton company would benefit both the movie industry and the community, making Santa Cruz "a City of Progress and Activity."[50]

In theory, at least, it was a strong argument. But implementing his plan proved harder than Ted imagined. According to contemporary newspaper accounts, in September 1925 he met with the Chamber of Commerce, which was chaired by Fred Garrison, to express his interest in acquiring several acres of the chamber's industrial site at Twin Lakes. Yet while members of the chamber were eager to bring a movie studio to their city, they were not unconditionally accepting of Ted's proposal. Just the opposite: they voted against him and "expressed very decided views against the use of the site by any persons who were not reasonably financed and ready to utilize the property for the purposes for which it was intended."[51]

Ted, though, was not discouraged by the chamber's decision. Instead, he pursued a new strategy. Negotiating the purchase of twenty acres in the so-called Barrett tract near Wagner Park and Horseback Hill, he began a campaign to raise funds for facilities and equipment. Progress, however, was slow—so slow that over the next year and a half, the *Santa Cruz Evening News* had few substantive developments to report.

Ultimately, nothing came of Ted's ambitious plan: the actual studio never materialized, and in the end he never got beyond the establishment of temporary offices on Pacific Avenue. The evolution of the film industry in the 1920s meant that the city of Santa Cruz, despite its many rich offerings, never became the "little Hollywood" envisioned by Wharton or by the city's leaders.[52] The increasingly elaborate sets being constructed on Hollywood lots diminished the need to travel beyond Los Angeles; and studios began to realize greater efficiency through centralization, making competition for smaller independents difficult at best.

So Ted returned to Hollywood without ever producing a single film in Santa Cruz. Anecdotal evidence suggests that he was able to secure employment again with other studios. Gerald M. Best, an award-winning Hollywood sound engineer who had worked for a time with the Whartons in Ithaca in the 1910s, for example, recalled seeing Ted on a studio lot at First National Studios in Burbank, where he was employed as an assistant director on a picture that was being filmed there.[53] But by then serials and silents were on the wane, and the exciting possibilities of sound production were changing and reshaping the film industry once again.

The Final Chapter

Sadly, little more is known about the Whartons' final years. Business records archived as part of the Wharton Collection in the Division of Rare and Manuscript Collections at Cornell University show that in the early to mid-1920s, Wharton associate Charles V. Henkel was still working out of the office the brothers had established back in 1917 as the New York City branch of their Ithaca studio. Under the auspices of the Wharton Releasing Company, Henkel and Arthur ("Archie") Feary oversaw the distribution of pictures by the Film Company of Ireland (FCOI) throughout the Northeast, an enterprise in which Ted or Leo might have been indirectly involved. Such distribution arrangements were not uncommon, especially as struggling silent filmmakers turned to exhibiting or road-showing pictures by other producers as a way of supporting their own film efforts. Late in his career, for example, after Florida-born and -based silent filmmaker Richard E. Norman tried unsuccessfully to make the leap to sound film production, he exhibited feature pictures by a former rival, the pioneering African American writer, director, and race film producer Oscar Micheaux, showing them in schools, auditoriums, and churches—the same audiences that the American office of FCOI tried to reach with its film rentals. If, however, any association between the Whartons and the FCOI existed, it can only be surmised, not confirmed.[54]

More certain, though, are the circumstances of the Whartons' deaths. Leo died first, on September 29, 1927 (reported in several obituaries as September 27), in New York City.[55] He was fifty-seven years old, and it is estimated that over the course of his career as actor, screenwriter, producer, and director, he had been involved in over a hundred films. Leo was survived by his sister Eugenia Buck (wife of the Wharton Studio's onetime general manager J. Whitworth Buck) and his second wife, Bessie Wharton (born Bessie Emrick, in Rochester, Indiana, in 1875), an actress who had appeared in a number of the Whartons' productions, including their popular serial *The Exploits of Elaine* (1914) and the controversial eugenics film *The Black Stork* (1917), as well as in Leo's San Antonio Motion Pictures film *Welcome to Our City* (1922). Bessie, popularly known as the "Famous 'Mother of the Screen,'" died a decade later, in Boston, on December 13, 1939.[56] Records indicate that the couple had divorced sometime before 1925.[57] Although it was not mentioned in any of the obituaries, Leo was also survived by a daughter, Marie Wharton Shaffer (1893–1979), from his brief first marriage to Jennie Leach, and a son, Leo Richmond Wharton (1899–1977), from his second marriage to Bessie.[58]

Ted died a few years after Leo, on November 28, 1931, reportedly of thyroid disease, in Hollywood. He was fifty-six years old, and by his own account he had been involved as screenwriter, producer, or director in six hundred or more films.[59] Ted, who had no children, was survived by his sister Eugenia Buck and by his wife Anna Disbrow Wharton, who died in the Bronx on May 6, 1947.[60] At one time, he was reputed to be very wealthy. More than a decade earlier, one paper had suggested that he was among "the highest salaried [producers]" and that he drew "a nice little check every week."[61] That fact was confirmed by his former Wharton Studio bookkeeper, who remembered that Ted's weekly salary during the Ithaca years was $500.[62] And Essanay colleague Louella Parsons recalled that, earlier in his career at that studio, he received "what was considered a huge salary for those days."[63] But, by his final years, Ted had dissipated any fortune that he may have amassed. According to one contemporary account, he, like his brother Leo (who fell into debt because of extravagant expenditures, including those for "wardrobe and gin" for second wife Bessie and "damages" incurred by his son Leo), had little financial sense, either personally or professionally; and a gambling habit relieved him of whatever money was left.[64] Consequently, as his obituary in *Variety* noted, Ted was buried by the Motion Picture Relief Fund, surely an inauspicious end for an early cinema pioneer.[65]

The posthumous accolades for Ted were numerous: the force behind such popular and lucrative films as *The Exploits of Elaine*, he was acclaimed (albeit a bit inaccurately) as the "originator of motion picture serials"[66] and hailed for essentially inventing the serial technique.[67] Most significantly, though, as the *International Photographer* affirmed, he was "a man of unusually high character and was respected accordingly by a host of men and women who were part of the motion picture industry in the earlier days."[68]

Yet despite Ted's many distinctions, the last decade of his life, like Leo's, was no doubt filled with disappointment. Perhaps *Variety* summed it up best, observing that, since their Ithaca studio had been "taken over," the brothers kept trying to return to the making of serials. "But the episode films were on the wane and they were unable to adapt themselves [fully] to feature production."[69]

The advent of sound film production, moreover, marked the beginning of a new chapter in the story of motion pictures—one that, for a time, seemed to turn the page on the Whartons. Yet the remarkable and enduring contributions that these prolific filmmakers made to the silent film industry confirm that they clearly deserve the attention they are finally receiving. A close examination of their careers reveals their profound impact on the early serial picture and their influence on later popular genres, from crime and mystery procedurals to sensation-filled blockbusters. It also restores Ted and Leo Wharton to the classical narrative of early filmmaking and celebrates the special magic that these silent serial sensations brought to early cinema.

Appendix 1

The Mysteries of Myra

"The Dagger of Dreams" (Episode One)

The Whartons' landmark serial *The Mysteries of Myra* (1916) explored daring themes of spiritualism and the occult and introduced film audiences to a world of supernatural phenomena that included astral projection, thought photography, and levitation. The scenarios were written by serial-picture veteran Charles W. Goddard, in collaboration with noted British-born American psychic investigator Hereward Carrington. In the opening episode, the Grand Master of the mysterious and sinister Black Order that is behind the deaths of her two older sisters plots the demise of young Myra Maynard. Should Myra die before reaching her eighteenth birthday, the fortune of her late father John Maynard would revert to the Order, of which Maynard was a member. But psychic investigator Dr. Payson Alden intervenes and, as he does throughout the serial, rescues her from the predations of the Master and of Arthur Varney, who acts as Myra's friend but is in fact a member of the Black Order that is plotting her death.

The version of the script that appears here was registered by the Whartons at the Library of Congress in 1916. Certain small changes were made when the script was filmed: in this version, for example, Myra is about to turn twenty; in the finished serial, she is seventeen. The original spellings and punctuation, even when inconsistent, incorrect, or idiosyncratic, have been retained. (Wharton Releasing Corporation Records, #3924, Division of Rare and Manuscript Collections, Cornell University Library.)

"Mysteries of Myra"

Story by
Hereward Carrington
&
Charles W. Goddard
Produced by Wharton, Inc.

Episode 1
April 17, 1916

Subtitle 1.
As daylight arrives the members of the Black Order finish their mysterious incantations.

Scene 1.
The Main Council chamber of the Black Order. A large room with a dirt or cement floor. Up stage heavy black curtains meet in the center over a black altar. Just below altar stands an incense burner on a tripod. From tripod two rows of kneeling worshippers extend obliquely down stage right and left. For their costumes see Mr. Carrington's illustrations. There ought to be about a dozen of these worshippers. In the space between the worshippers a diagram of the Sacred Pentogram [sic] (which Mr. Carrington will give you) is painted on the floor. Near the tripod is the leader of ceremonies. He puts a pinch of incense in the tripod. As the vapor arises they all chant.

"Ahmi Padmi Hom."

Subtitle.
The Grand Master whose face they seldom see.

Scene 2.
Close up of George Arliss type of man. He is resting his chin in his palms and his thumbs are sticking up. Only his face, hands, thumbs and arms from his elbows. If no foreground or background is shown and this scene is in red, it ought to be effective. The Masters eyes are closed at first. Then they suddenly open very wide look left then right. Then he shows his teeth in a sardonic smile, reaches off into darkness, brings a small gong and hammer into the light and taps it.

Scene 3.
Main council chamber. Everyone chanting as before. Leader of Ceremonies hears something and orders them to stop. They all pause and listen.

Scene 4.
Flash of Grand Master lilting the gong.

Scene 5.
Main council chamber. They all rise from their knees and begin to talk. Someone again holds up a hand in warning. They all look left toward door. One of them taps on door and listens to answering taps. They are evidently satisfactory and door is opened. (perhaps after a pass word has been given) Arthur Varney carrying hat and gown like others enters. He is the handsome heavy. He places his fists to his cheeks with his thumbs up. They all respond in like manner and shake hands. He evidently has something on his mind and glances anxiously at the big curtains while he puts on hat and gown. Finally he whispers to the Leader of Ceremonies saying that he must see the Grand Master. The Leader of Ceremonies is doubtful but finally steps behind the curtains while the others wait in awe. He returns at once and tells Varney to enter. Varney bows before the altar, spreads his hands over the burning incense and passes between the curtains.

Scene 6.
The other side of the curtains. It is dark but the silhouette of Varney parting the curtains and approaching the camera is seen by the light from the other chamber. As soon as he drops the curtains it is dark again.

Scene 7.
Close foreground of Varney's face slowly fading in red. His head and eyes turn slowly in the direction from which the light comes and he registers a start which he controls.

Scene 8.
Same opening up into larger set showing both Varney's face and what he is looking at. It is a glowing spectral head of the devil with horns etc. on the wall as if it were painted in phosphorescent paint. (I'll probably have to explain what I mean when I see you, but in Carrington's book "The Ghost of Opera" is an illustration of an effect just like what I mean.)

Spoken title.
"Master, where art thou?"

Continuing scene.
Varney speaks the above and registers that he sees something.

Scene 9.
Same as Scene 2. Grand Master resting on elbows, thumbs up, etc. in red. He asks "have you done your work?"

Scene 10.
Same as scene 8. Varney says that he has, hesitates and then speaks.

Spoken title.
"Master I beg you to let her live and marry me. I'll give her fortune to the Lodge.["]

Continuing scene.
Varney speaks the above earnestly.

Scene 11.
Same as scene 9. Grand Master refuses emphatically /

Scene 12.
Same as scene 10. Varney pleads.

Scene 13.
Same as scene 11. Grand Master refuses with even greater emphasis, and dismisses him.

Scene 15. [No Scene 14 in script.]
Main council chamber. Varney comes out of curtain showing emotion. He takes off his costume. Just as he starts to go another man is admitted. He is a sneaky looking young man and carries a costume which he puts on. He is hastily passed through the curtains. Varney goes out through door. The others start removing their costumes and going out.

Spoken title.
"Master I left your warning but see he suspects us of killing the other two Maynard sisters."

Scene 16.
Same as scene 8. Except that sneaky looking man is standing near the spectral head. Man speaks the above produces several papers from his pocket and

holds in front of him. A hand is seen taking them from him. Man registers that he sees something.

Scene 17.
Same as scene 2. The Grand Master above the light looks at papers takes from them an ordinary index card with two holes punched in it such as is used in card index cabinets. Very close foreground of card. It reads:

(printed) Payson Alden, M.D.

(Typewritten) "SUICIDE of the two daughters of John Maynard on their twentieth birthdays. If the third daughter dies in same manner fortune will go to Black Lodge. Suspect occult influences.["]

Continuing scene.
Full set. Master reads the above, registers brief surprise then smiles sardonically and dismisses the man.

Subtitle.
Payson Alden a young doctor who has given up his practice to investigate certain occult influences which science cannot fathom.

Scene 18.
A small neat bedroom. Dr. Payson Alden a man of about 27 or 28 in bed asleep. He is good looking, clean intellectual type of man. Alarm clock near bed goes off. Alden wakes up shuts off alarm, stretches himself, shakes sleep off rapidly and sits on the side of bed. He suddenly becomes aware of a piece of folded paper pinned to his pajamas right over his heart. In surprise he removes paper unfolds and starts to read:

Close foreground of paper.
   ["]Cease your investigations of the occult. The hand that placed this warning over your heart can also stop its beating." (It is signed with the Satanic double cross (see illustration in Mr. C.'s book.)

Continuing scene.
Full set. Dr. Alden reads the above with a slight shudder, tries door, sees it is locked, looks hastily at window and decides the warning was brought that way. He hastily slips on bath robe and hurries out.

Subtitle.
Dr. Alden's laboratory for testing all supernatural mysteries such as spirits, mediums, astral bodies, aura, etc.

Scene 19.

The laboratory see diagram and illustrations to be supplied by Mr. Carrington. Dr. Alden enters looks hurriedly around to see if anything has been disturbed, decides everything is all right and finally notices that one drawer of a small filing cabinet is open. He looks in, pulls out large envelope.

Close foreground of same shows written on it.

Maynard Case.

His hand opens it and shows it is empty.

Continuing scene.

Dr. Alden registers that he has been robbed of his records. He registers angry determination, rings messenger calls and hastily writes note.

Close foreground of his hand writing as follows:

Mrs. John Maynard:
My dear Madam:—
    Kindly allow me to call on you this morning on certain matters regarding your daughter's approaching birthday.
(it is signed) "Payson Alden."

Subtitle.
Miss Myra Maynard finds candle grease on one of her slippers—the other is missing.

Scene 20.

Myra's bedroom. A large tastefully and elegantly fitted girl's bedroom. On a table near the window stands a dying plant of some sort. The walls and furnishing should suggest an old house, but one that was furnished richly to begin with and kept well up. Myra the heroine, a girl of twenty, should have besides good looks prominent eyes, or some unusual feature that might suggest psychic powers. Myra is completely dressed in a house dress. She takes off her bedroom slippers, picks up a high heeled slipper, starts to put it on and notices something wrong with it. She looks over at a half burned candle standing on table unlit, and brings the slippers over beside it.

Close foreground of slipper and candle shows her finger picking spot of candle grease from slipper.

Continuing scene.
Full set. Myra says "candle grease" and registers wonder, finishes picking it off, puts on the slipper and then begins hunting for the other one.

Scene 21.
Library of a fine old fashioned house in keeping with bedroom of previous scene. Butler enters slowly sorting over a handful of letters. He hits his foot against a slipper lying on the floor. He looks down and picks it up.

Close foreground shows it to be the mate of the one in previous scene.

Continuing scene.
Full set. Butler examines slipper, looks puzzled and bends over to examine the rug. He notices something on the rug near the wall at a point where we will show later exists a secret door.

Close foreground of butler's fright, picking at candle grease spots on the rug.

Continuing scene.
Full set. Butler registers concern, lays down his letters and starts out scanning the carpet carefully for some traces of candle grease. He almost runs into Mrs. Maynard, Myra's mother. She is a well dressed handsome woman of refinement. She says "Good morning". Butler starts and hides slipper behind him. She registers slight curiosity at his behavior.

Spoken title.
"Willis please ask Miss Myra how soon she will be down to breakfast."

Continuing scene.
Mrs. Maynard speaks the above. Butler bows and exits concealing slipper from her.

Scene 22.
Myra's bedroom. She is prancing around looking under bed and all over for the missing slipper. She hears a knock at door, and crosses for it.

Scene 23.
Close up of outwide [*sic*] of her door. Butler, slipper in hand knocks and
waits, then he bends down and picks candle grease on floor. Door opens,
Myra appears, butler delivers his message. Myra points at her slipper and
says, "I can't find my other slipper."

Butler hands her its mate and says he found it in library. She looks surprised
and thanks him. He registers concern and goes.

Subtitle.
The cook is superstitious.

Scene 24.
The kitchen of the Maynard house, large clean, but not very new fangled. Cook
puttering at something on the stove. Young maid fixing her cap or hair in front
of small mirror which is placed in some insecure place. Crossing from the stove
to cupboard or some other place, cook knocks mirror over, which breaks. Then
cook shakes her fist at the broken mirror and then up at ceiling?

Spoken title.
"Old man Maynard was a Devil worshipper. Sure and there's been a curse on
this house ever since he died."

Continuing scene.
Cook speaks the above. The maid tries to hush her as if she were afraid to
have such words spoken. Maid hastily picks up the pieces? Something starts
to burn on the stove. Cook points to it as further evidence of the curse, then
rescues it. A black cat walks in front of the camera, and suddenly spits at the
empty air. The maid does not see it but the cook does and drops the pan she
has rescued from the stove. She calls the maid's attention to the cat's behavior and they find no cause for it.

Spoken title.
"The house is cursed. The two older daughters killed themselves on their
twentieth birthdays—walking in their sleep."

Continuing scene.
Cook speaks the above with conviction. Maid asks about it. They stop as
butler enters stroking his head and muttering to himself gloomily. The maid
asks what is the matter.

Spoken title.
"Miss Myra has begun walking in her sleep just like the others."

Continuing scene.
Butler speaks the above. The cook says: "I told you so—the place is cursed."

The butler agrees unwillingly. They all hear something and he hurries off in response.

Scene 25.
Dining room of same house. Mrs. Maynard at the table. Myra enters crosses to her mother and they exchange an affectionate morning kiss. Myra sits down and they begin breakfast as butler brings in something and goes out looking concernedly at Myra. She chuckles at his evident worry as soon as his back is turned and speaks to her mother.

Spoken title.
"Willis is so worried because I walked in my sleep last night."

Continuing scene.
Myra laughingly speaks the above. Mrs. M. registers great shock, controls herself with difficulty and asks about it. Myra starts to tell her as if it were of no consequence.

Scene 26.
Front door of Maynard house. Messenger boy ringing bell. Door opened by butler who takes Dr. Alden's letter, signs receipt and closes door, boy goes.

Scene 27.
Dining room. Mrs. M. very preoccupied is gazing into space. Myra is busily eating her breakfast. She looks up with a happy smile and speaks.

Spoken title.
"Day after tomorrow I'll be twenty years old."

Continuing scene.
Myra gayly speaks the above. Mother registers another shock. Myra asks what's the matter. She says: "nothing at all". Butler enters with note which he hands to Mrs. M. who opens and reads.

Very close foreground shows it to be the note which Payson Alden wrote in his laboratory.

Continuing scene.
Full set. Mrs. M. reads note with evident dismay. Myra asks her what it is, Mrs. M. evades a reply and hides the note away in her bosom of her dress or some other convenient place about her person. Myra wonderingly looks thoughtfully at her mother. She rests her chin on her hands and unconsciously raises her thumbs in the devil worshippers attitude. Mrs. M. still thinking about the letter, raises her coffee cup to her lips and happens to see her daughter sitting with her thumbs up. She screams, jumps up/ crosses to Myra, seizes her thumbs frantically and pushes them down. She tells her never to put her thumbs like that again, or it will d[r]ive her crazy. Myra does not understand what all this outburst is about and asks what is the matter with her thumbs.

Spoken title.
"Your father used to do that. It is the sign of the Devil Worshippers."

Continuing scene.
Mrs. M. speaks the above. Myra still wondering what she means looks up at her thumbs and places her chin in her hands with the thumbs up to see if that is what she means. This almost sends Mrs. M. into hysterics. She rushes out of the room. Myra watches her go and starts to follow. Butler enters.

Spoken title.
"Mr. Varney is calling."

Butler speaks the above. Myra registers pleased surprise and says: "I'll be right down," and proceeds to give her hair one or two little touches before a mirror on the sideboard.

Scene 28.
Parlor or drawing room. Varney standing with overcoat on. He lays hat down and takes off gloves, but does not remove coat. Butler enters gives message and exits. Varney as soon as he is gone, crosses to another door leading to library and exits.

Scene 29.
Varney enters, glances around to make sure nobody is looking, then hastily crosses to wall, looks for something on floor, sees candle grease, registers

evil satisfaction, cautiously feels along wall and touches secret spring. A door opens in the wall. He looks in, hears someone coming, hastily closes door and is discovered innocently examining a book or painting as Myra enters.

They greet each other with the affection of persons about to be engaged. She asks him to take off his coat, but he says he has only come for a moment to invite her to the opera on her birthday. She says "look" and mischievously, makes the sign of the Devil worshippers. He is startled and looks at her sharply for a moment, wondering how much she knows. She asks, what he knows about Devil Worshippers.

Spoken title.
"I don't know anything about Devil Worshippers. See. I am an ANGEL Worshipper."

Varney speaks the above, takes her thumbs away from her head, joins them together, drops on his knees and kisses them. She laughingly rebukes him. He hastily rises as Mrs. M. enters. They greet each other pleasantly. She has recovered her composure.

Spoken title.
"Arthur has invited us to the opera on my birthday."

Continuing scene.
Myra speaks the above joyously. Mrs. M. starts to accept until she hears the word 'birthday', then she looks troubled and says they can't go. Varney registers polite regret but Myra is surprised and disappointed, she wants to know why. Mrs. M. stalls. Myra demands a reason. Mrs. M. is embarrassed but still evades answering. Varney bids them good-bye pleasantly and goes. Myra becomes mutinous, stamps her foot and insists on her mother's reasons.

Spoken title.
"Your two sisters died on their twentieth birthdays—that's why you are going to stay in the house with me on yours."

Continuing scene.
Mrs. M. firmly speaks the above. Myra saddened by the recollection of her sisters for a moment, nevertheless protests. Mrs. M. forbids her to discuss it.

She sits down silent but mutinous and unconsciously assumes the thumbs up attitude. Mrs. M. sees it, screams at her to take them down. Myra goes out wrathfully.

Scene 30.
Parlor or drawing room. Butler ushers in Dr. Alden takes his card and goes out.

Scene 31.
Library. Mrs. M. pacing floor thoughtfully. Butler enters and hands her card.

Very close foreground of card. It reads:

"Payson Alden, M.D."

Continuing scene.
Full set. Mrs. Maynard reads card, doesn't remember who he is, suddenly recollects and produces letter from her dress and opens.

Very close foreground of flash of Alden's letter asking for an appointment.

Continuing scene.
Full set. Mrs. Maynard hesitates, then goes out.

Scene 32.
Parlor or drawing room. Dr. Alden is looking at large photo or painting of Myra with considerable interest. Mrs. Maynard enters rather suspiciously, asks what he wants. He points to Myra's picture and asks if that is the daughter. Mrs. Maynard quite stiffly says it is and asks his business.

Subtitle.
Mrs. Maynard is suspicious of anyone who ever investigates occult mysteries.

Continuing scene.
Dr. Alden informs her that he is an investigator of the occult. She freezes at the word and says that she does not care to discuss it with him. He tells her it is important, but she will not listen. He points to Myra's picture and says it is a matter of life and death. Mrs. Maynard refuses to hear anything at all, bows and goes. He follows her to the door pleading, then registers that he knows he is dismissed and that it is useless to butt in. Reluctantly he

picks up hat and gloves and starts to go. He crosses to picture and admires it again. Myra looks in door and sees him admiring her portrait. She watches mischievously—he starts somewhat guiltily at being discovered. She crosses to him and says in a whisper.

Spoken title.
"What's all this mystery about me?"

Continuing scene.
Myra speaks the above. Dr. Alden hesitates and does not know what to say. He finally says her mother has forbidden him. She teases and wheedles to know. He resists. Finally she assumes the thumbs up attitude and asks him mischievously if he knows what that means. He is startled and says it means devil worshippers. He places his chin in his hands with thumbs up at one end of a table to show her, while she does the same at the other. Mrs. Maynard enters at this point and sees this suspicious stranger practicing the abhorred devil's sign. She is almost beside herself and angrily orders him out. There is nothing for Dr. Alden to do but go. He does so with a regretful look at Myra who returns his glance with a sort of wistful smile. Butler enters to see what is the matter and Mrs. Maynard tells him to show Dr. Alden out. Butler and Dr. Alden go. Mrs. Maynard drops into chair and weeps. Myra wondering tries to comfort her.

Scene 33.
Outside front door Butler ushers Dr. Alden out and stiffly orders him not to return again. He walks down steps of house very sadly and regretfully, evidently wishing there were some way to get back.

Subtitle.
After worrying all day about Myra's case, Dr. Alden decides to test his theories at even at the risk of his arrest.

Scene 34.
Dr. Alden's laboratory. He is sitting at table reading a large book. Close foreground of book shows its title is "Sleep-walking."

Continuing scene.
Full set. Dr. Alden lays down book, says to himself "that's it, sleep-walking[.]" He paces floor, quickly registers decision, goes to cabinet, takes down jar, removes a little paste from it, puts it into a small glass box, slips box into pocket and goes out.

Subtitle.
That evening. Dr/ Alden plays burglar.

Scene 36 [for 35].
Moonlight effect. The grounds of the Maynard place. It is a large old fashioned house such as are quite common in Westchester County near New York City. Then follow one or two short scenes according to location of Dr. Alden entering grounds furtively approaching the house and looking in window.

Scene 36.
Dining room. A few feet of Mrs. Maynard, Myra and Varney in evening dress eating dinner.

Scene 37.
Outside window. Dr. Alden goes away from window and feels of the next one, finds it is not locked and carefully opens it.

Scene 38.
Library rather dimly lighted. Alden climbs in through window, looks about cautiously and goes out on tip-toe.

Scene 39.
Dining room. Varney acts as if he had heard or in some way sensed something in the next room. He asks if anything [*sic*] heard anything. They listen and say "NO" and soon resume their conversation."

Scene 40.
Stairway of same house. Dr. Alden sneaks up hurriedly and furtively.

Scene 41.
Hall near Myra's bedroom. Her door and another door near each other. Alden sneaks up, opens other door, looks in closes door carefully, then opens door of Myra's room.

Scene 42.
Myra's room dimly lighted by moonlight from window. Alden vaguely seen entering. He finds electric switch and lights room. He glances around hurriedly, then takes little glass box from pocket and smears paste from it thinly on inside door knob to her room. Then being careful to leave this door wide open, he puts out lights and exits.

Subtitle.
That night as Myra's clock struck 12.

Scene 43.
In blue. Very close foreground of pretty china clock. It is exactly 12 o'clock.
Move camera back on tracks and open up into full set of Myra's bedroom.
She is asleep in bed, moon dimly lights room. She slowly sits up in bed and
turns toward clock. She counts the strokes of twelve. Then with a dazed
look, she gets up talking to herself as if arguing with someone. She gets into
slippers, dons dressing gown, lights candle, opens door and hesitates seemingly arguing with the empty air.

Subtitle.
The combined evil influences of thirteen evil minds.

Scene 44.
The Main council chamber of Black Lodge. Same set as in early scenes.
Incense burning as before. Twelve worshippers in costumes led by same
leader of ceremonies are chanting.

"Ahmi Padmi Hom," over and over again.

Among the worshippers and kneeling next to the Leader is Varney.

Scene 45.
A flash in the red of Master of Ceremonies with head in hands and thumbs up
above his light same as in earlier scenes. He too, is chanting "Ahmi Padmi Hom."

Scene 46.
Myra's bedroom. She is still hesitating at the door but as if led by an unseen
influence, goes out.

Scene 47.
The stairway. Very dim, moonlight effect. Myra carrying candle and talking
to herself, descends in ghostlike manner. In her left hand she carries lighted
candle tipping so it drops grease, and her right hand on bannister.

Scene 48.
The council chamber of Black Lodge. A few feet showing some business of
chanting. Varney stands up and makes motions as if giving ~~instructi~~ direction
to some distant person, although he is facing a blank wall.

Scene 49.

Library. Faint moon, light from window. Scene lights gradually as Myra enters with candle in left hand. She is still talking to herself. She feels along the wall with her right hand until she reaches the secret spring. She presses this. Secret door opens and she enters leaving door open.

Scene 50.

Secret chamber. It is a small room with dust and cobwebs as if nobody had been there in years. It is a duplicate on a small scale, of the Black Lodge Council Chamber. Only there is no incense in the tripod and the black curtains are moth eaten, and almost ready to fall. There is no light except what comes from Myra's approaching candle. She descends a couple of steps, crosses to altar, sets down candle and picks up dagger and sheet of paper. She reads paper, registers shudder of horror, puts it and dagger where she found them and walks slowly up the steps pleading with someone unseen.

Scene 51.

Myra enters from secret door, closes it and slowly walks out of library.

Scene 52.

Flash of Council chamber. They are all chanting as before. Varney facing wall acts as if directing someone to ascend.

Scene 53.

Myra's bedroom. She enters, closes door, places candle where she found it and blows it out.

Subtitle.

Next morning Myra finds peculiar stains on her right hand.

Scene 54.

Myra's bedroom. The bed is thrown back as if she had just gotten up, but she is fully dressed. She looks at her hand and crosses to door to lavatory.

Scene 55.

Her lavatory adjoining room. She enters and scrubs her hands vigorously. Close foreground of her hands showing her trying to remove several stains on the tips of her fingers.

Scene 56.
Laboratory. Alden at phone.

Scene 57.
Dining room of the Maynard home. Mrs. Maynard and Myra at breakfast[.] Butler enters and says "Dr. Alden wants to speak to you." Myra looks rather pleasantly interested, but Mrs. Maynard says she will not speak to him. Butler goes out.

Scene 58.
Library. Butler enters, crosses to phone (receiver off hook) and says, "Mrs/ Maynard cannot talk to you." and hangs up.

Scene 59.
Laboratory. Dr. Alden registers disappointment, hangs up and paces floor anxiously.

Subtitle.
That afternoon the Maynards replenish their coal supply.

Scene 60.
The grounds of Maynard place. Several very dirty coal covered men carrying the coal across the grounds in bags on their backs and dumping it into a chute through a cellar window.

Scene 61.
Back door of Maynard house, a coal dust covered man with a dirty slouch hat pulled over his forehead so that his face is hard to recognize, and carrying a shovel, knocks at door. Maid admits him.

Scene 62.
Kitchen. Maid leads man across kitchen. Cook scolds him for walking with dirty feet across her clean floor. As soon as he is gone she mops up where he walked.

Scene 63.
Cellar. Maid leads man to coal bin. He gets in and starts to shovel the coal that comes from the chute to the four corners of the bin. As soon as maid is gone, he lays down shovel and sneaks after her.

Subtitle.
Varney's attentions to Miss Maynard are disturbed by the noisy coal men.

Scene 64.
Parlor. Myra and Varney sitting close together. Varney starts to make some sort of a love speech. Myra does not seem to hear him. He registers annoyance, goes to window and looks out.

Scene 65.
Flash of men dumping bag of coal into chute.

Scene 66.
Stairway. Coal man from cellar sneaks up stairs and examines banister. He discovers something and bends over.

Very close foreground of banister, showing pronounced finger marks.

Continuing scene.
Full set. Coal man descends registering that he finds more finger marks as he goes.

Scene 67.
Parlor. Varney is again trying to talk intimately against the noise of the coal/

Scene 68.
Library. Coal man enters furtively looking for trace of finger marks. In his doubt where to look, he scratches his head, and so doing, pushes his hat back, and reveals himself as Dr. Alden. He soon finds the finger prints and follows them along the wall toward the secret door.

Scene 69.
Parlor. Varney about to light a cigarette has no matches. Myra runs out to get him some.

Scene 70.
Alden has reached the secret door, and is trying to figure out where the finger prints went next. He stoops down and discovers candle grease on floor. At this moment Myra enters and catches him. She asks what he is doing there. He jumps up and begs her to keep quiet and starts to explain. She recognizes him and does not know what to make of it. She hesitates about

calling for help. Varney enters, registers that he knows who he is, but quickly conceals it. He starts to seize Alden who hurls him off. He starts to explain. Butler rushes in. Varney starts with help of butler to seize him, but Myra restrains them. His explanation is prevented by the arrival of Mrs. Maynard. At sight of him she screams arrest him. Butler and Varney fly at him. He knocks Varney down, dodges butler, and leaps through window.

Scene 71.
Outside library. Alden leaps out of window runs past the coal chute and off. The two coal men pause and ask each other who he is. Butler and Varney rush into scene followed by Mrs. Maynard and Myra. They ask who the man was.

Spoken title.
"He aint working with us lady. Most likely he is a burglar."

Continuing scene.
One of coal men speaks the above. Mrs. Maynard is aghast. Varney agrees with coal man, and is very anxious and indignant.

Subtitle.
In the evening. Mrs. Maynard hires a trusty watchman to guard the house against further intrusion.

Scene 72.
Library. Mrs. Maynard enters followed by big burly man who carries a club. She calls Myra who explains where Alden was caught and pantomine [*sic*] that he was kneeling near secret door. Watchman solemnly nods and pulls up chair to watch the spot. Mrs. Maynard indicates that he watch windows, etc. He assures her that he will. She and Myra go. He yawns and stretches himself comfortably in a chair and starts to doze. Butler enters backward giving instructions to a couple of expressmen who carry in a box and set it down. Butler stumbles over watchman who wakes up, draws gun and asks what they mean. Butler scornfully explains. He apologizes and makes himself comfortable while they go out. They wake him up again returning with a large and heavy rolled up rug. This they place alongside the wall or other convenient place and go. While they are doing this, the watchman goes to sleep again with his pistol in his hand. The butler watches him a moment in disgust, then he gently removes his club and gun and yells "wake up" in his ear. Watchman leaps to his feet and seeing butler armed, he holds up his

hands. Butler solemnly hands him back his gun and club and tells him to stay awake. He swears that he will. Butler goes out and watchman proceeds to go to sleep again.

Subtitle.
Just before midnight.

Scene 73.
Library. Watchman sound asleep. The rug suddenly unrolls and hits the watchman's feet. He slowly wakes up as Dr. Alden gets out of rug. At sight of Alden getting out of rug, the watchman is almost scared to death, drops gun and retreats to opposite wall. Alden grabs gun and covers him. Watchman starts to yell, but Alden makes him shut up.

Spoken title.
"I'm a detective you fool, keep quiet and watch what happens."

Continuing scene.
Alden speaks the above. Watchman has his doubts, but after some further argument subsides. Alden holds up his hand warning him to keep quiet. They both watch doorway. Myra enters in dressing gown over night dress, and slippers, carrying candle as before and talking to nobody.

Scene 74.
Flash of Council Chamber, Black Lodge chanting as before. Varney directing someone by gesture. His face registers anguish as if he hated to do it this time.

Scene 75.
Flash of Master in red light lilting gong.

Scene 76.
Council Chamber. Varney hears the gong, shows fear and goes on with his motioned instructions.

Scene 77.
Library. Myra watched intently by Alden and watchman, hesitates, starts to return, then goes on. She reaches secret spring and presses it. Secret door opens and she enters secret chamber followed by Alden and the trembling watchman.

Scene 78.

The secret chamber. It grows lighter as Myra enters with candle followed closely by Alden. She goes to altar, picks up paper and reads:

Very close foreground of paper.

It reads: "At midnight, on your twentieth birthday, you will pass into the next world. Here is the means."

Continuing scene.

Full set. Myra reads the above registers shudder of horror and pleads with some unseen person.

Scene 79.

Council Chamber black Lodge. Business as before. Varney hesitates upon something and nerves himself to continue. He makes gestures as if indicating to someone to stab herself.

Scene 80.

Secret chamber. Myra shudders, seizes dagger and starts to stab herself. Alden tears the dagger away from her. She screams, wakes, struggles an instant and then faints. He carries her out.

Scene 81.

Library. Alden aided by watchman, carries the moaning and half-conscious girl in from secret door and lays her on couch. She tries to talk, opens her eyes and seems to see things. Mrs. Maynard in night gown, slippers and dressing gown, rushes in with butler who has trousers over his pajamas. She is horrified at the sight, and starts to denounce Alden, but the watchman explains and Alden points to secret chamber. Mrs. Maynard then thinks Myra is dangerously ill and hurries to her. Myra does not recognize her.

Spoken title.

"No the girl is not sick. She is in a trance. I believe she is [a] natural psychic."

Continuing scene.

Alden speaks the above. Myra fumbles around with her right hand as if trying to write. Alden produces pencil and paper, puts pencil in her hand and paper under it. After some abortive attempts she writes.

Very close foreground of her handwriting.

"Someone from another world wishes to warn you that—"

Continuing scene.
Full set. They all bend over while she writes. Mrs. Maynard screams and breaks the trance. Myra wakes up, struggles, looks around wildly and wonders where she is. This scene fades out.

Scene 82.
Fade into close foreground of Grand Master in red with thumbs up glaring malevolently. Fade out.

Subtitle.
Next week the Second Episode of the MYSTERIES OF MYRA.

Appendix 2

Beatrice Fairfax

"The Opal Ring" (Suppressed Episode)

The Whartons' *Beatrice Fairfax* (1916), originally titled *Letters to Beatrice*, was a fifteen-part serial that featured the eponymous heroine, an independent modern newspaperwoman who was based on a Hearst newspaper advice columnist. In each episode, Beatrice receives a letter from a reader in need of her advice or assistance. Together with her colleague, reporter Jimmy Barton, she investigates and helps to resolve the reader's concern—always in time to write the story up for the late edition of their paper, the *New York Evening Journal*.

"The Opal Ring" was one of two episodes of the *Beatrice Fairfax* serial that the Whartons intended to film but never produced. According to correspondence in the Wharton Collection at the Division of Rare and Manuscript Collections, Cornell University Library, at the last moment Hearst insisted that this episode be replaced, reportedly because of the extreme violence against whites perpetrated by the Chinese villains. Although it was never filmed, the episode offers a valuable glimpse into the xenophobia that pervaded cinema and society at that time.

In the script that follows, the original spellings and punctuation, even when inconsistent or incorrect, have been retained. (Wharton Releasing Corporation Records, #3924, Division of Rare and Manuscript Collections, Cornell University Library.)

LETTERS TO BEATRICE

Episode # 8
The Opal Ring

Subtitle:
The Passing of Kwang-Si.

Scene 1.
INTERIOR OF PRIVATE DINING ROOM in rear of the Chop Suey restaurant of the Purple Dragon. Small room dimly lighted by a candle stick with two candles on a table in center of room. Usual Chinese furniture. At the table a middle-aged Chinaman. (Kwang-Si) is seated. A waiter enters and speaks. He nods without turning around, waiter retires and returns with young Chinaman Yung Kai loose Chinese clothes; white scar on his forehead. Waiter steps out. Kwang makes sign to the other to be seated. He remains standing however and presents Kwang with a slip of paper.

Close foreground. Kwang's hand holding letter. On his little finger is a ring set with a large opal.

Insert.
Note written in Chinese characters which fade into.

Kwang-Si is notified that he is deposed from leadership of the Seven Brothers and is ordered to hand to bearer, the Sacred Opal of office. The Seven Brothers.

Back.
Kwang raises his eye from paper and looks at the other with a crafty smile. He speaks slowly and his hand slowly pulls open the table drawer. The other sees the movement draws a knife and leaps forward. The candle stick falls, the room is in absolute darkness for a moment then spot of light from pocket torch flashes and falls on Kwang's hand lying on the floor. Close up of hand. Yung's hand comes in. Takes the ring from the finger of Kwang. The light goes out.

Scene 2.
OUTSIDE THE DOOR OF KWANG'S PRIVATE DINING ROOM. Yung Kai comes out closing door behind him.

Scene 3.
STAIRWAY. Yung Kai comes down. Meets the waiter of Scene 1, going up. As they pass waiter looks at him closely, then hurries up stairs.

Scene 4.
As 1. DARK. Waiter to door. Strikes a match, crosses in darkness, picks up and lights candle. Kwang likes [sic] face downward before him. He stoops and picks up note delivered by Yung Kai. Reads and puts in pocket, runs out of room.

Note. (Subsequent scenes blue for night up to and including Scene 20.)

Scene 5.
ALLEY ALONGSIDE THE PURPLE DRAGON. Yung Kai out. Looks up and down the alley. Starts to remove his clothes.

Scene 6.
As 4. Group of Chinamen around body of Kwang. They talk a moment, then hurry out.

Scene 7.
As 5. Yung Kai finishes removing clothes, under which he is dressed in American suit. He rolls clothes in a bundle and throws into shadows. Walks quickly away. A moment later. Four or five of Chinamen from room above come out. They talk a moment, separate, and some go one way, some the other up the alley.

Subtitle.
Alice Wayne.

Scene 8.
Close foreground. Alice seated in sight-seeing auto. She speaks to someone below.

Subtitle.
Bert Copeland.

Back.
Full set. Auto with number of passengers in Chinatown street. Bert standing beside it, helps Alice to alight. Others get down and stroll toward shops.

Subtitle.
The Closing Net.

Scene 9.
STREET ON CHINATOWN. Yung Kai along cautiously. (Camera behind him.) At next corner a crowd of Chinamen turn into street. Yung Kai stops, moves back the way he came. Others come on, apparently in no hurry.

Scene 10.
ANOTHER PART OF THE STREET. Front of a curio shop. Alice and Bert come out of shop and stand in doorway. Yung Kai passes, walking swiftly.

Same.
Shot from behind Yung Kai. Group of Chinamen coming from that direction. He stops and looks about him. Registers he is trapped.

Same.
Close to Alice and Bert. Yung Kai hurries on and runs into Bert.

Close foreground. Yung's hand puts ring in Bert's pocket.

Full set. Yung springs back, apologizes, and hurries off. Group of Chinamen go by, walking rapidly.

Scene 11.
STREET. Entrance to an Alley. Yung runs in.

Scene 12.
INSIDE ALLEY. As Yung comes in. Two Chinamen seize him. Fight ensues.

Scene 13.
As 11. Chinamen from both directions hurry in to alley.

Scene 14.
As 12. Chinamen have Yung down, and search him. One stands sentry at opening of alley.

Scene 15.
STREET. Two policemen on, and run toward alley. ~~Sight-seeing~~ Trolley car up and stops.

Scene 16.
CLOSE TO SENTRY. He shouts a warning to attackers. They break and scatter. Yung gets up and crouches in a doorway. Police run in thru alley. Yung out toward street.

Scene 17.
As 15. ~~Sight-seeing~~ Trolley auto about to start. Yung out and quickly along street. Runs around car, and as it starts, swings to running gear.

Subtitle.
Later.

Scene 18.
RESIDENCE STREET. EXTERIOR ALICE'S HOME. Alice and Bert on, and up steps. Yung following at short distance, in shadows, stops and waits.

Close.
Of Alice and Bert at door. He puts hand in pocket, starts. Brings out ring. Yung steals up, and crouches in shadow of steps.

Close foreground. Yung watching.

Close.
Alice and Bert. She shows great interest in ring. He says he doesn't know where it came from. She can have it. She takes it joyfully.

Full set. Yung raises his head, and looks as ring is passed. Alice says good-night. A quick embrace, and she enters, closing door. Bert goes down the steps and walks off. Yung takes two steps after him. Stops and steals by to shadows of porch.

Scene 19.
ALICE'S ROOM. She enters and switches on light. Nicely furnished bedroom. A window in wall opposite dresser. Alice throws off her things. Goes to dresser and stands admiring the opal ring.

Semi-close to include the dresser mirror, in which window behind her is reflected. Camera behind Alice. She raises her eyes, and looks into mirror. Yung Kai's face rises above sill and looks in at her. She whirls and looks, but while she turns he is gone. She stands gazing from window to mirror. Starts slowly to window.

Scene 20.

YARD OR COURT ALONGSIDE WAYNE HOUSE. Yung Kai drops from a water drain running up beside lighted window. He disappears in shadows. Alice looks out of window.

Scene 21.

As 19. Alice, doubting her eyesight, steps back from window. Drops into chair, staring at ring. A newspaper lying on floor in front of her attracts her attention. She picks it up and looks at it.

Insert.

Close foreground. Evening Journal page. Advice to Love-Lorn.

Back.

She sits a moment, looking from paper to the ring on her finger. Registers determination. Crosses to desk. Takes pen and paper.

Close to

Alice. She hesitates a moment, then begins to write. Fade out.

Subhead.
Morning.

Subtitle.
Beatrice Fairfax of the New York Evening Journal.

Insert.
Vignetted up close. Journal. Beatrice.

Subtitle.
Jimmy Barton. Reporter.

Insert.
Vignetted head of Jimmy.

Scene 22.

Open to full set. Beatrice at desk opening mail. Jimmy at desk, beating type-writer. Boy enters, goes to Jimmy, speaks.

Close
to Jimmy's desk. Boy says:—

Spoken title.
"Chief wants you."

Back.
Jimmy nods, gets up, and exits.

Close
to Beatrice. She tears open a letter, and reads.

Insert:—
Alice's letter.

> Dear Miss Fairfax.
>
> Is it true that opal rings bring bad luck to the wearer? I received one tonight, and had a terrible vision a few minutes afterwards. Shall I throw the ring away?
>
> Alice Wayne
> 2130 Carleton Avenue.

Scene 23.
OFFICE OF EDITOR, as in other episodes. Editor at desk. Jimmy in and speaks to him.

Spoken title.
"Kwang Si, proprietor of the Purple Dragon, has been killed. Jump down there and get a story."

Back.
Editor speaks above. Jimmy nods and exits.

Scene 24.
As 22. Jimmy returns to his desk and closes it. Beatrice asks him a question. He replies. She shows interest, and says:—

Spoken title.
"Take me with you."

Back.
Beatrice speaks above. Jimmy hesitates a moment, then agrees. Beatrice still has letter in her hand. She thrusts it in skirt pocket, gets hat. They exit.

Subtitle.
Hancho, the New Head of the Seven Brothers.

Scene 25.

AN ORIENTAL ROOM IN CHINATOWN. Hancho seated at an ebony inlaid table. Walls elaborately hung with Chinese tapestries, etc. Telephone on table. A Chinaman comes thru the curtains and speaks to him. Hancho makes a sign of assent. Chinaman holds back curtains. Yung Kai comes in, hat pulled well down over his eyes. He steps to table. Servant exits. Hancho holds out his hand, and speaks.

Spoken title.
"The Ring."

Back.
Hancho speaks the above.

Yung Kai says he hasn't it. Hancho angrily demands the reason.

Scene 26.

EXTERIOR OF THE "PURPLE DRAGON." Jimmy and Beatrice [pull] up in auto and enter.

Scene 27.

INTERIOR OF THE "PURPLE DRAGON." Typical Chop Suey Restaurant. Place deserted. Waiter of scene one, seats Jimmy and Beatrice as they enter, and takes order.

Scene 28.

As 25. Yung Kai explains. Fade out, and into

Scene 29.

As told by Yung Kai. EXTERIOR OF WAYNE HOME, as in #20. Level with Alice's window. (Blue for night). Yung supporting himself on down spout. Looks thru window. Camera shooting from behind him, takes in Alice before mirror, as in Scene 19. Fade out, and into

Scene 30.

As 28. Yung finishes and bows low. Hancho scowls at him. Orders him to sit down and strikes a gong. Servant appears. Hancho gives orders. Servant exits.

Scene 31.
As 27. Close to table. Waiter serves Jimmy and Beatrice. Jimmy touches him on arm, and whispers to him. Registers he doesn't know what he is talking about. Feigns stupidity[.] Jimmy puts his hand in his pocket and produces a bill. Waiter still hesitates. Jimmy shrugs, and starts to put up money. Waiter capitulates and takes money, looking about room. Whispers to Jimmy and walks off.

Jimmy follows with Beatrice.

Scene 32.
As 3. Waiter upstairs, followed by Jimmy and Beatrice.

Scene 33.
As 30. Hancho and Yung in picture. Servant brings in Chinaman in American clothes, Hancho makes him a sign to sit down. Tells Yung to tell him his story again. Yung begins to speak.

Scene 34.
As 1. Waiter in with Jimmy and Beatrice. Points to spot where Kwang lay when he found him. Jimmy speaks:—

Spoken title.
"Who killed him?"

Back.
Jimmy speaks above. Waiter registers that he has told all he knows. Jimmy produces another bill, and repeats his question. Waiter hesitates, searches his pockets, and hands Jimmy note.

Insert.
Note as in Scene 1. Chinese characters only.

Back.
Jimmy says he doesn't understand. Waiter takes note, and as Jimmy and Beatrice listen eagerly, he begins to translate.

Scene 35.
As 33. Yung finishes his story. Hancho gives orders. Yung and others start to leave. Hancho stops Yung, and speaks:—

Spoken title.
"Leave it to him. You have been seen."

Back.
Hancho speaks above. Yung writes address on slip of paper, and gives it to the other man, who exits.

Scene 36.
As 34. Waiter speaks to Jimmy, with gesture indicating scar on forehead.

Spoken title.
"Man with scar. Bring it. I come back. Kwang Si dead. Sacred opal gone."

Back.
Waiter speaks above to Jimmy. Waiter points to where Kwang lay, and shrugs shoulders. Beatrice, who has been listening, pulls letter from pocket, speaks to Jimmy, and shows it to him.

Insert.
Flash Alice's letter.

Back
Jimmy and Beatrice consult a moment. He says:—

Insert.
"Take the car, and see what she knows."

Back.
Beatrice agrees, and exits. Jimmy turns to waiter and speaks.

Insert:—

Spoken title:
"Now tell me where the Seven Brothers meet, or I'll call the police."

Back.
Jimmy speaks the above. Waiter registers fear, and pleads. Jimmy takes a step toward door. Waiter stops him and whispers.

Scene 37.
A STREET CORNER. Taxi cab up and stops.

Scene 38.
INTERIOR OF TAXI CAB. The man of scene 35 in cab. Takes a small suit case from floor of cab. Gets out.

Scene 39.
As 37. Chinaman out with grip [suitcase] and walks away. Cab waits.

Scene 40.
As 26. Jimmy comes out with waiter, and walks away.

Scene 41.
As 18. Chinaman with grip up to door, and rings bell.

Scene 42.
ENTRANCE HALL. ALICE'S HOUSE. She comes down stairs. Steps to door and opens it. The Chinaman steps in. Talking rapidly, he opens grip, pulling out pieces of lace and silk, which he tries to sell her. Alice, struck by their beauty and lowness of price, asked, becomes interested. Reaches out to take hold of a piece. His eyes fix on her hand.

Close foreground. Alice's hand, wearing the opal ring.

Back.
Chinaman, with laces draped over her hand, talks.

Scene 43.
STREET IN RESIDENCE DISTRICT. Beatrice drives thru in Jimmy's car.

Scene 44.
As 41. Semi-close. Chinaman moves his hand slightly. Barrel of revolver comes under edge of lace, pointing at Alice's breast. She sees it, and starts to spring back. He drops the laces to floor, catches her hand, and keeping gun pointed at her, strips the ring from her hand, threatening instant death if she screams. Alice shrinks, half-fainting against the wall. Keeping her covered, he calmly throws his goods into grip, and backs to door.

Scene 45.
As 41. Beatrice drives up, stops, goes up steps. Door opens, and Chinaman comes down. He bows low to Beatrice, and hurries up street. She looks after him a moment, hurries up steps.

Semi-close. Alice staggers out of doorway. Beatrice catches her arm, and questions her. Girl speaks excitedly, pointing in direction taken by Chinaman.

Spoken title.
"My ring! My opal ring!"

Back.
Alice speaks above. Beatrice runs down, jumps in car, and drives off.

Scene 46.
As 39. Chinaman on, and enters cab. Leans out, and speaks to chauffeur. Beatrice drives up. Sees him as cab drives off. Drops back to safe distance, and follows.

Scene 47.
STREET IN CHINATOWN. Jimmy and Waiter on, and in front of Curio shop, with sign—Hancho & Co. Waiter makes sign that this is the place, and hurries on. Jimmy stops and studies the place.

Subtitle.
The Double Traitor.

Scene 48.
INTERIOR OF PHONE BOOTH. The Waiter into booth, and exhibiting signs of fright. Calls number.

Scene 49.
As 35. Hancho and Yung Kai talking. Hancho and Yung Kai talking. [The line repeats in the script.] Hancho picks up phone, and answers call. Starts. Registers fury.

Scene 50.
As 48. Waiter, trembling, speaks.

Spoken title.
"I did wrong, Master, but I warn you in time."

Back.
Waiter speaks above. He listens a moment, trembling.

Scene 51.
As 49. Hancho hangs up receiver, and speaks quickly to Yung Kai, at same time striking bell. Servant enters. Hancho speaks to him.

Spoken title.
"A Gentleman will ask for me. Show him up here."

Back.
Hancho speaks above. Servant bows and exits.

Scene 52.
INTERIOR OF CURIO SHOP. Jimmy in, strolls about, looking at curios. Servant comes into shop from rear.

Scene 53.
As 51. Hancho makes motion to Yung Kai, who steps quickly behind the curtains. Servant brings in Jimmy. Hancho bows low. Brings chair forward and places it carefully with back to curtain, behind which Yung is hidden. Jimmy sits down. Hands a card to Hancho.

Insert.
Flash Jimmy's business card.
    James Barton
    N. Y. Eve. Journal

Back.
Hancho looks at card, and bows affably.

Scene 54.
Behind the tapestries. Close foreground of Yung Kai, peering thru aperture in curtain.

Scene 55.
Hancho smiling from across table, asks Jimmy what he can do for him.

Scene 56.
As 47. Taxi up and stops. Chinaman out and enters shop. Beatrice drives up and stops a short distance away. Gets out of car, looks about, motions to a policeman across street. He comes over.

Scene 57.
As 52. Chinaman from taxi, in, and thru to rear.

Scene 58.
As 56. Beatrice talks to policeman. He looks doubtful. She insists.

Spoken title.
"Kwang Si's murderers are in there."

Back.
Beatrice speaks above. Policeman shrugs shoulders and nods 'all right' as though to humor a child. They enter shop.

Scene 59.
As 55. Jimmy about to speak. Chinaman from taxi. Enters. Hancho asks a question with his eyes. Chinaman answers with almost imperceptable nod, and steps to one side. Jimmy leans across the table, and speaks to Hancho.

Scene 60.
Beatrice and policemen enter. Hancho's servant comes forward, smiling. Policeman questions him, pointing to Beatrice. Servant speaks.

Insert:—
Spoken title. "Madame is mistaken. No one has come in."

Back.
Servant speaks above. Beatrice insists. Officer looks doubtful.

Scene 61.
As 59. Jimmy speaks to Hancho.

Insert:—
Spoken title. "Mr. Hancho, who killed Kwang Si?"

Back.
Jimmy speaks above. Hancho is unmoved, and flashes a warning glance at the other Chinaman, who takes a step toward Jimmy, but stops. Hancho, smiling at Jimmy, replies:—

Insert:
Spoken title: "One who will do as much for you."

Back.
As Hancho speaks above, he makes a slight signal with his hand. Jimmy sees it, and drops to his knees as curtain behind him parts, and a knife buries itself on table. Jimmy draws gun, and fires at Yung Kai, as he comes thru the curtains. Yung crumples and falls.

The other Chinaman kicks the gun from Jimmy's hand, and he and Hancho jump for him.

Scene 62.
As 60. All register effect of shot. Servant throws himself in way. Officer knocks him down. Blows his whistle, and runs for rear, followed by Beatrice.

Scene 63.
As 61. Jimmy in rough and tumble fight with the two men, as policeman and Beatrice come in. Jimmy trips and throws Hancho. Policeman grabs the other. Prisoners are handcuffed. Policeman asks a question of Beatrice. Jimmy points to the dead man, and speaks.

Insert:
Spoken title.
"He killed Kwang Si."

Back.
Jimmy speaks above. Beatrice puts her hand in the handcuffed Chinaman's pocket, and brings out the ring, crosses and hands it to policeman. He grins and tells her to keep it. She shakes her head, and replies:—

Insert.
Spoken title.
"No, I'm sure they are unlucky."

Back.
Beatrice speaks above. Vignetted close up. Beatrice and Jimmy. Fade out.

Appendix 3

The Eagle's Eye

"The Hidden Death"
(Episode One)

The Eagle's Eye (1918), a twenty-part patriotic serial, was the last picture that the Whartons produced together. It was, they claimed, the true story "of the machinations of Germany, the intrigues, the plots, the counter-plots and the devilish ingenuity" by which the German government "sought to put America into a position where it would be helpless under the mailed fist of kaiserdom." A later version of the script noted explicitly: "Story from facts supplied by William J. Flynn, while Chief of the United States Secret Service. Arranged by Courtney Ryley Cooper. Produced by Whartons, Inc., Under the personal direction of The Whartons With George Lessey, Co-Director." That version also added a teaser at the end (which does not appear in the script that follows): "What devilish scheme did the Germans plot for the Ansonia Hotel Naval Ball? See episode two of 'THE EAGLE'S EYE.'"

In the first episode, "The Hidden Death," as German spies and agents plot to sink the *Lusitania*, Chief Flynn receives valuable assistance from Harrison Grant, president of the Criminology Club, and an undercover female agent for the Secret Service, whom Grant initially suspects of being in league with the Germans. The script reprinted here is an early version of that episode.

Certain changes were made before it was filmed: the name of the female lead, for example, was changed from Betty Lee to Dixie Mason.

Original spellings, capitalizations, and punctuation, even when inconsistent, incorrect, or idiosyncratic, have been retained. Thus, spellings such as "von Lertz," "von Lerts," and "Von Lertz" and "bombmaker," "bomb maker," and "bomb-maker" are used interchangeably and without correction. (Wharton Releasing Corporation Records, #3924, Division of Rare and Manuscript Collections, Cornell University Library.)

THE EAGLE'S EYE
An Exposure of Germany's intrigue in America

———

Episode 1.
THE HIDDEN DEATH

———

The Author
William J. Flynn
Chief of the U. S. S.

(This title fades to
View of Treasure [*sic*] Building
which fades to:

Introduction of:
The Chief seated at desk in office. He is reading letter:

(Insert Letter)
CRIMINOLOGY Club
Wm. J. Flynn, Chief–U. S. S.
Dear Sir:
  Tomorrow's papers will publish a message from the Kaiser, declaring his friendship for America. We have evidence to the contrary and offer our services.
                    Yours truly,
                    Harrison Grant,
                    President

The chief lays the letter down thoughtfully (IRIS)

Subtitle. The main action of our story is based on fact. The Secret service's methods of obtaining evidence are fictionized for obvious reasons. Therefore, we have introduced a typical character, the President of the Criminology Club: HARRISON GRANT—
                    (FADE TO)
Scene 1. CRIMINOLOGY CLUB–LOUNGING ROOM. Start with C. U. [close-up] of GRANT. He is apparently talking with some one. Open to full set. Disclosing the members, singly and in groups. There are various types and nationalities including a JAP and CHINAMAN of distinguished appearance. An attendant delivers a telegram to Grant, he reads and then

turns to members indicating a message of importance. As they gather about him he reads:

(TELEGRAM)
Harrison Grant, etc.
Shall be glad of your
Co-operation. W.J.F.

General indication of satisfaction.

Subtitle: The feminine element of the Secret Service is also shown in the person of a former actress, now a captain of human operatives: BETTY LEE. . . . . . .

Scene 2. Miss Lee's Apt. C. U. Miss Lee. She is reading letter.

(INSERT)
My dear Miss Lee:
Thanks for your letter. James is doing fine and by hard work has gotten into a position of trust in the private bank of two fine old Germans, Schneider and Wurtz. However, he intends to tell no one in his family until he receives his first raise.
Sincerely,
Wallace J. Claflynn
Universal Salvage Sales Co.

Back to motion as she places a bit of celluloid with holes cut in it over letter.

(INSERT)
LETTER UNDER CELLULOID
Work into trust of Germans. Tell no one.
W. J. Flynn, U. S. S.

Back to motion. She stands a moment in thought, then tosses letter on table after carefully concealing celluloid.

Subtitle: In 1914 Germany believed it would conquer the world. It first intended to crush France and England, then reach forth for America. It therefore assembled thousands of spies, headed by the German Ambassador.
Count Johann von Bernstorff. . . . . . .

Scene 3. Room in German Embassy. IRIS IN C. U. of von Bernstorff reading newspaper. The headlines of this paper show the Kaiser's declaration of friendship for America. Cut to full set. Von B. smiles cynically as he reads. IRIS OUT.

Subtitle. The plotting was done on American soil, even in the German Embassy itself. There Von Bernstorff often gathered with his chief aides.

FADE TO

Scene 4. Triple introductions of Albert, Boy Ed and von Papen.

SUBTITLE . . . The aim was to hamper supplies to the Allies, and cripple America, making it powerless in event of war.

Scene 5. Interior of Embassy. Albert, Boy Ed, von Papen enter. Greetings etc. Discuss and laugh over notice in paper. Von Papen begins to report activities. Rises and goes to concealed map in wall. Begins to point out various locations on map.

(INSERT)
Close up of map, as finger points to various locations there fades in

C. U. Blowing up of railroad bridge.
C. U. Elevator fire.

Continue action with full set. Von Papen turns laughingly from map and comes to table.
   (The map either concealed in wall or in false top of table.)

SUBTITLE . . . Every morning at 3 o'clock American time, instructions come direct from Germany, via the great wireless tower at Nauen, near Berlin.

Scene 6. Flash long shot of wireless tower.

Scene 7. Int[erior]. wireless station. The scene, with a change of furnishings, will be the same as that of the wireless station at Sayville, to be used in the future episodes. The wireless operators are in German uniform. The sending table is massed with papers and code messages. Officers are passing in and out and the scene is one of the greatest activity.

The wireless station is in full swing. An officer comes in with a wireless message. The operator looks at it.

CLOSE UP MESSAGE. (INSERT)
It reads: 4–11——21–2
7–3   12–5 etc.
NOTE: The above numbers are not correct as the message must
be made to conform to the dictionaries by which it is decoded.
(See decoding scenes later.)

Back to motion as the operator bends to his instrument.

Subtitle: While in America the message was caught by spies everywhere from the wharves to Fifth avenue.

Scene 8. On Deck of Interned Ship. Guard notes the time and locks up.

(INSERT)
Flash of wireless rigging.

Continue motion. He hurries to wireless room.

Scene 9. INT. Fifth Avenue home. Butler, fully dressed, asleep. Wakened by alarm clock, notes time.

(INSERT)

[The following repetition occurs in the manuscript of the script.]

Scene 10. Int. Fifth Avenue Home. Butler, fully dressed, asleep. Wakened by alarm clock, notes time.

(INSERT)

Flash wireless on roof of Fifth Avenue house. (Note: In each instance where wireless is flashed, we will show electrical flashes coming out of space toward wires.)

Continuation. Butler turns hurriedly as mistress comes down stairs in negligee. He indicates time and they exit hurriedly.

Scene 11. Basement. They enter and go to concealed wireless receiving apparatus. Butler receive [sic] message.

Subtitle: And in the morning, these messages all found their way to the Master Spy.

Scene 13. [No Scene 12 in script.] Int. Embassy. Von Bernstorff discovered with various messages in his hand.

(INSERT)
Several copies of same message.

Continue action. He gets code book and taking one of the messages, begins to decode it.

(INSERT)
C. U. of Dictionary and process of decoding. For example: Finger points to 4 on message, then page 4 on dictionary, then figure 11 on message, then to 11th word from top of page on dictionary. Etc.

Continue action. Von Bernstorff finishes decoding message, which he reads.

(INSERT)
Translation in German, which dissolves to
ALLIES SHIPMENTS INCREASING. MUST STOP
THEM BY ALL MEANS.
DO ANYTHING TO ACHIEVE THIS RESULT.
B 494

Continue action as he finishes reading message, he smiles cynically, presses button. Boy Ed enters and they discuss message.

Subtitle. AS THE MONTHS WENT BY, GERMANY GREW MORE DEFIANT.

Scene 14. German Embassy. Boy Ed and Bernstorff are in conference there. Bernstorff, going through messages, speaks:

Spoken title: "Berlin instructs that the Lusitania be sunk."

Boy Ed agrees. Bernstorff looks at calendar. Writes. Then speaks:

Spoken title: "Insert this advertisement to warn our friends. We don't want them drowned."

Boy Ed agrees.

Subtitle. At the German Club, New York. Heinrich von Lertz, another plotter . . .

Scene 15. Int. German Club. Iris in C. U. of Von Lertz. He is apparently talking to someone unseen. Open to full set, disclosing Papen as his companion. Papen says:

Spoken title: "The Atlantic fleet will be here soon. I leave the rest to you."

Continue action as von Lertz agrees. They rise and exit.

Scene 16. Ext[erior]. German Club. Grant is passing, observes Papen and von Lertz as they come out of the club. Registers interest and suspicion.

Scene 17. Int. Embassy. Bernstorff and Boy Ed conversing. Bernstorff says:

Spoken title: "We'll be sorry, of course, and sympathize with America. In the meantime arrange for someone to swear the Lusitania carries guns."

Boy Ed agrees and exits.

Scene 18. Lounging room of Criminology Club. Japanese boy brings paper to Grant, points to something which Grant reads.

(INSERT)
Lusitania warning.

Continue action. Grant calls one of the members, shows it to him, saying:

Spoken title: "This may mean more direct plots against the United States. Place a dictophone [sic] in the German club."

Member agrees and exits, while Grant discusses the advertisement with other members.

Subtitle. May 3rd, 1915. "The Lusitania sails away with its 1250 innocents to a deliberately planned whole-sale German murder."

Scenes 19, 20, 21, 22, 23. Flashes of Lusitania sinking. (LIBRARY)

Scene 24. Ext. Docks. Man in there watching.

Scene 25. Flash of Lusitania, outward bound. (LIBRARY)

SUBTITLE: Chance plays into the hands of Betty Lee.

Scene 26. Stenographer's stall in Hotel Lobby. Von Lertz dictating letter. Betty Lee enters, pauses to talk to an acquaintance.

Stenographer looks toward her.
    C. U. Stenographer, glance of regognition [*sic*].
    C. U. Betty returning glance.

Continue action. Stenographer takes finished letter from typewriter, and as von Lertz begins to read it, she begins to telegraph on the space bar.

Subtitle. A Novel telegraphic communication.
    C. U. Keyboard of typewriter. Stenographer's hand working the space bar as telegraph key.
    C. U. Betty listening.

(INSERT)
Telegraphic message. In space above keyboard. "This is the German I spoke of. Might I suggest? He thinks he is a lady killer."

    C. U. Betty registers she understands.

Continue action. Flirtation between Betty and von Lertz. He comes forward and speaks to her. They exit together.

Scene 27. Int. Telegraph office. Man who watched the Lusitania sail, enters and writes message.

(INSERT TELEGRAM)
L. H. Gerz,
Amsterdam, Holland

Lucy has entered last phase of illness. Doctor say progress
until Thursday normal. After that difficult to diagnose.
—Therbold.

Continue action. Files message. Orders it rushed.

Scene 28. Int. Hotel Café. Grant seated reading.

(INSERT)
LUSITANIA SAILS
DESPITE GERMAN THREATS

Continue actions. He looks up and von Lerts [sic] and Miss Lee enter. Is
impressed by her beauty. As they sit at nearby table, he recognizes von Lertz
as the man he saw coming from the German club with von Papen. IRIS OUT.

Scene 28 A. IRIS IN. Action of scene 16. IRIS OUT.

Scene 28 B. Continue action. Grant is puzzled and thoughtful.

SUBTITLE: IN A NEUTRAL COUNTRY . . . . THE BEGINNING OF THE
SYSTEMATIC ESPIONAGE OF THE LUSITANIA'S COURSE AT SEA.

Scene 29. A Room in Amsterdam. A man is waiting there, apparently nervous. Knock on the door and an old woman enters and hands him the message which he reads.

(INSERT MESSAGE)
This is the message sent to Thervold [sic] in Scene 27. This fades to.

Translation
L. H. Gerz,
Amsterdam, Holland

Lusitania has sailed. Normal progress until Thursday. After that don't
know course.
Therbold.

Continue action. He expresses some satisfaction and takes up telephone.
(Continental phone)

SUBTITLE . . . Nauen Tower.

Scene 30. Interior Tower. Operator answers phone and receives message from man in Amsterdam. He immediately goes to wireless and forwards message.

SUBTITLE. AT CUXHAVEN.

Translation from scene 29. Continue action. Operator hands message to visiting U. Boat captains. They go to map on table and study it.

(INSERT)

C. U. of map. North Coast of Ireland. The ocean is plotted in oblong. Each name after a fish peculiar to that region. In every square is also the number of a U. Boat.

Continue action. The captains converse for a few moments, then hurriedly exit.

Scene 31. Same as scene 28. Hotel safe.
Grant exits, closely observing Betty and von Lertz as he passes. Von Lertz invites Betty to attend the naval ball.

(NOTE: this by insert of original invitation if possible. Otherwise by a subtitle—"There's to be a Naval Ball at the Ansonia May 14th. May I have the pleasure of your company?")

Continue action. Betty accepts to the joy of von Lertz.

Scene 32. Int. Criminology Club. Lounging Room. Grant arrives. Is met by member he directed to install dictophone in German club. Letter says:

Spoken title. "I'll have that dictophone in before the end of the week."

Continue action as Grant express [sic] satisfaction and sits in deep thought. IRIS OUT.

Scene 33 A. IRIS IN. C. U. of Betty Lee smiling and laughing. IRIS OUT.

Scene 33 B. IRIS IN. Grant smiling to himself. He suddenly becomes thoughtful. IRIS OUT.

Scene 33 C. IRIS IN. C. U. Betty and von Lertz. IRIS OUT.

Scene 33 D. Grant frowns and shakes his head wonderingly.

SUBTITLE. Four days later the ill fated Lusitania started down the north coast of Ireland while German spies reported its progress.

Scene 34. Flash of Lusitania at sea.

Scene 35. On deck Fishing Smack at sea. German scours the horizon with high powered glasses.

Scene 36. Flash of Lusitania through glasses.

Scene 37. German gives hurried order and boat turns toward shore.

SUBTITLE. WHILE IN GERMANY THE SINKING OF THE BIG SHIP WAS BEING CELEBRATED BY A MEDAL ISSUED TWO DAYS BEFORE THE ACTUAL SINKING.

Scene 38. Int. Wireless tower at Nauen. Groups of officers are laughing and chatting. Another enters excitedly and displays:

(INSERT)
Actual medal

Continue action. They joyously drink to the success of the plan.

Scene 39. Int. Wireless Station in Ireland. The spy of the fishing smack enters and files message with operator.

(INSERT)
C. U. of message

Argus:
Antwerp
Shipping ten cases of Mackerel.
Sanders

Continue action. He pays for message and exits.

SUBTITLE . . . In America, strange things are happening in the vicinity of the German club.

Scene 40. Room, in building adjoining German Club. A couple of members of the Criminology Club have opened a section of the wall and loosened a waterpipe. The water begins to flow.

Scene 41. Int. German Club. The leak is discovered as it begins to discolor the wall and leak through the ceiling. Steward rushes to telephone.

Scene 42. Int. Plumber shop. Member of the Criminology Club is talking to the proprietor as the phone rings. A knowing glance flashes between the two as proprietor answers the phone. He receives message and says:

SPOKEN TITLE . . . "ALL RIGHT. I'LL HAVE A MAN UP RIGHT AWAY . . . AND HAVE HIM BRING A PLASTERER WITH HIM."

Continue action as he hangs up the phone.

Scene 43. Int. U. Boat. Wireless operator begins to catch message. Calls for captain, who reads:

(INSERT)
Message of Scene 29.
which dissolves into
Translation:
Lusitania entering mackerel.

Continue action. Captain looks at map of same kind as that on table as Cuxhaven. Points to oblong marked mackerel. Turns and orders full speed [a]head.

Scene 43. A. Flash of German submarine emerging. (Library).

Scene 44. Int. German Club. Plumber and plasterer enter with steward. He shows them the damage and leaves them to repair it. Business of dictograph.

SUBTITLE. With hundreds of fishing smacks, and their spies aboard to flash the news, the Lusitania dodged death throughout the night, only by its speed.

Scene 45. Flash of Lusitania at sea.

Scene 46. Int. submarine. (Note: Same interior can be used with different officers.) Action similar to Scene 43. Another message received reporting Lusitania entering HERRING. Business of map repeated.

SUBTITLE. BUT ESCAPE WAS IMPOSSIBLE. THE FATEFUL AFTER-NOON OF MAY 7TH, 1915.

Scene 47. Flash of Lusitania at sea.

Scene 48. Int. of U. 55. There all is excitement. The men are manning a torpedo bringing it to the tube. The captain is at the periscope.

(INSERT)

Scene 48 A. View through periscope. The Lusitania comes into it and when it centers.

Scene 48 B. The captain gives the signal.

Scene 49. Flash of Lusitania at sea.

Scene 50. Flash of torpedo going through water.

Scene 51. Same as 48. Int. submarine. Captain at periscope.

Scene 51 A. View through periscope. Blowing up of Lusitania.

Scene 51 B. The captain turns and congratulates his men. Gives instructions. Wireless operator begins sending message.

SUBTITLE. And when the news reached America . . .

Scene 52. Crowd around bulletin board. Signs of anger etc. A German in the crowd makes some cynical remark and is promptly placed in hors de combat by a patriotic American. Is finally rescued by a policeman.

Scene 53. Int. German Embassy. Reporter interviewing von Bernstorff, who is hypocritically sorry over the affair. As the reporters leave he smiles cynically to himself.

Scene 54. Int. German Club. Members grouped and discussing the affair. Reporters are announced. They interview von Papen.

Spoken title. "I think it was a famous American general who said: 'War is Hell.' That is my statement to the papers."

Reporters exit and von Papen and members drink a toast to Germany. (NOTE: It would be well to use double exposure Lusitania sinking in this scene.)

SUBTITLE: BUT IN A ROOM NEARBY . . .

Scene 55. Int. Room adjacent. Grant and members of the Criminology Club listening at dictophone. They apparently overhear the toasts and show signs of anger.

Scene 56. Int. German Club. Von Papen, von Hertz and others begin to talk in close conference.

Scene 57. Int. Room adjacent. Listener turns from dictophone, saying:

Spoken title. "They're speaking of the fleet . . . but I can't catch it all."

Continue action. All crowd around showing interest, while the listener is intently trying to catch conversation.

SUBTITLE. And the next day, the Great Atlantic Fleet dropped anchor in the Hudson to await the President's review.

Scene 58. Flash of fleet.

SUBTITLE. While Germany continued the plots of death and destruction.

Scene 59. Int. Tenement room. The scene is a chemical workroom. Work-table, reports and contrivances for making bombs. A German is finishing work on a large bomb. Gloats over his work.

Scene 60. Int. German Cub. Von Lertz and another member are having an argument. The member points to newspaper he is holding.

(INSERT)
LUSITANIA DISASTER MAY
CAUSE WAR WITH GERMANY.

Continue action. Von Lertz sneers, snaps his finger and snarls.

Spoken title. "We'll stop America's chances for that at the ball tonight. If that fails, there's still another means."

Continue action. He paces up and down the room glancing nervously at his watch.

Scene 61. Int. Room adjacent. The listener reports his remark and Grant hurriedly issues orders. Then turns to telephone.

Scene 61 A. Int. Chief Flynn's New York office. The chief answers phone.

Scene 62. Ext. Shack. Man is entering hurriedly and secretly.

Scene 63. Int. Shack. This is a workroom over a sewer manhole. There is a crane and other mechanical devices there. Men are discovered working on large torpedo as man enters. He speaks:

Spoken title. "You'll have to work faster. If the Hotel plot fails, everything depends on us when the fleet starts.["]

Scene 64. Int. Adjacent German Club. Grant turns from telephone.

Spoken title. "The Chief's sending fifty men to the Ansonia! We go as guests."

SUBTITLE. And while the officers of the United States Navy danced in happy ignorance of the plot to kill them all, the Secret Service was at work everywhere to protect them.

Scenes 65, 66, 67 and 68. Alternate views interior of ballroom, guests arriving, and so forth. Various members of the Criminology Club are in evidence. Grant is discovered talking to a lady.

SUBTITLE. The cordon of safety.

Scenes 69–70–71. Interior of hotel. Police and Secret Service men are in evidence all around it. Even on roof.

Scene 72. Int. Elevator shaft. Police and Secret Service men are there.

Scene 72 A. Basement of hotel. Everything dark. The rings of light begin to flash around the place finally disclosing the faces of the policemen who recognize each other, laugh quietly and turn away.

Scene 73. Entrance to ballroom. Von Lertz and Betty arrive. Are observed by club members as they pause to check their wraps. Club member exits.

Scene 73 A. Int. ballroom. Grant still with women. Club member of previous scene enters, passes quiet signal to him. Just as Von Lertz and Betty enter. The woman with Grant is an acquaintance of Betty's and stops her. Introductions. Grant talks to Betty while Von Lertz talks to the other women. Grant registers that he is impressed more than ever with her. Von Lertz eyes policemen standing in door. Shows annoyance. Grant catches the glance and at this moment Von Lertz offers his arm to Betty and they walk away. Grant watches after them wonderingly.

SUBTITLE. As midnight approaches, the German element quietly departs.

Scene 74. Int. Ballroom. Von Lertz and Betty have just finished a dance. One of the members of the German club appears nearby and taking out his watch quietly signals Von Lertz who also notes the time and nods to him. The German quickly begins to mingle with the guests.

Scenes 75–76–77. Alternate flashes of German stopping to give a quick nod to various guests of German type who immediately prepare to depart.

Scene 77 A. Von Lertz suggests to Betty that they depart. Betty wonderingly asks why and indicates she would like to remain a little longer. He argues with her and at this moment Grant arrives and asks Betty for the next dance, which is just starting. Betty indicates von Lertz wants her to go. Grant smilingly suggests that they remain a little longer, but von Lertz insists and carries his point. During this action von Lertz is apparently very nervous and keeps looking at his watch.

Scene 78. Ext. Hotel near the little park. Taxi pulls up to the curb. The German bomb-maker is inside.

Scene 79. Flash man seated on bench in park. He looks up quickly. Then exits.

Scene 80. Same as Scene 78. At taxi. As the bomb maker is about to get out of the taxi, the man arrives and stops him, saying:

Spoken title. "They got wind of it. There's a policeman or a secret service man every ten feet."

Angrily the bombmaker orders the driver to depart.

Scene 81. Ballroom. Grant still with Betty and von Lertz. Von Lertz still nervous and trying to induce Betty to leave. At this moment, the German who previously signalled Von Lertz passes and slips a card into his hand.

C. U. this action.

Von Lertz quietly looks at card.

(INSERT)
No need leaving as arranged. Affair abandoned. Too dangerous.

Von Lertz shows anger and annoyance for a moment, then turns smilingly to Betty and agrees to let her remain. The dance starts and Grant dances with Betty, leaving von Lertz gazing after them and nervously tearing the card to pieces. He places the torn fragments in his vest pocket.

SUBTITLE. Thus danger was averted for the time being. But on the night before the fleet review . . .

Scene 82. Room adjacent to German club. Man listening at dictophone.

Scene 83. German club. Papen and others talking.

Scene 84. Room adjacent. Man at dictophone registers he hears something.

Scene 85. Ext. Miss Lee's apartment. (Viewed through vestibule.) Betty and von Lertz alight from a taxi, evidently having come from theater or dance. Across the street a taxi stand is shown, with three or four cabs there. They come into the vestibule. Von Lertz starts to say goodnight and tries to kiss her. She plays with him and allows herself to come close for a second. As she does so:

C. U. Hand extracting a silver notebook from Von Lertz's pocket.

Back to action as von Lertz laughingly gives up his effort and leaves. Miss Lee looks hurriedly in the book.

(INSERT)
See Mueller 2 a.m. Urgent. Fleet affair.

Betty Lee looks out. Sees von Lertz's taxi just going out of picture. Hurries forth. Calls cab from across the street. It turns and comes to her as she watches nervously after cab which is going down the street. She enters taxi and follows.

Scene 86. Int. Criminology Club. One of the dictophone men enters hurriedly to Grant. He speaks:

Spoken title: "There's a plot to torpedo the flagship in the narrows and bottle up the fleet!"

Scene 87. Int. Harbor Police Station. Police chief answers phone, and assembles his men.

Scene 88. Ext. Road with winding road beneath it. Taxi stops. Betty gets out, looks around her. Sees machine passing below.

Scene 89. View of von Lertz machine on road below.

Scene 90. Same as 86. Betty gets into taxi. Instructs driver to go ahead.

Scene 91. Ext. Harbor Police station. Grant and several members of the club arrive, as the police come out. They enter the various police boats. One of Grant's men in each boat. They start out in various directions.

Scene 92. Int. Shack. Men are working feverishly on torpedo. They try the governor but it will not work. They keep on working. One of them looks at his watch.

Spoken title. "Von Lertz is an hour late now."

Continue action as the others keep working.

Scene 93. Ext. A road in front of shack. A machine stops. Von Lertz gets out and walks hurriedly forward.

Scene 94. Ext. Road nearby. <u>Closely shielded by trees</u>. Betty out of taxi observes.

Scene 95. Von Lertz entering shack.

Scene 96. Int. Shack. Von Lertz enters. Is very angry when he finds that work is not completed. He orders them to

Spoken title. "Get the torpedo into place before daylight. Schmidt can follow with the controller."

The men immediately prepare to attach torpedo to crane. Schmidt working very hard over controller, indicating that he is having a hard time of it. Von Lertz exits angrily exit. [*sic*]

Scene 97. Flash Betty watching.

Scene 98. Von Lertz comes from shack, enters auto and drives off.

Scene 99. Betty starts forward.

Scene 100. She arrives in front of shack (afoot). She finds a loose strip on the clapboarding. Very carefully she noiselessly works it loose.

Scene 101. C. U. View of men through hole under strip, lowering torpedo into sewer.

Scene 102. Same as 100. Betty sees and turns hurriedly away toward automobile.

Scene 103. Int. Sewer. Man lowering torpedo into it.

Scene 104. Ext. Shack. A pitfall. Betty Lee runs hurriedly toward auto. Just as she comes into foreground, she stumbles and falls, her vanity case flying out of her hand as she does so.

C. U. Betty on ground, registers extreme pain.

C. U. Vanity case where it has fallen.

Betty, registering that she has sprained her ankle badly, gets to her feet and starts to make her way to the taxi. The taxi driver who has seen her predicament hurries to her side.

Scene 105. Int. Sewer. The workmen have lowered the torpedo through the manhole, loaded it on a small wheel-car and are starting toward the mouth of the sewer.

Scene 106. Ext. Shack. Betty enters taxi, orders all haste ahead and exits in taxi at top speed.

Scene 107. Ext. Mouth of sewer. Men at mouth of sewer attach torpedo in wake of motor boat and start away with it, leaving another boat for Schmidt's use.

Scene 108. Ext. RIVER (CAMER [sic] IN GRANT'S BOAT). The boat speeds down the river. Meets another police boat which pauses a moment along side. Hurried orders. Then the police boat darts off in one direction while Grant's boat turns toward shore.

Scene 109. Ext. A Road. The taxi stops. Chauffeur gets out and looks under hood. Machine won't go. Betty in despair starts to limp across country.

Scene 110. Ext. Under Pier. The plotters are swinging into place under the pier. One of them orders caution. He speaks:

Spoken title . . . "Keep well under cover. It's broad daylight."

They begin to make their arrangements for placing the torpedo.

Scene 111. Ext. A Roadhouse. DAYLIGHT. Betty limps to door. Register Bell Telephone sign in plain evidence.

Scene 112. Int. Roadhouse. Proprietor asleep. Awakens as Betty limps in, locates the telephone booth and goes to it. He looks at her drowsily wondering. Betty picks up receiver and calls.

Scene 113. Int. Chief Flynn's Office. The Chief hears the call of the telephone and answers. Talks.

Scene 114. Ext. River. Grant's boat coming upstream, close to shore.

Scene 115. Int. Roadhouse. Betty talking over telephone. She says excitedly:

Spoken Title . . . "The shack's on the south shore, near Ft. Wadsworth."

Continues talking.

Scene 116. Int. Chief Flynn's office. The chief receives Betty's message, makes a note of it, hangs up, then picks up another phone.

Scene 117. Int. Harbor Police Station. The Captain there answers the phone.

Scene 118. Ext. Harbor Police Station. Grant's boat arrives there. Grant jumps out and goes into the station.

Scene 119. Int. Police station. Captain at phone as Grant enters. Turns and gives him the message that Chief has just given him. Grant exits hurriedly.

Scene 120. EXT. Police Dock. Grant out. Into boat and away with several of his men. Intensely excited.

Scene 121. Ext. Roadhouse. Betty also starts to make her way out, faints from ___[word illegible]. The proprietor rouses himself and hurries to the chair where she has sunk. Calls his wife.

Scene 122. Ext. River. Grant's boat tears across, approaching Staten Island.

Scene 123. Ext. Roadhouse. The proprietor's wife has come to Betty's assistance and revived her. She leads her away, apparently to bed and rest.

Scene 124. Int. Shack. Schmidt is working on controller. He is endeavoring feverishly to finish his work. A clock in the foreground shows that the time is nine o'clock.

Scene 125. Ext. River under pier. The plotters have placed their torpedo. They await Schmidt anxiously. One of them speaks:

Spoken title. "Is'nt [sic] Schmidt ever going to get her[e] with the controller?"

The men argue, then slink out of sight as they evade discovery.

Scene 126. Ext. Street near St. George's Ferry. Grant with his men run forth, hail a taxi and start away.

Scene 127. Int. Shack. Schmidt working on the controller. Is just finishing it. Registers delight that his work is nearly over. Is feverish in his haste.

SUBTITLE. THE START OF THE NAVAL REVIEW.

Scene 128. Ext. River. The fleet starts down to the sea. (LIBRARY.)

Scene 129. Int. Short distance from shack. Grant and his men alight from the taxi and start hurriedly toward the shack.

Scene 130. Int. Shack. Schmidt is starting down the manhole and just as it is closing over him, Grant and his men enter. They see the manhole top close and hurry in pursuit.

Scenes 131–132–133. Views of fleet with President reviewing it.

Scene 134. Int. Sewer. Schmidt, running along, is pounced upon by Grant. They fight.

SUBTITLE. AND WHILE THE FLEET DREW NEARER TO THE PLACE OF IT'S [sic] PLOTTED DEATH . . .

Scene 135. Flash of men under pier waiting for fleet.

Scene 136. Flash of fleet. (LIBRARY.)

Scene 137. Int. Sewer. The fight continues. Then reinforcements come to the aid of Grant. The German breaks free from them and plunges into the water. They rush forward through the sewer.

Scene 138. Ext. Shack. The chauffeur is wandering around when he sees something on the ground. Stops and looks at it and picks it up.

C. U. Vanity Case.

Continue action as the chauffeur stares at it wonderingly.

Scene 139. Ext. Mouth of river. The men arrive there. Grant orders them to take Schmidt's boat which they do and exit hurriedly. Grant watches them, then turns back.

Scene 140. Flash of Fleet.

Scene 141. Ext. River under Pier. The Germans see the scout boat approaching and angered, they dismantle the torpedo, plunge it in the river and scurry for safety among the barges and shipping. A moment later the boat with Grant's men come [sic] under the pier.

Scene 142. Ext. Shack. Grant with the chauffeur is looking around when the chauffeur remembers his find and telling Grant about it, pulls it forth from his pocket and shows it to him. Grant looks at it, opens it, then is amazed. Looks at calling card.

C. U. (INSERT)
Calling card bearing name
Miss Betty Lee

Continue action. Grant is surprised, angered, and hurt at the discovery. More, he is mystified as to how case should have gotten here . . . the discovery practically making Miss Lee a spy.

Scene 143. Ext. The Fleet goes sailing down the river (Library). Close diaphragm and dissolve into it fluttering American flag. This dissolves into

SUBTITLE . . . THIS WAS THE PLOT AGAINST AMERICA WITH WHICH GERMANY FOLLOWED THE SINKING OF THE LUSITANIA. ARE YOU GOING TO HELP AVENGE IT?

SUBTITLE . . . FIGHT OVER THERE! BUY BONDS OVER HERE. DO ONE—OR BOTH!

SUBTITLE . . . YOU'RE THE ONE WHO'S NEEDED TO HELP WIN THE WAR. EVERY ONE OF YOU!

SUBTITLE . . . IF YOU CAN'T GO ACROSS . . . COME ACROSS. BUY A LIBERTY BOND.

N O W !

NOTES

The following abbreviations are used in the notes:

BB   Miriam Hansen. *Babel and Babylon: Spectatorship in American Silent Film*. Cambridge, MA: Harvard University Press, 1991.

BG   Kalton C. Lahue. *Bound and Gagged: The Story of the Silent Serials*. New York: Castle Books, 1968.

CNW   Kalton C. Lahue. *Continued Next Week: A History of the Motion Picture Serial*. Norman: University of Oklahoma Press, 1964.

DD   Ed Hulse. *Distressed Damsels and Masked Marauders: Cliffhanger Serials of the Silent-Movie Era*. Morris Plains, NJ: Murania, 2014.

DM   *Dramatic Mirror*

IJ   *Ithaca Journal*

ISM   *Ithaca Silent Movies* (series of programs to accompany showings of silent films)

MM   Ben Singer. *Melodrama and Modernity: Early Sensational Cinema and Its Contexts*. New York: Columbia University Press, 2001.

MPN   *Motion Picture News*

MPW   *Moving Picture World*

MSG   Shelley Stamp. *Movie-Struck Girls: Women and Motion Picture Culture after the Nickelodeon*. Princeton, NJ: Princeton University Press, 2001.

NYT   *New York Times*

RAF   Lewis Jacobs. *The Rise of the American Film: A Critical History*. New York: Harcourt, Brace, 1939.

RW   Ally Acker. *Reel Women: Pioneers of the Cinema, 1896 to the Present*. New York: Continuum, 1991.

Serials   Raymond William Stedman. *The Serials: Suspense and Drama by Installment*. Norman: University of Oklahoma Press, 1971.

WC, Kroch The Wharton Collection, Division of Rare and Manuscript Collections, Carl A. Kroch Library, Cornell University

Introduction

1. Shelley Stamp, "Women and the Silent Screen," in *The Wiley-Blackwell History of American Film*, ed. Cynthia Lucia, Roy Grundman, and Art Simon (Oxford: Blackwell, 2012), 2.

2. Pamela Hutchinson, "Pianists Play It Again at Silent Movies," *Guardian*, April 12, 2011, online. At their height, in the United States, silent films were the largest source of employment for instrumental musicians, some of whom were women.

3. Rachel Friedman, "A History of Movie Theater Snacks in America," *Bon Appétit*, February 20, 2013, online.

4. Jared Gardner, *Projections: Comics and the History of Twenty-First-Century Storytelling* (Stanford, CA: Stanford University Press, 2012), 31.

5. Gerald Mast, *A Short History of the Movies* (New York: Macmillan, 1986), 498.

6. Ben Singer, *Melodrama and Modernity: Early Sensational Cinema and Its Contexts* (New York: Columbia University Press, 2001), 202.

7. Shelley Stamp, *Movie-Struck Girls: Women and Motion Picture Culture after the Nickelodeon* (Princeton, NJ: Princeton University Press, 2000), 3.

8. Richard Koszarski, *An Evening's Entertainment: The Age of the Silent Feature Picture, 1915–1928*, History of the American Cinema Series, vol. 3 (New York: Charles Scribner's Sons, 1990), 184.

9. As Shelley Stamp writes in *MSG*, 22, in addition to numerous tie-ins such as prizes and contests, the serial viewer's enjoyment was enhanced by other exploitation devices, from calendars and pincushions to puzzles and games.

10. Ed Hulse, *Distressed Damsels and Masked Marauders: Cliffhanger Serials of the Silent-Movie Era* (Morris Plains, NJ: Murania, 2014), 7.

11. Ed Hulse noted that serials rarely pretended to be anything but entertainment for the masses.

12. Stamp, "Women and the Silent Screen," 2.

13. Ibid.

14. Miriam Hansen, *Babel and Babylon: Spectatorship in American Silent Film* (Cambridge, MA: Harvard University Press, 1991), 116.

15. Lewis Jacobs, *The Rise of the American Film: A Critical History* (New York: Teachers College Press, 1975), 270.

16. Singer, *MM*, 222.

17. Koszarski, *Evening's Entertainment*, 164, and Kalton C. Lahue, *Bound and Gagged* (New York: Castle Books, 1968), 18.

18. Raymond William Stedman, *The Serials: Suspense and Drama by Installment* (Norman: University of Oklahoma Press, 1971), 4–5.

19. Ibid., 6; Singer, *MM*, 223.

20. Buck Rainey, *Those Fabulous Serial Heroines: Their Lives and Films* (Metuchen, NJ: Scarecrow, 1990), 307.

21. Stedman, *Serials*, 6, and Koszarski, *Evening's Entertainment*, 164.

22. Hulse, *DD*, 12.

23. Kalton C. Lahue, *Continued Next Week: A History of the Motion Picture Serial* (Norman: University of Oklahoma Press, 1964), 7; "*Adventures of Kathlyn,*" online at Chicagology; *MPN*, January 17, 1914. For more information on Selig see, for example, Andrew A. Frish, *Col. William N. Selig, the Man Who Invented Hollywood* (Austin: University of Texas Press, 2012).

24. Stedman, *Serials*, 8–9.

25. In a letter to *Films in Review* (February 1958), Pathé serial writer Frank Leon Smith differentiated between the "situation ending" of the series and the cliffhanger ending of the serial, in which "episodes wound up with sensational action or stunts, broken for holdover suspense . . . and gave the serial both the key to its success and the assurance of its doom."

26. *Motography*, September 6, 1913, cited in Mary Mallory, "Hollywood Heights: 'Adventures of Kathlyn,' Hollywood's First Cross-Promotional Stunt," in the *Daily Mirror*, June 3, 2013, online.

27. Singer, *MM*, 222.

28. Cunard had made her screen debut in one of William Randolph Hearst's weeklies. For more on Cunard see Ally Acker, *Reel Women: Pioneers of the Cinema, 1896 to the Present* (New York: Continuum, 1991), 161–164, and the Columbia University Women Film Pioneers Project.

29. Stamp, *MSG*, 114; Lahue, *CNW*, 20.

30. Terry Ramsaye, *A Million and One Nights: A History of the Motion Picture through 1925* (New York: Touchstone / Simon & Schuster, 1986), 661.

31. In "Extracts from the Diary of Mary Fuller" (dated April 6 and 10), *Motion Picture Magazine*, August, 1914, 97–98, Fuller recalled that one day "they blew me up with a Black Hand bomb." Another day "I was pulled up a coal-hole . . . and scrambled out with face and hands black with soot, hair down and dress torn, puffing and blowing like a grampus [dolphin]." Through it all, according to Fuller, audiences "[ate] her up."

32. Lahue, *CNW*, 15–16.

33. Rainey, *Those Fabulous Serial Heroines*, 417.

34. Stedman, *Serials*, 10–11. MacGrath had already been contracted to novelize *Zudora* for the newspapers.

35. Koszarski, *Evening's Entertainment*, 165.

36. Marina Dahlquist, *Exporting Perilous Pauline: Pearl White and the Serial Film Craze* (Urbana: University of Illinois Press, 2013), 3.

37. Louis Pizzitola, *Hearst over Hollywood: Power, Passion, and Propaganda in the Movies* (New York: Columbia University Press, 2002), 103.

38. Ibid., 104.

1. Seeking "Old Opportunity"

1. Although Jews were certainly prominent in what Neal Gabler in *An Empire of Their Own* called "the invention of Hollywood," many—like Ted and Leo, who at some point in the 1890s shed their Jewish surname and adopted their mother's maiden name of "Wharton"—downplayed their ethnicity.

2. According to census reports and other ancestry records, including *Select Births and Christenings, 1538–1975* [UK]. My great thanks to Karen Longley, Wharton-Rubenstein family historian, for sharing this and other valuable information about the Whartons' early lives.

3. Aaron Pichel, *ISM: The Lottery Man* (Ithaca, NY: Imagination Graphics, 2008), n.p. Wharton Studios Collection, the History Center in Tompkins County, Ithaca, NY.

4. *Dallas City Directory* (1891) (https://www.ancestry.com/search/collections/1890dallastx/) and *U.S. City Directories, 1822–1995* (https://www.ancestry.com/

search/collections/usdirectories/) [residence year 1891], William, who died by suicide, left behind a note to Fanny, in which he explained "I could not endure the sufferings in my head, but none of you would belief [sic] me." He left her $1,500, with the hope it "will enable you to fight your way through this world." With thanks to Karen Longley for this information.

5. For an excellent overview of the Whartons' work see Aaron Pichel, "The Wharton Brothers and Their Ithaca Studio," ISM: Beatrice Fairfax (Ithaca, NY: Imagination Graphics, 2007), n.p.

6. Motography, June 12, 1915, 981.

7. "Announcement," 1897–1898 theatrical season, Collection of the Missouri History Museum Archives, Saint Louis.

8. "The Theaters," Saint Louis Post-Dispatch, October 25, 1896, 4; "The Passing Show," Saint Louis Post-Dispatch, January 13, 1895, 24.

9. The Nebraska State Journal (March 2, 1894, 3) observed of the play after its Lansing performance, "It has plenty of thrilling situations and several climaxes that are both thrilling and legitimate."

10. "His Brother William," online essay, in "The Life & Times of Joseph Haworth."

11. Program for the Hopkins Theatre, week of January 3, 1896, Collection of the Missouri History Museum Archives, Saint Louis.

12. Hopkins, to be sure, was quite a showman. He made many wild claims, which may or may not have been true—for example, he alleged that he witnessed the assassination of Lincoln (Chicago Tribune, October 5, 1909) and that he was an associate of P. T. Barnum.

13. Sean Holmes, "All Work or No Play: Key Themes in the History of the American Stage Actor as Worker," European Journal of American Studies 3, no. 3 (Autumn 2008): 2.

14. New York Times, September 25, 1898, 14.

15. "Mr. Charles Frohman," Lusitania Resource: History, Passenger & Crew Biographies, and Lusitania Facts, www.rmslusitania.info/people/saloon/charles-frohman/.

16. Opera Glass: A Musical and Dramatic Magazine 4 (1897), 188.

17. Tammany Times, November 29, 1897, 11.

18. San Francisco Call, September 6, 1898.

19. "The Drama," NYT, July 25, 1897, SM8; "The Passing Show," Saint Louis Post-Dispatch, January 13, 1895, 24. In "My Years on the Stage," in the Ladies Home Journal of February 1911, John Drew recalled his experiences in A Marriage of Convenience as well as in other plays.

20. Lena Rubenstein (1868–1941), the daughter of Ted's uncle Solomon Rubenstein, had left her first husband Harry Prince and their two young children to run off with Clarke. With thanks to Karen Longley for the information about "Cousin Adelaide."

21. Boston Evening Transcript, February 10, 1914.

22. Argonaut (San Francisco), July 23, 1900, 4.

23. A. H. Saxon, "The Circus as Theatre: Astley's and Its Actors in the Age of Romanticism," Educational Theatre Journal 27, no. 3 (October 1975): 299. As Saxon writes, for much of the late eighteenth and nineteenth centuries, "the circus was theatre." By the late nineteenth century, it had become one of the most successful

forms of popular entertainment for all classes, not only because it incorporated performance techniques based on new inventions but also because it typically traveled from city to city, affording easy access to its wonders. And it also incorporated story lines taken from melodrama.

24. The Hanlons were also innovators who implemented such measures as the aerial safety net, still used today. See Mark Cosdon's definitive study, *The Hanlon Brothers: From Daredevil Acrobatics to Spectacle Pantomime, 1833–1931* (Carbondale: Southern Illinois University Press, 2009).

25. Richard Small, "Nothing Like It Ever Before Seen Here," *South Look* (supplement to the *Mariner Newspapers*), January 20–21, 1992.

26. Cosdon, *Hanlon Brothers*, 121–122.

27. "Magnificent Superba," *Boston Globe*, September 13, 1892.

28. As cited in Pichel, *ISM: The Lottery Man*, n.p.

29. *Motography*, June 12, 1915, 981. Pichel, in *ISM: The Lottery Man* (n.p.), writes that Ted Wharton had earlier called on the Kalem Company on Twenty-Fourth Street and suggested a story idea to them: "They liked it and told me to sit down and write it. In one hour's time I had left their office with fifteen dollars in my pocket."

30. The Kinetoscope, which had a magnifying lens and a rapidly rotating shutter, allowed viewers to watch a sequence of pictures on a band of film that moved continuously over a light source. That process created the illusion of motion.

31. A later biographical account in the trade journal *Motion Picture News* stated that—after leaving Edison and before joining Kalem—Ted was employed by another studio, Vitagraph. But that account cannot be confirmed.

32. "Why 'Ventures of Marguerite' Will Be Successful," *MPN*, October 16, 1915, 76.

33. A later story in *MPN* (July 12, 1919, 556) confirmed that Wharton had "built the first indoor studio for Pathé in 1911."

34. Donna Casella, in "Shaping the Craft of Screenwriting," an online essay for the Columbia University Women Pioneers Film Project, suggests that early writing was often skeletal at best, with stories consisting of outlines and a few words describing each scene (rather than actual scenarios). Early stories, she notes, took the form of a few lines of text, a paragraph, or a one-page plot summary, which producers / directors then took from page to screen, while a clerk on set "held the script," recording scenes, action, dialogue, and shooting directions.

35. Dated June 9, 1916, the contract between the Whartons and William Randolph Hearst stated: "It is understood and agreed that Wharton[s] will include in the cast of said series, Grace Darling, Creighton Hale, or Billy Quirk, or actors as equally as satisfactory [*sic*] to Film Service."

36. Sandra K. Sagala, *Buffalo Bill on the Silver Screen* (Norman: University of Oklahoma Press, 2013), 15.

37. "The Actor in the Early Days," *MPW*, March 10, 1917, 1509–1510. Other Pathé westerns that have been attributed to Ted (but not listed in the Fondation Jérôme-Seydoux-Pathé catalogue, which makes virtually no directorial attributions for Pathé 1910 films) include *The Girl from Arizona*, *The Cowboy's Sweetheart and the Bandit*, and *The Great Train Hold Up*.

38. *MPW*, September 10, 1910, 591. The attribution of this and a number of other films noted in this chapter is according to the *Catalogue général, Bibliothèque national de France*.

39. *MPW*, December 3, 1910, 308, and December 17, 1910, 1416.

40. *MPW*, September 24, 1910, 689.

41. Mary B. Davis, *Native America in the Twentieth Century: An Encyclopedia* (New York: Routledge, 1996), 197.

42. *MPW*, October 1, 1910, 762. The "hoodoo" was apparently a popular motif, featured in a spate of hoodoo films produced around that time, among them *The Hoodoo Lounge* (1908), starring Broncho Billy Anderson; *The Hoodoo* (1914); *Jake's Hoodoo* (1914); *The Hoodoo of Division B* (1916); and *Hoodoo Ann* (1916), directed by D. W. Griffith.

43. Although the *Rastus* picture is not cited in the Fondation Jérôme-Seydoux-Pathé catalogue, numerous other sources identify Ted Wharton as director of the film, among them the "Jim Crow Museum of Racist Memorabilia" (online) at Ferris State University, Daniel Stern's *Music Is My Life: Louis Armstrong, Autobiography, and American Jazz* (2012), and Todd McGowan's *Only a Joke Can Save Us: A Theory of Comedy* (2017). Daniel J. Leab, in *From Sambo to Superspade: The Black Experience in Motion Pictures* (Boston: Houghton Mifflin, 1975), and Donald Bogle, in *Toms, Coons, Mulattoes, Mammies, and Bucks: An Interpretive History of Blacks in American Films* (New York: Viking, 1973), explore the "Rastus" and other early film stereotypes.

44. *MPW*, November 26, 1910, 1247.

45. Ted Wharton included *Dad's Boy* and several other films noted in this chapter on the résumé of his films that he prepared as part of the "Wharton Film Studio Promotional Brochure," a proposal for a new studio in Santa Cruz.

46. *MPW*, July 15, 1911, 56.

47. *MPW*, July 9, 1910, 101.

48. Cited in Aaron Pichel, *ISM: Beatrice Fairfax*, n.p.

49. *MPW*, April 27, 1912, 356.

50. *MPW*, October 5, 1912, 66, and October 29, 1912, 342.

51. *MPW*, February 28, 1910, 806.

52. *MPW*, September 21, 1912, 1196.

53. Noted by Louella Parsons in her recollections of "young" Ted Wharton, as cited by Pichel. The film is also cited in Richard J. Maturi and Mary Buckingham Maturi, *Francis X. Bushman: A Biography and Filmography* (Jefferson, NC: McFarland, 1998), 120.

54. *MPW*, March 2, 1912, 796. Similarly sentimental was Ted's *The Snare*, in which Mary Clement, a "clever girl detective," tracks fugitive Tom Ransom to his mother's cottage in order to trap him; but when Tom is cleared, she offers a prayer of thanksgiving and then sadly "fades" from their lives (*MPW*, October 12, 1912, 164). As he did in *The Turning Point*, Bushman assumed many sympathetic roles in Ted's films—for example, as the helpful cyclist in *Two Men and a Girl*; as the consoler of a troubled and suicidal man in *Out of the Night*; and as an innocent laborer convicted of the death of his foreman in *Lost Years*.

55. Kate Carnell Watt and Kathleen C. Lonsdale, "Film and Television Adaptations 1897–2001," in John Glavin's *Dickens on Screen* (Cambridge: Cambridge University Press, 2003), 206, note that the film was both adapted and directed by Ted Wharton.

56. *MPW*, December 14, 1912, 1108.

57. *MPW*, May 11, 1912, 556. In that picture, investigator Howard Mayne (Bushman) disguises himself as a common thief in order to penetrate a gang of counterfeiters.

58. *MPW*, September 21, 1912, 1198; Maturi and Maturi, *Francis X. Bushman*, 122.

59. *MPW*, October 19, 1912, 270, and November 9, 1912, 552.

60. In one scene, according to Michael Glover Smith, as Joe confesses to Father O'Brien, the confession itself "appeared as an image within the same frame" (Smith, "The Secret History of Chicago Movies: *From the Submerged*," online essay@michael-gloversmith). See also Michael Glover Smith and Adam Selzer, *Flickering Empire: How Chicago Invented the U.S. Film Industry* (New York: Wallflower / Columbia University Press, 2015).

61. *MPW*, November 9, 1912, 588, and November 23, 1912, 767.

62. Michael Glover Smith writes that Kirsanoff's "avant-garde masterpiece Ménilmontant from 1926 features a nearly identical sequence in which a character is prevented from committing suicide by a stranger in a park."

2. Taking a Parallel Path

1. Diogenes was a family name (the name of Fanny Rubenstein's brother). Again, thanks to Karen Longley for this and for much of the family information that follows. *Billboard* (January 8, 1915, 53), reported that Leo "was brought to this country" from Manchester in 1872.

2. *The Handbook of Texas Online*, TSHA (Texas State Historical Association).

3. *MPW*, January 16, 1915, 378.

4. As per the *Dallas City Directories* (1889, 1891).

5. *MPW*, January 16, 1915, 378.

6. Although no documents are known to survive, Karen Longley notes that the marriage to Jennie likely occurred around 1891 and lasted only a few years. In 1898, Jennie married Harry Austin Shaffer; they moved together to Houston and later had three daughters. Over the years, Leo and Jennie's daughter Marie maintained connections to Leo and to the family, including her grandmother Fanny, her aunt Genie Buck, and her half brother Leo R. Wharton. After some early variations, she took Marie Wharton Shaffer as her legal name.

7. "The Standard," *Philadelphia Inquirer*, November 7, 1893, 5; *Worcester Daily Spy*, October 10, 1893, 6.

8. *Philadelphia Inquirer*, November 7, 1893, 5.

9. Program for the Hopkins Theatre, week of December 27, 1896 (Collection of the Missouri History Museum Archives, Saint Louis).

10. Program for the Hopkins Theatre, week of March 7, 1897 (Collection of the Missouri History Museum Archives, Saint Louis).

11. Program for the Hopkins Theatre, week of December 13, 1897 (Collection of the Missouri History Museum Archives, Saint Louis).

12. *Daily Picayune* (New Orleans), November 14, 1898, 2.

13. Credits for the play included Hollis E. Cooley (director), Harry James (musical director), and a cast of characters such as "Chef, Crappy Dan and Link Missing," "Little Weiner," and "Dusty Rhodes."

14. "Theaters," *Cleveland Plain Dealer*, October 17, 1899, 6.

15. Decades earlier, that theater (then known as Daly's Fifth Avenue or just Daly's Theatre) had been managed by Augustin Daly.

16. "'The Liberty Belles': A Pleasing Comedy," *NYT*, October 1, 1901, 8.

17. "Dramatical and Musical," *NYT*, September 2, 1900, 5. *The Great Ruby* was later filmed, in 1915, as a Lubin feature (reviewed in *MPN*, September 18, 1915).

18. *Rock Island (IL) Argus*, November 25, 1902; *Cornell Daily Sun*, December 12, 1901.

19. *Motion Picture Studio Directory and Trade Annual*, October 21, 1916, 1.

20. *MPW*, January 16, 1915, 378.

21. Hulse, *DD*, 91.

22. *MPW*, October 29, 1910, 993, and November 19, 1910, 1176, 1178.

23. William K. Everson et al., program notes for the Theodore Huff Memorial Film Society's showing of *The Rival Brothers' Patriotism*, part of a "Program of Early American Films: 1910–1916," January 5 and March 15, 1954, William K. Everson Archive, New York University.

24. *MPW*, July 27, 1912, 374. Cited, along with other dramas, including *The Frozen Trail* and *Social Highwaymen*, in *MPW* (January 16, 1915, 378) as part of Leo's early filmography.

25. "Leo Wharton, Director," *MPW*, January 16, 1915, 378.

26. *MPW*, November 2, 1912, 449.

27. *MPW*, August 31, 1912, 908.

28. An as-yet unrestored print of *An Exciting Honeymoon* is in the film collection of the George Eastman Museum, Rochester, New York.

29. *MPW*, April 26, 1913, 348.

30. *MPW*, May 10, 1913, 624.

31. *MPW*, November 29, 1913, 973 and 1044; Ray Istorico, *Greatness in Waiting: An Illustrated History of the Early New York Yankees, 1903–1919* (Jefferson, NC: McFarland, 2008), 110.

32. *Billboard*, January 9, 1915, 53; *MPW*, January 16, 1915, 378.

3. Bringing Essanay's "Special Eastern" to Ithaca

1. With thanks to "History Forge," the History Center in Tompkins County, and to *Cornell Alumni News* for some of this information. And special thanks to Donna Eschenbrenner, director of Archives and Research Services at the History Center, who noted that while the football team was always enthusiastically supported, in 1912 it had a losing season and "took a definite back seat to the national champion crew teams."

2. *MPW*, October 12, 1912, 352, and November 30, 1912, 902; *MPN*, December 7, 1912, 968, and December 21, 1912, 1183.

3. *IJ*, May 14, 1913, 6, and *MPW*, November 30, 1912, 902. Aaron Pichel, in *ISM: The Forgotten History* (Ithaca, NY: Imagination Graphics, 2009), writes that in order to get filming permission, Ted tendered a $300 donation to Cornell freshman athletics.

4. *MPW*, April 26, 1913, 335.

5. *MPW*, September 6, 1913, 186–187; also *IJ*, August 2, 1913.

6. Denise Lowe, "Beverly Bayne," in *An Encyclopedic Dictionary of Women in Early Films, 1895–1930* (New York: Routledge, 2005), 45.

7. *A Brother's Loyalty* was another film of mistaken identity, in which Bushman played a double role as Hal, who has been accused of counterfeiting, and Paul, the twin brother determined to exonerate him. And in the two-reel *The Power of Conscience*, he played a preacher whose sermon "The Power of Conscience" leads a guilty man to confess his crime (*MPW*, August 16, 1913, 766). According to *MPW* (August 3, 1913), Bushman's characterization of the preacher will remain "a model of its kind."

8. "Well-Known Player Recalls His Entrance to Screendom and Sees Great Things for Pictures," *MPN*, March 10, 1917, 1508.

9. *IJ*, May 14, 1913.

10. *IJ*, June 2, 1913, 6.

11. *IJ*, May 19, 1913, 6.

12. *IJ*, June 3, 1913.

13. According to the *IJ* (June 13, 1913), Ted often went to great lengths to "get as perfect a picture as possible," even climbing to the top of a steep cliff to cut away some foliage that was spoiling his shot.

14. *IJ*, June 12, 1913, June 13, 1913, and June 14, 1913, 7.

15. *IJ*, June 2, 1913, 6.

16. *IJ*, June 14, 1913, 3. Also noted by Walter R. Stainton, in "Pearl White in Ithaca: Films Were Once Made above Cayuga's Waters," *Films in Review*, May 1951, 20.

17. Felix Dodge, "The Hermit of Lonely Gulch," *Motion Picture Story Magazine*, October 1913, 17–23, 172.

18. To secure those scenes, Ted and his crew had to work on a Sunday. It was, *IJ* reported (June 23, 1913, 6), "the first time in three years he has had to work on a Sunday and it would probably be the last."

19. Maturi and Maturi, *Francis X. Bushman*, 130. See also *MPW*, September 6, 1913, 1088.

20. *IJ*, June 23, 1913, 7.

21. *MPW*, September 20, 1913, 1310; *MPN*, September 30, 1913, 25.

22. *IJ*, July 3, 1913, 3.

23. *MPN*, November 22, 1913. In that summary of the film, the title is given as *The Woman Scorned*, but Essanay's own ads list it as *A Woman Scorned*. Around the same time that the film was released, the *Ithaca Journal* reported on the local exhibition of another picture, *Little Ned* (set in the West and starring Bushman and young Louis Sumner Fuertes, the son of local Cornell professor Louis A. Fuertes, along with other Ithaca citizens, including Paul K. Clymer and Cornell proctor Dr. R. M. Vose). But there seems to be no evidence in the trade papers of *Little Ned*'s release, at least not under that title.

24. *Wilkes-Barre Times Leader*, December 2, 1913, 18. *IJ* (July 21, 1913, 6), however, described it as a "new one-reel photo-play."

25. *MPW*, September 27, 1913, 1414.

26. Dangers and perils were inherent in the new age of technology, especially as it extended to filmmaking.

27. *IJ*, July 24, 1913.

28. *IJ*, August 11, 1913, 6. According to Wharton, Walker (who assumed the role originally intended for Eugene Gladsby) performed "creditably."

29. *MPW*, October 4, 1913, 62, 64. In *Waiting*, there was also a sympathetic and devoted African American servant who assists the main character after his tragic loss.

30. Maturi and Maturi, *Francis X. Bushman*, 131.

31. *Photoplay*, May 1915, 22.

32. Hugh Hoffman, *MPW*, October 25, 1913, 367.

33. *IJ*, July 21, 1913, 6.

34. *IJ*, July 21, 1913, 6.

35. *IJ*, June 13, 1913, 7, and June 17, 1913, 6.

36. *IJ*, August 21, 1913, 6.

37. *IJ*, June 17, 1913, 6; *MPW*, August 16, 1913, 766.

38. *IJ*, July 5, 1913, 3. See also *IJ*, July 21, 1913.

39. *MPW*, October 18, 1913, 296.

40. *IJ* (August 8, 1913) described the fifty-eight-year-old Gladsby (occasionally cited in *IJ* as "Glasby") as a "colored man [who] took well in the pictures and for an amateur actor was especially fine."

41. *MPW* (September 13, 1913, 1205) gives the name as "Frank Robertson."

42. *IJ*, July 17, 1913.

43. Singer, *MM*, 12.

44. Christian Hale, "Phantom Rides," BFI ScreenOnline.

45. *IJ*, July 19, 1913, 2.

46. *IJ*, July 19, 1913, 2.

47. *MPW*, October 18, 1913, 296, 300.

48. *IJ*, August 1, 1913, 3.

49. *IJ*, August 1, 1913, 3.

50. *MPW*, November 15, 1913, 736.

51. *MPW*, October 25, 1913, 408; *MPN*, November 1, 1913, 18.

52. Review, *Anaconda (MT) Standard*, November 27, 1913, 3.

53. Review, *Salt Lake City Evening Telegram*, November 5, 1913, 5.

54. *IJ*, August 15, 1913.

55. *IJ*, August 21, 1913, 6.

56. *IJ*, August 21, 1913, 6.

57. *IJ*, August 11, 1913, 6.

58. *IJ*, August 18, 1913, 6.

59. *Cornell Alumni News*, August 13, 1913, 485.

60. Ted endeared himself to the community in ways large and small, even using his "magic" to effect a thrilling rescue of a trapped kitten in front of the Ithaca Hotel (*IJ*, August 6, 1913).

61. Hugh Hoffman, *MPW*, October 25, 1913, 367–368.

4. Taming and Reframing Buffalo Bill

1. The film was later released in various shorter versions. In his own filmography, Ted listed it as a seven-reeler.

2. Charles J. Ver Halen, "Bringing the Old West Back," *MPN*, November 22, 1913, 19. There is, however, some dispute about the matter of preservation. An

industry biography of Ted, citing the *Washington Post*, noted that "one complete set of reels [of the picture] will be preserved in the archives of the War Department as a record of the frontier campaigns." But, as Nancy M. Peterson writes in "Buffalo Bill's Lost Legacy" (*American History* magazine, October 2003), "Although the original documentary was reportedly donated to War and Interior Department archives, there is no record that it was ever received." Today only a fragment is extant.

3. *Motography*, July 20, 1912, 41–47.

4. *MPW*, October 25, 1913, 368.

5. Peterson, "Buffalo Bill's Lost Legacy," 51.

6. Buffalo Bill Museum and Grave, Golden, CO.

7. William F. Cody Archive, University of Nebraska at Lincoln.

8. The horse was purchased by a bidder at auction and returned to Cody (*NYT*, August 21, 1913).

9. The filming of his life story, writes Andrea I. Paul in "Buffalo Bill and Wounded Knee: The Movie" (*Nebraska History* 71 [1990]: 183), was, for Cody, a "last desperate attempt . . . to keep his legend alive in public consciousness (even after his death)" and "to help him regain financial solvency."

10. Peterson, "Buffalo Bill's Lost Legacy," 51.

11. David Burrell, "Buffalo Bill and Native Americans," online essay. Curiously, while Cody stoked racial antagonism and historical enmity, he himself apparently had respect for Native Americans, whom he cast for his popular shows directly from the reservations and generally treated well on tours.

12. Sandra K. Sagala, *Buffalo Bill on the Silver Screen: The Films of William F. Cody* (Norman: University of Oklahoma Press, 2013), 69.

13. Ibid., 69.

14. Ibid., 58–59.

15. Ibid., 71.

16. Paul, "Buffalo Bill and Wounded Knee," 183.

17. Peterson, "Buffalo Bill's Lost Legacy," 53.

18. Sagala, *Buffalo Bill on the Silver Screen*, 78–79.

19. Ibid., 84.

20. *MPW*, October 25, 1913, 368.

21. In the picture, according to Ver Halen, the warrior "Dewy Beard"—"still considered a hero among his tribe"—appeared "in his ghost shirt, which still bears the marks of five bullet holes."

22. Peterson, "Buffalo Bill's Lost Legacy," 55.

23. Ver Halen, "Bringing the Old West Back," 19.

24. Peterson, "Buffalo Bill's Lost Legacy," 55. Also noted in Sagala, *Buffalo Bill on the Silver Screen*, and elsewhere.

25. Sagala, *Buffalo Bill on the Silver Screen*, 88–89.

26. *Billboard*, October 25, 1913, 7.

27. Those "pictures of modern homes, schools, and farming practices," according to Paul, "Buffalo Bill and Wounded Knee" (185), would document "the progress of reservation Indians" over the last twenty years.

28. As indicated on the title card of the film (according to Sagala, *Buffalo Bill on the Silver Screen*, 107).

29. Ver Halen, "Bringing the Old West Back," 20. In her *Memories of Buffalo Bill*, Louisa Cody recalled the hours that she, her husband Buffalo Bill, Ted Wharton ("the director of the history"), and Mrs. Wharton spent in the "little tent" of Short Bull getting to know the Sioux and learning about the stories of "Indian politics." Afterward, Short Bull expressed his gratitude. Through his interpreter, "He say you the first white person ever ask that [i.e., the actual events of the last Indian Rebellion]. He say to thank you—now he get to tell the truth." The belief that Ted Wharton would tell the real stories obviously endeared him to the Sioux.

30. Ver Halen, "Bringing the Old West Back," 19.

31. "Buffalo Bill Picture Shown," *MPW*, March 14, 1914. The review also remarked on the "alternate handclapping cheers, and hisses which greeted individual action when viewed by the aforementioned gentlemen [Secretary of War Garrison, Secretary of the Interior Lane, congressmen, and other government officials]."

32. Peterson, "Buffalo Bill's Lost Legacy," 56.

33. Paul, "Buffalo Bill and Wounded Knee," 186, writes that the film was presented to two different Washington, DC, audiences on February 27, 1914. The first was composed of members of the National Press Club, who the producers hoped would provide extensive coverage in their publications and thus encourage large crowds as the film began touring the country. "The endorsements most dear to the film's producers, however, were those that followed the evening presentation to the New Home Club, a social organization hosted by the Interior Secretary Lane. Among the 1,000 persons in attendance were Secretary of War Garrison, numerous congressmen, Commissioner of Indian Affairs Cato Sell, and other government officials." That showing resulted in endorsements by both the Interior and War Departments. For more on the reception of the film at the New Home Club see *MPW*, March 14, 1914.

34. Curator of the Nebraska State Historical Society Museum Melvin R. Gilmore called the production "a disgrace to the government under whose sanction it was made," while Native Americans offered similar criticisms. Sioux Chauncey Yellow Robe, for example, castigated the film and argued that "history was being manipulated by Cody and Miles for their own self-aggrandizement." He called them pretenders who "went back and became heroes for a moving picture machine" (Paul, "Buffalo Bill and Wounded Knee," 188).

35. Advertisements for the edited version did not credit Ted Wharton's contribution, and one review (*MPN*, February 17, 1917, 1092) even insisted that most of the film's footage "has never been released before." *MPW* (February 10, 1917, 880) wrote that the film—a "special" with a running time of one hour and fifteen minutes—was one of the "real adventure films on the market." According to the Adventure Club of Chicago, the feature, "for the first time, puts American history on the screen. Thrilling adventures in Buffalo Bill's life have been filmed with great detail." *MPN* (January 17, 1917, 564) noted that "in this film production [called a "Film Autobiography of America's Most Picturesque Figure"], the American people have a legacy in which they may well take pride. The younger generation especially will be vitally interested in it."

5. Going Independent

1. *IJ*, February 19 and March 3, 1914.

2. *IJ*, March 18, 1914, 2.

3. *IJ*, March 18, 1914, 2.

4. *IJ*, March 18, 1914, 2.

5. Hulse, *DD*, 75–76.

6. *MPN*, June 12, 1914, 69. See also Richard Lewis Ward, *When the Cock Crows: A History of the Pathé Exchange* (Carbondale: Southern Illinois University Press, 2016).

7. As Martin L. Johnson wrote, a handful of small regional producers like the Paragon Feature Film Company of Omaha, Nebraska, tried unsuccessfully to move from municipal to more mainstream filmmaking. A few years later, though, other regional filmmakers had better luck—for instance, Henry Klutho and Richard E. Norman, who established permanent studios in Jacksonville, Florida. See Martin Johnson, "'Boost Your Town in the Movies': Municipal Film Companies in the United States, 1910–1917," in *Beyond the Screen: Institutions, Networks and Publics of Early Cinema*, ed. Marta Braun, Charlie Kiel, Rob King, Paul Moore, and Louis Pelletier (New Barnet, UK: John Libbey), 288.

8. Pichel, *ISM: The Lottery Man*, n.p.

9. *IJ*, April 24, 1914. The *Ithaca Daily News* (cited in Pichel, *ISM: The Lottery Man*) noted that both Bergen and Esmond, soon after their arrival to join the Wharton company in Ithaca, "agreed that the motion picture business had reached a development where it is attracting the best actors on the legitimate stage. A few years ago they would not consider propositions to act before the cameras, but now the best actors are securing engagements with picture producers."

10. *IJ*, May 8, 1914.

11. "Peppery" was an adjective frequently applied to Tracy. See, for example, *IJ*, August 8, 6, and August 21, 1913, 6.

12. *IJ*, April 14, 1914.

13. *IJ*, April 14, 1914. According to *IJ*, one site under consideration, but ultimately rejected, was the new baseball cage at Cornell University.

14. *IJ*, April 22, 1914.

15. *IJ*, April 20 and May 4, 1914.

16. *IJ*, May 5, 1914.

17. *IJ*, May 23 and 16, 1914. In fact, the division of labor was not always so clear.

18. Chadwick went on to become a professor of theater at Ithaca College, to which he donated his collection of Wharton Studio photographs.

19. Cited in Pichel, *ISM: Beatrice Fairfax*, n.p.

20. "Sylvan Ithaca Is Idyll Spot for Busy Whartons," *MPN*, August 14, 1915, 45.

21. *IJ*, May 12, 1914. Weather was not the only problem; according to another article in *IJ* (May 16, 1914), a mule used in the filming refused to cooperate, "and there was considerable fun in trying to make it conform to the requirements of moving pictures."

22. *IJ*, May 11, 1914.

23. In fact, in a later film, *The Lottery Man*, the accounting of Mrs. Wright's unfortunate finances is written on stationery from F. W. Stewart's actual brokerage company.

24. *DM*, August 5, 1914. The plot was similar to that of Ted's earlier picture *Into the North*.

25. *IJ*, June 2 and 3, 1914.

26. *MPN*, June 13, 1914, 54.

27. *IJ*, June 3, 1914.

28. *IJ*, August 13, 1914. Pathé explained that the factory where the film was developed received the "Ithaca, N.Y." trademark "rather late" and thus failed to include it on the picture.

29. *IJ*, June 2, 1914.

30. *DM*, August 5, 1914. Not all the reviews were that laudatory. *Variety* (September 11, 1914, 22), for instance, lamented that the producer "didn't make good use of the pruning fork and lop off several hundred feet of this feature."

31. *IJ*, May 23, 1914.

32. *IJ*, July 9, 1914.

33. *IJ*, July 7, 1914, and July 10, 1914.

34. Both *IJ* (July 10, 1914, 2) and an undated review, likely from the *Dramatic Mirror* (in the Wharton Studios Collection in the History Center in Tompkins County), described the filming.

35. *IJ*, June 23, 1913.

36. *IJ*, July 8, 1914.

37. *IJ*, July 9, 1914.

38. *IJ*, July 17, 1914.

39. *Variety*, October 10, 1914, 25; *IJ*, October 30, 1914.

40. *IJ*, August 1, 1914.

41. *IJ*, August 1, 1914, reported that two cameras were used; but another article in *IJ* suggested there might have been a third camera as well.

42. Reported in "Theo Wharton in Town," *MPW*, October 10, 1914, 171.

43. *IJ*, July 21, 1914, 6. Those faces included F. W. Stewart and other locals.

44. *IJ*, July 25, 1914.

45. *DM*, October 7, 1914.

46. *DM*, October 7, 1914.

47. *IJ*, November 3, 1914.

48. *IJ*, November 23, 1914. Things end well, though, and they are all later reunited in the city.

49. *IJ*, September 18, 1914, 3. *IJ* (November 23, 1914) later observed that the scene of the struggle "go[ing] over the Triphammer Falls and down through the rapids below" had to be reshot. And "anyone who knows the temperature of the water would not question Mr. Bergen's ability to earn a substantial salary."

50. Clifford H. Pangburn, *MPN*, November 28, 1914.

51. *IJ*, August 11 and 13, 1914, 3.

52. *DM*, December 2, 1914.

53. *Variety*, October 3, 1914, 21. The use of double exposure is noted in the *Dramatic Mirror* (October 21, 1914).

54. *Sis Hopkins*, a 1919 comedy film (directed by Clarence Badger) that starred Mabel Normand, was based on a character made famous by actress Rose Melville in the theater play *Zeb*.

55. *IJ*, November 7, 1914, 3.

56. *IJ*, November 7, 1914, 3.

57. *IJ*, November 7, 1914, 3.

58. *IJ*, August 6, 1914. Reportedly, after traveling to New York City, Ted brought back "assurance" that Wharton studio activity would continue, as evidenced by the

new three-reel production that Leo was beginning the following week. The "Effect of the War on the Making of Motion Pictures" was also discussed in *IJ* (August 17, 1914), which listed some of the measures the Whartons were taking.

59. *IJ*, August 19, 1914, 7, and September 5, 1914, 2.

60. According to *IJ* (February 23, 1915), Dubray wrote the Whartons from the front in France that the ideas for war stories he was collecting might make a good war installment in their new serial. They, in turn, promised Dubray to keep his old job open for him when he returned. See also *MPN* (February 27, 1915, 44) for an explanation of Dubray's readiness to fight after earlier having been "excused from service."

61. As Pichel noted in *ISM: Beatrice Fairfax*, n.p., June was "called away from the Wharton studio to serve in the Signal Corps during World War I," after which he went on to Hollywood, where he had a long career as a cinematographer at MGM and other studios, shooting over 160 feature films. Earlier, *IJ* (August 19, 1914) reported a rumor that had spread about actor Billy Mason being called up as well. "Billy, it appears, is a Swede, . . . If Sweden mobilizes her navy, Billy says he might have to go back to fight for his native land. But Mrs. Mason says different." Penn and Dubray's departures for service are noted in *IJ* (August 4, 1914, 7).

62. *IJ*, August 17, 1914.

6. Exploiting *Elaine*

1. *MPW*, January 23, 1915, 522. Also noted (often verbatim) in numerous other publications, including the *New York Clipper*, January 23, 1915, 13.

2. Shelley Stamp, "An Awful Struggle between Love and Ambition: Serial Heroines, Serial Stars and Their Female Fans," in *The Silent Cinema Reader*, ed. Lee Grieveson and Peter Krämer (London: Routledge, 2004), 211.

3. As Miriam Hansen noted in *BB*, 63, the "shaping" extended to the cinema as well.

4. Singer, *MM*, 243–244.

5. Singer, *MM*, 222.

6. *Variety*, April 10, 1914, as cited in Stamp, *MSG*, 104.

7. Stamp, "Awful Struggle," 212; also Sumiko Higashi, in *Virgins, Vamps, and Flappers: The Silent Movie Heroine* (Montreal: Eden, 1978), 106.

8. Stamp, *MSG*, 128.

9. Singer, *MM*, 238.

10. Arthur Benjamin Reeve, *The Exploits of Elaine* (New York: Harper and Bros., 1915), 3.

11. Marina Dahlquist, "Pearl White," *Columbia Women Film Pioneers Project*, online. See also Jennifer M. Bean, "Technologies of Early Stardom and the Extraordinary Body," *Camera Obscura* 16, no. 3 (2001); and Acker, *RW*.

12. See "How Pearl White, Pathé Star, Got Her Start," *MPN*, January 23, 1915, 34.

13. *The Macon (MO) Daily Herald*, October 6, 1915, 12.

14. *MPN*, December 19, 1914, 33. An earlier ad in *MPN* had explicitly called Arnold "The Highest Salaried Man in Pictures Today."

15. "Arnold Daly a Pathé Player," *MPW*, January 2, 1915, 54.

16. Subsequent "Kennedy" stories appeared between 1919 and 1935 in magazines such as *Dime Detective*, *Popular Detective*, and *Detective Story Magazine* and were

compiled in book form; but the later titles in the overall sequence, most of which were novels, generally did not have the same appeal as the early work.

17. *MPN*, December 19, 1914, 33, noted that Reeve "keeps so closely in touch with the newest discoveries that he is able to solve mysteries by means which are as ingenious as they are startling."

18. "Introducing Scientific Apparatus in Photoplay," *World's Advance* 30 (May 1915): 609.

19. Reeve, *Exploits*, 12.

20. Stedman, *Serials*, 16.

21. Elaine, too, had a song—"Elaine, My Moving Picture Queen"—which was sometimes performed by singers outside the theater as a way of attracting moviegoers to come in and watch the serial.

22. *MPN*, December 19, 1914, 33.

23. Lahue, *CNW*, 28.

24. The next year, Lewis would menace Pearl White again, this time in the non-Wharton chapter play *The Iron Claw*. For more on Lewis see *MPN*, January 23, 1915, 73; on Hale see *MPN*, January 23, 1915, 32.

25. Stedman, *Serials*, 17.

26. Margaret Hennefeld, in "The Exploits of Elaine," online essay for the National Film Registry, Library of Congress website, discusses "the obsessive desire to watch over Elaine, allegedly in order to protect her from her own pluckiness," which "quickly becomes a panoptic nightmare," and "the gendered media devices have been finely woven into the history of American cultural identity and entertainment pastimes."

27. Singer, *MM*, 14.

28. Singer, *MM*, 222, 255. See also Bean, "Technologies of Early Stardom and the Extraordinary Body," 20.

29. *MPW*, January 9, 1915, 276, 278; *MPN*, January 2, 1915, 48.

30. *MPW*, January 2, 1915, 80. See also *MPN*, January 2, 1915, 48.

31. *MPW*, January 9, 1915, 278; *MPW*, January 16, 1915, 388; *MPN*, January 15, 1915, 43.

32. *MPN*, January 23, 1915, 45, and January 30, 1915, 43. "The Vanishing Jewels" was alternatively titled "The Iron Prison."

33. *MPN*, February 6, 1915, 45; *MPW*, January 30, 1915, 740.

34. Hulse, *DD*, 95.

35. *MPN*, February 13, 1915, 45.

36. *MPW*, February 20, 1915, 1148. The episode also takes a predictable turn, as Elaine and Kennedy exchange their first kiss. The reviewer writes that "in this number there is less of science than in the previous ones," but there is also added interest in the introduction of several new characters.

37. *MPW*, February 6, 1915, 900; *MPN*, February 27, 1915, 52.

38. *MPW*, February 13, 1915, 1052; *MPN*, March 6, 1915, 50.

39. *MPN*, March 20, 1915, 53.

40. *MPW*, February 20, 1915, 1200; *MPN*, March 13, 1915, 53.

41. Reeve, *Exploits*, 235.

42. *MPW*, March 13, 1915, 1682; *MPN*, March 27, 1915, 56.

43. *MPW*, March 20, 1915, 1846; *MPN*, April 3, 1915, 68.

44. Reeve, *Exploits*, 294.

45. Stamp, *MSG*, 135.

46. *San Francisco Examiner*, January 19, 1915, 7, as cited in Stamp, *MSG*, 135.

47. Stamp, *MSG*, 135.

48. Stamp, *MSG*, 135–136.

49. Singer, *MM*, 262.

50. Similarly, in "The Devil Worshippers," when the phony medium Mme. Savetsky attempts to conjure the ghost of Elaine's father, she "levitates" a guitar and tambourine that appear to be superimposed on the frame (but later are shown to be attached with strings to the ceiling, in an attempt to deceive the participants).

51. Cited in Kristen Whissel, "Regulating Mobility: Technology, Modernity, and Feature-Length Narrativity in *Traffic in Souls*," *Camera Obscura* 17, no. 1 (2002): 1–30.

52. That same "sound wave"–like superimposition on the frame occurs in a later episode ("The Devil Worshippers") as well, when Mme. Savetsky "speaks" the lines "I'm sorry but I'm afraid my control will not work to-day."

53. *MPN*, April 10, 1915, 60–61, and December 19, 1914, 33. *World's Advance* 30, no. 5 (May 1915): 615, which praised Leo's direction, described the "film [as being] of quite an unusual nature, since it introduces new scientific invention in a thrilling manner."

54. Hulse, *DD*, 96. *MPN* (July 24, 1915, 43), reporting on the convention, noted that *The Exploits of Elaine* was only into its thirteenth episode when it reached the million-dollar mark.

55. *IJ*, July 14, 1915, 7.

7. Extending *Elaine*

1. As always, Hearst was quick to promote his own interests as well. In one of the *Elaine* episodes, as Wayne Schulz noted in "'Elaine' at Saginaw: A Foreword and a Finale" (*Classic Images*, September 1995, 51), "an issue of [Hearst's] the New York Journal is very prominently visible."

2. *MPN*, April 10, 1915, 61.

3. Reeve, *The Romance of Elaine* (Harper and Bros., 1916, for Hearst's International Library Company), 7; Stedman, *Serials*, 39.

4. The novelization truncated installments five through ten of the sequel-serial into a single chapter.

5. *MPW*, April 10, 1915, 306; *MPN*, April 17, 1915, 73.

6. *MPW*, April 17, 1915, 470; *MPN*, April 24, 1915.

7. *MPW*, April 24, 1915, 64. "The "combined Wharton forces," the reviewer noted, "are making a tremendous success of the big Pathé-Hearst serial." Also *MPN*, May 1, 1915, 65.

8. *MPW*, May 1, 1915, 808; *MPN*, May 8, 1915, 70. *IJ* (April 15, 1915) commented on the "remarkable pictures" of the "microbes of the disease" caused by the tick.

9. *MPW*, May 8, 1915, 986; *MPN*, May 15, 1915, 67; *Motography*, May 15, 1915, 787–788.

10. *MPW*, May 15, 1915, 1168.

11. *MPN*, May 29, 1915, 70.

12. *MPN*, June 5, 1915, 72.

13. *MPW*, June 5, 1915, 1690; In *MPN* (June 12, 1915, 76), Pangburn comments on the choice of title and makes the connection to Poe's story, "in which a criminal [also] betrayed himself by his own imagination."

14. *MPW*, June 12, 1915, 1856; *MPN*, June 19, 1915, 72.

15. Stamp, *MSG*, 9.

16. Stamp, "Awful Struggle," 213. See also Tom Gunning's essay "From the Opium Den to the Theatre of Morality: Moral Discourse and the Film Process in Early American Cinema," 145–154, and Ben Brewster's "*Traffic in Souls*: An Experiment in Feature Length Narrative Construction," 226–241, both in Grieveson and Krämer, *Silent Cinema Reader.* See also Kristen Whissel's "Regulating Mobility: Technology, Modernity, and Feature-Length Narrativity in *Traffic in Souls.*"

17. Marina Dahlquist, "Introduction: Why Pearl?," 3 and 13, in *Exporting Perilous Pauline: Pearl White and the Serial Film Craze*, ed. Dahlquist (Urbana: University of Illinois Press, 2013).

18. Hulse, *DD*, 99.

19. *MPN*, June 5, 1915, 48.

20. "Sylvan Ithaca Is Idyll Spot for Busy Whartons," *MPN*, August 14, 1915, 45.

21. Dickey had been selling real estate in Chicago when Goddard got in touch with him to tell him that Hearst had gone into the movie business and wanted to do a serial. So Goddard asked Dickey to help (Pichel, *ISM: Beatrice Fairfax*, n.p.).

22. Hulse, *DD*, 97.

23. Hulse, *DD*, 100. Walter H. Stainton, in "Pearl White in Ithaca," *Movies in Review* (May 1951, 23), noted that, in Ithaca, Barrymore kept to himself and read a great deal, to the point that the rest of the company nicknamed him "the Professor."

24. For more on Oland's many film roles see, for example, *MPW*, May 12, 1917, 972.

25. *MPW*, June 26, 1915, 2178.

26. *MPW*, June 26, 1915, 2176; *MPN*, July 3, 1915, 73.

27. *MPW*, July 10, 1915, 396.

28. *MPW*, July 10, 1915, 322.

29. *MPW*, July 17, 1915, 566; *MPW*, July 17, 1915, 509.

30. *MPW*, July 31, 1915, 904; *MPN*, July 31, 1915, 81.

31. *MPW*, July 24, 1915, 728.

32. *MPW*, July 31, 1915, 904; *MPN*, August 14, 1915, 92.

33. *MPW*, August 7, 1915, 1076; *MPW*, August 21, 1915, 1325.

34. *MPW*, August 14, 1915, 1231; *MPN*, September 4, 1915, 70.

35. *MPW*, August 21, 1915, 1396.

36. *MPW*, August 21, 1915, 1396. Also *MPN*, September 11, 1915, 90.

37. *MPN*, June 19, 1915, 8.

38. *MPN*, June 26, 1915, 72.

39. Hulse, *DD*, 101. Hulse observed that, in some cases, it was not even a weapon but merely the component of a weapon—a rare mineral, or perhaps a chemical compound.

40. *IJ*, May 17, 1915, 7.

41. This oft-repeated anecdote varied in the telling: sometimes it was a five-dollar fine; other times, it was ten dollars or more.

42. *IJ*, June 10, 1915, 6.

43. *IJ*, August 14, 1915, 2.

44. *IJ*, August 7, 1915, 3. The enthusiasm of the locals, moreover, extended beyond the theaters. According to *MPN* (August 14, 1915, 46), "the greatest wonder of all [occurred] when a waiter in a local hotel refused tips from those of the [*Romance*] company at his table, saying that the honor of serving required no fee."

45. *IJ*, August 7, 1915, 3.

46. *IJ*, August 7, 1915, 3.

47. *IJ*, August 14, 1915, 6.

48. *IJ*, August 28, 1915, 3.

49. Rudmer Canjels, "Changing Views and Perspectives: Translating Pearl White's American Adventures in Wartime France," in Dahlquist, *Exporting Perilous Pauline*, 30.

50. Ibid., 33–34.

51. Ibid., 27.

52. Monica Dall'Asta, "Pearl, the Swift One," in Dahlquist, *Exporting Perilous Pauline*, 82–83. Delluc also stated that White was one of the few actresses who "understood the costuming technique of the screen."

8. Establishing Roots in Renwick Park

1. *IJ*, February 3, 1915, 3. In addition to the outstanding mortgage, the various liens totaled approximately $6,000. See also *IJ*, December 19, 1914.

2. *IJ*, April 15, 1915. *Variety* (May 1915) commented on another special feature that the new studio offered: proximity to "the greatest 'class' of extras in the country"—that is, "the students at Cornell, who number 6,000 [including those nonmatriculating], embracing every race and nationality."

3. *IJ*, March 22, 1915. A later article in the *Ithaca Journal* (March 10, 1915) noted that an appeal of the foreclosure had been made. The court was asked to postpone the sale, scheduled for March 20. But the sale ultimately went forward as originally scheduled.

4. *IJ*, April 4, 1915.

5. According to *MPN*, August 14, 1915, 45, Buck had become interested in the Whartons' business and had "severed a twenty years' connection with the wholesale dry goods firm of Ely and Walker of St. Louis and become one of the Wharton organization." *Motography* (March 20, 1915, 454) described him as a "capitalist of St. Louis, Mo" who had taken up permanent residence in the East after allying himself with the Whartons in the "production of pictures for Pathé."

6. *DeWitt Historical Society Newsletter*, Summer 1995: 2–3. With special thanks to Todd Zwigard of Todd Zwigard Associates, who has worked with the Wharton Studio Museum, for some of these particulars.

7. *DeWitt Historical Society Newsletter*, Summer 1995: 3.

8. In May 1915, *Variety* wrote that the Whartons took possession on May 30.

9. An earlier story in *IJ* (January 27, 1915) had reported that the "new studio [would] keep three companies busy."

10. *IJ*, September 28, 1915, 6.

11. Pathé Exchange advertisement, *MPN*, October 16, 1915, 32–33.

12. "'Get-Rich-Quick-Wallingford' Is at Last in Films," *MPN*, July 17, 1915, 64.

13. Ibid.

14. *MPW*, October 9, 1915, 285.

15. *MPW*, October 16, 1915, 518. *MPN*, October 9, 1915, 91, lists the title as "A Bungalow Bungled."

16. *MPW*, November 20, 1915, 686; *MPN*, October 16, 1915, 89. The name appears in different forms in different publications. Both *MPN* and *Variety* list it as "Silas Bogger"; *MPW* lists it as "Elias Boggers"; and *Cosmopolitan* as "Elias Bogger."

17. *MPW*, October 30, 1915, 858; *MPN*, October 23, 1915, 102.

18. The many problems involving the skunks that were imported for the scene are detailed in *IJ* (September 15, 1915) under the headline "Humble Polecat Now Starring in Moviedom; HELP!" *IJ* (September 10, 1915) also described the problems.

19. *MPW*, October 30, 1915, 1028; *MPN*, October 30, 1915, 92. *MPN* lists the name of the episode as "The Master Touch."

20. *MPW*, November 6, 1915, 1204; *MPN*, November 6, 1915, 97.

21. *MPW*, November 20, 1915, 1558; *MPN*, November 13, 1915, 97.

22. *MPW*, November 27, 1915, 1728; *MPN*, November 27, 1915, 100.

23. *MPW*, December 4, 1915, pp. 1906–1907; *MPN*, December 4, 1915, 98.

24. *MPW*, December 4, 1915, p. 1907; *MPN*, December 11, 1915, 99–100.

25. *MPW*, December 11, 1915, 2086; *MPN*, December 25, 1915, 138.

26. *MPW*, December 18, 1915, 2258 (in which the name is listed as "Jones Squibble"). In *MPN*, December 25, 1915, 138, the title appears in a variant spelling, as "A Stoney Deal."

27. *MPW*, December 25, 2448.

28. *MPW*, January 1, 1916, 138.

29. *MPW*, January 8, 1916, 300.

30. *IJ*, October 1, 1916, 6.

31. *MPW*, October 9, 1915, 285.

32. *Variety*, October 15, 1915, 21, and October 22, 1915, 23.

33. *IJ*, September 3, 1915, 3, and September 7, 1915, 6.

34. *IJ*, September 22, 1915, 3, and September 10, 1915, 3. But, as *IJ* (November 24, 1915, 6) reported, McIntosh became a real hero when he outwitted a crook at a local fair with his expertise with a deck of cards. And Figman, too, played "a real hero's part" (*IJ*, August 16, 1915, 2) when he rescued two young women from a boat that was sinking.

35. *IJ*, October 1, 1915, 6.

36. Jacobs, *RAF*, 137, 76.

37. Brenda Murphy, *American Realism and American Drama, 1880–1940* (Cambridge: Cambridge University Press, 1987), 5.

38. *MPW*, February 5, 1916, 842.

39. See, for example, Geo. F. Worts, "At the Sign of the Rooster," *World's Advance* 30 (May 1915): 611–616, and "Golden Rooster a Sign of Quality Is Pathé Plan," *MPN*, September 25, 1915, 55–56.

40. *Billboard*, February 5, 1916, 61.

41. *Variety*, February 4, 1916, 25.

42. *Billboard*, February 5, 1916, 61.

43. Clyde Fitch, *The City: A Modern Play of American Life in Three Acts* (Boston: Little, Brown, 1915).

44. Laura Shea, Review of a Revival of *The City*, October 1, 2003, American TheaterWeb.com.

45. Ibid.

46. *Variety*, January 14, 1916, 19.

47. *IJ*, November 8, 1915, 6. As Pichel (*ISM: The Lottery Man*, n.p.) writes, "Bit players and extras were paid between $3 and $10 a day, a large sum in those days."

48. *IJ*, November 22, 1915, 7.

49. According to Internet Broadway Database.

50. Sherry D. Engle, "Rida Johnson Young," in *New Women Dramatists in America, 1890–1920* (New York: Palgrave, 2007), 159.

51. Edward F. O'Day, "As to 'The Lottery Man,'" *Town Talk: The Pacific Weekly* (San Francisco), August 27, 1910, 17.

52. Pichel, *ISM: The Lottery Man*, n.p.

53. Lotteries were a familiar theme in early films. In *Schultz's Lottery Ticket* (Universal/Crystal, 1913), for example, Schultz loses a $5,000 lottery ticket and goes through a series of misadventures in order to recover it before learning that it is a counterfeit. In that short, Pearl White starred as Mrs. Schultz.

54. *IJ*, September 30, 1915, 3.

55. *IJ*, September 3, 1915, 6.

56. *IJ*, September 7, 1915, 6.

57. Pichel, *ISM: The Lottery Man*, n.p.; *IJ*, September 30, 1915, 3.

58. According to *IJ* (September 30, 1915, 3), they included Joe Mitchell, Blondy Hart, Herb Snyder, and Howard Teachout.

59. Pichel, *ISM: The Lottery Man*, n.p.

60. *Billboard*, February 19, 1916, 52.

9. Unraveling *Myra*'s Mysteries

1. *IJ*, February 7, 1916, 7.

2. *Motography*, April 8, 1916, 791.

3. Aaron Pichel, in *ISM: Beatrice Fairfax*, n.p., described the evolution of Hearst's International Film Service, which began in 1915 as an early film animation studio.

4. Some of those films included *A Girl of To-Day*, *Red Robin*, *A Prince for a Day*, and *The Burma Pearl*. *IJ* (September 28, 1915, 6) reported that *Red Robin*, based on a Fred Jackson story published in *Argosy* magazine, would be a five-reeler and also noted that the Whartons had "secured an option on nine of Fred Jackson's stories."

5. *MPW*, April 26, 1916, 758.

6. "Estabrook Popular with College Boys," *MPW*, June 24, 1916, 2244.

7. Such "proof" had the allure of a carnival sideshow, also popular at the time. Sideshows often combined optic and scientific wonders with more grotesque freak shows and cabinets of curiosities and oddities. See, for example, "A Cabinet of Curiosities—a History of Side Show Exhibitions and Acts," National Fairground and Circus Archive, online, University of Sheffield.

8. Hulse, *DD* 115.

9. "Hereward Carrington—Psychic Extraordinary," *MPW*, July 1, 1916, 83; *Motography*, June 24, 1916, 1443.

10. Hulse, *DD*, 114.

11. *MPW*, July 1, 1916, 83.

12. Stedman, *Serials*, 10.

13. Advertising for "The Serial Squadron's" DVD version of the surviving episodes of *The Mysteries of Myra*, restored by Eric Stedman, with music by Kevin McLeod.

14. For instance, L. Ron Hubbard, the American founder of Scientology, was involved in Thelema in the early 1940s.

15. For more on Crowley's life see, for example, Richard Kaczynski's *Perdurabo: The Life of Aleister Crowley*; Tobias Churton's *Aleister Crowley: The Biography*; and Gary Lachman's *Aleister Crowley: Magick, Rock and Roll, and the Wickedest Man in the World*.

16. Hulse, *DD*, 114–115.

17. *Motography*, May 27, 1916, 1214. Many wild rumors swirled around the production: for example, that the Whartons "spent six months making a study of mental suggestion and thought transmission before filming Myra" (reported in *Motography*, May 6, 1916, 1021).

18. *Richmond (VA) Times-Dispatch*, April 23, 1916, 50.

19. Peter Milne, "The Mysteries of Myra," *MPN*, June 10, 1916, 3596.

20. For more on Murnane see *MPN*, July 8, 1916, 71.

21. Singer, *MM*, 229–230.

22. *MPW*, May 6, 1916, 1044. *Variety* (April 21, 1916) noted that "the first installment is in three reels," while the rest were in two.

23. *MPW*, May 6, 1916, 1044, 1046.

24. *MPW*, May 20, 1916, 1402.

25. *MPW*, June 3, 1916, 1762.

26. *MPW*, June 10, 1916, 1947.

27. *MPW*, June 3, 1916, 1762.

28. *MPW*, June 24, 1916, 2303–2304.

29. *MPW*, July 8, 1916, 309–310.

30. *MPW*, July 8, 1916, 310.

31. *MPW*, July 15, 1916, 534.

32. *MPW*, August 5, 1916, 1000.

33. *MPW*, August 5, 1916, 1000.

34. *MPW*, August 5, 1916, 1000.

35. Eric Stedman, foreword in Charles Goddard and Eustace Hale Ball, *The Mysteries of Myra* (Ithaca, NY: Serial Squadron Photonovel, 2010), 10.

36. *Motography*, April 8, 1916, 791. Hearst had earlier announced that he was moving even more "earnestly and seriously and extensively" into the film business because he felt that movies were the modern extension of the publishing business.

37. Stedman, *Serials*, 10–11. Stedman adds that Hearst "wanted his productions to be done his way, or else. And he got his way in his reworking of some of the Myra story, for better or worse. He would continue to meddle with scripts produced by the Whartons in the future."

38. Stedman, *Serials*, 10–11.

39. According to Hulse, *DD*, 120, a surviving scenario of chapter 15 ends with the Master and Varney still at large, and a final intertitle reads: "Next Week—The 16th episode of *The Mysteries of Myra*." But in the final episode, as released, both the Master and the Thought Monster were killed off.

40. In *Beyond the Gibson Girl: Reimagining the American New Woman, 1895–1915*, Martha H. Patterson observes that water, specifically "wave imagery," was associated with the New Woman.

41. Lahue, *CNW*, 44–45; *MPN*, May 6, 1916, 2720.

42. For more on the Méliès trick films see Richard Abel, "The Cinema of Attractions in France, 1896–1904," in Grieveson and Krämer, *Silent Cinema Reader*, 63–68.

43. Hulse, *DD*, 117. *Motography* (June 17, 1916, 1385) also comments on the special effects, including "the novelty in a set of Cooper-Hewitt lights," as does *MPN* (May 6, 1916, 2720).

44. As cited in Hulse, *DD*, 117.

45. Hulse, *DD*, 117.

46. *MPW*, May 6, 1916, 984.

47. *Motography*, June 10, 1916, 1339.

48. *MPN*, May 6, 1916, 2720.

49. *Variety*, May 26, 1916. See also *Variety* reviews of April 21 and May 19, 1916.

50. Advertisements in *MPW* (June 10, 1916, 1838) and other trade papers boasted a similar endorsement.

51. *Motography*, June 3, 1916, 1269.

52. As per the instructions on the Crolette itself.

53. Gardner, *Projections*, 37. As Gardner notes, such interactive promotions also blurred the lines between writers and filmmakers.

54. *MPW*, May 16, 1916, 984.

55. Ads in *MPN* (May 6, 1916) and other trade papers boasted that *Myra* "is the greatest *feature series* ever released."

56. Hulse, *DD*, 117–118; *Motography*, May 27, 1916, 1214.

57. *Atlanta Constitution*, May 7, 1916, C9.

58. As cited in Hulse, *DD*, 120.

59. Hulse, *DD*, 120.

60. *IJ*, March 23, 1916, 3.

61. *MPW*, June 24, 1916, 2244.

62. Stedman, *Serials*, 7.

63. Diana Anselmo-Sequeira, "Apparitional Girlhood: Material Ephemerality and the Historiography of Female Adolescence in Early American Film," *Spectator* 33, no. 1 (Spring 2013), accessed online.

64. Ibid.

65. Ibid.

66. Stamp, "Awful Struggle," 216.

67. *MPW*, May 6, 1916, 984.

10. Asking Beatrice

1. Singer, *MM*, 248–249.

2. According to Linda Rodriguez McRobbie in "Marie Manning: The Original Dear Abby" (published online in Mental Floss), the letters that Brisbane brought to Manning had originally been addressed to the "People's Forum," a common newspaper feature at the time that functioned as a public message board. But "the letters Brisbane carried didn't quite fit," and he wondered what Manning could do with them.

3. Manning tended to be vague about her age, often shaving off as much as a decade. She was likely twenty-six, not twenty, when she inaugurated her column.

4. Cynthia Crossen, "Dear Beatrice Fairfax, You Once Lent an Ear to Troubled Readers," *Wall Street Journal*, May 22, 2006, accessed online.

5. Ibid.

6. Apparently, as Aaron Pichel writes in *ISM: The Great White Trail*, not all the "Dear Beatrice" letters were authentic.

7. The prologue was not a separate episode but rather part of the opening episode.

8. Lynde Denig, *MPW*, August 26, 1916, 1391.

9. The contract between the Whartons and the International Film Service, signed June 9, 1916, stipulated that the Whartons would also receive an additional eighty dollars for each print (WC, Kroch).

10. "International Announces Several Coming Productions," *MPW*, August 19, 1916, 1224.

11. Peter Milne, "Beatrice Fairfax, Episodes One and Two," *MPN*, August 26, 1916, 1245.

12. Ibid., 1245.

13. Denig, *MPW*, August 26, 1916, 1391.

14. It was not Bacon's first appearance on screen. Earlier, he had appeared as Elaine's butler in the *Elaine* serial.

15. Denig, *MPW*, August 26, 1916, 1391.

16. Cited in Jim Catalano, "Back in Time: 1916 'Beatrice Fairfax' Series Offers Glimpse of Ithaca's Silent-Film Past," *Ithaca Times*, posted June 1, 2011, on Ithaca.com.

17. *MPN*, August 19, 1916, 1054.

18. *MPW*, September 9, 1916, 1754–1755.

19. *MPW*, September 9, 1916, 1755.

20. *MPW*, October 21, 1916, 450–451.

21. *MPW*, October 21, 1916, 450–451.

22. *MPW*, October 21, 1916, 451.

23. *MPW*, November 11, 1916, 916.

24. Edward Weitzel, *MPW*, November 18, 1916, 1000.

25. *MPW*, November 11, 1916, 915.

26. *MPW*, November 25, 1916, 1229.

27. *MPW*, September 23, 1916, 2030.

28. Letter from Ted Wharton to the IFS, August 10, 1916 (WC, Kroch). Also noted in the Serial Squadron DVD release of *The Mysteries of Myra*.

29. *MPW*, November 11, 1916, 915–916.

30. *MPW*, September 23, 1916, 2030–2031.

31. *MPW*, December 2, 1916, 1383 and 1349.

32. Billing from Wharton Inc. to the IFS, August 14, 1916 (WC, Kroch). As other billings confirm, the cost per episode, without overages, was $4,500. But in virtually every instance, excess charges had to be added by the Whartons to cover the changes.

33. As Ted wrote to the IFS, in a letter of August 10, 1916, "After due consideration, it has been decided to eliminate the seventh episode, GREY WOLVES, because of the censorship proposition" (WC, Kroch).

34. Letter from Basil Dickey to E. A. MacManus, February 29, [1916] (WC, Kroch).

35. *IJ*, August 14, 1916, noted that in the episode "Mrs. Leo Wharton took the part of a squaw."

36. That reference occurs in "The Stone God" episode, when Jimmy, disguised as a bumbling waiter, asks the prince what opinion he has of suffrage.

37. Like *Beatrice Fairfax*, *Perils* consisted of fifteen stories complete in themselves; each dealt with "a powerful incident in real newspaper life" that told "the story from the 'inside'—depicting in detail the way in which front page news is collected" and showed "girl reporters exposing the evils of the underworld—securing confessions from crooks—interviewing society debutantes—aiding the government in capturing counterfeiters and blackmailers—ferreting out strange crimes—foiling evil plots" (*MPW*, December 23, 1916, 1747).

11. Preparing for War

1. As *Motography* (December 2, 1916, 1256) reported, "the strenuous work" that Ted "was compelled to perform" on *Beatrice Fairfax* and on the first ten episodes of *Patria* made it "necessary" for him to spend two weeks in Honolulu before returning to complete the final episodes of *Patria* in California. Leo, on the other hand, traveled directly to the West Coast "with the entire Vernon Castle Company."

2. *MPW*, November 11, 1916, 876.

3. Jacobs, *RAF*, 250, 253.

4. Lahue, *CNW*, 38.

5. Lahue, *CNW*, 38. Mutual would go on to produce or distribute other patriotic preparedness pictures, including *Fighting for France, A Daughter of War, Manning Our Navy, A Zeppelin Attack on New York*, and *Uncle Sam's Defenders*. Many other companies did the same, among them General Film Company / Official War Films' *The War* and Defense or Tribute Film Company's *Defense or Tribute* (*MPW*, February 24, 1917, 1127).

6. Lahue, *CNW*, 40–41.

7. Lahue, *CNW*, 41.

8. Ad, *MPW*, December 9, 1916, 1423.

9. Ramsaye, *Million and One Nights*, 778. MacManus, whom *MPW* (August 4, 1917) described as "the originator of the moving picture serial running in novelized form in newspapers," would go on to become serial manager at Paramount.

10. Hulse, *DD*, 121, writes that "contrary to previously published reports, Vance's story never saw publication in hard covers."

11. Ramsaye, *Million and One Nights*, 778.

12. *MPW*, December 9, 1916, 1478.

13. Ramsaye, *Million and One Nights*, 779, and Hulse, *DD*, 121.

14. Hulse, *DD*, 121.

15. Hulse, *DD*, 120–121.

16. Lahue, *CNW*, 48–49.

17. For a more detailed account of Castle and especially her time in Ithaca see, for example, Walter H. Stainton, "Irene Castle," *Films in Review*, June–July 1962, 347–355.

18. Hillary Rettig, "They Made Movies in Ithaca," *Grapevine Weekly Magazine*, September 6–12, 1984, 13.

19. Hulse, *DD*, 121. Also noted by Arch Merrill in *Upstate Echoes* (New York: American Book–Knickerbocker, 1950), 90.

20. *IJ*, May 18, 1916, 7. Also noted in Rettig, "They Made Movies in Ithaca," 13, and Colleen M. Kaplin, *Take Two: The True Story of Ithaca's Movie-Making Era* (Cabin John, MD: Seven Locks, 1989), 46.

21. *MPW*, November 11, 1916, 876. According to George A. Katchmer, "Oland didn't particularly care to make serials, but at $1,000 per week the length and steadiness of the work, which could last four months, compensated for the negatives." See Katchmer, *Eighty Silent Film Stars: Biographies and Filmographies of the Obscure to the Well Known* (Jefferson, NC: McFarland, 1991), 732.

22. *Patria* was originally scheduled for release on January 1. But according to "Pathé and International Join Forces" (*MPW*, January 13, 1916, 202), a new consolidation agreement between Pathé and Hearst's IFS delayed the release for two weeks.

23. *MPW*, January 6, 1917, and December 9, 1916, 1510.

24. *MPW*, December 9, 1916, 1510; February 3, 1917, 707; January 13, 1917, 280.

25. *MPW*, January 27, 1917, 588, and February 3, 1917, 707.

26. *MPW*, February 10, 1917, 912 and 867; *MPN*, February 10, 1917, 921.

27. *MPW*, February 17, 1917, 1084, and February 24, 1917, 1213; *MPN*, February 17, 1917, 1090.

28. *MPW*, February 24, 1917, 1211 and 1213; *MPN*, February 24, 1917, 1255; *MPN*, March 10, 1917, 1254.

29. *MPW*, March 3, 1917, 1368, 1375, 1408.

30. *MPW*, March 10, 1917, 1676, 1593, 1585; *MPN*, March 10, 1917, 1571.

31. *IJ*, October 2, 1916, 3; *MPW*, April 14, 1917, 328. Gene Fernett, in *American Film Studios: An Historical Encyclopedia* (Jefferson, NC: McFarland, 1988), 264, writes that location shooting drove up production costs.

32. *MPW*, March 17, 1917, 1826; *MPN*, April 7, 1917, 2192.

33. *MPW*, March 31, 1917, 2118, 2124, 2160; *MPN*, March 31, 1917, 2034.

34. *MPN*, April 14, 1917, 2365.

35. *MPW*, April 21, 1917, 447 and 496.

36. *MPW*, April 28, 1917, 683. Notably, in its review of this episode, *MPN* praised "Director Jacques Jaccard" for producing "some of the best battle scenes ever." The failure even to note the Whartons suggests their radically diminished role.

37. *MPW*, April 28, 1917, 633.

38. *MPW*, May 5, 1917, 804 and 854; *MPN*, May 5, 1917, 2857. In the final episode, Huroki commits suicide.

39. *MPW*, May 5, 1917, 805.

40. Hulse, *DD*, 130. Hulse writes that in 1942, after the Hearst organization officially disbanded the IFS (which, for the most part, had been defunct for decades), a handful of *Patria* chapters—all that survived after a quarter century of careless storage and the resulting deterioration—were donated to New York's Museum of Modern Art, which eventually preserved them, but only after additional decomposition had taken place.

41. Singer, *MM*, 226.

42. Singer, *MM*, 226, 224.

43. Craig W. Campbell, *Reel America and World War I: A Comprehensive Filmography and History of Motion Pictures in the United States, 1914–1920* (Jefferson, NC: McFarland, 1985), 50–51.

44. Hulse, *DD*, 121.

45. *MPW*, December 23, 1916, 1738.

46. It was around this time that the public relations industry was evolving, in response to the technologies of mass influence and the increasingly broad but complex society.

47. "'Patria' Has Great Reception," *MPW*, December 9, 1916, 1478.

48. Ibid.

49. *MPN*, March 10, 1917, 1533.

50. *MPN*, March 10, 1917, 1563.

51. *MPN*, March 31, 1917, 1941.

52. *MPN*, March 31, 1917, 2022 and 2020.

53. *MPN*, April 28, 1917, 2654.

54. *MPW*, February 10, 1917, 895.

55. Cited in Pichel, *ISM: Beatrice Fairfax*, n.p.

56. Letter from Edward A. MacManus to L. D. Wharton, August 8, 1916 (WC, Kroch).

57. See "Wharton Releasing Company Records" (WC, Kroch).

58. Many of the excess costs are noted in invoices to the International Film Service (WC, Kroch).

59. Hulse, *DD*, 130. See also Pizzitola's *Hearst over Hollywood*.

60. Letter from the law firm of Griggs, Baldwin & Baldwin to Howard Cobb, August 9, 1919 (WC, Kroch).

61. Ted Wharton letter to E. A. MacManus, July 31, 1916 (WC, Kroch).

62. Hulse, *DD*, 126.

63. *MPW*, November 25, 1916, 1167.

64. *IJ*, November 14, 1916, 3.

65. G. von Harleman, "Wharton Brothers Working on 'Patria,'" *MPW*, December 30, 1916, 1948.

66. Ibid. Harleman remarked that Jaccard's cast "should produce a most unusual picture."

67. Hulse, *DD*, 126.

68. Campbell, *Reel America*, 50–51.

69. As cited in Hulse, *DD*, 129–130. *IJ* (April 12, 1917, 2) noted that the "U.S. government had issued an order saying that 'Patria' not be shown in this country," although "the Whartons say they have received no such order."

70. Lahue, *CNW*, 48–49.

71. Hulse, *DD*, 130. See also "National Issue When Pennsylvania Calls 3 Films Unpatriotic," *MPN*, May 5, 1917, 2809.

72. *MPW*, May 12, 1917, 1000. While all American industries were contributing to preparedness by "strengthen[ing] the sinews of government," filmmakers felt an especially keen obligation to assist in the patriotic activity.

73. *MPW*, February 10, 1917, 867.

74. Quoted in Kaplin, *Take Two*, 42.

75. *MPW*, December 9, 1916, 1510.

76. *MPW*, December 9, 1916, 1510.

77. Quoted in Stainton, "Irene Castle," 350.

78. *IJ*, August 22, 1916, 5.

79. Kaplin, *Take Two*, 46–48. Part of that "rescue" included Southern Comfort whiskey, which apparently was a common cure.

80. Lahue, *CNW*, 50.

81. Lahue, *CNW*, 50.

82. Hulse, *DD*, 125. According to Hulse, Sills "fully earned the $400 a week paid him by the Whartons." Katchmer, in *Eighty Silent Film Stars*, 873, though, reported that later Sills confessed a boyish delight in the thrillers and admitted that he had a good time performing in *Patria*.

83. Merrill, *Upstate Echoes*, 90.

84. Mary Richie, "They Made Movies in Ithaca," *culturefront*, Fall 1999, 36.

85. *Billboard*, October 14, 1916, 52.

86. As *IJ* (November 15, 1916, 3) noted, the Whartons "have already out-grown the Renwick Studio and have plans to build a new one." But the break with Hearst put an end to the ambitious expansion plan.

87. "Wharton to Establish Exchanges," *MPW*, February 24, 1917, 1188. The article added that "R. H. Hadfield, of Chicago, Ill., who has had a wide experience in the motion picture field," had been appointed general manager of Wharton Inc.

88. Branch offices, which were becoming more common, were one more innovation reflected and furthered by commercial moviemaking in response to the advancements in technology and business.

89. "Wharton Releasing Plans Are Now Under Way," *MPN*, August 4, 1917, 861, stated that Leo was president of the new corporation, with Charles S. Goetz (formerly with World, General, Artcraft, and Fox) as vice president and Edward Small (formerly with Loew and Master Drama Features) in an unspecified position. (While it is not clear just how long Goetz and Small staffed the office, Wharton associate Charles V. Henkel was soon assigned to manage the New York City–based releasing company.)

90. "Whartons Open Offices in New York," *MPW*, July 21, 1917, 470. The article listed Small and Goetz as "active managers."

91. *IJ*, January 17, 1918. At that time, G. Ervin Kent was serving as general manager of the studio.

92. According to *Exhibitors Herald*, June 30, 1917, 33, John Holbrook was head of the photography department, Leroy Baker was chief of the mechanical department, and Marshall Francisco was head of developing. Longtime Wharton associates Arch Chadwick and Courtney Ryley Cooper also headed their departments. And *IJ* (January 17, 1918) noted Kent's role as general manager.

93. Pichel, *ISM: The Forgotten History*, n.p.

94. *Wid's Year Book*, 1919–1920 (New York: Arno, 1971).

95. *MPW*, July 21, 1917, 394.

12. Moving into Feature Filmmaking

1. Martin S. Pernick, *The Black Stork: Eugenics and the Death of "Defective" Babies in American Medicine and Motion Pictures since 1915* (New York: Oxford University Press, 1995), 4.

2. Ibid., 5.

3. Ibid., 8.

4. *MPN*, February 24, 1917, 1256.

5. "The Black Stork," *AFI Catalog Online*. As *Variety* (April 6, 1917, 28) observed, some critics suggested avoiding the film entirely. The *Chicago Daily Tribune*, for

instance, "lambasted the Haiselden film to a frazzle and declared it was as pleasant to the eye as a running sore."

6. *MPN*, April 28, 1917, 2676.

7. *MPN*, February 24, 1917, 1244 and 1256.

8. *MPN*, February 24, 1917, 1244 and 1256.

9. That later version of the film, preserved by the University of Michigan Historical Health Film Collection, was reportedly "adapted from a story by W. H. Strafford by Jack Lait" and directed by Strafford, with no mention of the Whartons in the credits.

10. *MPW*, July 15, 1916, 481.

11. *MPN*, February 24, 1917, 1256.

12. Pernick, *Black Stork*, 56–57.

13. *MPW*, February 24, 1917, 1211.

14. Pernick, *Black Stork*, 57.

15. For a fuller discussion of these and other eugenics films see Pernick, *Black Stork*. See also Larry Langman, *American Film Cycles: The Silent Era* (Westport, CT: Greenwood, 1998), 211–218.

16. Pichel, *ISM: The Forgotten History*, n.p.

17. See "Gardner Hunting with Wharton," *MPW*, January 1, 1916, 56. Aaron Pichel, in *ISM: The Great White Trail*, notes that Hunting had been an editor and also a successful writer of popular boys' stories.

18. *Billboard*, June 16, 1917, 62.

19. Closely allied to the Cinderella-shoe motif is the theme of the missing mother, which is reinforced throughout the picture in ways both subtle (the mother dog who watches over her puppies) and overt (the promise Reverend Dean makes to a dying man to save his motherless daughter from the dance hall).

20. Jacobs, *RAF*, 147–148.

21. Stamp, *MSG*, 53.

22. Singer, *MM*, 261.

23. *Motography*, June 23, 1917, 33.

24. *IJ*, February 17, 1917, 7, and March 5, 1917, 3.

25. Pichel, *ISM: The Forgotten History*, n.p.

26. *IJ*, March 7, 1917, 7.

27. Pichel, *ISM: The Forgotten History*, n.p.

28. Kaplin, *Take Two*, 68.

29. Cutaways, too, were used well, almost incrementally, to advance the plot. For instance, the letter that Charles Carrington sends to his sister about the financial losses he has incurred on George's investments appears twice as an insert early in the film. Prudence's anxiety mounts with each reading of it. And that same letter, which Prudence thinks she has destroyed but which George pulls from the fire—by then the fire has burned off most of the text and left only a few harmless lines that George misinterprets—serves as the catalyst for his rejection of her and his proof of her adultery.

30. Pichel, *ISM: The Great White Trail*, n.p.

31. *IJ*, February 17, 1917, 7.

32. *MPW*, July 7, 1917, 101.

33. *Variety*, June 8, 1917, 23.

34. *MPW*, June 30, 2112.

35. Pichel, *ISM: The Forgotten History*, n.p.

36. Another Arctic film, *The Mints of Hell* (1919), used similar advertising that suggested "pictures produced in Alaskan atmosphere have invariably proved extremely fascinating, especially if such are shown during the summer months."

37. Pichel, *ISM: The Great White Trail*, n.p.

38. *MPN*, November 10, 1917, 3293; *IJ*, September 9, 1917.

39. *MPN*, August 4, 1917, 860.

40. Reportedly, the Whartons constructed a "special 'house'" on the 600 block of North Cayuga Street to be used in the comedy productions.

41. *IJ*, February 17, 1917, 7; Fred Allen, *Much Ado about Me* (Boston: Little, Brown / Atlantic Monthly Press Book, 1956), 130–131.

42. *Library of Congress Catalogue of Copyright Entries*, Part 1, Group 2 (Washington, DC: Government Printing Office, 1918), 1123, 1125, 1126. *Billboard* (June 16, 1917, 59) reported that the Eddie Vogt comedy (likely *The Missionary*, although it is never specifically named in the article) "concern[ed] the exciting adventures of a professional Jonah" and was based on a ten-year-old "laughmaker" script that Ted had written—his first comedy—and tucked away and only recently resurrected. According to *Billboard*, "He read it over. The first page sounded good, the second better and the third still better. And the result of it was that there was a conference, a hiring of a cast and a sudden beginning on a new comedy."

43. According to a summary prepared by the Whartons for the Library of Congress.

44. *Library of Congress Catalogue of Copyright Entries*, Part 1, Group 2 (Washington, DC: Government Printing Office, 1918), 1123, 1125, 1126. An ad in *MPN*, June 16, 1917, 3711, announced that three comedies were available "for early release": *Below Zero*, *The Missionary*, and *The Fatal Wedding*. It is almost certain that *The Fatal Wedding* was an alternative or earlier title for *Marriage à la Mode*.

45. See, for example, the Wharton Inc. billing dated September 2, 1918 (WC, Kroch).

46. According to an ad in *MPW* for the Fox Sunshine Comedies.

47. Cooper's career is described in *MPW*, December 22, 1917, 1788.

48. *MPN*, June 30, 1917, 4089. An interesting anecdote about Ted Wharton and Cooper appeared in *Billboard* (May 26, 1917, 77). Apparently, the two men had just met and were in search of entertainment when they stopped in front of a movie house, where *Tapped Wires* was playing. Cooper said, "I'm the fellow who wrote it." Ted replied, "That's nothing. I'm the man who produced it."

49. The contract between Wharton Inc. and F. W. Stewart and J. K. Holbrook, signed September 3, 1917, stipulated that the "studio and equipment at Renwick Park" would be leased to Stewart and Holbrook from September 10 until October 1, 1917, at a cost of $100 per week. The leasees would also "pay for all materials used in construction dept." (WC, Kroch).

50. *IJ*, September 7, 1917.

51. *IJ* noted that even the dog, "which made a big hit," was a local.

52. *IJ*, October 5, 1917.

53. *IJ*, September 7, 1917.

54. *IJ*, May 9, 1919, 3.

55. *IJ*, January 11, 1917.

56. *IJ*, January 13, 1917, 5.

57. *IJ*, January 16, 1917, 3.

58. Pichel, *ISM: The Forgotten History*, n.p.

59. *IJ*, January 18, 1917, 7. The Whartons did not object directly to the notion of a National Board of Censorship. But like most of their fellow filmmakers, they believed in the concept (if not always the actual practice) of self-censorship. For more on NAMPI and its "Thirteen Points" resolution see Ruth Vasey's "The Open Door: Hollywood's Public Relations at Home and Abroad, 1922–1928," in Grieveson and Krämer, *Silent Cinema Reader*.

60. *MPW*, February 17, 1917, 989.

61. *IJ*, January 25, 1917.

62. Reported in *IJ*, January 31, 1917.

63. *MPW*, February 17, 1917, 998.

64. Adding to the financial problems were problems of health. As *Motography* (September 8, 1917) reported, Leo Wharton was hospitalized for two weeks in the Post Graduate Hospital in New York City, following an unspecified operation.

65. Pernick (*Black Stork*, 156) noted that Sherriot Pictures, a large company with offices in New York and Chicago, initially handled the sale of state rights. But after Sherriot went out of business, all unsold franchises reverted to Hadfield.

66. *IJ*, February 3, 1917, 3.

67. *MPW*, February 24, 1917, 1147.

68. *IJ*, February 17, 1917, 7.

69. *MPN*, July 21, 1917, 372.

70. *MPW*, July 14, 1917, 217.

71. *IJ*, April 23, 1917, 2.

72. *IJ*, November 1, 1917.

73. The agents who purchased the pictures from producers on a state-rights basis would typically play the films until they literally fell apart. (The producers made their profit from the initial sale of the pictures, while the state-rights buyers made theirs from exhibition.)

74. *MPN*, September 29, 1917, 2184. *MPW* (September 29, 1917, 2013), however, reported that it was Leo, not Ted, who was elected to the office.

13. Staring into *The Eagle's Eye*

1. As Kaplin (*Take Two*, 53) wrote, the film ultimately cost $400,000 to make, "an extraordinary amount" for the time.

2. "German Plots and Pictures," *MPW*, November 3, 1917, 704.

3. *IJ*, January 22, 1918, 5.

4. *MPN*, January 5, 1918, 130.

5. Campbell, *Reel America*, 88.

6. *MPW*, November 3, 1917, 704.

7. *MPW*, December 1, 1917, 1304. See also Sally A. Dumaux, *King Baggot: A Biography and Filmography of the First King of the Movies* (Jefferson, NC: McFarland, 2010), 99–103. According to Dumaux, the Whartons' relationship with Baggot went back at least as far as 1913, "when Theodore was a member of the screen club." But

it is likely that Ted (and possibly Leo) first crossed paths with Baggot much earlier than that—in Saint Louis, where Baggot was part of the Hopkins stock company in the early 1900s.

8. *IJ*, November 15, 1917, 3.

9. Dumaux, *King Baggot*, 100. Also noted in "'Eagle's Eye' to Expose Menace," *MPN*, January 19, 1918, 434.

10. *Billboard*, January 26, 1918, 66.

11. Kaplin, *Take Two*, 50.

12. *IJ*, January 22, 1918.

13. *MPN*, December 29, 1917, 4514.

14. The *IJ* (March 19, 1918) provided some of the details of the episode.

15. *IJ*, March 19, 1918.

16. *IJ*, March 19, 1918.

17. *MPN*, February 16, 1918, 1007.

18. *IJ*, April 13, 1918, 2.

19. *IJ*, April 20, 1918, 7.

20. *IJ*, April 20, 1918, 7.

21. Stedman, *Serials*, 42–43. *IJ* (January 17, 1918) similarly noted how Germany had plotted "against this country while accepting its friendship."

22. *IJ*, December 3, 1917, 3.

23. *IJ*, November 12, 1917.

24. *MPN*, January 12, 1918, 276.

25. *IJ*, May 1, 1918, 3.

26. *MPW*, December 15, 1917, 1656.

27. *MPW*, December 15, 1917, 1656.

28. *MPN*, February 9, 1918, 877.

29. *IJ* reported that Baker had been urged to patent his invention but, "being nothing if not a patriot," preferred to donate it to the country at large without demanding royalties (undated clipping, Wharton Studios Collection at the History Center in Tompkins County, Ithaca, NY). The "revolution in sham warfare" was also noted by *MPN*, November 22, 1917, 4393.

30. "Wharton 'Prop' Expert Invents Paper Bullet," *MPW*, December 22, 1917, 1774.

31. *MPN*, February 23, 1918, 1152. D. H. Turner, Leo's assistant, was present during the shooting of the waterfront scenes.

32. *MPN*, February 2, 1918, 688.

33. "Hoffman Leaves for Tour of the United States," *MPN*, December 15, 1917, 4210.

34. *MPW*, December 29, 1917, 1964.

35. *MPN*, December 29, 1917, 475.

36. *IJ*, January 22, 1918.

37. *Billboard*, January 26, 1918, 66.

38. *IJ*, January 29, 1918, 5.

39. *IJ*, January 29, 1918, 5. Also reported in *IJ*, February 19, 1918, 5.

40. In a letter to Howard Cobb (August 3, 1918), Charles V. Henkel wrote that he met personally with Creel to discuss using *The Eagle's Eye* as propaganda overseas (WC, Kroch).

41. According to *IJ* (January 29, 1918, 5), the newspapermen who attended the National Press Club exhibition also "denounced severely the action of the New York theater magnate [Loew]."

42. *MPN*, March 2, 1918, 1264.

43. "Not expecting that all of the recipients would respond en masse," the Whartons had issued four thousand invitations. If that was a publicity gimmick on the Whartons' part, it certainly proved effective.

44. *IJ*, March 23, 1918.

45. *IJ*, January 21, 1918.

46. Advertisement in *MPW*, February 1918.

47. *MPN*, January 12, 1918, 282.

48. "Flynn Serial Rouses Country," *MPN*, April 27, 1918, 2546.

49. Campbell, *Reel America*, 95.

50. Letter from Charles V. Henkel to Howard Cobb, August 3, 1918 (WC, Kroch). For more on Hoffman Inc. see *MPN*, December 1, 1917, 3818, and December 29, 1917, 4359.

51. *IJ*, March 21, 1918, 2.

52. *Canadian Moving Picture Digest*, July 27, 1918, 10.

53. According to Charles V. Henkel, letter to Howard Cobb, April 1, 1919 (WC, Kroch).

54. Letter from Charles V. Henkel to Howard Cobb, April 5, 1919 (WC, Kroch).

55. *MPN*, February 9, 1918, 877.

56. Lahue, *CNW*, 61.

57. Letter to Wharton Releasing Company, March 7, 1919 (WC, Kroch).

58. *MPW*, August 25, 1917, 1205.

59. *Exhibitors Herald*, June 30, 1917, 33. Holbrook was head of the photography department; Levi Bacon, cameraman; Marshall Francisco, head of the developing department; and Leroy Baker, chief of the mechanical department. According to *IJ* (April 25, 1918, 3), Baggot and Snow also teamed up to sell Liberty bonds.

60. *Variety*, May 24, 1918, 42.

61. Letter from George Eastman, March 11, 1918, cited in Carl W. Ackerman's *George Eastman: Founder of Kodak and the Photography Business* (Boston: Houghton Mifflin, 1930), 411.

62. *Variety*, May 24, 1918, 42.

63. "Whartons Work on Reel for the County," *MPW*, June 1, 1918, 3300.

64. *MPW*, June 30, 1917, 2098.

65. *MPW*, June 30, 1917, 2098.

66. *MPW*, June 9, 1917, 1605.

67. *MPW*, July 21, 1917, 472.

68. Campbell, *Reel America*, 86; see also 85–90.

69. *MPW*, September 15, 1917, 1635.

70. *MPW*, September 22, 1917, 1822–1823.

71. One company, Universal Film, even organized a "Miss Preparedness Contest" (Uncle Sam's prettiest and most popular daughter, to be designated as "America's future goddess"), who would then be invited to star in a series of motion pictures to encourage the war effort (*MPW*, February 10, 1917, 826).

72. There were even mercy drives to support the horses in service to the Red Cross overseas.

73. *Cornell Daily Sun*, March 27, 1918; *IJ*, March 20, 1918.

74. *IJ*, October 20, 1919, 7.

75. *IJ*, October 20, 1919, 7.

76. "Whartons Busy," *Wid's Daily*, March 31, 1919. There is, however, no record of Leo's engagement in *The Red Peril*.

77. *IJ*, November 15, 1919, 5. Lusk believed that the moving picture was an agent of publicity for the dangers of Bolshevism and could reach those citizens who cannot be influenced by the press and start them "on the right lines of reasoning."

78. Letter from Charles V. Henkel to Howard Cobb, April 21, 1919 (WC, Kroch). Henkel also noted that the film, as it stood, would have no chance of going "through any of the big organizations" but, with some work, might actually be handled "through independent exchanges and get a considerable sum." One thing was clear: owing to the various disagreements, Leo and Ted were rarely speaking directly to each other anymore.

79. *MPN*, February 9, 1918, 877. According to Henkel, such sentiments, the foundation of which was already "smouldering" in this country, could easily be fanned "into the flames of riot and destruction of property or lives."

80. Charles V. Henkel, correspondence and notes on the film (WC, Kroch).

14. Leaving Ithaca

1. Robert Sklar, *Movie-Made America: A Cultural History of American Movies* (New York: Random House, 1975), 68.

2. *IJ*, May 9, 1919, 3.

3. *Classic Images*, November 1983, 49–50; *IJ*, November 6, 1917, 5. The releasing company was being run under the direction of Wharton associate Charles V. Henkel, former manager of Universal City, who took over for original managers Edward Small and Charles J. Goetz.

4. "They Made Movies in Ithaca," *Grapevine Weekly Magazine*, August 30–September 5, 1984, 8.

5. *IJ*, February 20, 1958, 5.

6. In "A Saga in the Motion Picture Industry in the Finger Lake [*sic*] Region," an essay in the archives of the Wharton Studios Collection in the History Center in Tompkins County, Ithaca, New York, the anonymous author (drawing on the recollections of Ben Jones, who supposedly moved from New York City to Ithaca to work for Leo Wharton and who "furnished most of the material about the private lives of the Whartons" therein), the brothers were lavish spenders, both personally and professionally. Allegedly, all who knew them and their brother-in-law Buck "agree[d] that he [Buck] was the only one with a sense of the meaning of money."

7. *IJ*, March 22, 1918; *Classic Images*, November 1983, 49.

8. "Whartons, of Ithica [*sic*], Rest on Oars," *MPW*, January 25, 1919, 470.

9. *IJ*, May 9, 1919, 3.

10. *IJ*, May 12, 1919, 3.

11. *IJ*, May 9, 1919, 3.

12. Letter from Howard Cobb to J. W. Buck, dated February 20, 1923; letter from Ted Wharton in California to Howard Cobb, dated December 7, 1923; letter from Howard Cobb to Ted Wharton in California, dated December 22, 1923 (all in WC, Kroch). Wharton noted that while Cobb held the Wharton Inc. stock under a five-year voting agreement, the agreement "has since expired."

13. Cobb, in his letter of December 22, 1923, also detailed the various accounts and settlements, noting that "creditors were notified and received all they were entitled to. They had received interest upon their accounts up to the time of the payment of the dividend. That had used up a great deal of the moneys as they were something like $30,000. There is also an unpaid judgment of over $4000.00 against Grossman for rent. Grossman has gone through bankruptcy and the judgment is no good. This would have helped out considerably had we been able to collect, but he like most of the other producers at that time went by the board. The stock is of absolutely no value, neither is the Wharton Releasing stock. When I can receive releases in full satisfaction I will turn over all of the stock in my hands." He also wondered "if you [Ted] are in position to return to me the moneys which I loaned to you in New York about the last time I saw you. I think you remember the occasion and the amount" (WC, Kroch).

14. Letter from Howard Cobb to Leo Wharton, February 16, 1923, and from Howard Cobb to J. W. Buck, February 20, 1923 (WC, Kroch).

15. Some film historians, like Walter R. Stainton in "Pearl White in Ithaca" (*Films in Review*, May 1951, 19), mention the rumor that "the last of *The Perils* [along with many Wharton films] went to the bottom of Cayuga's waters when the studio at Renwick Park was closed. It seems that the temptation of the unguarded store of reels was too great to be endured by small boys without appropriate action. The fire chief, fearful of what nitrate films might do in the attics and cellars of those small boys' homes, did away with all the reels that remained." Hillary Rettig, in "They Made Movies in Ithaca" (*Grapevine Weekly Magazine*, September 6–12, 1984, 11), repeats the story. But the rumor of disposal of the films in Cayuga Lake seems to be just that. It is far more likely that the films were destroyed in 1929 by a fire in Cobb's storage shed.

16. *IJ*, May 17, 1919, 3.

17. The preparations and remodeling of the studio were reported in *Exhibitors Herald*, June 28, 1919, 39, and *Wid's Daily*, June 23, 1919, 965.

18. Although *MPN* (June 1, 1918, 3300) makes reference to two different pictures—"a picture which was made by the Whartons especially for the Red Cross Drive last fall" that raised "a great part of the $1,000,000 total in Rochester" and a "new picture being made in response to a request from the committee of Rochester who are interested in a War Chest Fund"—it would appear that the two films are actually one and the same.

19. According to "A Saga in the Motion Picture Industry in the Finger Lake Region," both brothers were "erratic" yet "hard-working, irascible" men. "Theo" was said to be less apt than his brother to "go all to pieces."

20. Among the many lawsuits they faced was one from their own employee. As noted in *Variety*, January 31, 1919, 51, Charles S. Goetz—who was, according to *MPW* (July 21, 1917), "active manager" of the Wharton Releasing Company in New York City in 1917—successfully sued the Whartons "for recovery of "$1,000 in

commission for services rendered in disposing of the right" to *The Great White Trail*. He received a judgment of $1,085, which included interest.

21. As *Classic Images* (November 1983, 50) reports, from mid-July on, whenever Ted returned to Ithaca, he was alone. According to a letter (April 21, 1919) from Charles V. Henkel to attorney Howard Cobb, there was already a breakdown in communications between the brothers. As Henkel and Ted were editing *The Red Peril*, "Ted called Leo into consultation" and arranged for him to attend a screening of the picture. "But Leo did not show up and [Henkel] was instructed to make a point to inform Leo" when the film would be run again, so that he could see it. Apparently Henkel never did.

22. *MPW*, April 5, 1919, 104–105. According to documents filed on March 22, "The incorporators are Maclyn Arbuckle, W. H. Furlong, and L. D. Wharton."

23. *MPW*, July 12, 1919, 556, featured a picture of Ted, one of several "Noted Writers and Directors" working for Pathé. The accompanying article stated that Ted "has long been associated with serial making" and "will produce and direct for the Pathé program."

24. *IJ*, July 23, 1919, 5. Driscoll Brothers, the same local company that was responsible for the renovations on the Renwick Park studio, was awarded the contract for remodeling the skating rink.

25. *IJ*, July 23, 1919, 5.

26. *IJ*, September 3, 1919. Notably, the Whartons had earlier purchased rights to other of Jackson's works, including *The Burma Pearl* and *Red Robin*, with the intention of producing them through Wharton Inc. They intended to film Jackson's story *Red Robin* several times over the years. In fact, it was announced as "forthcoming" by the Wharton Studio as far back as January 1, 1916; and it was one of the first pictures they hoped to film as independent producers. Jackson was also the author of *The Fatal Ring*, a non-Wharton twenty-part serial (1917) directed by George B. Seitz and starring Pearl White and Warner Oland.

27. Norworth (best known for the songs he wrote, among them "Take Me Out to the Ballgame"), according to the *Trenton Evening Times* ("Deserts Stage to Join Screen Stars," September 1, 1919, 7), had "never appeared before motion pic-camera in his life." But he "signed on the dotted line" because he greatly admired Ted Wharton.

28. "Movie Star Makes High Record in Trap Shoot," *IJ*, August 27, 1919, 3.

29. *IJ*, October 20, 1919, 7. In an interesting coincidence, Norworth was the second husband of Nora Bayes, who divorced him and married vaudevillian entertainer Harry Clarke (originally Harry Prince Clarke). Clarke was the son of the Whartons' cousin Adelaide Prince (née Lena Rubenstein in 1868) and her first husband Harry Prince. Adelaide later married noted actor Creston Clarke, whose surname her son assumed. Bayes went on to marry two more times.

30. Nares, according to *Variety* (September 1919, 5), had appeared in the cast of *The Great Train Robbery*, "the first so-called feature picture in the history of the screen, which was made by the Edison Company sixteen years" earlier. His "Ithaca engagement made possible a visit to his birthplace, Geneva [NY], for the first time in thirty years."

31. *IJ*, July 30, 1919, 5. The performers in *The Crooked Dagger* reportedly composed a "company of 15 well known actors."

32. *IJ*, August 4, 1919, 2.

33. According to *Classic Images* (November 1983, 51), Wharton had already made arrangements with the local firm Thomas-Morse Corporation to "have planes bomb and destroy the dirigible [to be burned while flying high above Cayuga Lake], all to add a touch of realism and some further thrills to *The Crooked Dagger*." *IJ* (October 17, 1919) reported that the injured Adair would be replaced by Alice Mann of New York City, who would assume the "vampire part in the production."

34. *IJ*, November 20, 1919, 3.

35. Lahue, *CNW*, 82. Notably, Ted did not include the serial picture in his "Wharton Film Studio Promotional Brochure," in which he enumerated his completed productions.

36. *IJ*, July 12, 1919, 3.

37. *IJ*, July 16, 1919, 3.

38. "What of the Serial?," in *Wid's Year Book, 1919–1920* (New York: Arno, 1971). Grossman's dislike of "impossible impossibilities" in favor of "probable probabilities" may have been a veiled reference to Aristotle, who, in his *Poetics*, told writers that audiences would prefer "the impossible" to "the improbable."

39. *Cornell Daily Sun*, January 13, 1920; also "Grossman to Leave Ithaca," *MPN*, February 28, 1920.

40. Kaplin, *Take Two*, 65. In an interview with *IJ* (January 3, 1920, 5), Grossman estimated that the cost of the production of that serial was between $125,000 and $140,000, which would "give the motion picture public some idea of the financial outlay required for serial productions."

41. "Grossman Gets Reeve Stories," *MPN*, August 31, 1918, 1406. Reeve was also behind an earlier Grossman production, the fifteen-part serial *The Master Mystery*, which he cowrote with Charles Logue and which starred Harry Houdini as Justice Department agent Quentin Locke, who was investigating "International Patents, Inc.," a powerful cartel protected by a robot known as "Q, the Automaton."

42. In the story, Helen Marsley (Marsh), who employs a dictaphone and other mechanical devices similar to those popularized in the Whartons' serials, ultimately traps the criminal who was responsible for her father's death. But, in an interesting twist, the whole story turns out be a fiction, penned by the heroine, who is a writer. The picture thus linked Helen to other independent "New Woman" heroines in popular productions such as *The Exploits of Elaine* and *Beatrice Fairfax*.

43. *IJ*, June 3, 1920, 5. Naulty, the paper wrote, "has been for 22 years in the motion picture industry." He had worked for Thomas A. Edison; for the General Film Company (as general manager); for the Mutual Film Corporation (as vice president and manager); and for Famous Players–Lasky (as producer and head of the eastern studio). Hunting, too, had significant experience, as a successful fiction writer and author of plays, books, and stories. After serving as a magazine editor, he went into the movie business, working for the World Film Corporation and then for Famous Players–Lasky, for whom he wrote "a succession and great variety of pictures for leading stars and directors which established for him a national reputation."

44. *IJ*, June 25, 1920.

45. *Cornell Alumni News*, October 13, 1921.

46. *IJ*, October 5, 1916, 6.

47. *IJ*, August 12, 1949, 7.

15. Heading West

1. Thompson, *The Star Film Ranch: Texas' First Picture Show* (Lanham, MD: Republic of Texas Press, 1996), 15, 17, 19.

2. Ibid., 26–27.

3. Ibid., 25–27.

4. According to James R. Buchanan, "Early Pioneers of Silent Films in Texas" (*Film Texas*, September 1972, 9), Paul Tilley wrote that he left San Antonio because "the Motion Picture Patents Corporation was putting all [independent] filmmaking out of business by agreeing with the major film supply company not to sell perforate film to anyone who did not have a license from them."

5. "Erecting Gotham City," *Motography*, November 25, 1916, 1194.

6. Frank Thompson, *Texas Hollywood: Filmmaking in San Antonio since 1910* (San Antonio, TX: Maverick, 2002), 10–11.

7. *MPN*, December 20, 1919, 4439.

8. *IJ*, June 19, 1919.

9. *MPW*, May 31, 1919, 1312.

10. *Exhibitors Herald*, June 28, 1919, 39.

11. *MPW*, July 31, 1920, 632.

12. According to *IJ* (June 19, 1919), Townley was going to be both manager and head director of the Texas studio. An earlier report in *IJ* (May 17, 1919), however, noted that Leo would be general manager and vice president of the new concern, while Ted would be supervising director.

13. According to *AFI Catalog*.

14. *Theatre Magazine Advertiser*, 11–12, xv.

15. *MPN*, October 25, 1919, 3171.

16. *MPN*, December 27, 1919, 148.

17. *MPN*, December 20, 1919, 4439.

18. *MPN*, December 27, 1919, 148.

19. *Motion Picture News Booking Guide*, 3:49 (October 1922).

20. The reincorporation was recorded in 1922 and was reported in *MPW*, June 17, 1922, 664. According to census records, Leo R. Wharton moved to San Antonio around the same time that his father did; in the 1920 state census, his position was listed as assistant treasurer of the Majestic. After moving to New York, Leo R. married Margaret R. Glen. On his marriage license (January 1922) his profession was listed as "clerk." At the time, Genie and her husband James (J. Whitworth) Buck, former studio manager for the Whartons, were living just outside New York City, in Westchester County.

21. "'Scenario Revisers' Indicted as Frauds," *Washington Post*, November 4, 1924. The indictments were widely reported in the trade papers as well; see, for example, *Film Daily*, November 5, 1924, 6.

22. *Classic Images*, November 1924, 53.

23. The names of the principals in the indictment were spelled differently in various accounts: Kunzinger, for example, was sometimes cited as Cunziger or C. Kuninger; Hoagland as Hoaglund; Hallamore as Hallamare or Hallermore.

24. *Endicott (NY) Bulletin*, September 19, 1924, 1.

25. "Scenario Writer Finds Rejected Story Produced," *Republican-Journal*, Ogdensburg, NY, June 20, 1924, 1. The same story was also carried in other papers, including the *Plattsburgh Sentinel*, June 20, 1924, 3, under the headline "'Romance' Worries Miss Mary Sweeney."

26. *Endicott Bulletin*, September 19, 1924, 1.

27. *MPW*, as cited in *IJ*, April 9, 1920, 7.

28. For more on Acord see Katchmer, *Eighty Silent Film Stars*, 1–8.

29. *New York Dramatic Mirror*, December 11, 1915, 23, as cited in Grange B. McKinney, *Art Acord and the Movies* (Raleigh, NC: Wyatt Classics), 9–10.

30. The detailed summary of *The Moon Riders* is drawn from the filmography in McKinney, *Art Acord and the Movies*, 104–107.

31. According to various ads for the serial in *MPW*, April–June 1920.

32. "Lloyd in Pictures," *Variety*, April 8, 1921, 47. Apparently, the film was never produced by Morosco, though a later film, *Perils of the Rail* (Morris R. Schlank Productions, 1925), directed by J. McGowan, starred Helen Holmes and Dan Crimmins ("Slippery McGee").

33. "George Rigas to Be Seen in Zenith's 'Besetting Sin,'" *New York Tribune*, July 3, 1921. There is no evidence that the film was ever made, but Rigas went on to play numerous film roles, usually as a Native American or an ethnic Latino or Italian, between 1921 and 1940. And Leota Morgan wrote the story or scenario for at least eleven films between 1921 and 1928.

34. "Theo. Wharton's Co.," *Variety*, May 27, 1921, 38, and "Coast Film Notes," *Variety*, June 24, 1921, 35.

35. As reported in the *Story World and Photodramatist*, May 1923, 88: "The Scenario staff at Universal has been increased to include Zach Sanderson, formerly of the Putnam Publishing Company, Theodore Wharton of serial fame, Tommy Grey, author of vaudeville and comedy sketches, and Joseph La Brandt, author of many stage plays."

36. Fred Schader, "Coast Film Notes," *Variety*, May 6, 1921.

37. The names of these and other well-known film professionals associated with the company were touted in the various Palmer publications, including *The Secret of Successful Photoplay Writing* (1920) and *The New Road to Authorship* (1924).

38. Ann Morey offers an excellent overview of the Palmer Photoplay Company and its operation in "'Have You the Power?' The Palmer Photoplay Corporation and the Film Viewer/Author in the 1920s," *Film History* 9, no. 3, Screenwriters and Screenwriting (1997): 300–319.

39. Review of *His Forgotten Wife*, *Variety*, June 25, 1924; also cited in Morey, "'Have You the Power?,'" 311 and 319.

40. Theodore Wharton, four-part "Wharton Film Studio Promotional Brochure, Part I: Why Santa Cruz," online publication of the Santa Cruz Public Library.

41. Ann Young, "Early Film Studios in Santa Cruz County, Part II: The Beginnings: A Western Pioneer Village," online publication of the Santa Cruz Public Library. That set continued to be used intermittently over the next decade for other films, including *Broken Chains*, *Ten Ton Love*, and a remake of *Salomy Jane*.

42. Ann Young, "Early Film Studios in Santa Cruz County, Part III: The Establishment of the DeLaveaga Park Studio," online publication of the Santa Cruz Public Library. The Fer Dal Motion Picture Company never completed a single feature film—or even the building of its studio—before leaving town.

43. Ann Young, "Early Film Studios in Santa Cruz County, Part V: The 1920's: Two Boardwalk Studios and Theodore Wharton," online publication of the Santa Cruz Public Library.

44. Writing in the *Santa Cruz Evening News* (August 25, 1923, 2), Preston Sawyer observed that "the ambitious young company possesses the uncommon ability to 'deliver the goods.'"

45. According to the *Santa Cruz Evening News* (August 14, 1923, 20), *His Weekend* screened locally in an early three-reel version for members of the cast on August 14, 1925, but it appears that the final two-reel version was never released.

46. *Santa Cruz Evening News*, January 15, 1923, 4.

47. Theodore Wharton, "Part I: Why Santa Cruz." According to Wharton, associated with him in the new enterprise were Michael J. Leonard, secretary, and Mrs. Helene Card, treasurer, "both of whom are well known and bear enviable reputations."

48. Ibid.

49. Ibid.

50. Theodore Wharton, "Part II: The Production Plan," and "Part IV: A Word to the People of Santa Cruz County."

51. *Santa Cruz Evening News*, September 28, 1925.

52. Young, "Part V."

53. Gerald M. Best, "The Shooting of Serials," *Cornell Alumni News*, March 1977, 27.

54. The fact that Ted Wharton had been associated with Essanay, the first American company to produce films in Ireland, only increases the possibility of that connection.

55. In the trade paper obituaries, the date of Leo's death is often listed as September 27. But his death certificate (the information for which was supplied by his son, Leo R. Wharton) states that he died on September 29 in Astoria, Queens. Whereas the 1925 census had identified him as "motion picture producer," the death certificate listed his occupation as "actor."

56. According to her obituary in the *Rochester (IN) Sentinel* (December 12, 1939), Bessie L. Emrick was "educated in schools in Rochester [Indiana] and in a New York conservatory. She was one of the first actresses to enter the films with the old Pathé Company. She appeared in a number of musical comedies before entering the movies" and is reported to have made pictures "with such well known performers as Lionel Barrymore, Warner Baxter, Irene Castle and Pearl White." There is, however, no mention of her son, Leo R. Wharton. The reference to Bessie as "mother of the screen" occurs in numerous trade journals, such as *MPN*, December 27, 1919, 148.

57. According to Leo's death certificate, his marital status was "divorced." (According to the 1925 New York State Census, he was already "living alone" in Brooklyn.)

58. Marie Rubenstein later assumed the surname of Jennie's second husband, Harry Austin Shaffer. In the 1900 census, she was listed as Maricia Shaffer and in a later census as Maree Shaffer. Eventually she took "Marie Wharton Shaffer" as her legal name. She worked as an office manager in a large law office in Houston and supported the Alley Theater in Houston during its early days.

59. According to Julie Simmons-Lynch, "Ithaca and the Silver Screen," Wharton Studio Museum website, and Theodore Wharton, "Wharton Film Studio Promotional Brochure."

60. Obituary, Mrs. Theodore Wharton, *New York Herald Tribune*, May 7, 1947, 26. Ted and Anna had married in 1905.

61. "[Theodore Wharton] Brains of Pathé Pictures," *Olympia (WA) Daily Recorder*, July 16, 1915, 4.

62. Colleen Kaplin (*Take Two*, 31) writes that Harriett Phillips Bass, who worked as bookkeeper, receptionist, and stenographer in the Whartons' office from 1915 to 1917, recalled that "each of the Whartons and their brother-in-law and investor and general manager J. Whitworth Buck pulled down $500 a week."

63. Pichel, *ISM: Beatrice Fairfax*, n.p.

64. "A Saga in the Motion Picture Industry in the Finger Lake Region," n.p.

65. Obituary of "Theo. Wharton," *Variety*, December 1, 1931, 55.

66. Ibid. An obituary for Ted in the *Washington Post* (November 29, 1931, M4) mistakenly wrote that Ted had "first conceived the motion picture serial" and that he "directed Pearl White in the first venture in that direction." It also overlooked perhaps the Wharton brothers' greatest accomplishment, concluding that "in later years he [Ted] and his brother Leopold, who died several years ago, started an independent studio, but it was not successful."

67. Obituary, Mrs. Theodore Wharton, *New York Herald Tribune*, May 7, 1947, 26.

68. *International Photographer*, December 1931, 36.

69. *Variety*, December 1, 1931, 55.

SELECTED BIBLIOGRAPHY

Archives of Wharton Materials

The Wharton Collections, The History Center in Tompkins County, Ithaca, New York.

Wharton Releasing Corporation Records, Carl A. Kroch Library, Cornell University, Ithaca, New York.

Wharton Studio Photographs Collection. Archelaus D. Chadwick Collection, Ithaca College, Ithaca, New York.

Secondary Sources

Some of the best and most interesting information about the Whartons and their work appears in the Ithaca, New York, newspapers, especially the *Ithaca Journal* (1913–1920), the *Cornell Daily Sun*, and the *Cornell Alumni News*, as well as in the trade papers and journals, including *Moving Picture World*, *Motion Picture News*, *Motography*, *Billboard*, *Dramatic Mirror*, *Variety*, and *Photoplay*. Articles and reviews that I have referenced from these sources are indicated in the text and notes.

Abel, Richard. *The Red Rooster Scare: Making Cinema American, 1900–1910*. Berkeley: University of California Press, 1999.

Abel, Richard, and Rick Altman, eds. *The Sounds of Early Cinema*. Bloomington: Indiana University Press, 2001.

Acker, Ally. *Reel Women: Pioneers of the Cinema, 1896 to the Present*. New York: Continuum, 1991.

Anselmo-Sequeira, Diana. "Apparitional Girlhood: Material Ephemerality and the Historiography of Female Adolescence in Early American Film." *Spectator 33*, no. 1 (Spring 2013): 25–35.

Barbour, Alan G. *Cliffhanger: A Pictorial History of the Motion Picture Serial*. New York: A&W, 1977.

——. *Days of Thrills and Adventure*. New York: Collier Books, 1970.

Bean, Jennifer, ed. *Flickers of Desire: Movie Stars of the 1910s*. New Brunswick, NJ: Rutgers University Press, 2011.

——. "Technologies of Early Stardom and the Extraordinary Body." *Camera Obscura* 16, no. 3 (2001): 8–57.

Bean, Jennifer M., Anupama Kapse, and Laura Horak, eds. *Silent Cinema and the Politics of Space*. Bloomington: Indiana University Press, 2014.

Bean, Jennifer M., and Diane Negra, eds. *A Feminist Reader in Early Cinema*. Durham, NC: Duke University Press, 2002.

Best, Gerald. "Making Movies." *Cornell Alumni News*, February 1972, 20–23.

———. "The Shooting of Serials." *Cornell Alumni News*, March 1977, 23–27.

Blum, Daniel. *A Pictorial History of the Silent Screen*. New York: G. P. Putnam's Sons, 1953.

Bordwell, David, Janet Staiger, and Kristin Thompson. *The Classical Hollywood Cinema: Film Style and Mode of Production to 1960*. New York: Routledge, 1985.

Bowser, Eileen. *The Transformation of Cinema, 1907–1915*. Berkeley: University of California Press, 1990.

Braff, Richard E. *The Braff Silent Short Film Working Papers: 1903–1929*. Jefferson, NC: McFarland, 2002.

Braun, Marta, Charlie Kiel, Rob King, Paul Moore, and Louis Pelletier, eds. *Beyond the Screen: Institutions, Networks and Publics of Early Cinema*. New Barnet, UK: John Libbey, 2012.

Bridges, Melody, and Cheryl Robson, eds. *Silent Women: Pioneers of Cinema*. Twickenham, UK: Supernova Books, 2016.

Brownlow, Kevin, and John Kobal. *Hollywood: The Pioneers*. New York: Knopf, 1979.

Campbell, Craig W. *Reel America and World War I: A Comprehensive Filmography and History of Motion Pictures in the United States, 1914–1920*. Jefferson, NC: McFarland, 1985.

Canjels, Rudmer. *Distributing Silent Serials: Local Practices, Changing Forms, Cultural Transformation*. New York: Routledge, 2011.

Cline, William C. *In the Nick of Time: Motion Picture Sound Serials*. Jefferson, NC: McFarland, 1984.

Columbia Women Pioneers Project. Columbia University. Online.

Dahlquist, Marina, ed. *Exporting Perilous Pauline: Pearl White and the Serial Film Craze*. Urbana: University of Illinois Press, 2013.

Ellis, Jack C., and Virginia Wright Wexman. *A History of Film*. 5th ed. Boston: Allyn and Bacon, 2002.

Elsaesser, Thomas, and Adam Barker, eds. *Early Cinema: Space, Frame, and Narrative*. London: British Film Institute, 1990.

Everson, William K. *American Silent Film*. New York: Oxford University Press, 1978.

Fernett, Gene. *American Film Studies: An Historical Encyclopedia*. Jefferson, NC: McFarland, 1988.

Finch, Christopher, and Linda Rosenkrantz. *Gone Hollywood*. Garden City, NY: Doubleday, 1979.

Freedland, Michael. *The Men Who Made Hollywood: The Lives of the Great Movie Moguls*. London: JR Books, 2009.

Gabler, Neal. *An Empire of Their Own: How the Jews Invented Hollywood*. New York: Crown, 1988.

Gardner, Jared. *Projections: Comics and the History of Twenty-First Century Storytelling*. Stanford, CA: Stanford University Press, 2012.

Gledhill, Christine, and Linda Williams, eds. *Reinventing Film Studies*. London: Arnold, 2000.

Goddard, Charles, and Eustace Hale Ball. *The Mysteries of Myra*. Foreword by Eric Stedman. Ithaca, NY: Serial Squadron Photonovel, 2010.

Gomery, Douglas. *Shared Pleasures: History of Movie Presentation in the United States*. Madison: University of Wisconsin Press, 1992.

Gregory, Mollie. *Stuntwomen: The Untold Hollywood Story*. Louisville: University of Kentucky Press, 2015.

Grieveson, Lee, and Peter Krämer, eds. *The Silent Cinema Reader*. New York: Routledge, 2004.

Gunning, Tom. *D. W. Griffith and the Origins of American Narrative Film: The Early Years at Biograph*. Champaign: University of Illinois Press, 1994.

Hansen, Miriam. *Babel and Babylon: Spectatorship in American Silent Film*. Cambridge, MA: Harvard University Press, 1991.

Harbin, Terry. *Ithaca Made Movies*. Website and videos. Online.

Harmon, Jim, and Donald F. Glut. *The Great Movie Serials: Their Sound and Fury*. New York: Doubleday, 1972.

Hennefeld, Margaret. "The Exploits of Elaine." Online essay for the National Film Registry, Library of Congress website.

Higashi, Sumiko. *Virgins, Vamps, and Flappers: The American Silent Movie Heroine*. Montreal: Eden, 1978.

Horak, Jan-Christopher. *Lovers of Cinema: The First American Film Avant-Garde, 1919–1945*. Madison: University of Wisconsin Press, 1995.

Hulse, Ed. *Distressed Damsels and Masked Marauders: Cliffhanger Serials of the Silent-Movie Era*. Morris Plains, NJ: Murania, 2014.

"Ithaca-Made Films and Their Stars." *Bulletin of the DeWitt Historical Society of Tompkins County* 14, no. 4 (June 1966): 59–60.

Ithaca, NY: The Original Movie Capital of the World. Ithaca, NY: Chamber of Commerce, n.d.

Jacobs, Lewis. *The Rise of the American Film: A Critical History*. New York: Harcourt, Brace, 1939.

Kaplin, Colleen M. *Take Two: The True Story of Ithaca's Movie-Making Era*. Cabin John, MD: Seven Locks, 1989.

Katchmer, George. *Eighty Silent Film Stars: Biographies and Filmographies of the Obscure to the Well Known*. Jefferson, NC: McFarland, 1991.

Keil, Charlie. *Early American Cinema in Transition: Story, Style, and Filmmaking, 1907–1913*. Madison: University of Wisconsin Press, 2001.

Keil, Charlie, and Shelley Stamp, eds. *American Cinema's Transitional Era: Audiences, Institutions, Practices*. Berkeley: University of California Press, 2004.

Keim, Norman O., with David Marc. *Our Movie Houses: A History of Film and Cinematic Innovation in Central New York*. Syracuse, NY: Syracuse University Press, 2008.

Kinnard, Roy. *Horror in Silent Films: A Filmography, 1896–1929*. Jefferson, NC: McFarland, 1995.

Klepper, Robert K. *Silent Films, 1877–1996: A Critical Guide to 646 Movies*. Jefferson, NC: McFarland, 1999.

Kobel, Peter. *Silent Movies: The Birth of Film and the Triumph of Movie Culture*. Boston: Little, Brown, 2007.

Koszarski, Richard. *An Evening's Entertainment: The Age of the Silent Feature Picture, 1915–1928.* History of the American Cinema series, vol. 3. New York: Charles Scribner's Sons, 1990.

Lahue, Kalton C. *Bound and Gagged.* New York: Castle Books, 1968.

——. *Continued Next Week: A History of the Motion Picture Serial.* Norman: University of Oklahoma Press, 1964.

——. *Gentlemen to the Rescue: The Heroes of the Silent Screen.* New York: Castle Books, 1972.

Langman, Larry. *American Film Cycles: The Silent Era.* Westport, CT: Greenwood, 1998.

Langman, Larry, and Daniel Finn. *A Guide to American Silent Crime Films.* Westport, CT: Greenwood, 1994.

Ledger, Sally. *The New Woman: Fiction and Feminism at the Fin-de-Siècle.* Manchester, UK: Manchester University Press, 1997.

Lewis, Jon, and Eric Smoodin, eds. *Looking Past the Screen: Case Studies in American Film History and Methods.* Durham, NC: Duke University Press, 2007.

Margolies, John, and Emily Gwathmey. *Ticket to Paradise: American Movie Theaters and How We Had Fun.* Boston: Little Brown, 1991.

Mast, Gerald. *A Short History of the Movies.* 4th ed. New York: Macmillan, 1986.

McCaffrey, Donald W., and Christopher P. Jacobs. *Guide to the Silent Years of American Cinema.* Westport, CT: Greenwood, 1999.

Menefee, David W. *The First Female Stars: Women of the Silent Era.* Westport, CT: Praeger, 2004.

Merrill, Arch. *Upstate Echoes,* 84–93. New York: Knickerbocker, 1950.

Musser, Charles. *Before the Nickelodeon: Edwin S. Porter and the Edison Manufacturing Company.* Berkeley: University of California Press, 1991.

——. *The Emergence of Cinema: The American Screen to 1907.* Berkeley: University of California Press, 1994.

Otto, Elizabeth, and Vanessa Rocco, eds. *The New Woman International: Representations in Photography and Film from the 1870s through the 1960s.* Ann Arbor: University of Michigan Press, 2011.

Peiss, Kathy. *Cheap Amusements: Working Women and Leisure in Turn-of-the-Century New York.* Philadelphia: Temple University Press, 1986.

Pichel, Aaron. *Ithaca Silent Movies.* Program to accompany the Ithaca Film Festival, with a showing of *Beatrice Fairfax,* June 2, 2007. Ithaca, NY: Imagination Graphics, 2007.

——. *Ithaca Silent Movies.* Program for a June 2008 showing of *The Lottery Man* in Ithaca, NY. Ithaca, NY: Imagination Graphics, 2008.

——. *Ithaca Silent Movies: The Forgotten History.* Program to accompany a May 2009 showing of silent films, including *The Great White Trail,* in Ithaca, NY. Ithaca, NY: Imagination Graphics, 2009.

——. *Ithaca Silent Movies: The 100th Anniversary.* Program to accompany a May 2013 showing of silent films, including episodes 2 and 12 of *Beatrice Fairfax,* in Ithaca, NY. Ithaca, NY: Imagination Graphics, 2013.

Pizzitola, Louis. *Hearst over Hollywood: Power, Passion, and Propaganda in the Movies.* New York: Columbia University Press, 2013.

Rabinowitz, Lauren. *For the Love of Pleasure: Women, Movies, and Culture in Turn-of-the-Century Chicago.* New Brunswick, NJ: Rutgers University Press, 1998.

Rainey, Buck. *Those Fabulous Serial Heroines: Their Lives and Films*. Metuchen, NJ: Scarecrow, 1990.

Ramsaye, Terry. *A Million and One Nights: A History of the Motion Picture through 1925*. New York: Simon & Schuster / Touchstone Books, 1986.

Rettig, Hillary. "They Made Movies in Ithaca." *Grapevine Weekly Magazine*, August 30–September 5 and September 6–12, 1984.

Richardson, Angelique, and Chris Willis, eds. *The New Woman in Fiction and in Fact: Fin-de-Siècle Feminisms*. London: Institute of English Studies / School of Advanced Study, 2002.

Richie, Mary. "They Made Movies in Ithaca." *Culturefront*, Fall 1999: 36–41.

Robinson, David. *From Peep Show to Palace: The Birth of the American Film*. New York: Columbia University Press, 1996.

Rossell, Deac. *Living Pictures: The Origins of the Movies*. Albany: SUNY Press, 1996.

Sachse, Gretchen. "A Tour of the Wharton Studio." *DeWitt Historical Society Newsletter* 2 (Summer 1995): 1–3.

Savada, Elias. *The American Film Institute Catalog of Motion Pictures Produced in the United States: Film Beginnings, 1893–1910*. Metuchen, NJ: Scarecrow, 1995.

Schickel, Richard. *D. W. Griffith: An American Life*. New York: Simon & Schuster, 1984.

Schneider, Dorothy, and Carl J. Schneider. *American Women in the Progressive Era, 1900–1920*. New York: Facts on File, 1993.

Selzer, Adam, and Michael Glover Smith. *Flickering Empire: How Chicago Invented the U.S. Film Industry*. New York: Wallflower / Columbia University Press, 2015.

Simmons-Lynch, Julie. "Ithaca and the Silver Screen." Wharton Studio Museum website.

Singer, Ben. *Melodrama and Modernity: Early Sensational Cinema and Its Contexts*. New York: Columbia University Press, 2001.

Sklar, Robert. *Movie-Made America: A Social History of American Movies*. New York: Random House, 1975.

——. *The New Historical Dictionary of the American Film Industry*. Lanham, MD: Scarecrow, 2001.

Slide, Anthony. *The American Film Industry: A Historical Dictionary*. Westport, CT: Greenwood, 1986.

——. *Aspects of American Film History prior to 1920*. Metuchen, NJ: Scarecrow, 1978.

Spehr, Paul C., with Gunnar Lundquist. *American Film and Company Credits, 1908–1920*. Jefferson, NC: McFarland, 1996.

Staiger, Janet. *Bad Women: Regulating Sexuality in Early American Cinema*. Minneapolis: University of Minnesota Press, 1995.

Stainton, Walter H. "Irene Castle's Movie Career." *Films in Review*, June–July 1962, 347–355.

——. "Pearl White in Ithaca." *Films in Review*, May 1951, 19–25.

Stamp, Shelley. "An Awful Struggle between Love and Ambition: Serial Heroines, Serial Stars and Their Female Fans." In *The Silent Cinema Reader*, edited by Lee Grieveson and Peter Krämer, 210–225. New York: Routledge, 2004.

——. *Movie-Struck Girls: Women and Motion Picture Culture after the Nickelodeon*. Princeton, NJ: Princeton University Press, 2001.

Stedman, Raymond William. *The Serials: Suspense and Drama by Installment*. Norman: University of Oklahoma Press, 1971.

Strauven, Wanda, ed. *The Cinema of Attractions Reloaded*. Amsterdam: Amsterdam University Press, 2006.

They Made Movies in Ithaca. Documentary film, produced under the auspices of the Ithaca College School of Communications, 1975.

Usai, Paolo Cherchi. *Silent Cinema: An Introduction*. London: BFI, 2000.

Waller, Gregory A. *Main Street Amusements: Movies and Commercial Entertainment in a Southern City, 1896–1930*. Washington, DC: Smithsonian Institution Press, 1995.

Ward, Richard Lewis. *When the Cock Crows: A History of the Pathé Exchange*. Carbondale: Southern Illinois University Press, 2016.

Weaver, John T. *Twenty Years of Silents: 1908–1928*. Metuchen, NJ: Scarecrow, 1971.

Weiss, Ken, and Ed Goodgold. *To Be Continued . . .* New York: Crown, 1972.

Wharton Studio Museum website. Ithaca, NY.

Wharton, Theodore. *Wharton Film Studio Promotional Brochure*. Four parts. N.p.: n.d. [ca. early 1920s].

"The Whartons Set Up in Ithica [*sic*]." Part 1. *Classic Images*, October 1983, 33–35.

"The Wharton Studios." Part 2. *Classic Images*, November 1983, 47–51.

Young, Ann. "Early Film Studios in Santa Cruz County." Parts 1–5. Online publication of the Santa Cruz Public Library, n.d.

ILLUSTRATION CREDITS

0.1. Map by Bill Nelson

I.1. *Moving Picture World*, January 24, 1914. Courtesy of George Eastman Museum.

1.1. Playbill. Image #A1624-00018, the State Historical Society of Missouri, Photograph Collection.

1.2. Billy Rose Theatre Division, The New York Public Library, "Hanlon's superba, the grotto," New York Public Library Digital Collections, http://digitalcollections.nypl.org/items/5e66b3e8-e5b1-d471-e040-e00a180654d7.

1.3. Courtesy of The History Center at Tompkins County, Ithaca, New York, Wharton Studios Collections.

1.4. Screen grab retrieved from https://www.dailymotion.com/video/xep3rt.

2.1. *Moving Picture World*, October 29, 1910. Courtesy of George Eastman Museum.

2.2. *Moving Picture World*, January 18, 1913. Courtesy of George Eastman Museum.

3.1. Playbill courtesy of the Division of Rare and Manuscript Collections, Cornell University.

3.2. Photograph courtesy of the Division of Rare and Manuscript Collections, Cornell University.

3.3. Photograph courtesy of the Division of Rare and Manuscript Collections, Cornell University.

3.4. Photograph courtesy of the Division of Rare and Manuscript Collections, Cornell University.

3.5. *Moving Picture World*, October 25, 1913. Courtesy of George Eastman Museum.

3.6. Photograph courtesy of the Division of Rare and Manuscript Collections, Cornell University.

4.1. Photograph courtesy of Buffalo Bill Museum and Grave, Golden, Colorado.

4.2. *Moving Picture World*, November 7, 1914. Courtesy of George Eastman Museum.

5.1. Courtesy of the Division of Rare and Manuscript Collections, Cornell University.

5.2. Photograph courtesy of The History Center in Tompkins County, Ithaca, New York, Wharton Studios Collections.

5.3. Photograph courtesy of The History Center in Tompkins County, Ithaca, New York Wharton Studios Collection.

6.1. Photograph courtesy of the Division of Rare and Manuscript Collections, Cornell University.

6.2. *Moving Picture World*, January 30, 1915. Courtesy of George Eastman Museum.

6.3. *Moving Picture World*, 1915. Courtesy of George Eastman Museum.

6.4. *Moving Picture World*, December 26, 1914. Courtesy of the Division of Rare and Manuscript Collections, Cornell University.

7.1. *Motion Picture News*, May 29, 1915. Courtesy of George Eastman Museum.

7.2. *Moving Picture News*, July 3, 1915. Courtesy of the Division of Rare and Manuscript Collections, Cornell University.

7.3. Photograph courtesy of the Division of Rare and Manuscript Collections, Cornell University.

7.4. Photograph courtesy of The History Center in Tompkins County, Ithaca, New York, Wharton Studios Collections.

7.5. Cover of *Les Mystères de New-York* (1915), published by La Renaissance du Livre, Paris. From the author's collection.

8.1. Photograph courtesy of The History Center in Tompkins County, Ithaca, New York, Wharton Studios Collections.

8.2. Photograph courtesy of The History Center in Tompkins County, Ithaca, New York, Wharton Studios Collections.

8.3. Photograph courtesy of The History Center in Tompkins County, Ithaca, New York, Wharton Studios Collections.

8.4. Photograph courtesy of the Division of Rare and Manuscript Collections, Cornell University.

8.5. Photograph courtesy of The History Center in Tompkins County, Ithaca, New York, Wharton Studios Collections.

8.6. Photograph courtesy of the Division of Rare and Manuscript Collections, Cornell University.

9.1. Photograph courtesy of The History Center in Tompkins County, Ithaca, New York, Wharton Studios Collections.

9.2. Photograph courtesy of the Division of Rare and Manuscript Collections, Cornell University

9.3. *Moving Picture World*, June 17, 1916. Courtesy of George Eastman Museum.

10.1. Photograph courtesy of the Division of Rare and Manuscript Collections, Cornell University.

10.2. Photograph courtesy of the Division of Rare and Manuscript Collections, Cornell University.

10.3. *Moving Picture World*, August 26, 1916. Courtesy of George Eastman Museum.

11.1. Photograph courtesy of The History Center in Tompkins County, Ithaca, New York, Wharton Studios Collections.

11.2. Photograph courtesy of The History Center in Tompkins County, Ithaca, New York, Wharton Studios Collections.

11.3. Photograph courtesy of The History Center in Tompkins County, Ithaca, New York, Wharton Studios Collections.

11.4. *Moving Picture World*, February 3, 1917. Courtesy of George Eastman Museum.

11.5. Photographs courtesy of The History Center in Tompkins County, Ithaca, New York and the Division of Rare and Manuscript Collections, Cornell University.

12.1. Photograph courtesy of the Division of Rare and Manuscript Collections, Cornell University.

12.2. Photograph courtesy of the Division of Rare and Manuscript Collections, Cornell University.

12.3. Photograph courtesy of the Division of Rare and Manuscript Collections, Cornell University.

12.4. *Moving Picture News*, June 16, 1917. Courtesy of George Eastman Museum.

12.5. Photograph courtesy of the Division of Rare and Manuscript Collections, Cornell University.

12.6. Photograph courtesy of the Division of Rare and Manuscript Collections, Cornell University.

12.7. Photograph courtesy of the Division of Rare and Manuscript Collections, Cornell University.

13.1. Photograph courtesy of the Division of Rare and Manuscript Collections, Cornell University.

13.2. Photograph courtesy of the Division of Rare and Manuscript Collections, Cornell University.

13.3. *Moving Picture News*, December 22, 1917. Courtesy of George East-man Museum.

13.4. Photograph courtesy of the Division of Rare and Manuscript Collections, Cornell University.

13.5. Program courtesy of the Division of Rare and Manuscript Collections, Cornell University.

14.1. Photograph courtesy of the Division of Rare and Manuscript Collections, Cornell University.

15.1. *Moving Picture World*, December 27, 1919. Courtesy of George East-man Museum.

15.2. Cover of *Moving Picture Weekly*, May 8, 1920, retrieved from Media History Digital Library, https://archive.org/stream/movingpicture we1014movi_1#page/n300/mode/2up.

INDEX